DATE DUE

MY 30 '96			

THE ECONOMIC DEVELOPMENT OF JAPAN

THE ECONOMIC DEVELOPMENT OF JAPAN

A Quantitative Study

Second Edition

Ryōshin Minami

Professor of Economics, Institute of Economic Research
Hitotsubashi University, Tokyo

Translated by Ralph Thompson, Kumie Fujimori and Ryōshin Minami
with assistance from David Merriman

St. Martin's Press   New York

© The Oriental Economist 1986, 1994

First edition published in the United States of America in 1986
Second edition 1994

The economic development of Japan : a quantitative study / Ryōshin
Minami ; translated by Ralph Thompson, Kumie Fujimori, and Ryōshin
Minami with assistance from David Merriman. —2nd ed.
    p.   cm.
Includes bibliographical references and index.
ISBN 0–312–09956–8 (cl.). — ISBN 0–312–09958–4 (pbk.)
1. Japan—Economic conditions—1868–   I. Title.
HC462.7M47513   1994
330.952—dc20
                                                            93–10467
                                                                CIP

Publication has been sponsored by the Japan Foundation and the
Suntory Foundation.

Contents

PART I

AN OVERVIEW OF ECONOMIC HISTORY

PART II

MODERN ECONOMIC GROWTH: PRODUCTION AND DEMAND

PART III

MODERN ECONOMIC GROWTH: CAUSES AND RESULTS

PART IV

SUMMARY AND CONCLUSIONS

List of Tables

xiii

List of Figures

Preface to the First Edition

The Japanese economy has never before attracted as much attention as it does today. In countries that have felt the full force of Japan's export drive, and whose own industries are in decline, there is a growing interest in discovering the secret of Japanese industry's sustained growth. Japanese management techniques, labour-management relations and the qualities of the labour force are all attracting interest. Developing countries, as well as placing great hopes on financial assistance and the introduction of technology from Japan, are attempting to learn from the economic development of what is the only developed country outside the west. Meanwhile in Japan the period of rapid economic growth hás come to an end, and the economy is struggling to find its way along a new path. It is generally accepted here that problems such as the supply of raw materials, pollution, how to improve social welfare, an ageing population and friction with other countries will have to be tackled when formulating future economic policy.

We believe that it is therefore of great value to analyze the last hundred years of economic development and use our evaluation of these years in plotting the future course. Hence this book consists of three main themes:

1. Why was Japan able to 'take off' successfully – to achieve modern economic growth initially? The view that the decisive factor was the Meiji government's forthright economic policies has often been put forward. Recent empirical research has, however, emphasized the economic and cultural inheritance from the Tokugawa Period. Yet, had it not been for the introduction of modern technology, which had its beginnings in the late Tokugawa Period but was not significant until the Meiji Period, industrialization might never have got off the ground. We suggest in Chapter 2 that the Tokugawa inheritance and Meiji modernization deserve equal consideration.

2. Why was Japan able to achieve a more rapid rate of economic

growth than other developed countries? The answers to this question constitute the major part of the book. In this section we particularly emphasize two points. First, while economic growth was indeed rapid, it was by no means constant. There were a series of long swings in the growth rate, and overall it was showing a tendency to accelerate. Second, major structural changes accompanied economic growth. Manufacturing industry's and services' shares of output rose, at the expense of agriculture's share. Consumption expenditure's share of GNP declined and capital formation's share increased significantly. Since the Second World War the surplus on the labour market has changed to a shortage. We discuss the economic growth rate in Chapter 3, the structural changes in Chapters 4 to 11.

3. What is the probable future of the economy? To answer this, first it is necessary to evaluate correctly the results of the last hundred years of economic growth. We do this, using the results of analyses from earlier in the book, and then attempt to say something about the future.

We believe that this book differs from several books already published in English on the Japanese economy in that it contains:

1. Long-term analysis, beginning with premodern economic growth and covering the long process of industrialization from its very beginnings.

2. Detailed structural analysis. It covers not only the overall growth of the economy, but also the structural changes that accompanied it. It is for this reason that we have used the word development, rather than growth, in the title.

3. Quantitative analysis. It does not simply enumerate a series of historical facts. We have used abundant statistical sources and have discussed the theory behind modern economic growth. *The Long-Term Economic Statistics* compiled at the Hitotsubashi University Institute of Economic Research have been particularly valuable.

4. An overall analysis. We have given, we believe, a balanced picture of all the major controversies and important aspects of Japan's economic development. We have tried to include as wide a range of opinion as possible, and have introduced the views of some economists who have been perhaps unjustly ignored in the past.

5. Comparisons with other countries, in an attempt to illuminate the similarities and differences between them and Japan. Some previous studies have not done this to a sufficient extent, and have tended to exaggerate Japan's uniqueness.

6. A mention of all the important research which has been done, and an evaluation of what has been achieved and problems that have still to be solved.

This is the English version of a book of the same title in Japanese published in 1981 by Tōyōkeizai Shinpōsha (Tōkyō). The content is the same except for the following changes:

1. At the beginning of Chapter 1 a new section entitled An Introduction to Japan has been inserted for those whose present knowledge of Japan is limited (Section 1.1).
2. Some of the comments from the reviews of the Japanese version have been included, and a new section, Industrial Organization and Industrial Policies, has been added to Chapter 5 (Section 5.5).
3. Tables, figures and the text have all been updated.
4. We have tried to quote mainly English language sources, and the further reading after each chapter contains only English language works. This means that many sources published in Japanese could not be included, and those who read Japanese are asked to refer to the bibliography of that version.

Readers are advised to read Chapter 12 first, as this will help them grasp the overall structure of the book and further their understanding. Similarly it is suggested that they read the summary at the end of each chapter, before beginning the chapter itself.

The author has great pleasure in seeing his book on the Japanese economy printed in English, but without the kind assistance of many people this might never have been realized. He would like to express gratitude to Professors Kazushi Ohkawa, Miyohei Shinohara, Mataji Umemura, Hugh Patrick, Saburō Yamada and Kōzō Yamamura for their encouragement and support. Thanks are due to Professor M. E. Falkus for his invaluable comments and to Professor Masao Baba for including this book in the present series – Studies in the Modern Japanese Economy. The author is particularly indebted to Mr Ralph Thompson and Mr David Merriman for their devoted efforts at translation and to the Japan Foundation and the Suntory Foundation for their financial aid. Finally he would like to express gratitude to Mr Yoshimaru Tadokoro of the Macmillan Shuppansha for his support in facilitating the translation and to Tōyōkeizai Shinpōsha for their permission to have the book translated. I hope that this, as well as the Korean, Chinese and Thai versions, will be read widely and help people in other countries to have a better understanding of Japan.

Institute of Economic Research   RYŌSHIN MINAMI
Hitotsubashi University
Tōkyō
1985

Preface to the Second Edition

Seven years have passed since the publication of the first edition (and twelve years since the first edition written in Japanese).

During this period a large change has occurred in the world economy. The USA, which has suffered constant deficits in both budget and trade balance, has become by the middle of the 1980s the largest borrower in the world with Japan becoming the biggest creditor nation; the USA could not now survive without the flow of credit from Japan. These relative changes between the American economy and the Japanese economy triggered great reversals in American perceptions about Japan. Yet at the same time as Japan is being praised, alarms and criticisms have also arisen. A new trend of the latter is the appearance of people called 'revisionists'. According to them, the success of Japan is due to its unique social and economic systems, which are completely different from any others in the world, and therefore there is no basis for fair competition.

In the past the uniqueness of the Japanese experience was stressed. Before Second World War, Marxist economists thought that a critical boost had been given to the performance of the Japanese economy by the intervention of the government in the private sectors and by the huge industry reserves (the excess labour forces). However, after the Second World War, as research by modern economists extended, they became aware that the Japanese experience was in fact not so different from that of the advanced Euro-American countries. It appears that the opinions of overseas Japanologists, mainly those in the USA, have played a significant role in this growing awareness.

It may be said, in this context, that the views of recent revisionists seem to be against history. Although there are some persuasive points in their opinions, it is difficult to avoid the impression that their views are often superficial and emotional. As has been mentioned in the Preface to the first edition, it is necessary to properly analyze both the 'common points' and the 'unique points' of the Japanese experience to evaluate it clearly. For this purpose, doing elaborate quantitative research is becoming ever more important. The necessity of writing a revised edition comes from this consideration.

The great difference between the first and second editions is the addition of descriptions of recent economic situations based on analyses extended to up to 1990. But in order to maintain a reasonable length, significant reductions have been made to the text, figures, footnotes and references. This may have reduced the number of pages a little, but the merit is that the book has become easier to read.

The first edition written in Japanese was also published in English as well as in China (in Chinese) and in Korea (in Korean). There are plans to publish the translated versions of the revised edition in China, Brazil and Thailand. I wish that the revised edition could be read by even more people in the world. Finally, I would like to thank Professor Malcolm E. Falkus and Yoshimaru Tadokoro, who actively promoted the publication of the revised edition in English.

Institute of Economic Research   RYŌSHIN MINAMI
Hitotsubashi University
Tōkyō
1993

BIBLIOGRAPHICAL SOURCES

Periodically published volumes of statistics (mainly by government organs) are abbreviated in the text, where the relevant years are also stated. Their full titles, and publishers, are shown in Part A of the Bibliography. For other sources, the author's name and the year of publication appear in the text; the full titles and publishers are found in Part B of the Bibliography.

After each chapter the most important bibliographical sources are listed. They are marked with an asterisk in Part B of the Bibliography.

ABBREVIATIONS

r = correlation coefficient
$\bar{r}$ = correlation coefficient adjusted by the degrees of freedom
R = multiple correlation coefficient
$\bar{R}$ = multiple correlation coefficient adjusted by the degrees of freedom
F = F-value
d = Durbin-Watson statistic
$G(\ )$ = the growth rate of the symbol in parentheses
t-statistics appear in parentheses below estimated coefficients

Part I

An Overview of Economic History

1 Introduction

When, after closing her shores to the world for more than two hundred years (1641–1854), Japan recommenced intercourse with other countries the majority of the world's people did not even know of her existence. Economically Japan, was a long way behind the advanced nations of the west. According to one estimate, in 1870 Japan's GNP per capita was only a quarter of that of the UK and one third of that of the USA. After several wars and phenomenal economic growth, particularly after the Second World War, Japan has gradually made itself known to the peoples of the world. Her GNP per capita is now on a par with the advanced industrial nations of the west, and today a description of the state of the world's economy without reference to Japan would be impossible.

Section 1.1 of this chapter is an introduction to Japan's geography, culture, society and politics. Some knowledge of these areas is essential to an understanding of the economy. Readers who already know Japan well are advised to begin from Section 1.2, in which Japan's economic development is divided into stages, and modern economic growth and its beginnings are discussed.

1.1 AN INTRODUCTION TO JAPAN[1]

1.1.1 The Land and the People

Japan is an island country off the east coast of Asia. It is made up of four main islands – Honshū, Hokkaidō, Kyūshū, Shikoku – and a host of smaller ones (see Appx B). Their total area is 372 000 square kilometres; one and a half times the size of the UK, one twenty-fifth of the USA, and three thousandths of the world's area.

Japan is surrounded by sea, and has a mild, damp climate peculiar to the temperate zones. However, because it is next to a massive

3

continent the summers are hot and humid, the winters cold. The year divides itself clearly into four seasons. This is a source of stimulation and refreshment for the people, and could be said to account partially for their energetic nature. Japan is also on the edge of the monsoon area, so that there is a rainy season in early summer, and a typhoon season in early autumn. Considerable damage is caused by the strong winds and floods, but substantial rainfall enables the cultivation of wet rice. Three-quarters of the country is mountainous; the remainder is made up of small plains scattered around the coast. The country is long and narrow, stretching from north to south. Mountain ranges run from north to south right through the middle of the country, and the climate is quite different on the opposing sides of these mountains. In winter the Pacific Ocean side is fine and dry, while the Sea of Japan side has heavy snowfalls. As a result cultural and economic development on the Sea of Japan side has been much slower. The major cities – Tōkyō, Ōsaka, Kyōto, Nagoya (Aichi Prefecture) – are all on the Pacific side. The Sea of Japan side has come to be called *Ura Nihon* – Reverse Japan, the Pacific Ocean side *Omote Nihon* – Obverse Japan.

In 1990 the population was 123 600 000, about twice that of the UK, half that of the USA, and slightly less than 3 per cent of the world's population. Population density (number of people per square kilometre) was 330, nine times higher than the world average. Moreover, the vast majority of people live on the plains, which make up only a quarter of the land, so that population density there is as high as anywhere in the world. This has affected Japan's society and her economy in many ways. The labour–land ratio is high, and labour productivity in the agricultural is much lower than in the non-agricultural sector. Contacts between people are very frequent, so that an efficient communication network has developed naturally. This has contributed greatly to the people's ability to come to a consensus of opinion, and also to the diffusion of technology in agriculture. It has also given Japan a great advantage in the accomplishment of 'national projects' (whether it be military expansion or economic growth). It is this aspect which sometimes makes other countries look upon Japan as a potential source of trouble.

1.1.2 The People and their Culture

One characteristic of the Japanese is their high degree of homogeneity. If the *Ainu* minority is excluded, all Japanese belong to the same race (Mongoloid) and speak only one distinctive language. Several religions are practised – Shintō, the traditional folk religion, Buddhism, Christianity – but their influence on everyday life is minimal. The Japanese have no qualms about participating in the ceremonies of more than one religion. It is quite common for the same person to have a Shintō wedding ceremony, pray for his children's health at a Shintō shrine during the *Shichi-Go-San* (Seven-Five-Three; for girls aged seven and three, boys aged five) festival, celebrate the Christian Christmas Eve at home with his family, and have a Buddhist funeral service when he dies.

The old social class system (*samurai*, farmers, artizans, merchants – in descending order) was abolished after the Meiji Restoration (1868), and the occupation army's measures to introduce democracy after the Second World War (agricultural land reforms, the break-up of the *zaibatsu* – the giant business conglomerations, the formation of labour unions) created a high degree of equality, both socially and economically. Today the majority of the population believe they belong to the middle classes.

Another characteristic of Japan's culture and society is the coexistence of traditional and modern elements. Japanese people's ideals were greatly influenced by Confucian teaching in the Tokugawa Period (1603–1867), so that even today more importance is attached to the interests of the group than to those of the individual. Loyalty to the extended family and its head, to one's company and one's country, all stem from Confucian thought. It is the same teaching that encourages the Japanese to save rather than consume, which accounts basically for the high level of savings. After the Meiji Restoration western ideals were introduced, but they did not spread until after the Second World War, when they began to supplant traditional ones. Today the nuclear family is gradually replacing the extended family. Loyalty to the company is still the rule, but there is little evidence of patriotism among the generations brought up since the war. Thus, for example, the national anthem *Kimigayo* and the national flag (*Hinomaru*) are even regarded as symbols of the political right wing.

The coexistence of old and new can also be seen in living styles. Traditional Japanese-style houses are found next door to western-style ones, and most houses have both western- and Japanese-style rooms.[2] The people's diet saw very few changes before the Second World War, but thereafter the popularity of western food quickly grew. Nowadays Japanese food is eaten at some meals and western food at others, and it is not uncommon to see both at the same table. Generally speaking young people prefer western food and the elderly Japanese food, and there is a curious tendency for people to come to prefer Japanese food as they grow older. Overall, however, there has been a significant increase in the consumption of western food, and one beneficial result is that the Japanese are now taller than in the pre-war period.

In the Tokugawa Period, literature, art, music and drama reached levels of excellence that Japan could be proud of. *Nō, kyōgen* and *kabuki* plays, and traditional dances, are still highly regarded all over the world. From the Meiji Restoration (1868), however, western culture began to spread quickly, and since the war it has become much more popular than traditional culture. Today the Japanese listen to Mozart and Beethoven rather than to the *koto* or the *shamisen*.[3] It is even said that the custom of playing Beethoven's Ninth Symphony as a part of the year-end festivities began in Japan and was then 'exported' to Europe.

Science and technology made progress in the Tokugawa Period as a result of Dutch studies,[4] but they were a long way behind Europe and America. After the Restoration students were dispatched to Europe and America, and teachers invited in return, in a determined effort to introduce western science and technology. These efforts, and improvements in higher education, did improve matters, but progress in the field of production technology was much faster than in the field of science. Japan's backwardness in radar and nuclear power was one of the causes of her defeat in the war. This trend continues today. While Japan's products flood world markets, the number of Nobel Prizes Japan's scientists receive is embarrassingly low compared with those of other advanced nations.

There are two major reasons why Japan was able to transplant western culture so quickly after the Meiji Restoration:

1. Japan's long history of intercourse with the countries of the Asian continent, especially China. Much of Japan's traditional culture came from the continent. It is significant, however, that the transplanted elements were often modified by the Japanese. One example is the writing system. In the fourth century, *kanji* – Chinese characters – were introduced to Japan, and used to write the Japanese language. Then in the ninth century a fifty-letter phonetic alphabet was invented to supplement them. Since then the two have been used in conjunction; this has given the writing system a greater

variety of expression, contributing to the excellence of Japanese literature.

2. Education. The Meiji government quickly introduced, first, compulsory primary education, and then voluntary secondary and higher education systems. In the latter, modern culture was taught alongside moral education. After the Second World War the American system of education – six years at primary school, three at middle school, three at high school and four at university – was adopted. Surveys have shown that the mathematics taught in Japan's primary and middle schools is very advanced compared with world levels. Also, the percentage of children who go on to high school and university is very high.

Despite their contacts with western culture the Japanese are still very insular; marriages between Japanese and foreigners are rare. On the other hand foreigners' knowledge of Japan is inadequate and full of misconceptions. This situation is the result of a combination of Japan's geographical isolation, the long period in which her shores were closed, and her unique language.

1.1.3 Politics and Economics

With the Meiji Restoration in 1868, Japan became a constitutional monarchy; government passed from the hands of the Shōgun (military governor) to the Emperor Meiji. The constitution was promulgated in 1889 and a parliament established in 1890. Popular demand for a more democratic system grew, and the first election took place in 1925. But suffrage was limited to men, and it was the Emperor who held power. In the 1930s military influence in government increased, and this led to first the China Incident,[5] then the Pacific War and finally the country's complete collapse. After Japan's defeat the occupation forces enforced demilitarization and democratization: in 1946 the new constitution was promulgated, declaring that the country would be governed democratically by a constitutionally elected parliament, and that arms would be renounced completely. (Suffrage was given to all adults and the Emperor was prohibited from participating in politics.) In 1951 Japan and the USA signed a mutual co-operation and security treaty, and in 1952 occupation came to an end. Under the treaty Japan agreed to the stationing of American troops in Japan and in return received military protection. As a result Japan's expenditure on defence is considerably lower than in other advanced countries, which may facilitate economic growth. The American people, however, have had to pay heavy taxes to support defence. The American economy has been relatively stagnant and dissatisfaction is widespread. The US government has, therefore, exerted strong pressure on Japan to increase its defence spending.

With the Liberal Democrat Party (LDP) in power continuously since 1955 (up until October 1955 the country was governed by a coalition of the Liberal Party and the Democratic Party) government has been stable. The LDP has continued to promote co-operation with the USA, while domestically economic growth has been the main priority. The LDP works in close connection with the civil service and the business world. These connections lead to corruption and occasional scandals, but they are very useful when it comes to the execution of economic policies.

Japan has few raw materials. Rainfall is abundant, but it is concentrated into relatively short periods of time, and because of the steepness of the land most of it flows quickly to sea and cannot be used for hydro-electric power schemes. For minerals Japan is almost completely dependent on imports. But human resources are abundant, and have been particularly valuable. In the early period of modern economic growth, when capital accumulation was inadequate, it could even have been said that human resources were the only resources available. Excellent entrepreneurs and technicians made possible the introduction of modern industry and technology, and the skilled labour force quickly mastered the new techniques. Many people believe that Japan's growth rate is higher than western countries' because of the difference in their managers – Japan is positive, prepared to take risks with new technology; the west is always putting safety first – and its respective labour forces – Japan's diligent and co-operative; the west's concerned only with asserting their rights, and putting their companies in difficult straits with continual strikes.

Social overhead capital linked with production activities has increased considerably. During the Tokugawa Period the necessary irrigation facilities for agriculture were virtually completed, roads of some sort extended to all parts of the country, and coastal shipping services improved considerably. From the Meiji Restoration the government has put a lot of effort into the construction of railways, ports, roads and communication systems. Coastal shipping used to carry the greatest share of freight, with railways second and roads third. Since the 1970s road transport has taken the lead, with shipping second and railways third. Railways carried the most passengers for a long time, but again since the 1970s road transport has been carrying most. Postal and telephone services and telecommunications are highly developed, while broadcasting, journalism and publishing have improved greatly, thus giving Japan one of the world's most advanced communications networks. This also has contributed to the people's ability to form a consensus of opinion.

Japan's lack of resources has meant that to industrialize successfully she has had to import enormous quantities of raw materials (in the past mainly raw cotton and iron ore, nowadays oil and natural gas) and export manufactured products. Industrialization (pre-war mainly light industry, post-war heavy and chemical industry) has, except during the long recession caused by the war, proceeded since the Meiji Period (1868–1912), and Japan has caught up with the leading countries of the west. In 1964 Japan became a member of the OECD, thus joining the brotherhood of advanced industrial nations. In the late 1960s Japan's GNP overtook West Germany's, making Japan second only to the USA in the free world. Japan's economic growth has been without equal, particularly since the war, and has attracted a great deal of attention in other countries. One person referred to Japan as the risen sun, and another has prophesied that the twenty-first century will be Japan's. Yet another, referring to Japan's policy of putting economic growth before everything else, described the Japanese as economic animals, and a certain prime minister referred to Japan's prime minister as a transistor radio salesman. How did Japan manage to industrialize so rapidly? The main purpose of this book is to attempt to answer this question.

In recent years, however, a number of problems have reared their heads. Demands for the social overhead capital which benefits people's lives (educational facilities, parks, etc.) and for social security (pensions, sickness benefits) have increased. The concentration of people in the cities and rapid economic growth have caused worsening pollution of the environment. Political problems in some countries have made raw materials more difficult to obtain, and the rapid increase in Japanese exports continues to cause friction. All these factors suggest that the economy has entered a new phase; the miracle period of high growth has come to an end.

1.2 MODERN ECONOMIC GROWTH

1.2.1 The Concept

The concept of a 'modern economic growth' era has been found useful in studying Japan's economic development.[6] The distinguishing feature of this era was the application of modern science and technology in all fields of production. Science and technology have been applied most often, and with greatest effect, in industry (here we include transport, communications and public works) and thus industry's growth rate has been the highest. 'Industrialization' was the engine of modern economic growth; in fact industrialization and modern economic growth are only different sides of the same coin.[7] Moreover the starting-point of modern economic growth coincided with the start of what is often referred to as the 'industrial revolution', the period when modern industry suddenly rose to prominence.[8] The most important feature of this 'revolution' was the increased use of the steam engine in transport and industry, which in the latter was inextricably tied up with the development of the modern factory system.

1.2.2 The Transition Period

The introduction of western science and technology had already begun in the closing stages of the Tokugawa Period; the Satsuma Clan in southern Kyūshū had begun building factories and importing machinery. Then, with the Restoration and truly centralized government, the great effort to catch up with the west began. Modern economic growth or industrialization, became what K. Ohkawa and H. Rosovsky called the 'national objective'.[9]

The economic growth of the early Meiji Period cannot, however, be called 'modern' in the strict sense of the word. As this period is called 'the blank quarter century', the economic situation in this period is not always clear. However, unstable price variations stemmed from the weak currency system and symbolizes the confusion of the economy. We do know, that agriculture accounted for the larger part of the economy, that what industry existed was usually only a by-employment in agricultural communities, and that it involved mainly manual labour. There were very few modern factories. According to Kazuo Yamaguchi's estimates in 1881–7 only 3.6 per cent of all factories were powered by steam,[10] and the author has estimated that in 1884 steam engines only accounted for 38.3 per cent of the total horse-power capacity employed in the manufacturing industry.[11] Thus the early Meiji Period was a transition period leading up to, not the beginning of, modern economic growth.

1.2.3 The Beginning of Modern Economic Growth

I would like to follow Ohkawa–Rosovsky and set the year in which modern economic development (industrialization) began as 1886.[12] During this year private firms began to develop rapidly. The success of Japan Railways in 1881 encouraged capitalists, and other private railways were constructed in quick succession. In the area of sea transportation, Ōsaka Mercantile Steamship Company (Ōsaka Shōsen) and the Japan Mail Steamship Company (Nihon Yūsen) were established in 1884 and 1885, respectively, and they extended the sea lanes steadily. In industry, prominent developments were centred around cotton-spinning. Strong evidence for this is the fact that the horsepower of steam engines, which were the driving force of the new industries, increased rapidly after 1885.[13] Also, the real output of the manufacturing industries recorded a growth of 18.3 per cent in 1886, although it had been depressed between 1881 and 1885 during the Matsukata inflation.[14]

However, it was after the beginning of the twentieth century that modern economic development assumed a substantial shape. It is possible to evaluate the economic development after 1886 as being of a primitive form compared to the economic development of the twentieth century. The following two points are the basis of this period division.

1. There is proof that such systems of information/transportation as the mail, telecommunications and railway systems had been developed throughout the nineteenth century and that the national market for products, finance and labour was formed at the beginning of the twentieth century. Differences among the regions in prices and in the interest on savings were reduced in the nineteenth century and differences virtually disappeared by the beginning of the twentieth century.[15]

2. In 1896 the government passed laws granting subsidies to shipbuilding and shipping services. This resulted in the increased construction of large merchant vessels, and also increased the demand for motors and electrical machinery, thus stimulating the growth of the machinery industry. By the beginning of the twentieth century the

machinery industry was on a firm foundation. The founding of the public Yawata Iron Works in 1897 (it began operating in 1901) was another important development; domestic production of iron and steel was essential for substantial industrialization.

SUMMARY OF THE CHAPTER

The Meiji Restoration signified the birth of a modern nation, but not the beginning of modern economic development. This first required social and economic reforms, the formation of social overhead capital and the introduction of modern science and technology. These things took about twenty years and necessitated several government projects. The period 1868 to 1885 was one of transition from pre-modern to modern development. Japan finally entered the modern economic growth era, between twenty and 120 years behind the advanced nations of the west. The UK had been the first, beginning her Industrial Revolution in the second half of the eighteenth century (Table 1.1). In the first half of the nineteenth century the Netherlands, Belgium, France and the USA entered the modern growth era, and in the middle of the nineteenth century Germany, Sweden and Italy. Japan was the first country outside the west, but was one of the 'latest starters' among present-day advanced industrial nations.

Our periodization of Japan's economic development is as follows:

Pre-modern – pre-1868
Transition Period – 1868 to 1885
Modern economic growth – from 1886 to present (1886 to beginning of twentieth century = early phase of growth)

Thus, by our calculations, Japan has already experienced a full century of modern economic growth. The main objective of this book is to analyze this growth.

FURTHER READING

Introduction to Japan:
  Encyclopaedia Britannica, 1974 edn
  Ministry of Foreign Affairs, 1980
Periodization:
  Ohkawa and Rosovsky, 1965

TABLE 1.1 Per capita GNP in the developed countries at their modern
economic growth starting-points, and in 1965, 1989

	MEG starting-point (1965 dollars)	1965 (1965 dollars)	1989 (1989 dollars)
Australia	760 (1861–9)	2 023	17 338
Switzerland	529 (1865)	2 354	26 348
Canada	508 (1870–4)	2 507	20 783
USA	474 (1834–43)	3 580	20 629
Denmark	370 (1865–9)	2 238	20 402
Netherlands	347 (1831–40)	1 609	15 061
Belgium	326 (1831–40)	1 835	15 393
Germany[a]	302 (1850–9)	1 939	19 183
Norway	287 (1865–9)	1 912	21 500
Italy	261 (1861–9)	1 100	15 051
France	242 (1831–40)	2 047	17 061
Great Britain[b]	227 (1765–85)	1 870	14 646
Sweden	215 (1861–9)	2 713	22 303
Japan	136 (1886)	876	23 296

Notes:
[a] The post-war figures are for (the former) West Germany, as opposed to Germany.
[b] The post-war figures are for the UK, as opposed to Great Britain.

Sources:
Starting-points and 1965: Figures are, with the exception of Japan, from Kuznets,
1971, p. 24, table 2. Per capita GNP in Japan at the starting-point was estimated by
the same method as in Kuznets, 1971 and that in 1989 is from KKKK, No. 89, June
1991, p. 184.

2 Readiness for Modern Economic Growth

Why was Japan the first country outside the west to accomplish modern economic growth? To answer this is no simple matter, but an attempt to do so will we hope provide some lessons for present-day developing countries. Some economists assert that it was mainly because of traditional elements – the inheritance from pre-modern society – others emphasize the Meiji government's policy of introducing modern elements from the west. In this chapter we discuss the contribution of these two elements to political and economic organization, human resources and social overhead capital in Section 2.1, and to agriculture, manufacturing industries and commerce in Section 2.2. Finally in Section 2.3 we attempt to evaluate the state of Japan's readiness for modern economic growth.

2.1 POLITICAL AND ECONOMIC ORGANIZATION, HUMAN RESOURCES AND SOCIAL OVERHEAD CAPITAL

2.1.1 Political and Economic Organization

Tokugawa Japan was a 'feudal society'.[1] The country was divided into more than 260 territories known as *han*, which were ruled by lords known as *daimyō*. The *daimyō* were kept under close scrutiny by the central government, the Tokugawa Shogunate. They were allowed to take a certain proportion of the rice yield from their *han* and to have a certain number of warriors – *samurai*. The *samurai* were at the top of the social scale (followed by farmers, artisans, and lastly merchants), but they were generally not prosperous. Their expenditure increased with the rising cost of living, but their income remained virtually constant (they were paid a certain number of *koku* of rice, which usually remained unchanged), so that they fell increasingly in debt to merchants. Agricultural and industrial development brought about an increase in the economic powers of the other classes. It was this process that eventually brought about the collapse of feudalism, from within.

In 1867 the Shōgun abdicated and in 1868 imperial rule was restored. Finally in 1869 the *daimyō* surrendered their lands and subjects to the imperial government. Thus a modern nation with a centralized government was born. As we shall see later, the government abolished the social class system and most of the feudal elements which had been hindering the development of industry. The armed forces, which had of course been made up totally of *samurai*, were modernized, and universal conscription was introduced. Western technology and western political, educational, military, and company systems were introduced. Before the overthrow of the Shogunate, the slogan of the rebel leaders had been 'Respect the Emperor, keep out the barbarians'. After, it became 'Wealthy country, strong army'.

The new government, however, inherited the financial problems of the late Tokugawa Period. In 1868 central government expenditure amounted to thirty million yen; the revenue from land taxes and other traditional sources was only three million. The remainder was made up by twenty-four million in issues of unconvertible notes, and three million in forced loans (*goyōkin*) from rich merchants (three in particular – Mitsui, Ono, Kōnoike). Issues of unconvertible notes continued to support government finances until land tax reforms began to take effect. The income from the note issue was used to pay for the campaign against rebellious elements in the south-west, the formation of social overhead capital and the promotion of industry. It could also be said that these issues contributed to industrialization by enabling private saving and investment to be carried out smoothly before the development of modern financial organizations.[2]

The land tax reforms of 1873–81 greatly increased the stability of the Meiji government's finances, for three reasons. First, they reduced fluctuations due to the size of the harvest. The old taxes had been based on the yield, whereas the new ones were based on the value of the land. Second, they eradicated regional variations in the rate of taxation; under the new system it was fixed at 3 per cent of the value of the land for all the country (in 1877 this was reduced to 2.5 per cent). Third, under the new system the taxes were paid in cash instead of in kind (rice). As a result of these reforms revenue from land taxes as a proportion of total government revenue rose from 22.5 per cent in 1868–71 to 70.3 per cent in 1872–5, and 64.4 per cent in 1875–85.[3] Furthermore they meant that a money economy was forced on agricultural villages as farmers needed currency to pay their taxes. Farmers who were unable to pay the taxes gave up their land and became tenants or factory labourers.

Although government income increased, the issue of more than 40 million yen in unconvertible notes had resulted in inflation. Inflation increased the cost of imports and thus led to an excessive trade deficit and the outflow of specie. This inflation was the first crisis the new government faced; the first major trial of the feasibility of modernization in Japan. At first Shigenobu Ōkuma, the minister of finance, did not recognize the true nature of the problem. He believed that it was the excessive imports, caused by slow domestic production, which had increased the demand for, and hence the value of, silver coins. Thus his policy was to give further support to industry. This, however, had little effect on inflation, and eventually he changed to a policy of deflation. Masayoshi Matsukata, who became minister of finance in 1881, continued this policy.[4] Furthermore he realized that unconvertible notes were the real culprit, and that increased imports and the outflow of gold and silver were merely the consequences. Thus his policy was to redeem unconvertible notes and issue convertible ones. He balanced the budget by increasing taxes on tobacco and alcohol, and greatly reducing expenditure with the closing of government-run factories. During the period 1881–5 the government was able to save 28 per cent of its income; cash currency in circulation decreased by 15 per cent, and general prices in 1885 were only 79 per cent of their 1881 level. There was also a trade surplus, after several years of deficits.

Having stabilized its finances the government established the Bank of Japan in 1882. Thus by the 1880s the government had modernized the political system, their own and the country's financial structure.

2.1.2 Human Resources

Meiji Japan's greatest inheritance from the Tokugawa Period was an abundance of eligible labour. In 1872 the population was 34 million and the labour force 21 million, both manifestly excessive for such a small country (Ch. 8, Sec. 1). The quality of the labour force, however, was excellent. It was able to adapt easily to the new social and economic order, and meet the needs of modern industries when they began to expand rapidly.

The extent of education is, we believe, the major reason for the quality of the labour force. In the Tokugawa Period the ordinary people were educated in *terakoya*, classrooms set up in people's houses in which reading, writing, and the abacus[5] were taught. Most *terakoya* were run by priests or *samurai*, and they usually had between twenty and fifty pupils. By 1868 there were between 12 000 and 13 000 *terakoya* with a total of 837 000 pupils.[6] It is estimated that at this time 43 per cent of male children and 10 per cent of female children received education in these institutions.[7] According to R. P. Dore 'the literacy rate in 1868 was considerably higher than in present-day developing countries and probably compared favourably even then with some contemporary European countries'. He says that in the UK in 1837 'only one child in four or five was ever getting to school in the major industrial towns', and quotes a certain Frenchman in 1877 as saying that 'primary education in Japan has reached a level which should make us blush'.[8] Without the basic skills of reading and writing the introduction of the new land system and the new registration system of births, marriages and deaths could not have been carried out so smoothly and the remarkable progress in farming methods described later would have been impossible. According to Dore *terakoya* education 'constituted at the very least a training in being trained'. It was probably because of their education that labourers from agricultural areas were able to absorb the necessary training and become skilled at their new jobs. Dore said that 'the wide diffusion of basic education implanted in people's minds the simple notion of a possibility of improvement, so that Japan had already got over the first hurdle in a process of purposeful development'.[9] E. S. Crawcour, talking about the education of merchants and businessmen in the Tokugawa Period, says that 'larger businesses ran schools for their apprentices', and that 'a high level of accounting technique and the uniformity of accounting procedures suggests widespread formal teaching'.[10]

In 1872 the government introduced universal compulsory (primary school) education, but its progress owed much to the traditional *terakoya* system. Many existing *terakoya* were permitted to become 'acting' national schools, and the majority of the teachers at national schools had formerly been teachers at *terakoya*. In 1873 the rate of primary school attendance was 28 per cent; by the early 1890s it had risen to over 50 per cent.[11] To put this into perspective let us compare it with education in developed countries at the time. Compulsory education in Germany (Prussia) began in 1763, about a century before the beginning of modern economic growth there. By the 1860s the rate of primary school attendance was 98 per cent in Prussia, and 100 per cent in Saxony.[12] In the USA (the state of Massachusetts), the UK and France, however, compulsory education was not introduced until after the beginning of modern economic growth, in the 1850s, the 1870s and the 1880s respectively. Thus, from the point of view of the stage of economic development, compulsory education in Japan, as in Germany, began very early. However in 1873 the total number of pupils attending school in Japan represented a mere 4 per cent of the population. This was slightly less than the UK and considerably less than the USA in the 1870s. It was in fact not until the 1910s that Japan reached the USA figure for the 1870s. If, however, we bear in mind the economic stage of development, the difference is minimal.

The early start of compulsory education must certainly have helped to provide the necessary supply of trained people. However at the beginning of modern economic growth only 935 000 people, in other words only 2.5 per cent of the population, had received education under the new system.[13] Even if we add to this the number of people who were then attending school (3 195 000), it still only represents 10.9 per cent of the population. Thus at the starting-point of modern economic growth the contribution of the traditional *terakoya* was of greater significance than that of the newly introduced educational system.

The capable leaders of the Meiji Period were a further legacy from the Tokugawa Period. Most of the leaders of the new government came from the *han* (e.g. Chōshū, Satsuma) which had played the greatest part in the overthrow of the Shogunate (e.g. Hirobumi Itō, Taisuke Itagaki, Toshimichi Ōkubo, Shigenobu Ōkuma). The effect of Confucian teaching on the behaviour of the new leaders has often been cited. By the late Tokugawa Period nearly all the *han* had their own schools, and there were also many independent schools for *samurai*. In these schools they were imbued with Confucian ethics, particularly the idea of self sacrifice in the public interest, as well as a feeling of racial superiority from nationalistic Shintō teaching.[14] Takao Tsuchiya's theory on the background and the motives of the entrepreneurs who pioneered capitalism was generally accepted for many years.[15] He said that most of the Meiji Period entrepreneurs were of *samurai* extraction, and that their way of thinking was 'group-oriented' and 'community-centred' rather than concerned with personal profit; they were prepared to give everything for the sake of their country. Eiichi Shibusawa was a good example of this type. Born the son of a wealthy farmer, he became a lower-ranked *samurai* and worked in the Shōgun's personal service. When the Shōgun's younger brother went to Paris in 1867 Shibusawa accompanied him. In the new government he was made a high official in the ministry of finance, but later went into the private sector and helped to found several modern enterprises, many of which he was made president of (e.g. Daiichi Bank, Ōsaka Spinning Company, Ōji Paper Manufacturing Company, Tōkyō Marine Insurance Company). He explained both management techniques and Confucius's *Analects* to entrepreneurs, emphasizing to them the importance of serving their country as well as the pursuit of profits.

In recent years, however, Tsuchiya's theory has come in for criticism. It has been asserted, mainly by two non-Japanese scholars (Y. Hirschmeier and K. Yamamura), that Meiji entrepreneurs were by no means exclusively *samurai*; that in fact they came from a variety of backgrounds.[16] Yamamura said, for example, that the founders of the Mitsubishi and Yasuda *zaibatsu*, Yatarō Iwasaki and Zenjirō Yasuda, were both from farming families. Kenjirō Ishikawa traced the backgrounds of 219 Meiji entrepreneurs. He found that the greatest number (48 per cent) were *samurai*, followed by merchants (23 per cent).[17] These figures appear to substantiate Yamamura's criticism, but the fact that *samurai* account for almost half the total suggests that there was a kernel of truth in Tsuchiya's theory.

Yamamura also criticized Tsuchiya's views on entrepreneurial motives. From his research into Iwasaki's and Yasuda's business methods he concluded that their motives were ruled not by any public-spiritedness, but by a desire for personal gain.[18] Iwasaki, for example, made enormous profits by very devious means. When the demand for shipping services increased, Iwasaki, who by conspiring with the government had gained a monopoly of the country's shipping services, reduced the number of ships in service by six, and charged exorbitant prices. This infuriated the public. At a mass protest meeting they beheaded a 'sea monster' with Iwasaki's face. Certainly one of the motives of Meiji entrepreneurs was personal profit. However entrepreneurs of *samurai* extraction had received Confucian moral training, and the others had also been influenced to some extent by Confucian thought. Yasuzō Horie says that Confucianism 'was a way of life and thought widely disseminated through every stratum of society'. Confucianism was not a reactionary moral code; it stimulated the pursuit of knowledge and awakened a love of learning. Horie concluded that 'while I would hesitate to say that Confucianism helped to breed the entrepreneural spirit as actively as did the Protestant ethic in Europe, it certainly provided an intellectual and moral climate that favored the emergence of this new leadership'.[19]

The threat of invasion by the powerful nations of the west, combined with their educational background must have made many of the entrepreneurs of the Meiji Period deeply concerned with the interests of the nation.

2.1.3 Social Overhead Capital

Japan's road network improved considerably during the Tokugawa Period largely because of the *sankinkōtai* system – the *daimyō* were required to reside alternately in Edo (the name of Tōkyō in the Tokugawa Period) and their *han*, and the constant coming and going of *daimyō* and their entourages meant that roads had to be maintained. However, the ordinary roads away from the main trunk roads were left, being disrupted by the mountain ridges and rivers. In addition, since Japan is in the monsoon zone, the roads tend to turn to mud, and the Shogunate's policy of restricting the building of bridges as part of their military strategy, meant that wheeled transport was virtually useless for long journeys. Commodities were transported by pack horse or coolies, but water transport was probably more important. Although the ban on voyages overseas precluded any major improvement in sailing methods, coastal and river transport were well developed and organized.

Irrigation facilities for agriculture also improved considerably in the Tokugawa Period. The quality of construction varied considerably, but by the late Tokugawa Period most agricultural land was reaping the benefits of irrigation.[20]

The sweeping away of the restrictions which had hampered travel (checkpoints for travellers, enforced changing of horses and boats at certain points, etc.) at the beginning of the Meiji Period allowed traditional methods of transport to develop rapidly. Furthermore the government's industrial policies included the formation of modern social overhead capital. In 1870 they inaugurated a telegraph service between Tōkyō and Yokohama (Kanagawa Prefecture), in 1871 the postal service, and in 1872 the Yokohama-Shinbashi (Tōkyō) Railway was opened.

To demonstrate the significance of the new social overhead capital,

TABLE 2.1   Changes in travel time and expenses resulting from the opening of railways in Japan

(A) Travel time

	Before the opening of railways (days)	By rail (hours and minutes)		
		1890	1909	1912
Tōkyō–Ōsaka	19 (palanquin)	18'52"	12'00"	11'55"
Tōkyō–Sendai	5 (carriage)	12'18"	9'10"	8'58"

(B) Travel expenses

(yen)

	Before the opening of railways				Railway fares
	Palanquin fares	Miscellaneous	Lodging charges	Total	
Tōkyō–Yokohama	0.68	0	0	0.68	0.32
Tōkyō–Nagoya	6.53	0.09	1.16	7.79	2.76
Tōkyō–Ōsaka	9.45	0.13	1.89	11.36	3.67

Sources: Minami, 1965, p. 7, table 1.2; p. 8, table 1.4.

TABLE 2.2   Changes in time and charges for transporting *habutae* silk from Fukui to Tōkyō with the opening of railways

	Before the opening of railways	By rail	
		Between Tsuruga and Sekigahara, opened 1883	Entire Tōkaidō Line, opened 1889
Number of days	10	8	4
Charges (yen/100 *kan*)	13.2	10.0	6.2

Sources: Minami, 1965, p. 8, table 1.3.

let us look at how the development of land transport affected the economy. By palanquin the journey from Tōkyō to Ōsaka had taken nineteen days; with the advent of the railway this was reduced to nineteen hours in 1890 and to only twelve hours in 1912 as locomotives improved (Table 2.1). The cost primarily for this journey by palanquin (primarily for transport and lodging) had been more than eleven yen; by 1890 it was reduced by two-thirds. Table 2.2 gives an indication of how freight transport was affected, the example here being the transportation of *habutae* silk from Fukui City to Tōkyō. Before the railways it had taken ten days.

Railways over part of the journey reduced this to four days by 1889 and the cost was halved. Thus these improvements, particularly the building up of a rail network, reduced the time and cost of both freight and passenger transport. Reduced freight costs meant a corresponding fall in commodity prices, and the increase in speed reduced production costs by accelerating the circulation of working capital. These developments hastened the formation of nationwide commodity markets. They also facilitated population mobility and contributed to the formation of labour markets, especially in the cities. The railway network was, however, far from complete, and it was not until the twentieth century that truly nationwide markets became a reality.

Thus, traditional and modern social overhead capital both developed rapidly in the early Meiji Period, and formed the foundations for the economic growth which followed.

2.2 ECONOMIC DEVELOPMENT

2.2.1 Agriculture

In the Tokugawa Period agricultural production made up the overwhelming part of the economy. (As late as 1872 15 400 000 people, 72 per cent of the total working population, were employed in agriculture.)[21] Farmers were theoretically tied to the land by the rigid social class system; they were officially forbidden to move to another area or forsake agriculture. Agricultural products were increasingly being sold rather than consumed by the farmers. By the late Tokugawa Period three-quarters of the rice shipped to Ōsaka came from the storehouses of the *daimyō*, the remainder from the farmers themselves. Cotton, rape-seed, indigo, tobacco, tea and sugar cane were also cash crops. By the 1860s the degree of commercialization in advanced areas had reached 80 per cent, and in backward areas 10 per cent, so that for the country as a whole it was probably about 60 per cent.[22] This was very significant, because as Crawcour says, 'the degree of commercialization is . . . of great relevance to the responsiveness of the economy'.[23] Landes said that the significance of commercialization and industrialization in rural areas lay in 'the evidence they offer of a rational economizing mind at work' and that 'this was probably the greatest achievement and legacy of the late Tokugawa Period: the rise and spread of attitudes conducive to adaptation and growth'.[24] Adjustment of output in response to changes in demand (in Japan this meant in the long-term the reclamation of land for rice, and technical progress) works well provided the price mechanism functions properly. This mechanism cannot function without the progress of commercialization and where self-sufficiency prevails.

The *daimyō* and the landowners' eager attempts at reclamation increased the area of arable land considerably, and the spread of double-cropping and improvements in agricultural technology increased land productivity. The most important improvement during the period 1600–1850 was the increased use of commercial fertilizers (mainly dried sardines, oil cakes). Commercial fertilizers were used before the Tokugawa Period, but only in certain areas. With the improvements in land transport and the expansion of local markets during the seventeenth and eighteenth centuries they came to be used widely. By the beginning of the nineteenth century they were used in almost every part of the country. The second most important improvement was in plant varieties. At the beginning of the seventeenth century there were 177 different species of rice being cultivated. This increased to 2363 by the middle of the nineteenth century. As has already been mentioned irrigation improved considerably, and there were two other important changes: improved methods of planting rice – from the early nineteenth century farmers planted it at equal distances in neat rows – and a new method of selecting rice seeds – putting the seeds in salt water and taking the heavier ones.[25]

In 1869 the government abolished the four-tier social ranking system. From 1871 farmers were officially permitted to sell rice and grow the crops of their choice. In 1872 the ban on the sale of farmland was lifted, the division of farmers into three classes was abolished, and farmers were officially given permission to engage in industry and commerce. Thus farmers could leave their land and move into commerce or industry in the towns whenever they wished. These reforms, together with the newly acquired freedom of movement from place to place, helped lay the foundations for industrialization. According to the author's estimates, during 1876–80 59 000 people per year, and during 1881–5 73 000 people per year, moved from primary to non-primary industries. These people accounted for 75 per cent of the increase in the non-primary industries labour force during 1876–85 (Table 9.5).

To stimulate agricultural production the government tried to transplant western agricultural technology, but the attempt failed, except in Hokkaidō – a new frontier with smaller population density. In such a densely populated country capital-intensive, labour-saving methods could hardly be expected to take root; farmers continued to use traditional methods. The growth rate of agricultural output, however, was high. It averaged 1.7 per cent for 1878–85.[26] Thus agricultural productivity was comparatively high at the starting-point of modern economic growth. Furthermore the high rate of agricultural growth continued, assisting modern economic growth in its early years.

2.2.2 Manufacturing Industry

What industry there was in the Tokugawa Period was carried on as a by-employment in agricultural areas, mainly through the domestic system. This can be seen in the spinning, reeling (silk), weaving and ceramics industries. Merchants in the towns supplied spinning-frames, reeling-machines and looms to farmers, and paid them by the piece. Cotton spinning and weaving was common in Kinai (present-day Kinki region), Mikawa and Owari (these two make up present-day Aichi Prefecture); silk reeling in Fukushima, Gunma and Shinshū (present-day Nagano Prefecture). However, true 'manufacture' could only be found in a few places: silk weaving in Kiryū (Gunma Prefecture), silk reeling in Shinshū, *sake* brewing in Nada (Hyōgo Prefecture).[27] The use of mechanical power (i.e. the water wheel) was very rare, and limited to simple operations such as grinding or crushing (of rice, wheat, rape-seed, earth, minerals). Other operations where machinery was used involved only simple implements moved by hand or foot, for example the *zakuri* (sedentary reeling) technique, in which the left hand takes the silk thread from a cocoon while the right hand turns a machine which winds it on to the bobbin. This suggests that in the Tokugawa Period production was not on a sufficient scale, and production techniques were not advanced enough, to necessitate the development of mechanization and the factory system.[28]

In the late Tokugawa Period the more forward-looking *han* attempted to introduce western technology. In 1857 Nariakira Shimazu, the *daimyō* of Satsuma *Han* (present-day Kagoshima Prefecture), had a western-style factory built. It consisted of a blast furnace, a glass works and a ceramics works, and the machinery was driven by water power. For the Kagoshima Spinning Works, built in 1867, Satsuma *Han* imported spinning-frames from the UK, which were steam driven. The Sakai Spinning Works, also founded by Satsuma *Han*, was completed in 1870, and the Kashima Spinning Works in 1872. These three factories are known as *Shisosanbōseki*, the three founders of spinning in Japan.

In the Meiji Period the development of traditional industries, particularly cotton and silk, gained momentum. One reason for the development of the former was the advent of *gara-bō* (throstle spinning).[29] It was invented in 1876 by a Buddhist priest from Nagano, Gaun Tatsuchi, and it received the first prize at Japan's first industrial exhibition in the following year. Although it was merely an extension of the old hand-spinning technique it meant a considerable increase in output, and the frames for throstle spinning were easy to produce and inexpensive. From 1878 it was used with the water wheel, further improving productivity. Throstle spinning spread quickly in agricultural areas in the 1880s. Meanwhile the government was trying to introduce modern spinning techniques from the west. In 1878 spinning factories were built in Aichi and Hiroshima Prefectures, and run by the government. In 1879 ten 2000-spindle spinning-frames were imported, and sold or rented to private concerns. Three spinning works were built with government loans for the frames. These enterprises, however, found it difficult to make a profit, and modern techniques were not adopted widely.

The government also fostered the silk-reeling industry, encouraging it to become a major exporter. In 1870 a government-run model factory was built at Tomioka (Gunma Prefecture) with the most up-to-date machines, driven by steam. However, this factory also was unable to run at a profit and private concerns did not build similar factories, perhaps because such production methods were too capital-intensive for the needs of the day. In the late 1870s, however, modern methods were tried in conjunction with the *zakuri* technique, and the resulting combination was used widely. The demand for silk increased in Europe, and, from the latter half of the 1880s, in the USA. The output of raw silk increased rapidly, as did exports. Raw silk accounted for 6 per cent of manufacturing industry's output in the 1870s, and raw silk exports for 36 per cent of commodity exports.[30] The expansion of the silk-reeling industry in this period was very significant.

The government also tried to introduce modern technology to other areas. They took over the mines and armament and machinery factories which had been run by Shogunate and the various *han*, for example the Ishikawajima Shipbuilding Yards (Hyōgo Prefecture), Yokosuka Iron Works (Kanagawa Prefecture) and Nagasaki Iron Works. Also, in 1873 they built the Akabane Engineering Works (Tōkyō). In these factories, not only ships, iron and weapons, but also machine tools, motors and general machinery were manufactured and repaired. At this time the private machinery industry was still at a very early stage of development; the government produced what the private sector was not yet able to. They built a cement works at Fukagawa (Tōkyō) in 1874 and a glass works at Shinagawa (Tōkyō) in 1876. However the preoccupation with foreign technology was eventually succeeded by a period of reflection; the government's industrial policies underwent a sharp turnabout. Many government-run mines and factories were either closed or sold to private concerns.[31]

The state of industry at this time is reflected by real output figures.[32] The growth rate for 1878–85 averaged 3 per cent. However, of the increase in output during the period 1877–85 the increase in the production of foodstuffs accounted for 43.5 per cent and the increase in the production of textiles 32.9 per cent. What modern industry existed was run or sponsored by the government, and its contribution to industrial output was still tiny. The traditional industries of the Tokugawa Period, carried out on a small scale in agricultural areas, still formed the nucleus of Japan's industry.[33] Their accelerated growth in the Meiji Period was an important factor in preparing Japan for the industrialization which followed.

2.2.3 Commerce and Finance

Although the merchants were the lowest rung on the social ladder in the Tokugawa Period, they held the real power. The progress of commercial and financial activities in the castle towns was striking. The *daimyō* had warehouses and offices in Edo or Ōsaka in which they employed merchants and financiers who sold the commodities from the *han* and were charged with the safekeeping and disposal of the money received for them. Other merchants received the rice allowance from the Shogunate on behalf of the *daimyō*, and sold it for them. As time went by the merchants increasingly made high-interest loans to *samurai* with the latter's rice allowances as collateral. With the capital they built up, merchants and financiers also invested in land reclamation and the cottage industry, improving their position socially and economically, and contributing not a little to economic growth. Commerce made great progress in agricultural communities, because of increased agricultural productivity and expanding rural markets.

In the Tokugawa Period coins – gold, silver, and copper – were minted exclusively by the Tokugawa government for use in all the *han*. Money supply was a source of revenue for the government. In addition, not a few *han* issued unconvertible paper money. This was authorized by the government in order to help the *han* overcome the increasing shortage of coinage (minting could not keep pace with economic development), but the *han* frequently used this privilege to supplement their finances. The main financial institutions in this period were private exchange houses. They played a similar role to the modern bank; they not only exchanged money but also carried out general financial transactions.

The contribution of commercial capital to economic development increased in the Meiji Period. Capital for the government's industrial policies was raised by land taxes and bonds, from landowners and merchants. In 1872 the government authorized the establishment of National Banks, modelled on the US system, but only four banks were actually founded under the initial regulations (the First National Bank was founded in 1873). In 1876 the regulations were revised, and new banks were founded in rapid succession. These banks facilitated the collection of land taxes, absorbed landowners' and merchants' capital and supplied funds for industrialization. In 1882 the Bank of Japan was founded, and it began issuing convertible notes in 1885. Thus the government created a modern financial structure.

Before the mid-1880s commerce and finance had already made considerable progress, and therefore helped to prepare the way for industrialization. At least one aspect of commercialization, however, lagged behind. Because Japan had had virtually no experience of foreign trade during the Tokugawa Period, the necessary organization for it (e.g. general trading companies) had to be built up after industrialization had begun in earnest (Ch. 7, Sec. 3).

Finally we must mention changes in the management of companies in mining, manufacturing, transport, commerce and finance. The new government was anxious to introduce a more modern company system. The First National Bank was the first joint-stock company in Japan, but the joint-stock company was not strictly legal until 1899 with the revision of the laws on commerce. The advent of the joint-stock company meant that savings could be drawn from a wider

sphere and it freed the management from considerations such as
risk-bearing and saving. The joint-stock company was in fact the basis
of modern capitalism, and its introduction was therefore vital to the
success of modern economic growth.[34]

2.2.4 The Economy and Population before Modern Economic Growth

Traditionally, historians have considered that in the seventeenth
century both the economy and the population grew rapidly, but that
during the following 150 years the economy was stagnant and the
population remained stationary.[35] However this view, both of economic and demographic movements, needs revision in the light of
recent research.

Throughout the Tokugawa Period the economy was by no means
stagnant, as was made clear in our analysis of industry above. Output
in the most important branch of activity, agriculture, increased
steadily. Industrial activity in agricultural areas increased, and commerce made significant progress. S. Hanley and K. Yamamura said,
'the economy grew throughout the entire Tokugawa Period, though
slowly by modern standards, and unevenly . . . the rate of economic
growth tended to exceed the rate of population growth even in the
poorer regions, thus raising the living standard of the large majority
of the population throughout the Tokugawa Period despite major
famines'.[36] Hiroshi Shinbo and Mataji Umemura concentrated their
attentions on the late Tokugawa Period. Shinbo argued that in this
period the Shogunate, through the medium of government expenditure, invested the profits it made from successive debasements of the
coinage, and that this and the multiplier effect worked to increase
both prices (from 1820 prices began to rise) and output. In this way,
he said, economic growth was achieved.[37] Umemura went a step
further. He said that these price rises caused real wages to fall and
profits to increase. This increased entrepreneurs' propensity to invest, and also made it possible for them to accumulate the necessary
capital. Thus private investment was stimulated, and economic
growth achieved.[38]

The economic growth of the Tokugawa Period (or at least the late
Tokugawa Period) not only continued into the Meiji Period, it
accelerated due to the 'opening' of the country and the reforms which
were carried out.[39] However growth before the mid-1880s was the
result of the expansion of traditional industries (agriculture, the

cottage industry in agricultural areas, service industries), not modern ones (i.e. those with factories operating on a large scale and using modern production methods). This is why we have suggested that modern economic growth did not begin until the mid-1880s, although the former growth was of great significance for the latter.

Population increased over the Tokugawa Period as a whole. In the first half it increased at a rate of 0.6–0.8 per cent; in the second half there was an increase, but the rate of increase was slower.[40] The population census initiated in 1721 by the eighth Tokugawa Shōgun, Yoshimune, was repeated at approximately six-year intervals thereafter. These censuses did not cover the whole population, but they give a good indication of overall trends. From them, Umemura concluded that the population remained stationary in the eighteenth century, but increased in the nineteenth century.[41] He also made the interesting assertion that these demographic changes were linked to the reclamation of land and agricultural output. There were, he said, three periods of prodigious reclamation – the middle of the seventeenth century, the end of the seventeenth and the beginning of the eighteenth centuries, and the nineteenth century – but that little reclamation took place during the greater part of the seventeenth and eighteenth centuries.[42]

If Umemura's assertions about the nineteenth century are correct, the old view of the population remaining stationary in the late Tokugawa Period must be revised. However, the rate of increase in the nineteenth century appears to have been lower than in the seventeenth century. According to demographers' estimates the natural rate of population growth in the early Meiji Period was 0.5–0.7 per cent, and the rate of increase did not rise until after the beginning of modern economic growth. The fact that Japan's population growth rate was low at the starting-point of modern economic growth meant that she was at a distinct advantage over present-day developing countries, where the population growth rate is often about 3 per cent.

2.3 AN ASSESSMENT OF JAPAN'S READINESS FOR MODERN ECONOMIC GROWTH

2.3.1 Relative Backwardness

With the accelerated development of traditional elements and the addition of modern ones in the early Meiji Period Japan had, by the mid-1880s, attained a high level of development, both socially and economically, and was thus in a comparatively favourable position for her modern economic 'take-off'. Certainly she was in a much better position than present-day developing countries.[43] How then did Japan in the 1880s compare with the leading nations of the west? Industry in the UK had made considerable progress even before her industrial revolution. Landmarks included the expansion of the woollen industry and the use of the water wheel in the fulling process from at least the thirteenth century, while from the middle of the sixteenth century the coal-mining industry grew rapidly and stimulated expansion in several manufacturing industries (e.g. glass, salt, metallurgy). In contrast mechanization had hardly begun in Japan in the Tokugawa Period, and though it progressed somewhat in the Meiji Period it was on a much smaller scale that it had been in England. Thus the indications are that before modern economic growth industrial development in Japan was much slower that it had been in England, and also in other European areas where new industrial technology was slowly developing.[44] To put it another way, Japan was in a state of 'relative backwardness'.[45] Assuming that there is a correlation between industrial development and economic growth – and in most cases there is – industrial backwardness necessarily implies economic backwardness. Let us then compare economic development in Japan and the west, first in 1870, using GNP per capita, and the number of agricultural workers as a proportion of the total number in employment, as our indicators.[46] This is slightly before Japan's 'starting-point', but this should cause no serious discrepancy. Japan's GNP per capita was only 25 per cent of the UK's and 36 per cent of the USA's.[47] Agricultural employees still accounted for 72 per cent of the total in Japan, whereas this figure had already fallen to 19 per cent in the UK and 51 per cent in the USA. The difference between a country which had already completed an industrial revolution and one which was about to embark on one was manifest.

Next let us compare Japan and other countries at their respective modern economic growth's starting-points. Japan's GNP per capita (1886) was 60 per cent of the UK's (1765–85), 29 per cent of the USA's (1834–43) and 18 per cent of Australia's (1861–9) (Table 1.1). Unfortunately there are virtually no figures available on the labour forces employed in different industries during these periods. We do have a figure for the UK in 1801; the number of workers employed in agriculture and fishing accounted for 36 per cent of the total number employed.[48] The figure must have been higher at the starting-point of modern economic growth, but it was almost certainly lower than the figure for Japan in 1886, 71 per cent.[49] Thus, when compared at the same stage of development also, it is clear that Japan was 'relatively backward'.

SUMMARY OF THE CHAPTER

The institutional and economic developments in the Tokugawa Period and the early Meiji Period laid the foundations for modern economic growth, which began in the 1880s, say 1881. The growth which occurred prior to, and continued after this turning-point, particularly in agriculture, traditional industries and service industries, also assisted the 'take-off'. Two important points emerged from this:

1. It contradicts the view, put forward mainly by Marxist economists, that the economy was stagnant in the Tokugawa Period, and that economic growth was achieved by the political reforms and economic policies adopted after the Meiji Restoration. This view exaggerates the contribution of modern elements in the Meiji Period and understates the significance of traditional ones; it fails to take into account the continuity of history.

2. It suggests that Japan at that time was in a much more favourable position for 'take-off' than are present-day developing countries. This seems to be the most likely explanation of Japan's successful take-off, and the difficulties being experienced by present-day developing countries trying to emulate her.

Japan, however, had less favourable conditions for take-off than the west. To overcome Japan's relative backwardness the Meiji government took a series of measures in rapid succession to sweep away feudal elements and introduce modern ones. Recently there have been several empirical studies of the economy in the Tokugawa Period and the early Meiji Period. Most of them emphasize the continuity of traditional elements, and stress the high level of economic development attained in this period. The old view of a complete reversal of historical trends must be radically revised. However, we must be careful not to go too far in the opposite direction. Japan's relative backwardness must be recognized, as must the contribution of modern elements in various fields from the late Tokugawa Period onwards.

FURTHER READING

Allen, 1972, chs 1–5
Crawcour, 1965
Landes, 1965
Lockwood, 1968, ch. 1
Rosovsky, 1966; 1972
Smith, 1955; 1959; 1973

3 An Analysis of the Growth Rate during Modern Economic Growth

Despite the setback caused by the Second World War, Japan's modern economic growth has continued from 1886 until the present day – in other words for a full century. The purpose of this chapter is to survey the process of modern economic growth by discussing the level and changes of the growth rate of GNP. In Section 3.1 we put forward a theory (the 'relative backwardness hypothesis') to explain why Japan's economic growth rate in this period has been higher than the growth rates of the developed countries of the west. In Section 3.2 we analyze cyclical fluctuations in the growth rate, 'long swings', looking at historical events and their relationship with the 'upswings' and 'downswings'. In Section 3.3 we turn our attention to long-term trends for the growth rate, and the phenomenon of 'trend acceleration'.

3.1 ECONOMIC GROWTH RATE LEVELS

3.1.1 An International Comparison

Table 3.1 shows the growth rates of GNP, population and per capita GNP of major developed countries including Japan.[1] Periods differ for each country because they are calculated from their respective modern economic growth starting-points. Highest economic growth rates were achieved by Japan (3.6 per cent) and the USA, followed by Canada, Sweden and Australia. It is significant that three of these

TABLE 3.1   Economic growth rate, population growth and growth of per capita GNP during the modern economic growth phase in the developed countries (%)

	Period	Duration (years)	Average annual growth rate		
			G(Y)	G(N)	G(Y/N)
Japan	1885/9–1963/7	78	3.6	1.1	2.5
USA	1834/43–1963/7	125.5	3.6	2.0	1.6
Canada	1870/4–1963/7	93	3.5	1.8	1.7
Sweden	1861/9–1963/7	100	3.2	0.6	2.6
Australia	1861/9–1963/7	100.5	3.2	2.2	1.0
Denmark	1865/9–1963/7	98	2.9	1.0	1.9
Norway	1865/9–1963/7	98	2.8	0.8	2.0
Italy	1895/9–1963/7	68	2.8	0.7	2.1
Germany[a]	1850/9–1963/7	110.5	2.7	1.0	1.7
Netherlands	1860/70–1963/7	100.5	2.5	1.3	1.2
Switzerland	1910–1963/7	55	2.3	0.8	1.5
Great Britain[b]	1765/85–1963/7	180.5	2.2	1.0	1.2
France	1831/40–1963/7	128.5	2.0	0.3	1.7
Belgium	1900/4–1963/7	63	1.9	0.5	1.4

Notes:
Y = real GNP (or GDP, NNP, national income).
N = total population.
Y/N = per capita GNP.
[a] The post-war figures are for the former West Germany.
[b] The post-war figures are for the UK.

Sources:
$G(Y)$, $G(N)$, $G(Y/N)$: All countries except Japan – Kuznets, 1971, pp. 11–14, table 1. Japan – see Figure 3.3.

(the USA, Canada, Australia) are countries that were 'opened up' by European settlers comparatively recently. Belgium, France, and the UK had the lowest average growth rates. If the countries were placed according to the population growth rate, Japan (1.1 per cent) would be about halfway, Japan's population growth rate is in fact equal to the simple average of all the countries in Table 3.1. The growth rate of output per capita was much higher in Sweden and Japan (2.5 per cent) than in any of the countries. Population growth was rapid in the USA, Canada and Australia, whereas it was gentle in Sweden and Japan. This accounts for the difference between the former and the latter in terms of output per capita.

As a result of Japan's all-out efforts to catch up with the developed countries of the west, her GNP per capita, which was 60 per cent of the

UK's and 29 per cent of the USA's at their respective modern economic growth starting-points, has exceeded that at these countries in the late 1980s (see Table 1.1).

3.1.2 The Relative Backwardness Hypothesis

How are we to account for the difference in the economic growth rates of these countries? It is, of course, the result of countless social and economic factors, but it appears that the lower a country's economic level (measured by GNP per capita) at its modern economic growth starting-point, the higher its economic growth rate is thereafter. This is, we believe, because 'latecomers' are able to adopt the advanced technology developed in the advanced countries (Ch. 5, Sec. 3). We have called this the 'relative backwardness hypothesis', and it was first presented by Gershenkron to explain the history of industrialization in Europe.[2]

The upper half of Figure 3.1 shows the correlation between the GNP per capita of twelve countries in 1870 and their GNP growth rates during the period 1870–1965. Apart from the USA and Canada, the lower a country's GNP per capita was in 1870 the higher its subsequent GNP growth rate was Japan's proximity to the regression line indicates that her high growth need not be seen as abnormal. The USA and Canada's distance from the regression line is mainly because the influx of immigrants from Europe helped to raise the economic growth rate and this in turn stimulated further immigration. The lower half of Figure 3.1 reveals the close correlation between GNP per capita in 1870 and subsequent growth rates of GNP per capita. In it, the USA and Canada are closer to the regression line, which supports our hypothesis that their distance from the regression line in the upper half of the figure is due to the effect of the population growth rate.

Figure 3.2 shows the correlation between the GNP per capita of the fourteen countries in Table 3.1 at their modern economic growth starting-points and their subsequent growth rates. The upper half shows the correlation with the growth rate of GNP, the lower half the correlation with the growth rate of GNP per capita. In the upper half, the USA, Canada and Australia are a long way from the regression line, but even if we exclude these three countries, there is still no significant statistical correlation. In the lower half, however, there is a significant correlation even when we include all the countries.

There appears, therefore, to be a clear correlation between relative

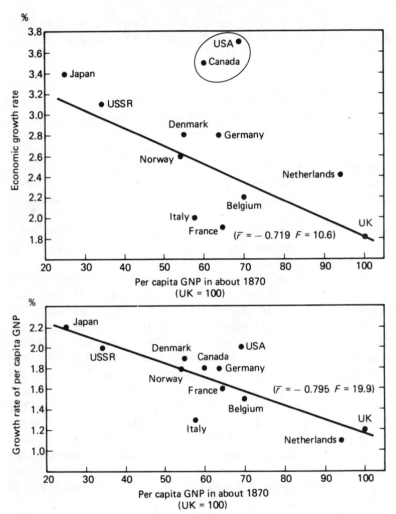

FIGURE 3.1   Relationships between economic growth rates during
the modern economic growth phase and per capita GNP in 1870

Notes:
Rates of growth (for the period 1870–1965) are calculated from real GNP figures.

The regression shown in the upper diagram was estimated excluding the USA and
   Canada.

Sources:
Economic growth rates: Maddison, 1969, p. xxi, table 4.
Per capita GNP: Maddison, 1969, p. xvi, table 1.

40

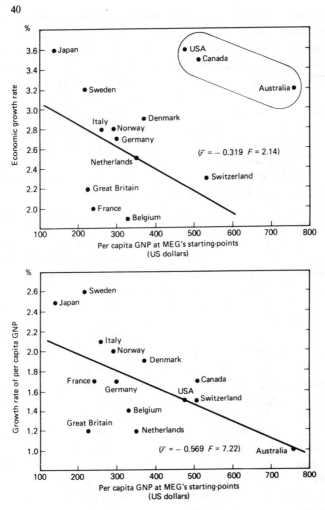

FIGURE 3.2   Relationships between economic growth rates during
the modern economic growth phase and per capita GNP at its
starting-point

Notes:
Growth rates are for the period from the starting-point of the modern economic
  growth until 1963/7, and they are calculated from real GNP.
Per capita GNP is in 1965 dollars.
The regression shown in the upper diagram was estimated excluding the USA, Canada
  and Australia.

Sources:
Tables 1.1, 3.1.

backwardness as measured in the same year (1870) and subsequent growth rates than between relative backwardness at modern economic growth starting-points and subsequent growth rates. This is because in 1870 the developed countries' GNP per capita was higher than it had been at their modern economic growth starting-points; the gap between them and the latecomers had widened. In this respect the analysis using modern economic growth starting-points could be said to be a more meaningful test for our hypothesis. In both figures there is a stronger correlation when we use the growth rate of GNP per capita than when we use the economic growth rate. This is because the population growth rate, and hence the economic growth rate, is affected by such factors as immigration.

From this analysis we conclude that the pace of economic growth in these countries has been considerably affected by the economic level at their respective economic growth starting-points; the greater the degree of relative backwardness of the latecomers the faster their economies grew subsequently. To this we would like to add three comments. First, while the GNP per capita gap between the developed countries has tended to shrink during the process of modern economic growth, the gap between developed and developing countries has widened, mainly as the result of economic growth in the former.[3] Second, if a country is to take advantage of its relative backwardness it must have what Kuznets called the 'social capability' to adopt and assimilate technology. In Japan this social capability developed before and during modern economic growth (Ch. 5, Sec. 3). Third, it should not be forgotten that relative backwardness also entails disadvantages. The introduction of new medicine and methods of hygiene may lead to rapid population growth due to a fall in the death-rate, and hence increased consumption and a fall in the propensity to save. Adoption of the same consumption patterns as developed countries would also cause a rapid increase in consumption. These things are actually taking place in present-day developing countries, whereas they did not happen in Japan. The death-rate did decline, but gradually, as a result of an improvement in the standard of living (Ch. 8, Sec. 1). The 'demonstration effect' did not affect consumption until after the Second World War (Ch. 11, Sec. 3). Thus it might be said that the decisive factor in Japan's economic success was that the demonstration effect operated effectively in the area of production technology, but did not affect consumption.

3.2   FLUCTUATIONS IN THE ECONOMIC GROWTH RATE

3.2.1   Long Swings

Research on Europe and the USA has revealed the existence of various types of business cycles: Kitchin cycles (2–3 years), Juglar cycles (7–8 years), Kuznets cycles (about 20 years) and Kondratieff cycles (50–60 years). Kitchin cycles are said to occur because of inventory cycles, Juglar cycles because of equipment cycles and Kuznets cycles because of building and construction cycles. In other words, the longer the gestation period for investment, the longer the cycle created. Kondratieff cycles are said to be connected with technological revolutions.

Some of these cycles have been identified in Japan's economic history. We will concentrate on Kuznets cycles, otherwise known as 'long swings'.[4]

We have chosen the growth rate of GNP (or GNE) for our attempt to identify long swings, because GNP is an aggregate indicator of economic activity. The fluctuations in $G(Y)$ and $G(Y/N)$ are shown clearly in Figure 3.3 and Table 3.2. We have presented the long swings in graphical form in Figure 3.3, choosing where possible the years with the highest growth rates for the peaks (P), and those with the lowest for the troughs (T).[5] According to our periodization the average length of time from P to P is 23 years, and from T to T 21 years. The average duration of long swings is therefore about 22 years. The economic growth rate has been high during the upswings (from T to P) and low during the downswings (from P to T).

Our periodization of the long swings is similar to that of other authors.[6] As for the mechanism which causes them, however, there is not an established theory. Shinohara stresses the effect of exogenous factors such as wars and exports.[7] Fujino explains it by a model incorporating financial markets.[8] However, long swings are probably, as Ohkawa and Rosovsky suggest, the product of a variety of factors – economic, non-economic, exogenous and endogenous.[9]

Next we will look briefly at each upswing and downswing and the events which took place during it, and thus trace the way in which the economy evolved. It will become clear that these swings were affected not only by domestic economic factors, but also by political, military and international ones.

TABLE 3.2   Economic growth rate $G(Y)$, population growth $G(N)$ and growth of per capita *GNE* $G(Y/N)$ in Japan 1876–1988 (%)

	$G(Y)$	$G(N)$	$G(Y/N)$
1889–90	3.53	0.85	2.68
1891–5	3.12	0.92	2.19
1896–1900	2.25	1.10	1.15
1901–5	1.84	1.18	0.66
1906–10	2.29	1.14	1.16
1911–15	3.35	1.36	1.99
1916–20	4.77	1.11	3.66
1921–5	1.93	1.26	0.67
1926–30	2.53	1.50	1.03
1931–5	4.98	1.36	3.62
1936–8	5.07	0.95	4.12
(1889–1938)	3.15	1.01	2.14
1955–60	8.35	1.01	7.34
1961–65	9.98	0.99	8.99
1966–70	9.67	1.25	8.42
1971–75	5.30	1.33	3.97
1976–80	4.06	0.92	3.14
1981–85	3.90	0.67	3.23
1986–88	4.45	0.50	3.95
(1955–88)	6.71	0.98	5.73

Note:
The figures are the simple averages of the annual growth rates.

Sources:
Same as Figure 3.3.

3.2.2   Pre-war

1885–96 (upswing)   In this period modern industries expanded remarkably. From the founding of the Japan Railways Company in 1881 the private railway network expanded rapidly, covering 2731 kilometers in 1895, compared with only 955 kilometres belonging to the National Railways.[10] The use of electricity spread rapidly after the founding of the Tōkyō Electric Light Company in 1887. The Ōsaka Mercantile Steamship Company and the Japan Mail Steamship Company, founded in 1884 and 1885 respectively, grew steadily with aid from the government. The most important development, however, was the growth of a modern spinning industry. The Ōsaka Spinning Company, founded in 1883, was very successful, and from 1887 several large spinning factories were built in other areas.

Japan was to all intents and purposes on the silver standard, and during this period world silver prices fell. This reduced the exchange rate of the yen, stimulating exports. (Imports did not decrease in spite of the reduced exchange rate, because industrialization caused an increase in the supply of goods.) The reparations China was obliged to pay Japan after the Sino-Japanese War (1894–5) were equal to a quarter of the national income, and greatly contributed to industrial activity and economic growth.

1897–1903 (downswing)   The rapid industrial development of the previous phase peaked, and the growth rate fell. In 1897 Japan adopted the gold standard, which stopped the fall in the exchange rate and improved the terms of trade. This adversely affected the balance of payments, causing several financial crises.

1904–18 (upswing)   The Russo-Japanese War (1904–5) and the foreign loans obtained after it stimulated Japan's modern industries, but because of the increasing burden of interest on these loans and an increase in imports, the trade balance worsened further. However, Japan's chronic trade deficit changed to a large surplus almost overnight with the outbreak of the First World War. The countries involved in the war were unable to meet the demand for their products, and Japan's share of world markets greatly increased. The unprecedented expansion of exports stimulated investment activity. The investment ratio increased, and the economic growth rate rose to 5–6 per cent (Figure 3.3 and Figure 6.2). Not only did textiles and other light industries expand rapidly, heavy industries – iron and steel, machinery, shipbuilding – at last began to make significant progress. The demand for labour increased, temporarily absorbing the surplus which had existed in both rural and urban areas.

1919–28 (downswing)   Exports peaked in 1917 and fell rapidly; percentage of exports in GNE decreased from 27 to 14 during 1917–21 (based on non-smoothed statistics), so that there was again a balance-of-payments deficit. In 1920 there was the 'post-war financial crisis', sparked off by a collapse in the silk market. The Great Kantō Earthquake of 1923 exacerbated the situation. In 1927 there was a run on the banks, and a severe financial crisis. In this period modern industries were strengthened by mergers and takeovers, moves towards monopoly, the growth of the *zaibatsu* and efforts to make management more efficient. Thus the productivity gap between modern and traditional industries widened. Companies in modern industries began to introduce the lifetime employment system and the seniority

42

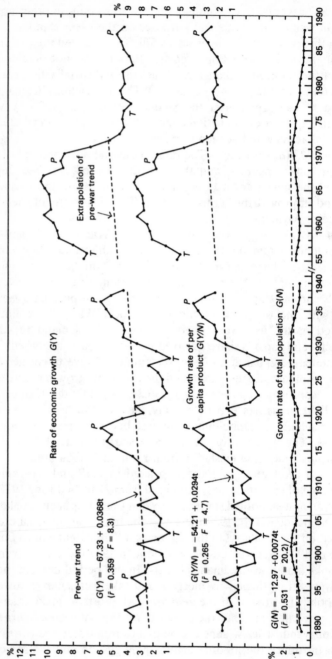

FIGURE 3.3 Economic growth rate, population growth and growth of per capita GNE in Japan 1889–1988

Notes:

Y = real GNE (1934–6 prices for the pre-war period, 1985 prices for the post-war period).

N = total population.

$G(Y/N) = G(Y) - G(N)$.

Figures for Y and N are seven-year moving averages (five-year averages for 1938, 1954 and 1988).

Sources:

Y for the pre-war period: Ohkawa and Shinohara 1979, pp. 256–8.

Y for 1970–90 is based on new SNA figures at 1985 prices; 1970–89: KKKN, 1991, pp. 118–21; 1990: KKKK, no. 88, p. 165.

Y for 1952–69 is old SNA figures in 1965 prices (Ohkawa and Shinohara 1979, pp. 260, 365) with adjustment to make a continuity to the new SNA series from 1970. Adjustment was made from the components of GNE.

N: Until 1964 – Nippon Ginkō, Tōkeikyoku, 1966, pp. 12–13; Ohkawa and Shinohara, 1979, pp. 392–3. Since 1965 – KTN, 1991, p. 290.

wage system (Ch. 9, Sec. 3); they made all possible efforts to retain their skilled workers and take on less unskilled ones. Thus there was again a surplus of the latter, and the difference between skilled and unskilled workers' wages increased.

1929–36 (*upswing*)   In 1929 Junnosuke Inoue, the minister of finance, introduced a policy of austerity, with the aim of strengthening the economy and improving Japan's ability to compete in world markets. Since 1917 the export of gold had been forbidden; in 1930 the embargo was lifted, and gold was sold at the old price. This meant an effective rise of 15 per cent in the value of the yen. The worldwide panic which had begun in the USA in 1929 spread to Japan 1930–1. Companies went bankrupt and unemployment increased. In December 1931 the new minister of finance, Korekiyo Takahashi, reimposed the gold embargo, and embarked on a policy of reflation, including an increase in the national debt. As the exchange rate of the yen fell, the terms of trade deteriorated and exports increased rapidly. Industrial output expanded sharply, particularly in the heavy and chemical industries. Demand for labour increased and the level of unemployment fell.

3.2.3   Wartime and Post-war

1937–56 (*downswing*)   With the beginning of the war with China in 1937 and the Pacific War in 1941 the economy went increasingly on to a wartime footing. In 1938 the National General Mobilization Law gave the government power to direct resources to military objectives, and in 1941 rationing was introduced. In 1943 factories still being used for 'peacetime industries' were converted to munitions factories. However, the economic situation became critical when Japan lost command of the seas, and hence could not import raw materials.

With defeat in 1945 began the long road to recovery. The war had drastically reduced productive capacity, and the distribution of all remaining funds to soldiers returning to their homes (to prevent them falling into the hands of the occupation forces) immediately after the war helped bring about violent inflation. Emergency financial measures by the occupation forces (SCAP) to combat this inflation in 1946 included freezing a large proportion of bank deposits and limiting the amount that could be withdrawn to a mere 300 yen a month for the head of a household and 100 yen for each other member. Meanwhile SCAP ordered the Japanese government to introduce democratic practices to all areas of the economy. As early as 1945 they ordered the dissolution of the *zaibatsu*, land reforms[11] and the passing of a law which gave full rights to trade unions. It is said that these reforms laid the foundations for subsequent economic growth by guaranteeing the operation of the principle of free competition throughout both the economy and society in general. In 1946 the Differential Production Scheme was introduced by the government; coal mines were given first claim to iron and steel, and the extra coal produced as a result was used for the production of iron and steel. It was believed that expansion in these two industries would lead to growth in other industries. By about 1948 the economy was on the road to recovery, but inflation still persisted. In 1949 under the direction of J. M. Dodge, an adviser brought in by the occupation authorities, a tight money policy was implemented, and inflation was at last brought under control. Then in 1950 the Korean War broke out, and the emergency demand for large amounts of military supplies gave impetus to the economic recovery. The peace treaty signed with the Allied Powers in 1951 restored Japan's independence.

1957–69 (upswing)   This is the period now referred to as the high economic growth period, when the economy grew at unprecedented rate of over 10 per cent. The immediate cause of this growth was a sharp rise in investment; in 1969 the private fixed investment ratio had reached 27.3 per cent of GNE, and the overall investment ratio (including government investment) 35.3 per cent.[12] The increase in investment could not have taken place without the introduction of technology; new products and technology developed in the developed countries during and after the war came into Japan in great waves. New industries sprung up – synthetic fibres, petrochemicals, electronics – and existing ones completely renewed their equipment. The government's Double the National Income Plan (1960) also stimulated investment. Improved productivity as a result of the technological revolution, and the maintenance of the $1 = 360 yen exchange rate (set up in 1949, under-valuing the yen) brought about a rapid increase in exports. By the late 1960s there was a consistent balance-of-payments surplus on current account. The demand for labour, particularly young labour, increased and from about 1960 there was a shortage. Wages increased sharply, even in low-productivity sectors, so that the rise in production costs and consumer prices gained momentum. Inflation and certain social costs, such as pollution, detracted from the benefits high growth brought.

1970–5 (downswing)   The USA's worsening trade balance led to massive sales of dollars, which shook the international currency structure. In 1971 and again in 1973 the exchange rate of the yen to the dollar was raised. On the first of these two occasions the government, fearing a reduction in exports, and a recession, greatly increased government expenditure and made credit easier. There was, however, no reduction in exports, and 'excess liquidity' ensued. The 'oil shock' of 1973 (OPEC's restrictions on crude oil exports and the big price increase which accompanied them) exacerbated the situation. There was speculation on assets such as land, and prices increased remarkably. This was the 'runaway inflation' of 1973–4. The government's reaction was a very tight money policy. This succeeded in controlling inflation, but equipment investment stagnated and economic growth declined significantly. The labour shortage was interrupted for a time as companies took on fewer new employees and unemployment increased.

1976–1987 (upswing) The tight money policy was lifted in 1975, but the expected business revival did not transpire. Demand remained slack, and only the expansion of exports (particularly cars and electrical products) kept the economy from stagnating. In 1976 a surplus was achieved, but export-led economic growth was becoming more difficult as Japan's expanding exports met with increasing criticism abroad. In 1977 the government embarked on a bold expansionist policy. The economy at last began to improve and the labour market situation became more hopeful.

The characteristic aspect to be pointed out for this period is that there was a great change in relationship between Japan and overseas countries. By the continuous expansion of exports, the trade balance, with deficits in 1974–5 became a surplus in 1976. After that, the surplus rapidly increased. As the result the foreign currency reserve increased rapidly, and the exchange rate against US dollars went up (the yen was evaluated). In particular, as the result of the Plaza agreement in 1985 this trend was enhanced. Furthermore, although the price of oil suddenly increased due to the second oil crisis of 1979–80, exports did not decrease due to technological innovations by industry and to management efforts. This further aggravated trade frictions.

1987 (downswing) By 'Black Monday' (the extraordinary fall of share prices on the New York Stock Market) in October 1987, the trend of cheaper dollar – higher yen was accelerated. The yen reached 122 to the dollar in November 1988. Because of this, the lowering of the official interest rate became impossible (it had been expected that the trend of cheaper dollar – higher yen would be encouraged if the official interest rate was raised). As a result, the rate was to be set at an extraordinarily low level of 2.5 per cent until April 1989. Against the background of this low interest rate, financial firms loaned large sums of money without questioning their use if land was offered as security, resulting in an increase in both land prices and share prices. This so-called 'Bubble Economy' (from the latter half of 1986 until the beginning of 1990) had a deleterious effect on the capital market and on the lives of the Japanese.

The growth rates of real GNP and real fixed capital formation (seven-year average) reached a peak in 1987 (see Figures 3.3 and 6.1).[13] However, the fluctuation was not large and the fundamental condition of the economy was not much different from that in the previous period. However, less dependence of economic growth on external demand (exports) was expected.

The reasons for this are: first, a situation exists in which Japan has to expand fiscal expenses and domestic demand because of requests from foreign countries; and secondly, because of direct investment during the previous period, productivity in consumer countries had been increased even more and exports from Japan had become less.

Also, the expansion of domestic demand has caused increased imports, and the increase of off-shore production has contributed to the decrease of the trade surplus because of the re-importation of off-shore products into Japan. The decrease in the trade surplus started in 1986 and this trend is expected to continue. Nevertheless, the American trade deficit with Japan has not been decreased significantly. Therefore, in the USA, there is a feeling that the trade imbalance is due to unfair Japanese economic rules and trade practices, and its unique economic and social structure (the Unique Japan Theory). The US government demanded fundamental structural improvements from Japan in the US–Japan Structural Conference.

3.3 ECONOMIC GROWTH TRENDS

3.3.1 Trend Acceleration in the Pre-war Period

Ohkawa and Rosovsky discovered that Japan's 'trend rate of growth' has been rising – the economic growth rate has been higher in each succeeding upswing. They christened this phenomenon 'trend acceleration'.[14]

The best way to examine this phenomenon is to calculate the trend for the annual growth rate using the method of least squares. Figure 3.3 shows the equation we used, and the trend (the dotted line) calculated from it. It indicates that trend acceleration did take place in the pre-war period. The parameter of the equation shows a 0.368 percentage point increase in $G(Y)$, a 0.294 percentage point increase in $G(Y/N)$, and a 0.074 percentage point increase in $G(N)$ every ten years. This suggests that the trend acceleration of the economic growth rate in the pre-war period was to some extent due to the population growth rate (and the consequent growth rate of the labour force), but the main factor for the trend acceleration was a trend in the growth rate of output per capita. The growth of output per capita was the result of the acceleration of the growth rate of productivity in industry (particularly the manufacturing industry, transport and communications, and public works), which was in turn caused by increased capital formation and the increased momentum of the technological revolution (Ch. 5, Sec. 1). The increase in capital formation was the result of increased returns to capital, as the labour surplus held wages down and reduced the relative income share of labour (Ch. 6, Sec. 1).

Thus, pre-war trend acceleration can be explained by the increase in the growth of the labour force, increased capital formation and the increased pace of technological progress.

3.3.2   Growth Rate in the Post-war Period

We believe that in the post-war period there were several completely new factors which increased the economic growth rate. The average growth rate for the post-war period was 6.7 per cent, compared with only 3.2 per cent for the pre-war period (Table 3.2). These figures indicate significant differences between the two periods.

In Figure 3.3 we have presented a simple extrapolation of the calculated pre-war trend, our objective being to determine whether the high post-war growth rate (or part of it) can be seen as a simple continuation of pre-war trend acceleration. It is clear that growth in the 1950s and 1960s was well above the pre-war trend. The actual economic growth rates for 1960 and 1970 were approximately double the figure gained from a simple extrapolation of the pre-war trend, while for output per capita the extrapolated trend only accounts for about 40 per cent of the actual post-war trend (see the following table).

	Actual figure	*Extrapolation of the pre-war trend*	*Deviations from the extrapolated trend*
	Economic growth rate		
	%	%	%
1960	9.50	4.80	4.70
1970	9.03	5.17	3.86
	Growth rate of per capita output		
	%	%	%
1960	8.58	3.41	5.17
1970	7.63	3.71	3.92

In other words, much of the post-war growth rate cannot be explained simply as a continuation of the pre-war trend; it was the result of factors peculiar to the post-war period. There were several growth-promoting factors which began before the war and continued after:

1. Despite Japan's efforts to catch up the west, she was still well behind the end of the war, and this factor continued to facilitate technological progress (Ch. 5, Sec. 3).

2. The increase in the investment ratio continued, which indicates that there was no basic change in investors' desire to invest (Ch. 6, Secs 1 and 2). Two factors helped convert this desire into increased investment: the continued increase in the personal savings rate (Ch. 6, Sec. 4) and Japan's distinctive 'indirect financing system', which not only continued but developed further after the war (Ch. 10, Sec. 3).

3. The continued contribution of Japan's abundant and excellent human resources.

What then were the new factors?

1. The recovery from the exceeding low levels of production immediately after the war, and the massive American demand for supplies during the Korean War (1950–3) kept the growth rate high during the early post-war period (probably until about 1960).[15]

2. 'Democratization' (land reforms, the dissolution of the *zaibatsu*, trade unions) improved companies' competitiveness and increased the purchasing power of the people.

3. The government's economic growth policy included keeping interest rates low to encourage private equipment investment (Ch. 10, Sec. 4). Successive economic plans were designed to encourage

entrepreneurs and investors to increase equipment investment (Ch. 6, Sec. 1).

4. The reduction in defence spending meant that a much larger proportion of government expenditure could be directed into productive areas (Ch. 10, Sec. 1).

5. The generous patronage afforded to export industries and the undervaluation of the yen-stimulated exports (Ch. 7, Sec. 3).

6. Having lost their military power and their international position the Japanese made economic growth their new national objective. The 'pursuit of economic growth' as 'the highest national goal' originated at the managerial level and spread to all strata of society.[16]

7. Japanese-style employment practices, particularly lifetime employment, were adopted generally, and helped to maintain stable management-labour relations (Ch. 9, Sec. 3).

8. Japan's isolation in the war, and the rapid post-war technological progress in the developed countries, widened the technological gap between them and Japan. Much of the new technology was subsequently introduced in Japan (Ch. 5, Sec. 3).

9. Because the international economy was buoyant the growth rate of the developed countries increased. As a result international commodity markets expanded, and Japanese exports increased (Ch. 7, Secs 1 and 3).

However, the growth rate of the economy and the growth rate of per capita product decreased rapidly at the beginning of 1970s and they became even lower in the latter half of the 1970s than the trend before the Second World War.

The following three factors in particular should be emphasised:

1. A global trend of technology innovations. As mentioned in item 8 above, the technological improvement which continued until the 1960s slowed down and no prominent technological innovations have appeared since then. Because of the slowdown in technological improvement, the rate of improvement of industries in the world slowed down, and economical growth dwindled. Japan, which has borrowed fundamental technologies from the rest of the world, could not be separated from this global phenomenon and as a result (as will be analysed later) Japan's rate of industrial technology improvement decreased dramatically. This became one of the major reasons for the lowering of the economic growth rate. In addition to this, the opportunity of borrowing technologies has disappeared, due to the closing

of technological gaps between Japan and such advanced countries as the USA (the disappearance of the 'catch-up' technologies) made the lowering of the rate of technological improvement of Japanese industries inevitable.[17]

2. Changes in economic policies in the advanced countries. By the beginning of the 1970s the economies of the OECD countries had reached their capacity and were already feeling the pressure of inflation. The two oil crises in the 1970s confirmed this fact. As a consequence, governments of these countries abandoned their Keynesian economic policies, which aimed at full employment, and were forced to place the highest priority on suppressing inflation.[18] Thus factor in item 9 relating to the economic growth of Japan had disappeared.

3. Deterioration of resource distribution due to the rapid rise of the price of oil. During the first oil crisis, the price of oil and primary products jumped threefold in a short period of time. Because of this, the basis for the growth of heavy and chemical industries, which demanded great consumption of resources due to the rapid pace of development, was lost. In order to establish a new resource distribution mechanism which conformed to the new pricing system, an adjustment of the industrial structure became necessary. It was inevitable that production efficiency continued to decrease until this adjustment was finally completed.

By the mid-1980s, the world economy began to recover and the economy in Japan expanded during this period. However, because of reasons mentioned below, it did not recover to its previous high rate of growth and it appeared that it was impossible to have such high growth rates again in the future.

1. The opportunity of 'catching up' by borrowing technologies has diminished even more. Rather, Japan is placed in the position of leading the world in development research. As a result, the uncertainty associated with the necessary trial-and-error process in developing technologies has increased. Therefore the investment in R & D has inevitably been reduced when compared to that of the previous period. This is the disappearance of the so-called 'merit of relative backwardness'.

2. A few variations in industrial (employment) structure have contributed to the slowdown in growth. First, the trend that the labour force tends to be concentrated in the low productivity service sectors may continue in the future. Also in manufacturing industry, the heavy, bulky and lengthy types of industry which pursued huge

scales (the scale merit) has declined, and the proportion of the machinery industry which is characterised by the production of small quantities of a variety of items is increasing. Because of the multi-purpose nature of the industry, productivity becomes lower than previously, and it requires a larger equipment investment.

3. The excess supply of labour, which was one of the factors in the acceleration of the improvement, has already diminished and in recent years the shortage of labour has become apparent. This trend will slow down economic development along with the lowering of the birth rate and the ageing of the society. In particular, the ageing of the population lowers the per capita savings rate, and gradually reducing the source of the investment.

4. Confronted by the tightening of international economic relations, Japan could no longer continue with its previous 'small country' economics. Therefore, on the one hand it will be more difficult to export, and on the other the demands for the opening up of and participation in the domestic market by overseas countries will be stronger. Also, overseas investments by Japanese manufacturing industries will be further accelerated and this will cause a reduction of productive activities in Japan.

5. Together with the increased seriousness of global environmental issues, overseas countries will strongly demand that Japan adopt an economic mechanism based on consumer-oriented rather than production-oriented attitudes.

In conclusion, those factors that used to sustain high level of economic growth have become things of the past, and it appears that the Japanese economy will continue to follow the track of 'stable economic growth' as it has been doing since the 1970s.

3.3.3 Trend Acceleration in Other Countries

The acceleration of economic growth is not a phenomenon unique to Japan. Let us focus on the economic growth rate of the UK shown in Figure 3.4. The two trends (A and B) are of a different nature, but when they are combined, there is a clear upward trend from the middle of the eighteenth century to the end of the nineteenth century. It goes without saying that the driving force for this acceleration was the Industrial Revolution.

It is possible to look up the GNP data for the main European countries since the end of the nineteenth century.[19] When the relative growth rate $G(Y)$ of the real GNP (the 7-year moving average) is examined, it is found that the upward trends are in Norway and Italy. For Norway, the following equation can be drawn when the $G(Y)$ is calculated by using the time-trend for the period between 1880 and 1936,

$$G(Y) = -79.39 + 0.0429t \; \bar{r} = 0.601, \; F = 28.7$$

For the period of 1865–1910 in Italy, the following equation applies,

$$G(Y) = -105.94 + 0.0568t \; \bar{r} = 0.699, \; F = 43.9$$

The acceleration trend in the two countries has continued after the Second World War. The following equations are drawn for the periods 1880–1936 and 1950–74 for Norway, and 1865–1910 and 1955–74 for Italy:

$$G(Y) = -69.46 + 0.0377t \; \bar{r} = 0.835, \; F = 16.9$$

$$G(Y) = -128.15 + 0.0686t \; \bar{r} = 0.959, \; F = 739.3$$

That is, in Norway and in Italy, the acceleration phenomena have been observed over about 90 years and 110 years, respectively.

This means that the acceleration phenomenon is not unique to Japan, but it is worthwhile to recognize that several development accelerations can be found in the histories of developed countries.[20] According to these examples it seems that the development acceleration tends to appear in those 'young countries' where industry is expanding rapidly. When industrialization proceeds quickly, the share of industry in the national economy will increase and because of the high growth rate of industry, the economic growth rate will, of course, also increase. (As in the case of Japan, if there is a development acceleration in the growth rate of industry itself, the economic growth rate will accelerate even faster.) The high growth rate of manufacturing industry depends on such factors as rapid technological progress, high investment rate and ample labour force. Therefore when a few of these factors disappear, the development acceleration comes to an end. In the case of Japan the disappearance of the opportunity of borrowing technologies via 'catch up' and the disappearance of the excess labour force have brought to an end development acceleration. When a 'young country' continues to de-

54

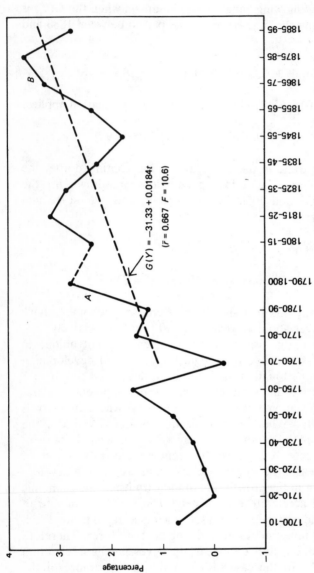

FIGURE 3.4 Economic growth rate for Great Britain in the eighteenth and nineteenth centuries

$$G(Y) = -31.33 + 0.0184t$$
$$(\bar{r} = 0.667 \quad F = 10.6)$$

Notes:
A: Annual compound rate of growth of the output index in England and Wales (1700-base).
B: Annual compound rate of growth of gross national income in Great Britain (1865–85 prices).

Sources:
A: Deane and Cole, 1962, p. 78, table 19.
B: Deane and Cole, 1962, p. 282, table 72.

velop, the technological difference between it and the developed countries will diminish. The labour force becomes increasingly in short supply, causing an increase in wages, which makes direct investment in overseas countries more extensively damaging to the growth of domestic manufacturing industries. Therefore it is not possible for development to continue for ever. This is the way in which the drama of the flourishing and diminishing of the world economy is played out.

SUMMARY OF THE CHAPTER

At Japan's modern economic growth starting-point output per capita was lower than it had been in other developed countries; subsequently her economic growth rate was higher than in the latter. This appears to fit the general pattern; an inverse correlation can be seen between countries' output per capita at the starting-point of modern economic growth and their subsequent economic growth rates.

Economic growth rates naturally exhibit sharp fluctuations. In this chapter we have focused on long swings, cycles of approximately twenty years in length. In the pre-war period, despite these long swings the economic growth rate showed an upward trend (trend acceleration), which we believe continued into the post-war period. The post-war growth rate was, however, much higher than a simple extrapolation of the calculated pre-war trend, due to several new growth-promoting factors. This indicates that post-war growth cannot be seen simply as a continuation of the pre-war trend.

In the 1970s the economic growth rate fell sharply. This was due to the fact that the global trend of technological progress had slowed down, and that Japan had lost the opportunity to 'borrow' technologies because of the disappearance of the level difference between the technologically-advanced countries and Japan. The phenomenon of trend acceleration has not been confined to Japan. It can also be seen in the UK from the late eighteenth century to the late nineteenth century (a period of over a hundred years), in Norway from the late nineteenth century until the mid-seventies (a period of about 100 years), and in Italy from the late nineteenth century to the early twentieth century (a period of about fifty years).

FURTHER READING

Trend acceleration:
  Ohkawa and Rosovsky, 1973, chs 2 and 8

Long swings and business cycles:
  Fujino, 1966; 1968
  Ohkawa and Rosovsky, 1962
  Shinohara, 1962, part 2; 1982, ch. 11

Pre-war and wartime economic growth:
  Allen, 1972
  Cohen, 1949
  Lockwood, 1968, ch. 2
  Nakamura, 1983

Post-war economic growth:
  Allen, 1965; 1972, supplementary chapter
  Itō, 1992
  Kōsai and Ogino, 1984
  Nakamura, 1981
  Patrick and Rosovsky, 1976b

Part II

Modern Economic Growth: Production and Demand

4 Agriculture during Industrialization

In most countries modern economic development has centred on industry and has been accompanied by increased agricultural output. In countries where industrialization has not been accompanied by agricultural expansion the result has been the hindrance of economic development, as increases in agricultural prices have led to rising wages and falling profits. In this chapter we will consider whether agricultural growth contributed to early modern economic growth in Japan, and if it did, in what ways? This analysis will, we hope, provide some valuable lessons for developing countries.

Section 4.1 will examine agricultural growth patterns during modern economic growth (from about 1886) and the main factors behind this growth. Section 4.2 will deal with the most important of these factors, technological progress. Section 4.3 will examine the validity of two hypotheses on the relationship between agricultural development and industrialization and Section 4.4 will analyze agriculture's contribution to industrialization in detail.

4.1 THE AGRICULTURAL GROWTH RATE

4.1.1 An Analysis of the Growth Rate

From a close look at the movements of $G(Y)$, the growth rate of primary industry (Table 4.1), four generalizations can be made:

1. From 1889 to 1920 the annual growth rate was comparatively high, between 1.4 per cent and 1.7 per cent.
2. During the 1920s it fell by half.
3. During the high-growth period from the end of the Second World War until the end of the 1960s, agriculture maintained high growth rates of 2–3 per cent.

59

TABLE 4.1   A breakdown of the primary industry growth rate in Japan
1889–1987 (%)

	$G(Y)$	$G(L)$	$G(Y/L)$	$E_K G\ (K/L)$ $+ E_B G\ (B/L)$	λ	$\dfrac{\lambda}{G(Y/L)}$
1889–1900	1.37	–0.03	1.40	0.44	0.96	69
1901–10	1.66	–0.33	1.99	0.88	1.11	56
1911–20	1.62	–0.56	2.18	1.08	1.10	50
1921–30	0.75	0.04	0.71	0.16	0.55	77
1931–8	1.30	–0.28	1.58	0.55	1.03	65
Pre-war average	1.34	–0.22	1.56	0.62	0.94	60
1956–60	3.34	–2.35	5.69	2.48	3.21	56
1961–70	2.10	–4.10	6.20	3.69	2.51	40
1971–80	–0.29	–3.95	3.66	3.63	0.03	1
1981–7	0.71	–2.61	3.32	2.10	1.22	37
Post-war average	1.24	–3.45	4.69	3.13	1.56	33

Notes:
Y = GDP (1934–6 prices for pre-war, 1985 prices for post-war).
K = gross capital stock (1934–6 prices for pre-war, 1985 prices for post-war).
L = labour force.
B = area of arable land.
E_K = output elasticity of capital.
E_B = output elasticity of land.
λ = See text.

The figures are simple averages of the annual growth rate calculated from seven-year
    moving averages (five-year averages for 1938, 1955 and 1987).

Sources:
Y: Same as the Table 5.1.
K: Pre-war – Ohkawa *et al.*, 1966, pp. 152–3
1953–4 – Estimated by extrapolating from the 1955 figure based on the series at 1965
    prices (Keizai Kikakuchō, Keizai Kenkyūjo, 1972, p. 6).
1955–64 – Estimated by extrapolating from the 1964 figure based on the series at 1970
    prices (Keizai Kikakuchō, Keizai Kenkyūjo, 1977, pp. 42–3).
1965–89 – Keizai Kikakuchō, Keizai Kenkyūjo, 1991, pp. 84–90.
L: Pre-war – Minami, 1973, pp. 312–3.
    Post-war – *Rōdōryoku Chōsa* (Labour Force Survey) in RTN, several issues.
B: Pre-war – Umemura *et al.*, 1966, pp. 216–7.
    Post-war – NTN, several issues.
E_K, E_B: Pre-war – Minami, 1981a, p. 359, table 1.
        Post-war – Minami, 1981a, p. 361, table 5.

4. After this high-growth period, its growth rates diminished greatly in the 1970s and 1980s, to 0–1 per cent.

How are we to account for these movements? First, let us divide $G(Y)$ into $G(L)$, the growth rate of labour force, and $G(Y/L)$, the growth rate of labour productivity.

$$G(Y) = G(L) + G(Y/L) \qquad (1)$$

Assuming a production function $Y = F(L, K, B, t)$, $G(Y/L)$ is expressed as follows:

$$G(Y/L) = \lambda + E_K G(K/L) + E_B G(B/L) \qquad (2)$$

K and B stand for capital stock and area of land respectively, and E_K and E_B represent the output elasticities of capital and land. $E_K G(K/L)$ and $E_B G(B/L)$ are the increases in productivity due to increases in the capital–labour ratio and the land–labour ratio. Thus they represent the contribution of increased inputs of production. λ or $(dF/dt)/F$ stands for shifts in the production function due to technological progress and changes in demand. λ is the 'residual', found by subtracting the contribution of increased inputs from $G(Y/L)$. Figures for the components of equations (1) and (2) are shown in Table 4.1.

4.1.2 Rapid Growth in the Early Period

From 1889 to 1920 $G(Y)$ remained high because of the improvement in productivity, $G(Y/L)$. During this period $G(L)$ was slightly below zero, while $G(Y/L)$ was 1.4 per cent in the 1890s, about 2 per cent in the 1900s and 2.2 per cent in 1910s. It was high mainly because of the 'residual', λ. λ was slightly less than 1 per cent in the 1890s, but it accounted for 69 per cent of $G(Y/L)$. In the first two decades of this century it was above 1 per cent, again accounting for more than half of $G(Y/L)$. The 'residual' includes several elements, but the most important was technical improvements, particularly in the area of plant varieties. The farming methods of this period are known as the 'veteran farmers' techniques (*rōnō gijutsu*).[1] By veteran farmers (*rōnō*) we mean the conscientious and wealthy farmers and landlords who had a very thorough knowledge of traditional farming methods. Using their leading position in the agricultural community, they selected the most effective methods and did their utmost to disseminate them. It was the veteran farmers of Hyōgo Prefecture and Yamagata Prefecture who, in 1877 and 1893 respectively, introduced the species of rice *Shinriki* and *Kameno-o*. These species afterwards spread throughout western and eastern Japan respectively, and greatly increased rice production.

The government's attempt to introduce western farming techniques in the 1870s ended in failure, because 'extensive' agriculture was simply not suited to Japan's factor endowment – the low land–labour ratio and the small units of land. Policy changed in the following decade and the state began seeking ways to develop methods which did suit Japan. The veteran farmers were instrumental in bringing about the success of this new policy. The government found that they had no choice but to focus on the veteran farmers' methods in the experimental centres they established, and the veteran farmers played a major role at the government-sponsored 'seed exchange meetings' and 'agricultural discussion meetings'.

4.1.3 Stagnation in the 1920s

In the 1920s a fall in the contribution of inputs and of the residual brought about a considerable drop in $G(Y/L)$, and this in turn caused a fall in $G(Y)$. Why did the contribution of inputs fall off? One factor was the fall in $G(B/L)$, the growth rate of the land–labour ratio. Until 1920 it had been above 1 per cent, but in the 1920s it fell almost to zero. $G(L)$, the growth rate of the agricultural labour force, increased, as the recession brought about a reduction in the demand for labour in the non-agricultural sector (Ch. 9, Sec. 1). This stemmed the flow of agricultural labour to the towns. The other factor was the fall in $G(B)$, the growth rate of the amount of land under cultivation (Table 4.2). In the 1910s a considerable amount of land reclamation for rice took place, especially in Hokkaidō, and $G(B)$ was between 0.5 per cent and 0.7 per cent. In the 1920s, however, reclamation virtually ceased.

The residual, which had also been above 1 per cent in the 1900s and 1910s, fell to 0.6 per cent in the 1920s. Several explanations have been put forward to explain the fall-off in technical progress, but the following two are the most widely accepted:

1. Technical improvements based on the veteran farmers' traditional methods had reached their limit, because by this time these techniques had spread to virtually every part of the country. The

TABLE 4.2 Growth rates of factor inputs, factor ratios and productivity in primary industry in Japan 1889–1987 (%)

	Factor inputs				Factor ratios		Productivity	
	Capital stock K	Area of arable land B	Intermediate goods	Fertilizers only	Capital–labour ratio K/L	Land–labour ratio B/L	Productivity of capital Y/K	Productivity of land Y/B
1889–1900	0.39	0.51	1.31	3.37	0.42	0.54	0.98	0.86
1901–10	0.86	0.72	2.50	9.65	1.19	1.05	0.80	0.94
1911–20	1.11	0.69	2.28	5.51	1.67	1.25	0.51	0.93
1921–30	1.67	0.02	2.19	4.09	1.63	−0.02	−0.92	0.73
1931–8	1.04	0.31	1.87	3.14	1.32	0.59	0.26	0.99
Pre-war average	0.99	0.46	2.01	5.16	1.21	0.68	0.35	0.88
1956–60	6.24	0.31	7.02	4.37	8.59	2.66	−2.90	3.03
1961–70	9.01	−0.46	–	–	13.11	3.64	−6.91	2.56
1971–80	9.15	−0.59	–	–	13.10	3.36	−9.44	0.30
1981–87	4.66	−0.33	–	–	7.27	2.28	−3.95	1.04
Post-war average	7.67	−0.35	–	–	11.12	3.10	−6.43	1.59

Note:
As Table 4.1.

Sources:
Y, K, B, L: as Table 4.1.
Intermediate goods and fertilizers; Umemura et al., 1966, pp. 186–7.

proportion of the total rice area in which veteran farmers' varieties (e.g. *Shinriki, Kameno-o, Aikoku*) were planted began to rise sharply from about 1895. It reached almost 50 per cent in the late 1910s, but after that remained virtually constant.[2] In the second half of the 1920s the government initiated the development of new techniques based on modern science, but it was not until after the Second World War that these efforts were substantially rewarded. (The proportion of land in which government experimental station varieties of rice were planted began to increase in the 1930s, and rose sharply during and after the war.) Thus it might be said that the stagnation of the 1920s occurred because there was a time-lag before modern methods took over from traditional ones.[3]

2. The importation of cheap rice from Korea and Taiwan was a disincentive to Japanese farmers. At the beginning of this century the supply of rice was often insufficient to meet demand, as witness the rice riots of 1918. The government thereafter attempted to relieve the problem by increasing rice production in the colonies of Taiwan and Korea. The growth rate of rice production within Japan fell significantly after 1920, while in Taiwan and Korea rice production increased rapidly between 1925 and 1935.[4] The increase in the flow of cheap foreign and colonial rice began at the beginning of the century, but was particularly noticeable in the 1920s (Table 4.3) and it seems reasonable to assume that these developments discouraged domestic farmers.[5]

TABLE 4.3   Rice – supply and demand in Japan 1878–1937 (per cent)

	Ratio of imports to consumption
1878–87	– 0.8
1888–97	0.0
1898–1907	6.2
1908–17	4.5
1918–27	11.3
1928–37	15.1

Notes:
Net imports = imports – exports.
Consumption = output + net imports.
The figures are annual averages.

Sources:
Output: Umemura *et al.*, 1966, pp. 166, 168.
Imports and exports: Kayō, 1958, p. 338.

It is difficult to say which of these two factors was the more important. Hayami and Ruttan produced a model of the balance of supply and demand and used it to analyze the effect of rice imports from the colonies.[6] Their conclusion was that this was a secondary factor and that the decline in technical progress more important.

The growth rate of rice production for the Japanese Empire as a whole remained high between 1915 and 1938 (except for 1921–5). It was 1.3 per cent in 1915–20 and 1926–30, and 1.8 per cent in 1931–8.[7] This was because the growth rate of rice production in Taiwan and Korea was high throughout this period, a factor of particular importance when the domestic growth rate fell. In other words, it could be said that the stagnation of domestic agricultural production in the 1920s was simply the result of regional changes in the Empire's production network; there are, indeed, many examples of the opening of new land in one part of a country causing a fall in the production in other parts.

4.1.4 Rapid Growth and Retardation in the Post-war Period

Agriculture showed a high growth rate in the 1950s and 1960s. This was accounted for by a rapid increase in Y/L, which was dependent on a rapid increase in inputs and a high level of λ.

The rapid increase in inputs was due to a rapid increase in capital stock, which reflected the full-scale mechanization of agriculture: $G(K)$ was 6–9 per cent and $G(K/L)$ was 9–14 per cent. The residual was large because of continuing improvements in plant varieties and the rapid spread of the use of chemicals after the war. Technical progress was also stimulated by the liberation of many farmers from the restraints of the landlord–tenant system immediately after the war (the agricultural land reforms of 1946–7),[8] and the rise in agricultural prices, which exceeded the average rate of inflation.

After the 1970s $G(Y)$ fell to 0–1 per cent, because of a decrease in $G(L)$ and $G(B)$. The decrease in $G(L)$ was caused by retardation of growth of labour supply and increased outflow of agricultural labourers. The decrease in $G(B)$ was due to a decrease in the ratio of land under cultivation to total land area.[9]

4.2   CHOICE OF TECHNOLOGY AND TECHNOLOGICAL PROGRESS

4.2.1   Japan

As already explained, pre-war technical progress was mainly the result of the dissemination of the veteran farmers' rice varieties. The main attribute of these varieties was their ability to take considerable quantities of fertilizer,[10] so that the yield could be greatly increased. This, however, necessitated an adequate supply of fertilizer. The amount of nitrogenous fertilizer used per *tan* (1 *tan* = 0.245 acre) during 1928–37 was double that for 1883–97, and the yield was 40 per cent greater (Table 4.4). The majority of fertilizers used were at first self-supplied (manure, human excrement, grass and leaves), but the amount of commercial fertilizers used gradually increased, from 11 per cent in 1883–97 to 46 per cent in 1928–37. The increased use of inorganic (i.e. chemical) fertilizers was particularly noticeable, from 0 per cent in 1883–97 to 25 per cent in 1928–37. This was due to the development of the fertilizer industry, especially the chemical fertilizer sector. The relative price of fertilizers to agricultural products fell rapidly and consistently from the 1890s until the Second World War (Table 4.4). This was mainly because productivity in the fertilizer industry improved much more quickly than productivity in agriculture and was, perhaps, industrialization's most important contribution to agriculture.[11]

Ohkawa and others have termed the pre-war combination of improvements in plant varieties and increased use of fertilizer, 'BC (biological and chemical) technology.[12] BC technology was characterized by two features:

1. Labour-intensiveness and land-economy. In other words it increased the output per *tan* (Y/B) without reducing the labour force per *tan* (L/B). The growth rate of Y/B averaged 0.9 per cent from 1889 until the Second World War (Table 4.2). From the 1920s further expansion of the area of agricultural land became virtually impossible, so increased output could only be achieved by increasing the yield. Because labour was cheap and abundant, and most farms were run on a family basis, labour-saving techniques served no purpose. Thus BC technology was the natural choice for Japan.

2. A high degree of divisibility. However small the unit of land a good yield was attainable. Therefore as long as BC technology pre-

TABLE 4.4 Rice yield, amount of fertilizer used, and relative prices of fertilizers to agricultural products in Japan 1883–1937

	Wet rice yield (koku per tan)	Amount of nitrogenous fertilizer used (kg per tan)	Commercial fertilizers used–as proportion of nitrogenous (%)	Inorganic only	Commercial fertilizer prices relative to agricultural products[a]	Inorganic only
1883–97	1.40	5.02	10.8	0.0	94	88[b]
1898–1907	1.58	5.54	15.7	1.3	71	61
1908–17	1.79	6.67	30.4	5.2	56	51
1918–27	1.91	8.26	42.1	10.8	39	31
1928–37	1.96	10.34	46.2	24.8	29	21

Notes:
[a] 1883–92 = 100.
[b] 1893–7.

Sources:
Hayami, 1973, p. 103, table 5.1; p. 104, table 5.2.

vailed there was nothing to be gained by increasing the size of farms.[13]

After the Second World War 'M (mechanical) technology' or mechanization was used in addition to BC technology. In direct contrast to BC technology, M technology was labour-saving; it raised the capital–labour ratio (K/L) and increased labour productivity. The flow of labour from agriculture to industry and the rise in agricultural wages prompted the introduction of labour-saving techniques, while the rapid development of the machinery industries improved the quality and reduced the prices of farm machinery.[14] K/L's post-war growth rate was a remarkable 11.1 per cent, so that capital productivity (Y/K) fell (-6.4 per cent) while labour productivity (Y/L) rose significantly (4.7 per cent) (Tables 4.1, 4.2). With M technology large-scale farms were, of course, more efficient.[15] This prompted an upheaval in the organizational structure of agriculture.

4.2.2   International Comparison

Is the agricultural technology of Japan a unique one when compared internationally? To answer this question, let me introduce the study by Saburō Yamada and V. W. Ruttan.

Let us look at Figure 4.1, an analysis of the relationship between land and labour productivities for one year, 1970. The forty-one countries in Figure 4.1 are divided into three groups:

1. Countries whose agricultural technology resembles Japan's, i.e. where Y/B is great in comparison with Y/L. This group includes several other Asian countries – Taiwan, the Philippines, India, etc.

2. Countries whose agricultural technology resembles the USA's, i.e. Y/L is great in comparison with Y/B. This group includes Canada and Australia.

3. European-type countries, where Y/B and Y/L are evenly-balanced, e.g. West Germany, France and the UK.

In Group 1 countries Y/B is high, but because B/L is low Y/L is also low. In Group 2 countries Y/B is low, but because B/L is high Y/L is high. Group 3 countries fall between the two extremes. In other words, Group 1 countries are significantly different from Group 2 countries in that they rely mainly on BC technology while the latter rely mainly on M technology.

One lesson developing countries of Asia can learn from Japan's

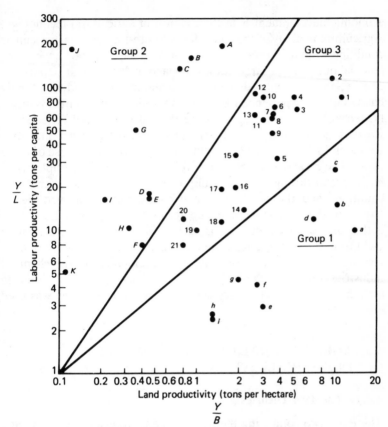

FIGURE 4.1   Relationships between productivity of agricultural labour and land 1970

Notes:
Y – calculated on wheat units.
L – male workers only.
B – includes all agricultural land.

Group 1 countries: *a* – Taiwan, *b* – Japan, *c* – Surinam, *d* – Mauritius, *e* – Bangladesh, *f* – Sri Lanka, *g* – the Philippines, *h* – Pakistan, *i* – India.
Group 2 countries: *A* – New Zealand, *B* – USA, *C* – Canada, *D* – Chile, *E* – Venezuela, *F* – Mexico, *G* – Argentina, *H* – Peru, *I* – South Africa, *J* – Australia, *K* – Paraguay.
Group 3 countries: 1 – the Netherlands, 2 – Belgium, 3 – West Germany, 4 – Denmark, 5 – Italy, 6 – Israel, 7 – France, 8 – Norway, 9 – Switzerland, 10 – Sweden, 11 – Austria, 12 – UK, 13 – Finland, 14 – Portugal, 15 – Ireland, 16 – Greece. 17 – Spain, 18 – Yugoslavia, 19 – Colombia, 20 – Brazil, 21 – Turkey.

Source:
Yamada and Ruttan, 1980, pp. 530–1.

economic development is in their choice of agricultural technology. Agriculture in many of the countries of South-East Asia is in a similar condition to that of pre-Second World War Japan. They have a low land–labour ratio, a large surplus of labour due to high population density, and the land is divided into small units managed on a family basis. Japan's experience has shown that under these circumstances BC technology is more appropriate than M technology. The Green Revolution, which resulted from a project of the International Rice Research Institute in the Philippines with US aid, makes use of these ideas. The new species of rice developed there (for example, *IR*8) have spread throughout the Philippines, Thailand and other Asian countries, and the result has been considerably improved yields. However, this project has come up against two major problems. One is that the supply of fertilizer is insufficient to extract the maximum yield from the new species. The other is that irrigation and drainage facilities are inadequate. In Japan the development of the chemical industries provided cheap fertilizers, and irrigation and drainage system were constructed very early, so that BC technology was used effectively.[16]

4.3 AGRICULTURAL GROWTH AND EARLY INDUSTRIALIZATION

4.3.1 The Two Theories

There are two conflicting theories on the relationship between early industrialization and agricultural growth in Japan.

1. The Concurrent Growth Theory
According to Kazushi Ohkawa, from the beginning of modern economic development in about 1886 until about 1920 the agricultural growth rate was high. Thus, agricultural and industrial expansion took place concurrently, in sharp contrast to western countries, where significant agrarian growth occurred before, and was a prerequisite for industrialization.[17] Ohkawa also concluded that the example today's developing countries should follow was that of Japan rather than Europe.[18] Hayami and Yamada agreed with Ohkawa's theory.[19]

2. The Prerequisite Theory
T. C. Smith, however, asserted that between 1600 and 1850 the

character of Japan's agriculture was transformed, that the productivity of land rose significantly and that this provided the foundations for the modernization of Japan.[20] J. Nakamura went a step further. His argument stemmed from doubts about the accuracy of agricultural growth rate figures in the early period of industrialization (the last twenty years of the nineteenth century), which formed the basis of the concurrent growth theory. The old Hitotsubashi Series figures for agricultural output, which hitherto had been widely accepted, were based on official government statistics. These statistics, he said, were excessively low for the early period. This was because agricultural production statistics were the basis for assessment of taxes, and farmers kept them lower than they really were to avoid paying taxes. The underestimation of agricultural output gave rise naturally to an over-estimation of the growth rate.[21] His criticism of the official statistics was justified to some extent, and these were revised. The revised statistics were published in *Long-Term Economic Statistics* (hereafter referred to as *LTES*), vol. 9[22] and it is these figures which are used in this chapter. Meanwhile Nakamura made his own calculations. He estimated that the agricultural yield had reached 1.6 *koku* (1 *koku* = 4.96 bushels) per *tan* by the early part of the Meiji Period (1878–82), much greater than that of present-day South-East Asia. This was considerably higher than the old government statistics figure of 1.2 *koku* per *tan*. From this figure Nakamura made new estimates of agricultural output.[23] According to these new estimates the growth rate of agricultural production for the period 1878/82 to 1898/1902 was 0.9 per cent, compared with 2.8 per cent according to the old Hitotsubashi Series. Based on the *LTES* revised figures it works out to 1.8 per cent.[24] In other words, before industrialization began agriculture had already made considerable progress, and output per capita had already reached a high level. Thus, although the growth rate of agriculture was low during the industrialization period, because output per capita was high, agriculture was able to supply industry with the funds it needed.[25]

In short, Ohkawa asserted that before industrialization began agricultural production was not expanding, and that the productivity at labour and land was low. When industrialization began, however, there was a period of rapid agrarian growth, so that agriculture was able to support industrialization. Nakamura asserted that agricultural production had increased considerably prior to industrialization, and therefore agricultural productivity was already high at the start of industrialization. This factor, he said, was the key to the success of industrialization.

4.3.2   The Facts

Let us examine the accuracy of these conflicting theories by answering three questions:

1. What was the agricultural growth rate prior to industrialization? One estimate shows a slow increase in agricultural output, 0.3 per cent, from 1600 to 1872. This increase depended on the increased use of commercial fertilizers (dried fish and oil cakes), improvements in rice varieties, the construction of extensive irrigation systems and inventions such as the *senba-koki*, a device for threshing rice.[26] An analysis of various agricultural treatises used in the Tokugawa Period led Smith to conclude that the prototypes of rice cultivation methods used from the Meiji Period until recent years were extant in the Tokugawa Period. Ideas for improvement of rice varieties appeared in the first half of the Tokugawa Period and the use of fertilizers increased as the period went on. Commercial fertilizers were first used in upland farming, but came to be used increasingly with rice as well.

Population trends can be of some assistance as an indirect indicator, for in an economy without access to large food imports a population increase cannot take place without an increase in agricultural production. We know, however, that in the seventeenth century the population increased, in the eighteenth century it remained constant and in the nineteenth century it increased again (Ch. 2, Sec. 1).

We have statistics for the growth rate of agricultural production after the Meiji Restoration, which show a rate of 1.6 per cent for 1878–85 (based on 7-year moving averages).[27] This shows that agricultural growth had started before the beginning of industrialization.

Thus steady agrarian growth began in the Tokugawa Period and continued into the Meiji Period. Agriculture before industrialization could hardly be described as stagnant.

2. How high was agricultural productivity before industrialization? According to the old government statistics the yield for the first few years of the Meiji Period was 1.2 *koku* per *tan*, well below Nakamura's figure of 1.6. According to the *LTES* figures it was 1.3.

Nakamura's estimates have received widespread criticism, for example, from Hayami and Yamada, who carried out the revision of the old government statistics. They criticized Nakamura on two scores.[28]

(a) They estimated a kind of production function in which the rice yield was explained by two variables; an indicator of improvements in plant varieties and the input of fertilizer per *tan*. They found that Nakamura's figures were much higher than those predicted by the production function.

(b) If Nakamura's estimates of rice production for 1878–87 to 1913–17 are converted into calorie intake per capita, they show no increase in this period whatsoever. This leads to an unrealistic supposition that the income elasticity of calorie intake is zero.

Nakamura's estimates cannot be accepted as they stand, but his contribution in calling attention to the agricultural growth of the Tokugawa Period and pointing out the necessity of the revision of the old government statistics should be recognized.

3. How great was agricultural growth during the early period of industrialization (1886–1920)? If both the old government statistics and also the *LTES* figures (which were based on the government statistics) underestimated the yield at the starting-point of industrialization, the growth rate for the early period of industrialization has been exaggerated. If we use Nakamura's estimates for the starting-point figure, the growth rate in this period is lower.[29] If, however, Hayami and Yamada's criticism is justified, and their *LTES* figures are reliable, agricultural growth was quite rapid in this period. Growth rate of agricultural production was 1.5 per cent for 1886–1900, 2.1 per cent for 1901–10, and 1.6 per cent for 1911–20.[30]

We believe that neither Ohkawa's view of stagnation in the pre-industrial period, nor Nakamura's denial of rapid growth in the early industrialization period fits the facts. Agriculture had expanded considerably before industrialization began and that growth continued into the early period of industrialization; this was the key· to its success. This fact is also true of the UK. According to recent studies, progress in agriculture began earlier than had been thought, and continued longer.[31] The fact that agricultural and industrial improvement overlapped one another brought about the success of the industrial improvement.

4.4 AGRICULTURE'S CONTRIBUTION TO INDUSTRY

4.4.1 Relative Importance of Agricultural Growth

The proportion of the contribution of Japanese primary industry to GNP was 43 per cent in 1885 and it is thought that the proportion had been about 45 per cent in 1880.[32] The proportion in the UK was only 11 per cent in 1880, and 19 per cent in the USA. In Norway, Germany and Sweden it was between 30 and 40 per cent and a little more than 40 per cent in France.[33] The proportion of agriculture in Japan was above that of those countries. Then how is it compared with the proportions in other countries at a similar stage of economic development? In order to do this comparison, the most distant year was looked at. The proportion was 33 per cent in the UK (1801), and 49 per cent in France (1789). That is, the proportion of the 'A' (for agriculture) industry in Japan in 1880 was much larger than that in the UK 80 years before.

When the proportion of agriculture is large at the initial stage, the relative rate of agricultural development to economic development or the development of non-agricultural sectors will also be large. The proportion of the GDP increment of primary industry to the increment of real GDP (the relative degree of contribution)[34] was 18–21 per cent in the period 1888–1910 (see Table 5.3). The relative degree of contribution of primary industry in the UK was 13.4 per cent[35] during 1805–1835, which was slightly smaller than that in Japan. It may be said that the contribution of the development in its agriculture to Japanese industrialization was larger than that in the UK at least. The details of the contribution of agriculture to industrialization will be discussed below.

4.4.2 The Supply of Foodstuffs

Agriculture's greatest contribution to industrialization was probably as a supplier of foodstuffs. Population growth and rising wages increased the demand for foodstuffs. Had agricultural production been unable to meet this demand, the pace of industrialization would have slowed. This would have occurred in one of two ways:

1. A shortage of agricultural products leading to rising prices and wages, bringing about a fall in profits and capital accumulation. As we will discuss later (Ch. 9, Sec. 2), until the 1950s the surplus of labour kept agricultural labourers' wages at subsistence levels. Assuming for the sake of simplicity that labourers consume only foodstuffs, therefore we have

$$w = SL \cdot P_A$$

where w, SL and P_A stand for nominal agricultural wages, subsistence level and agricultural prices respectively. If movement of labour between agriculture and industry takes place freely, industrial wages will also be w.[36] From this equation it can be seen that a rise in agricultural prices will lead to a corresponding rise in wages. If we divide the equation by P_M (industrial commodity prices) it becomes:

$$w/P_M = SL \cdot P_A/P_M$$

Thus a rise in P_A/P_M (the relative price of agricultural and industrial products) will cause w/P_M (real wages calculated on the basis of industrial products) to rise.[37] Thus if agriculture had not kept pace with industrialization, industrial prices would have fallen in relation to agricultural prices and real industrial wages would have risen. This would have reduced profit margins and hindered capital formation. These problems were recognized by D. Ricardo, and again by W. A. Lewis, and J. C. H. Fei and G. Ranis in the 'classical theory' of economic development evolved from Ricardian theory.[38]

2. International balance-of-payments difficulties. Had imports of foodstuffs to relieve domestic shortages put pressure on the balance of payments, the production equipment, raw materials and fuel necessary for industrialization could not have been imported.

Did either of these adverse features occur in Japan? As we have already seen, rice production exceeded consumption until the 1880s, and the surplus was exported (Table 4.3). In the 1890s output and consumption were about the same. Imports of rice did begin to increase at the beginning of this century, but in the first two decades they accounted for only 5–6 per cent of total rice consumption. Thus in the early stages of economic development, domestic agriculture was able to meet increasing demand. The relative price of agricultural and industrial products remained virtually constant[39] and agriculture did not impede industrialization.

There are four conditions which can bring about self-sufficiency:

1. The agricultural growth rate is high.
2. Agriculture occupies a very important position in the economy.
3. Growth in the non-agricultural sector is sluggish.
4. The increase in the population is minimal.

For Japan 3 can clearly be discounted, but the other three factors were all applicable to some extent. It was a combination of these

three factors that prevented a shortage of foodstuffs, and a consequent slowing down of industrialization in its early stages. Factors 2
and 4 are considered to have been the most important. In other
words, the difference between the agricultural and industrial growth
rates could easily have led to a shortage, but agriculture's large share
of the economy and the relatively gentle increase in population
prevented one.

With rapid industrialization and an acceleration of population
growth, the demand for foodstuffs eventually exceeded supply. As
has already been mentioned the government responded by promoting
the production of rice in the colonies. As a result the change in the
relative price of agricultural and industrial products in the 1920s was
only slight.[40] Lewis pointed out that several capitalist countries'
potential food-supply problems during industrialization were relieved
by the importation of food from their colonies. Japan in the 1920s and
1930s could be said to be one such example. In the past, Marxist
economists in Japan stressed the connection between cheap rice and
low wages. In 1961 Miyohei Shinohara revived their ideas within the
framework of neoclassical economic theory. He asserted that the
importation of cheap rice from the colonies prevented a rise in
agricultural prices, a corresponding increase in wages and thus a fall
in profits and a slowing down of economic growth.[41] The author and
Akira Ono used a dual-structured model incorporating surplus labour
to simulate Japanese economic growth for 1906–40. Our conclusion
was that increased imports of agricultural products did keep down the
increase in industrial real wages and that this resulted in increased
capital formation and faster economic growth.[42]

After the Second World War rice production increased significantly. The consumption of bread in place of rice also increased, so
that the shortage of rice became a surplus. In 1970 the government
decided to decrease rice acreage by 7.4 per cent, and since that time
rice production has been controlled. For wheat, barley and soybeans,
however, Japan depends almost entirely on imports. The proportion
of all agricultural products produced domestically fell from 91 per
cent in 1960 to 68 per cent in 1989.[43] The government's policy is to
support farmers by maintaining agricultural prices, especially rice
prices, at profitable levels. As a result the relative price of agricultural products has increased significantly,[44] and agriculture has come
to be a burden on the economy. Protection of non-competitive sectors is of course wasteful, but this policy might be justified to some
extent by the ever-present fear of a worldwide food shortage. In

formulating agricultural policy, both the forecasts for world supply and demand of foodstuffs and inflationary pressures should be taken into account.

Agriculture's share of the economy has fallen considerably. Primary industry's share of GDP fell from 18 per cent in 1938 to 3 per cent in the late 1980s (see Table 5.4). Their relative contribution to economic growth fell from 5 per cent in the 1930s, to almost zero in the 1970s (see Table 5.3).

4.4.3 Agriculture and Exports

Agriculture also earned foreign currency for industrialization through its contribution to exports. Primary industry's share of commodity exports was 47 per cent in the 1870s and 22 per cent in the 1890s (Table 7.3). For agricultural products only, the figures were 38 per cent and 11 per cent. The main agricultural export products were tea, silkworm egg-cards and cocoons. Later, agriculture's share of exports decreased rapidly, to 3 per cent in the 1930s.[45]

However, agriculture's contribution to exports was greater than these figures suggest. The improvements in sericulture enabled the silk reeling industry to expand and increase its exports. Exports of raw silk remained at a high level. Their share of total exports was more than 30 per cent for 1868–1900 and 1921–33, and 36 per cent for 1901–20. If exports of raw silk are included, agriculture's contribution becomes considerable. Thus its role can be likened to that of wool in Australia's exports (Ch. 7, Sec. 1).

Increased production of cocoons promoted such a rapid growth in the silk-reeling industry. Also improvements in the quality of silkworms themselves, through the spread of hybridization, increased the amount of silk produced per cocoon, thus improving productivity.[46] The new breeds, especially the First Filial Hybrid which appeared during the Taishō Period (1912–26), required much less labour because the silk was easier to unravel and the individual threads were longer.

4.4.4 Flow of Farmers' Savings to Industry

Foreign capital coming into Japan was minimal until the Second World War (Ch. 6, Sec. 4) and funds for industrialization had to be raised internally. Japanese Marxist economists, and later non-Marxist economists like Ranis, asserted that agriculture was the main source of capital for industrialization. Later, however, this hypothesis was criticized, and this issue is still a point of contention.

The 'agricultural surplus' (AS) funds for industrialization consisted of two items; the difference between farmers' savings (S_f) and farmers' investment (I_f), and the farmers' tax burden (T_f).[47] Thus,

$$AS = (S_f - I_f) + T_f$$

$S_f - I_f$ went directly to industry, but the same cannot be said about T_f. If the latter did go to industry it must have been through the medium of government expenditure. We must ask therefore:

1. Was S_f greater than I_f and did it account for a large proportion of the investment in the non-agricultural sector?
2. How much of T_f was transferred to industry by the government?

Let us examine the first question by looking at the controversial area of farmers' savings. Ohkawa, Nobukiyo Takamatsu, Ranis and others assert that farmers' savings provided funds for industry, but Shōzaburō Fujino and Jūrō Teranishi deny this.[48] Ohkawa and Takamatsu made estimates of farmers' income and expenditure from 1888 to 1940, and calculated S_f as the difference between them. From this they subtracted I_f (Table 4.5). They found that farmers' net savings $(S_f - I_f)$ were slightly negative in the 1890s, but were positive for the rest of the period, so that there should have been a continuous flow of capital from agriculture to industry. Net savings were particularly large in the 1910s and the 1930s. What was significant was that the proportion of farmers' net savings to non-agricultural investment was 40–50 per cent in the first twenty years of this century. As agriculture's importance declined this figure fell, but it was still 7–10 per cent in the 1930s.

Teranishi obtained rather different results from his studies of financial institutions' records. The basis for his calculations was that farmers' net savings were equal to the difference between the increase in their credit (ΔA_f) and their liabilities (ΔD_f); that is to say

$$S_f - I_f = \Delta A_f - \Delta D_f$$

A_f was calculated from statistics on cash, securities and deposits at banks and other financial institutions, D_f from loans by the latter. His calculations for the value of $S_f - I_f$ are much lower than those of Ohkawa and Takamatsu, except for the 1920s. According to Tera-

TABLE 4.5 Flow of savings from the agricultural sector to the non-agricultural sector in Japan 1888–1940 (millions of yen)

	Ohkawa and Takamatsu					Teranishi			
	1888–97	1898–1907	1908–17	1918–27	1928–40	1899–1907	1908–17	1918–27	1928–37
S_f	73	197	407	524	614	142	208	590	491
I_f	78	130	178	431	405	134	184	475	386
$S_f - I_f$	−5	67	229	93	209	8	24	115	105
T_f	62	106	161	299	203	110	160	291	167
AS	57	173	390	392	412	118	184	406	272
$(S_f - I_f)/I_n$ (%)	−5.9	42.1	52.2	6.6	10.1	5.0	5.5	8.2	8.0

Notes:

S_f = farmers' savings.
I_f = farmers' investment.
T_f = farmers' tax burden.
AS = agricultural surplus = $S_f - I_f + T_f$.
I_n = non-agricultural investment.
The figures represent the average value for each period.

Sources:
Ohkawa et al., 1978, p. 402. Teranishi, 1982, p. 255, table 4.4 and p. 258, table 4.5. Non-agricultural investment – Ohkawa and Shinohara, 1979, pp. 346, 348.

nishi, agriculture's share of investment in the non-agricultural sector was only 5–8 per cent for 1899–1937, suggesting that the flow of capital from agriculture to industry played a minor role in industrialization, and that most of the necessary capital was raised by industry itself. If this is true, the assertion that agriculture provided the funds for industrialization collapses.

As shown, the two estimates lead to quite different conclusions. According to the estimate by Ohkawa and Takamatsu, the farmers' consumption is increasingly underestimated as the years go by. As a consequence the farmers' savings, and therefore the transfer of the savings also, is estimated too high.[49] On the other hand, in the Teranishi estimation, although it is based on firm data, there are some problems:[50] the savings of non-resident landowners is not included in the farmers' savings; the fact that such real capital items as carts, water-mills and barns were used for commercial and industrial purposes is not included in the transfer of the savings; and the funding of commerce and industry by borrowing from such traditional financing sources as *tanomoshikō*[51] or from acquaintances is not included. It is necessary to find the problems in the two estimations and to solve these problems.

The historical experiences of Euro-American countries may be useful but there is no comparable study to match the studies by the Japanese mentioned above. Here, the viewpoint by Deane on the UK during its industrial revolution will be cited. Deane asserts that a large part of the funds for the industrialization in the UK were supplied by agriculture.[52] She points out that the early iron works were nearly all built by landowners, and agriculturalists were the main supporters of improvement schemes for roads, rivers and canals. Moreover, she says, many of the new managers in industry were from agricultural communities, and they had raised capital on their land or borrowed from farmer friends and neighbours. She uses these factors to refute Rostow's prerequisite theory and conclusion that the overlapping of the agricultural and industrial revolutions was the key to the success of the latter.

Deducing from this, it may be said that in Japan also the transfer of agricultural savings was playing a role which should not be overlooked. Because, as has been mentioned already, Japan is in the category in which the development of industry and the development of agriculture overlapped each other. However, it is possible that the viewpoint on the UK by Deane may be altered in the future when quantitative research such as that for Japan is carried out. Facts similar to the Teranishi estimation may be found when research about other countries progresses. International research is greatly needed on this point.[53]

4.4.5 Transfer of Agricultural Surplus by the Government

Although Ohkawa and Takamatsu's figures for $S_f - I_f$ are much higher, the two estimates for T_f are virtually the same (Table 4.5). Here we will discuss T_f's contribution to industrialization through an analysis of two factors:

1. Different Sectors' Tax Burdens[54]

During 1883–7 tax paid as a proportion of net production was 20 per cent for agriculture, and only 2 per cent for the non-agricultural sector. The difference gradually shrank; the figures were 10 per cent and 4 per cent respectively in the 1910s and 7 per cent and 4 per cent in the 1930s. Agriculture's relative tax burden was heavier than that of the non-agricultural sector.

2. Government Expenditure on Different Sectors

In 1880 (i.e. the average for 1877–83) 84 per cent of government subsidies went to non-primary industries, and virtually nothing to primary industry. For 1910 (average for 1907–13) these figures were 81 per cent and 4 per cent respectively (Table 10.7). Thus, until the second decade of this century, agriculture received almost no financial aid from the government.[55] Moreover, the government's considerable investment in construction indirectly aided industrialization.

Thus taxes were extracted from agriculture and this money was invested in the non-agricultural sector and the infrastructure. It seems clear that the agricultural surplus was transferred to industry by the government. Similar phenomena can be found in the UK. According to Deane, the Land Tax had been the main source of the government's income throughout the eighteenth century. This was because the proportion of agriculture was large and also because it was easier to assess and collect taxes in a stable agricultural society.[56]

Thus we believe that the agricultural surplus did contribute to industrialization, partly through farmers' savings, but particularly through government expenditure. Although the former does not appear to have been as great as Marxist economists claimed, it seems certain that there was indeed a flow of farmers' savings to industry resulting from agriculture's relatively high growth rate and its large share of the economy.

SUMMARY OF THE CHAPTER

If we exclude the 1920s and recent years (since the 1970s) we can say that agriculture has continued to expand fairly rapidly throughout the modern period. This growth has stemmed from technical progress and increased input of fertilizers. The most important aspect of technical progress has been the improvement in plant varieties, which was closely tied up with the increased use of fertilizers. The choice of this labour-intensive, land-saving technology was appropriate for a country with abundant labour and scarce land. The introduction of mechanical technology (mechanization of agriculture) was a natural consequence of the labour shortage which occurred since the sixties.

The agricultural growth rate from 1889 to 1920 was 1.4–1.7 per cent. This growth has been part of the development of agriculture since the preceding Tokugawa Period. This throws doubt on the validity of Ohkawa's concurrent growth theory and his assertion that Japan's experience was different to that of the UK. As we have observed, the agrarian revolution in the UK continued alongside the industrial revolution, as in Japan.

Agriculture's growth rate was lower than that of industry, but because its share of the economy was large in the early stages of industrial development, agriculture's relative contribution to economic growth was significant. It contributed to industrialization in three ways. First, it provided an abundant supply of foodstuffs. This prevented an increase in the relative price of agricultural products and the occurrence of a pattern of rising wages inducing reduced profits, and in turn leading to a falling growth rate. Second, its contribution to exports helped provide the necessary foreign currency. Third, the agricultural surplus was an important source of funds for the non-agricultural sector. These funds were transferred via two channels: farmers' savings and taxes on farmers. The former do not seem to have been as great as has been believed in the past.

The relationship between agriculture and industry was by no means one-sided. Industry provided large amounts of increasingly cheap fertilizers and reduced the prices of agricultural machinery and implements. It also drew more and more labour away from agriculture

FURTHER READING

Hayami, 1975
Hayami and Ruttan, 1971
Hayami and Yamada, 1991
Johnston, 1962; 1966; 1969
Ogura, 1967
Ohkawa, 1972, parts 2–4
Ohkawa, Johnston and Kaneda, 1969
Ohkawa and Rosovsky, 1964
Van der Meer and Yamada, 1990
Yamada and Ruttan, 1980

5 Industrialization

The history of the developed countries shows that industrialization has formed the core of modern economic growth. Industrialization refers to the growth of 'industry' – mining, manufacturing, construction and infrastructure industries (transportation, communication and public utilities) – and the increase in its share of the total economy. Manufacturing is the most important component of industry. The development of modern factories, equipped with imported machinery and steam engines, marked the beginning of industrialization in the mid-1880s in Japan.

In Section 5.1 we compare the process of industrialization in Japan with other developed countries. Section 5.2 contains a study of the growth of manufacturing. We identify factors accounting for its growth, analyze its contribution to economic development and examine changes in its structure. Section 5.3 deals with technological progress; we examine the pattern of adaptation of borrowed technology and research and development activities. Section 5.4 investigates industrial organization and industrial policies.

5.1 A SURVEY OF THE INDUSTRIALIZATION PROCESS

5.1.1 The Industrial Growth Rate

'Industry' (the M Sector) grew much faster than both the primary and service industries (the A and S Sectors, respectively), and hence the entire economy $(A + M + S)$ in both the pre-war and post-war periods (Table 5.1). During the pre-war period there was an upward trend in the M Sector's growth rate, a factor responsible for the trend acceleration (the increasing growth rate of the total economy) discussed earlier.[1] This trend continued during the 1950s and 1960s, when the M Sector growth rate exceeded 13 per cent. However, in

TABLE 5.1 Percentage of real GDP growth accounted for by various industry groups in Japan 1889–1987 (%)

	Primary (A)	Mining & manufacturing	Construction	Transportation communication & utilities	M Sector	S Sector	Non-primary (M + S)	All industries (A + M + S)
1889–1900	1.37	5.91	5.35	9.06	6.25	3.16	3.88	2.92
1901–10	1.66	5.82	4.17	10.30	6.44	1.55	3.10	2.62
1911–20	1.62	6.40	2.30	8.74	6.46	4.26	5.13	4.13
1921–30	0.75	4.82	6.33	6.79	5.57	0.44	2.91	2.41
1931–8	1.30	8.88	9.47	2.85	7.17	3.64	5.68	4.86
Pre-war average	1.34	6.25	5.36	7.80	6.34	2.59	4.07	3.31
1956–60	3.34	16.18	12.56	13.69	14.47	7.83	10.35	9.30
1961–70	2.10	14.50	11.85	10.98	12.93	9.25	10.94	10.12
1971–80	-0.29	5.37	2.93	3.62	4.43	5.72	5.09	4.83
1981–7	0.71	5.21	1.73	4.08	4.29	4.32	4.31	4.19
Post-war average	1.24	9.88	6.96	7.59	8.63	6.85	7.57	7.04

Notes:
All the figures are simple averages of the annual growth rate based on seven-year moving averages of real GDP (five-year averages for 1938, 1955 and 1987).

A = agriculture, forestry and fisheries.
M = mining, manufacturing, construction, transportation, communication and public utilities.
S = commerce and services.

Sources:
Pre-war period: Ohkawa and Shinohara, 1979, pp. 278–80.
Post-war period: 1953–69 – Extrapolated from the 1970 figure based on the old SNA series at 1965 prices (Ohkawa and Shinohara, 1979, pp. 281–2). 1970–89 – New SNA series (KKKN, 1991, pp. 158–61).

the 1970s the growth rate of the M Sector decreased sharply to 4 per cent, and became smaller than that of the S Sector. The growth rate of mining and manufacturing closely paralleled the growth rate of the M Sector as a whole, and was the second highest of the various industry groups (next to the infrastructure industries) in the pre-war period, and the highest in the post-war period excluding the 1970s.

Japanese manufacturing grew rapidly in both the pre-war and the post-war periods relative to other developed countries. In the pre-war period (1881–1937) Japan's growth rate (5.4 per cent) was higher than the USA (3.7 per cent), Italy (3.1 per cent), Germany (2.9 per cent), and the UK (1.6 per cent).[2] In Germany and Japan the growth rate increased during the period 1850–1910. In the 1950s and 1960s the growth rate was high in Germany, Italy and Austria. This supports Shinohara's hypothesis that the growth rate was higher in the countries that were defeated in the Second World War and experienced a sharp drop in production just after the war.[3] The growth rate of many developed countries decreased during the 1970s.

5.1.2 An Analysis of the Growth Rate

Employing a procedure similar to that used in our study of agriculture (Ch. 4, Sec. 1) we obtain equations which explain the growth rates of real GDP (Y) and labour productivity (Y/L):

$$G(Y) = G(L) + G(Y/L) \tag{1}$$

$$G(Y/L) = \lambda + E_K G(K/L) \tag{2}$$

Here L, K and E_K denote employment, capital stock and output elasticity of capital respectively. λ, a 'residual' of the growth rate, is an index of the rate of technological progress.

These equations were used to derive the breakdown of the growth rate $G(Y)$, shown in Table 5.2. The figures for each of three industry groups, mining and manufacturing, M Sector and non-primary ($M + S$) are shown. The mining and manufacturing figures demonstrate that:

1. The large change in $G(Y)$ from the pre-war to the post-war period ($9.90 - 6.94 = 2.96$ per cent) was mainly attributable to the change in $G(Y/L)$ ($7.80 - 4.44 = 3.36$ per cent).
2. The increase in $G(Y/L)$, in turn, resulted from the increases in $E_K G(K/L)$ (the growth rate accounted for by an increase in the

capital–labour ratio and in λ. The increase in λ $(5.89 - 2.89 = 3.00$ per cent) was of greater significance than the increase in $E_K G$ (K/L).

3. The ratio of λ to $G(Y/L)$ was a little larger in the post-war period than in the pre-war period.

4. The increases in $G(Y)$ and $G(Y/L)$ in the pre-war period resulted from an increase in λ. (The 1930s was an exception to this generalization. The decrease in λ in this decade was cancelled out by an increase in $E_K G(K/L)$ which resulted in an increase in $G(Y)$ and $G(Y/L)$.)

5. The decrease in $G(Y)$ and $G(Y/L)$ since the 1970s is attributable mainly to a decrease in λ; λ was 8.2 per cent until the 1960s, and 3.9 per cent since the 1970s.

These findings are also applicable to the M Sector. Technological progress played a significant role in the growth of mining and manufacturing and the M Sector. In contrast, λ was small in the $M + S$ Sector, especially in the pre-war period. This suggests that technological progress was slow in the S Sector.

Of course the 'residual' contains factors other than technological progress. Two important determinants of λ are increases in labour hours (h) and the rate of capital utilization (π). Substituting hL for L and πK for K in equation (2) and assuming that E_K is unchanged, we obtain

$$G(Y/hL) = \lambda' + E_K G(\pi K/hL). \tag{3}$$

From equations (2) and (3) we have

$$\lambda' = \lambda - E_K G(\pi) - (1 - E_K)G(h)$$

The value of the new variable λ' is unaffected by changes in labour hours and capital utilization and hence is a better index for the rate of technological progress than λ. However, our estimates of λ and λ' are similar except in the period from the 1920s to the 1930s when λ' fell a lot more than λ. As a result there is no apparent increase in λ' for the entire pre-war period.

Another factor that influences the value of λ is the quality of labour and capital. Unfortunately, because of difficulties in quantifying quality we cannot obtain independent estimates of the importance of changes in the quality of labour and capital over time.[4]

A study by Kendrick found that a comparable estimate of the 'residual' of manufacturing growth (λ') in the USA was 2.5 per cent

TABLE 5.2 A breakdown of the non-primary industry growth rate in Japan 1908–87 (%)

	G(Y)	G(L)	G(K)	G(Y/L)	G(K/L)	$E_K G(K/L)$	λ	λ'	λ / G(Y/L)
(A) Private mining and manufacturing									
1908–10	4.47	1.56	8.40	2.91	6.84	2.59	0.32	0.30	11
1911–20	7.36	3.39	6.69	3.97	3.30	1.46	2.51	2.58	63
1921–30	5.00	0.59	2.06	4.41	1.47	0.57	3.84	4.28	87
1931–8	9.78	4.14	9.15	5.64	5.01	2.49	3.15	2.61	56
Pre-war average	6.94	2.50	6.00	4.44	3.50	1.55	2.89	2.92	65
1956–60	16.20	5.54	11.49	10.66	5.95	2.03	8.63	8.79	81
1961–70	14.54	3.26	13.40	11.28	10.14	3.35	7.93	6.11	70
1971–80	5.42	-0.00	7.50	5.42	7.50	1.39	4.03	5.80	74
1981–7	5.17	0.99	5.60	4.18	4.61	0.52	3.66	3.44	88
Post-war average	9.90	2.10	9.55	7.80	7.45	1.91	5.89	5.85	76
(B) Private M Sector									
1908–10	5.41	1.56	9.94	3.85	8.38	3.39	0.46	0.44	12
1911–20	7.85	3.20	9.83	4.65	6.63	3.19	1.46	1.55	32
1921–30	5.03	0.93	4.35	4.10	3.42	1.54	2.56	2.96	62
1931–8	7.86	3.17	4.52	4.69	1.35	0.72	3.97	3.42	85
Pre-war average	6.71	2.31	6.70	4.40	4.39	2.03	2.37	2.38	54
1956–60	15.36	6.03	10.88	9.33	4.85	1.56	7.77	7.68	83
1961–70	13.30	3.77	12.65	9.53	8.88	2.74	6.79	6.72	71
1971–80	4.57	0.75	7.85	3.82	7.10	1.32	2.50	3.46	65
1981–7	4.63	1.07	6.91	3.56	5.84	0.82	2.74	2.64	77
Post-war average	9.00	2.59	9.62	6.41	7.03	1.69	4.72	4.96	74
(C) Private non-primary (M + S) Sector									
1908–10	3.24	2.18	7.69	1.06	5.51	2.04	-0.98	-1.00	-92

	Y	K	L	π	h	E_K			
1911–20	5.92	2.07	7.89	3.85	5.82	2.60	1.25	1.32	32
1921–30	2.21	1.64	4.47	0.57	2.83	1.12	-0.55	-0.13	-96
1931–8	5.87	1.88	4.32	3.99	2.44	1.21	2.78	2.25	70
Pre-war average	4.45	1.89	5.85	2.56	3.96	1.71	0.85	0.87	33
1956–60	11.10	4.97	8.63	6.13	3.66	1.17	4.96	4.81	81
1961–70	11.31	3.91	11.79	7.40	7.88	2.63	4.77	4.60	64
1971–80	5.09	2.01	8.43	3.08	6.42	1.55	1.53	2.34	50
1981–7	4.52	1.07	7.43	3.45	6.36	1.32	2.13	2.03	62
Post-war average	7.85	2.86	9.29	4.99	6.43	1.78	3.21	3.37	64

Notes:

Y = GDP (1934–6 prices for the pre-war period, 1985 prices for the post-war period).

K = gross capital stock (1934–6 prices for the pre-war, 1985 prices for the post-war period).

L = labour force.

π = rate of capital utilization.

h = labour hours (1934–6 = 1 for the pre-war period, 1985 = 1 for the post-war period).

E_K = output elasticity of capital.

λ, λ': See text.

All the figures are simple averages of the annual growth rates based on seven-year moving averages (five-year averages for 1907, 1938, 1955 and 1987).

Sources:

Y: Pre-war period – Ohkawa and Rosovsky, 1973, p. 284. Post-war period – Calculated by subtracting GDP for the government from GDP figures in Table 5.1.

K: Pre-war period – Keizai Kikakuchō, Keizai Kenkyūjo, 1968, p. 158. Post-war period – Same as Table 4.1.

L: Pre-war period and 1953–70 – Minami and Ono, 1978a, pp. 168–9. 1971–90 – Calculated by subtracting the labour force at the government from the figure in Rōdōryoku Chōsa (Labour Force Survey) (RTN, various issues).

E_K: Estimated by Minami and Ono see Figure 9.5.

π: Pre-war period – Ohkawa and Minami, 1975, p. 575. Post-war period – Survey of the Tsūshō Sangyōshō (Ministry of International Trade and Industry) taken from KTN, various issues.

h: Pre-war period – Minami and Ono, 1978b. Post-war period – Maigetsu Kinrō Tōkei (Monthly Labour Survey) taken from RTN, various issues.

during the period 1909–37.[5] This was smaller than that in Japan during the analogous period (2.9 per cent for the period 1908–38). However, the difference in the growth rates of the two countries is largely attributable to the difference in the growth of the capital–labour ratio, that is $E_K G(K/L)$. For the post-war period Kendrick's estimate of λ' (2.5 per cent) for 1948–53 is much smaller than Japan's figure (8.8 per cent) for 1956–60. In spite of the difference in the period of estimation there is no doubt that Japan's residual is much larger than the USA's in the post-war period.[6]

5.1.3 The Contribution of 'Industry' to Economic Growth

For the pre-war period as a whole the relative contribution of the M Sector to economic growth (as measured by the ratio of the increase of this sector's GDP to the total increase in GDP) was 62 per cent, and tended to increase during the period (Table 5.3). This shows that pre-war economic growth depended on industrialization to a large and growing extent. In the post-war period this ratio was 53 per cent; post-war economic growth depended on industrialization to a lesser extent than in the pre-war period. This means that the contribution of the S Sector increased during the post-war period.

The relative contribution of mining and manufacturing was the largest among the various industry groups during the pre-war period (38 per cent) and the second largest, next to the S Sector, for the post-war period (33 per cent).

Thus, the M Sector, especially mining and manufacturing, has been the largest contributor to the growth of the economy. However, the increasing role of the service industry in the post-war period has also been important.

5.1.4 Changes in the Industrial Structure

The proportions of real GDP with respect to each kind of industry are shown in Table 5.4. First, the proportion of Sector A had been declining steadily, from 42 per cent in 1888 to only 3 per cent in 1987. Between the M and S Sectors, the rise in M was noticeable. It started from 12 per cent and increased, reaching 52 per cent in 1938. It declined a little after the Second World War, but climbed again to 48 per cent by 1970. However, it declined slightly to 46 per cent in 1987. This indicates a qualitative transformation of modern economic growth after 1970, which until then depended on industrialization. In

TABLE 5.3 Relative contributions to economic growth by industry group in Japan 1888–1987 (%)

	Primary (A)	Mining & manufacturing	Construction	Transportation communication & utilities	M Sector	S Sector	Non-primary (M + S)	All industries (A + M + S)
1888–1900	17.8	19.3	5.5	6.8	31.6	50.6	82.2	100.0
1900–10	20.8	29.2	5.9	17.3	52.4	26.8	79.2	100.0
1910–20	11.0	26.5	2.0	16.5	45.0	44.0	89.0	100.0
1920–30	7.1	42.4	10.5	33.0	85.9	7.0	92.9	100.0
1930–8	4.9	50.5	11.2	8.0	69.7	25.4	95.1	100.0
Pre-war average	9.6	38.4	7.9	15.2	61.5	28.9	90.4	100.0
1955–60	5.9	28.1	13.7	14.8	56.6	37.5	94.1	100.0
1960–70	2.0	33.5	13.9	12.5	59.9	38.1	98.0	100.0
1970–80	-0.3	32.0	7.1	8.5	47.6	52.7	100.3	100.0
1980–7	0.6	36.0	3.8	9.9	49.7	49.4	99.4	100.0
Post-war average	1.1	33.4	8.8	10.6	52.8	46.1	98.9	100.0

Notes:
The figures in the table were calculated by dividing the increase in real GDP accounted for by the respective industry groups by the increase in total real GDP. GDP figures are seven-year moving averages (five-year averages for 1938, 1955 and 1987).

Sources:
Same as table 5.6.

TABLE 5.4 Industry groups' share of GDP in Japan 1888–1987 (%)

	Primary (A)	Mining & manufacturing	Construction	Transportation communication & utilities	M Sector	S Sector	Non-primary (M + S)	All industries (A + M + S)
1888	41.5	8.1	2.6	1.5	12.2	46.3	58.5	100.0
1900	34.6	11.3	3.5	3.1	17.9	47.5	65.4	100.0
1910	31.5	15.4	4.0	6.3	25.7	42.8	68.5	100.0
1920	24.7	19.0	3.4	9.7	32.1	43.2	75.3	100.0
1930	20.9	24.0	4.9	14.6	43.5	35.6	79.1	100.0
1938	15.9	32.4	6.9	12.5	51.8	32.3	84.1	100.0
1955	16.7	12.6	8.5	8.2	29.3	54.0	83.3	100.0
1960	12.6	17.1	9.9	10.0	37.0	50.4	87.4	100.0
1970	5.9	25.2	11.5	10.8	47.5	46.6	94.1	100.0
1980	3.6	26.5	9.6	9.6	45.7	50.1	96.4	100.0
1987	2.8	28.4	8.1	9.5	46.0	51.2	97.2	100.0

Note:: Composition at real GDP.
The figures are based on seven-year moving averages of GDP (five-year averages for 1938, 1955 and 1987).

Sources:
Same as Table 5.1.

contrast to this, the proportion of the *S* Sector had experienced a long-term decline before the Second World War; it maintained a level of about 50 per cent after the war. However, when it is examined in terms of specific values, the proportion of the *S* Sector has been continuously increasing after the Second World War (Figure 5.1). (It increased from 37 per cent to 52 per cent during the period 1955–87.) This is because the product price in that Sector increased relatively when compared with that in the *M* Sector.

5.1.5 A Comparison with Other Countries

Figure 5.1 illustrates a decreasing share of the *A* Sector in nominal GDP (and an increasing share of the *M* + *S* Sector) in all eleven countries, including Japan. Only in the UK in this century do we find an exception to this trend. This is attributable to the fact that in the

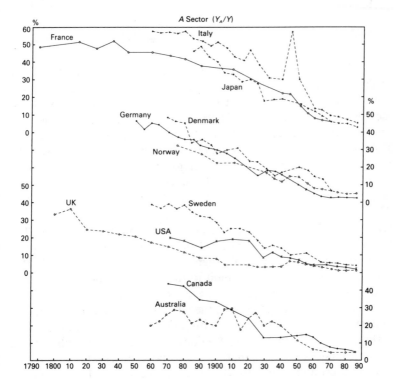

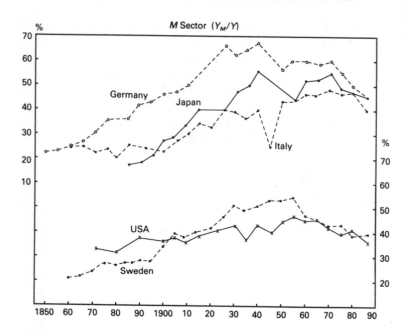

UK industrialization had already reached saturation point by the end of the last century. The share of both the M and S Sectors increased until about 1940 in all countries, but thereafter only the S Sector increased. Thus, the industrial structure changed first from the A to the M Sector and later from the M to the S Sector.

An international comparison of recent years is also of interest. The relationships between the three major industry groups' shares of GDP, $Y_A/Y, Y_M/Y$ and Y_S/Y, and per capita GDP (an index of the degree of economic development) for 1987 are shown in Figure 5.2. The figure indicates that Y_A/Y tends to decrease while Y_M/Y and Y_S/Y tend to increase as the result of an increase in per capita income. The lower the per capita income level the larger are these changes. At higher-income levels Y_M/Y falls slightly whereas Y_S/Y increases slightly. This suggests that there is a limit to the transformation of industrial structure even though the structure of an industry is changed by economic growth. In particular, the curve fitted to the Y_M/Y values is almost horizontal for countries with high income. In contrast to this, it should be noted that the Y_S/Y values (however gently) still show an upward tendency. In summarizing the above observations, it is said that with economic growth, the A Sector declines relatively and M

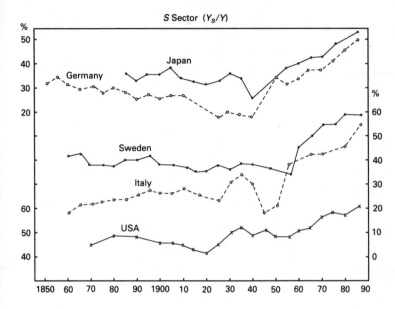

FIGURE 5.1   Major industry group's shares of GDP in the developed
countries 1790–1987

Notes:
All the figures are at current prices.
Figures for Germany in the post-war period are for former West Germany.

Sources:
Japan: Pre-war period: Nominal GDP is calculated by multiplying real GDP by NDP
deflator. Real GDP is from Table 5.1. NDP deflator is obtained by dividing nominal NDP
(Ohkawa *et al.*, 1974, p. 202) by real NDP (*Ibid.*, p. 226).
Post-war period (new SNA base): 1953–69 – Extrapolated from the 1970 figure based on
the old SNA series (Ohkawa and Shinohara, 1979, p. 281). 1970–89 – KKKN 1991, pp.
150–3.
USA: US, Department of Commerce, Bureau of the Census, 1975, pp. 239–40.
Canada: Firestone, 1958, p. 189.
Australia: Butlin, 1962, pp. 12–13.
European countries: Mitchell, 1978, pp. 428–33.
Figures for Canada since 1955, Australia since 1950, and the other countries for 1975,
1980, and 1987: YNAS, 1988.

and *S* Sectors expand relatively, and that the variation becomes
smaller and smaller with time, resulting in the *M* Sector having a
decreasing proportion. However, the proportion of the *S* Sector can
still afford to go upward. These conclusions agree with the ones
obtained from the historical data on Japan.

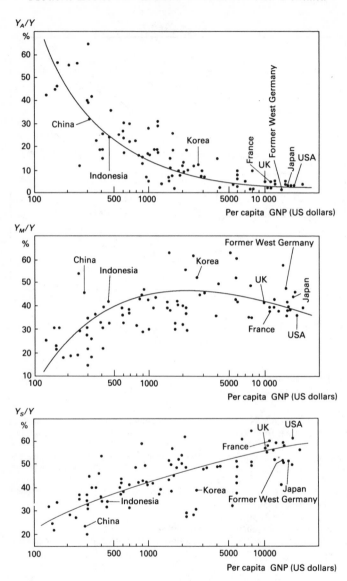

FIGURE 5.2   Relationships between major industry group's shares of GDP and per capita GNP 1987

Note:
For some countries where figures for 1987 are not available, figures for 1986 or 1985 have been used. Sample size is 84 countries.

Sources:
GDP by industry groups: YNAS, 1988. Per capita GNP: WDR, 1989, pp. 164–5.

5.1.6 Factors Responsible for the Change in the Industrial Structure

Two factors may account for a decrease in the share of the *A* Sector and an increase in the shares of the *M* and *S* Sectors. The first is on the production side; growth in labour productivity over time is small in agriculture because land area is inherently limited. In the non-agricultural industries growth in labour productivity is large because of the ease of introducing new technology. Under these conditions the rate of profit tends to be higher in the non-agricultural industries, and this sector is able to attract more capital investment. Thus the capital labour ratio increases much faster in the non-agricultural industries and this accelerates the growth of labour productivity still further.

The second is a change in consumption patterns. As per capita consumption (O/N) increases, the share of food consumption (O_A/O) tends to fall and the share of industrial products (O_M/O) and services (O_S/O) tends to increase. ($O_A + O_M + O_S = O$) These changes can be explained in the following way. Suppose that the demand functions for the three sectors' products are given by:

$$\frac{O_A}{N} = \Lambda_A \left(\frac{O}{N} \right)^{\eta_A}$$

$$\frac{O_M}{N} = \Lambda_M \left(\frac{O}{N} \right)^{\eta_M}$$

$$\frac{O_S}{N} = \Lambda_S \left(\frac{O}{N} \right)^{\eta_S}$$

where Λ_i and η_i denote constants and income elasticities of demand, respectively. These functions can be rewritten as:

$$\frac{O_A}{O} = \Lambda_A \left(\frac{O}{N} \right)^{\eta_A - 1}$$

$$\frac{O_M}{O} = \Lambda_M \left(\frac{O}{N} \right)^{\eta_M - 1}$$

$$\frac{O_S}{O} = \Lambda_S \left(\frac{O}{N} \right)^{\eta_S - 1}$$

From these relationships we learn that O_A/O must decrease and O_M/O and O_S/O must increase as the result of an increase in O/N, because of the conditions, $\eta_A < 1$, $\eta_M > 1$ and $\eta_S > 1$.[7] The changes in consumption patterns necessitate a change in the industrial structure.[8]

Due to these two factors the growth rate of the non-agricultural industries tend to be higher than agriculture. This tendency is usually counterbalanced, to some extent, by a change in relative output prices favourable to the slowly growing industry (Ch. 11, Sec. 2). Consequently the difference in the growth rates of various sectors tends to be smaller at current prices than at constant prices. In spite of this phenomenon the share of agriculture in nominal GDP has decreased and the shares of non-agricultural industries have increased, in all developed countries.

5.2   THE DEVELOPMENT OF MANUFACTURING

5.2.1   Early Industrialization

Although by interpreting the industrialization in a broad sense and regarding it as the development of the *M* Sector (mining industry, construction industry, transport and telecommunication industries and other public utilities), the growth was mainly caused by the development of manufacturing industries. When the contribution to the real GDP for the period 1888–1938 is examined, the *M* Sector as a whole contributed 61.5 per cent of which the mining and manufacturing industry contributed 38.4 per cent (see Table 5.3). Therefore, the contribution by the mining and manufacturing industry to the real GDP increment of the *M* Sector was 62.4 per cent (that is, 100 × 38.4/61.5). And during the period 1955–87, it was 63.3 per cent (that is, 100 × 33.4/52.8). Manufacturing industries were the main industries of industrialization. In this Section, the structural transformation of the manufacturing industry will be discussed.

Manufacturing industries are a collection of numerous enterprises. These enterprises are usually categorized into a few groups of work categories. In Table 5.5, the growth rates of each work category in the real industrial product are shown. Here, manufacturing industries are placed in eight categories (textiles, food, etc.). Table 5.6 shows the relative contributions of the eight categories to the increase of real industrial production; and Table 5.7 shows the proportions of the enterprises in the real amount of industrial production.

In both tables, the sum of the contributions by the textiles and food enterprises is cited as the indicator for light industries, and the sum of

TABLE 5.5   Growth rate of real manufacturing output by sub-industry group in Japan 1878–1987 (%)

	1878–1900	1901–20	1921–38	1956–70	1971–87
Textiles	6.93	5.88	5.59	8.47	−0.05
Foods	3.64	3.13	2.16	7.73	1.55
Metals and metal products	3.98	14.82	10.23	15.16	2.17
Machinery	11.36	14.01	9.40	19.34	7.31
Chemicals	3.98	5.39	10.31	13.41	4.39
Ceramics	4.23	7.30	7.51	11.25	1.86
Wood and wood products	3.89	2.53	7.26	4.55	−1.97
Miscellaneous	3.13	4.33	5.01	17.54	2.60
Light industries*a*	4.51	4.25	4.01	7.97	1.07
Heavy and chemical industries*b*	4.93	9.92	9.83	15.80	5.20
All manufacturing	4.38	5.41	6.53	11.83	3.85

Notes:
All the figures are simple averages of the annual growth rate based on seven-year moving averages of real output (five-year average for 1938).
Real output is represented by the value of production at 1934–6 prices for the pre-war period and 1985 prices for the post-war period.
a Textiles and foods.
b Metals and metal products, machinery and chemicals.

Sources:
Pre-war period: Shinohara, 1972, pp. 144–7.
Post-war period: Total value of shipments in 1985 is taken as the bench-mark for real output. For the other years real output is calculated by linking with the production index (1985 = 1). The production index is from the *Tsūshō Sangyōshō* (Ministry of International Trade and Industry) (KTN, 1963, pp. 217–8; 1970, pp. 185–6; 1978, pp. 237–8; 1990, pp. 267–8).

the contribution by metals, machinery and chemicals enterprises is cited as the indicator for heavy industries, for reference purposes.

First let us observe the structure of the manufacturing industries at the beginning of industrialization. During the period 1877–1900, the contributions by the food industry (40 per cent) and textiles industry (35 per cent) were overwhelming in the growth of manufacturing industry as a whole: 75 per cent in total. In other words, more than two-thirds of the growth in the manufacturing industry in the nineteenth century was due to developments in light industry. The rate of growth was 4.5 per cent close to the average for industry, but the proportion of light industries in industrial production increased from 69 per cent in 1877 to 73 per cent by 1900.

The development in the light industries was led by the textiles industry. There, as will be mentioned in the next Section, modern

TABLE 5.6   Sub-industry groups' relative contributions to manufacturing growth in Japan 1877–1987 (%)

	1877–1900	1900–20	1920–38	1956–70	1970–87
Textiles	34.9	28.9	21.6	6.4	–0.1
Foods	40.3	21.6	6.8	12.3	5.0
Metals and metal products	1.5	11.3	17.5	19.5	8.7
Machinery	4.0	19.4	23.6	27.1	60.4
Chemicals	7.5	8.9	20.3	19.7	22.7
Ceramics	1.2	2.5	2.8	4.4	1.8
Wood and wood products	2.5	1.4	2.8	3.9	–2.1
Miscellaneous	8.1	6.0	4.6	6.7	3.6
Light industries	75.2	50.2	28.4	18.7	4.9
Heavy and chemical industries	13.0	39.6	61.4	66.3	91.8
All manufacturing	100.0	100.0	100.0	100.0	100.0

Note:
The figures are for the increase in the real output of respective sub-industry groups divided by the increase in the total real output of all manufacturing industries.

Sources:
Same as Table 5.5.

TABLE 5.7   Sub-industry groups' shares of manufacturing output in Japan 1877–1987 (%)

	1877	1900	1920	1938	1955	1970	1987
Textiles	10.1	25.5	27.8	23.6	13.2	7.5	3.9
Foods	58.5	47.2	30.6	14.5	22.2	15.2	10.4
Metals and metal products	1.4	1.4	7.8	14.4	12.1	17.9	13.5
Machinery	1.1	2.9	13.7	20.4	11.3	23.5	41.0
Chemicals	11.1	9.0	8.9	16.6	15.7	18.9	20.7
Ceramics	2.1	1.5	2.2	2.6	4.8	4.5	3.2
Wood and wood products	6.6	4.1	2.3	2.6	16.8	6.6	2.5
Miscellaneous	9.1	8.4	6.7	5.3	3.9	5.9	4.8
Light industries	68.6	72.7	58.4	38.1	35.4	22.7	14.3
Heavy and chemical industries	13.6	13.3	30.4	51.4	39.1	60.3	75.2
All manufacturing	100.0	100.0	100.0	100.0	100.0	100.0	100.0

Note:
Figures are a composition of real output. The figures are based on seven-year moving averages of output (five-year averages for 1938).

Sources:
Same as Table 5.5.

technology was introduced and modified skilfully, and then import and export were subsequently successfully carried out. For example, the export of silk had taken up 30–36 per cent of total product exports in the nineteenth century.[9] Also, the domestic production of cotton thread exceeded the import of cotton thread in 1891, and in 1897, the exported amount exceeded the imported amount. Woven fabric production grew to occupy 15 per cent of the total amount of production by manufacturing industries as a whole in the 1880s and 1890s. Its export reached 9 per cent of total product exports during the corresponding period.[10]

This parallels the British experience during the industrial revolution. The relatively high growth rate of heavy and chemical industries during the early stage of industrialization in Japan, however, led some economists to conclude that Japan's pattern of industrialization differed from the British one. E. H. Norman, for example, said that a 'metal and machinery first' policy was pursued by the Meiji government,[11] whereas our study confirms Yūichi Shionoya's view that the early industrialization of Japan was characterized by the traditional 'textiles first' pattern.[12] According to D. S. Landes the development of European latecomers such as Germany centred on the heavy and chemical industries, because the timing of their growth coincided with the age of coal and iron.[13] Japan's departure from this pattern is attributable to her slow progress in the field of modern science, her capital shortage and her labour surplus. The slow progress of modern science made the absorption of sophisticated technology difficult, while the capital shortage and labour surplus favoured labour-intensive technology.

Japan's experience of industrialization contrasts sharply with what happened in some developing countries which attempted to carry out import substitution in the 1950s. They were unsuccessful, largely because domestic demand was not great enough for them to maintain large-scale production. Because import substitution failed, export expansion was impossible. As a result their balance-of-payments position worsened because of increased imports of raw materials, production equipment and technology. In Japan the domestic market for consumer goods was already well-developed as a result of the expansion of agriculture, commerce and the traditional industries before the start of industrialization, and exports of primary products such as copper, coal, tea and raw silk paid for the importation of the raw materials, production equipment and technology for industrialization.

5.2.2   The Acceleration of Manufacturing Growth

The growth rate of the manufacturing industry increased from 4.4 per cent in the period 1878–1900 to 5.4 per cent in the period 1901–20 and 6.5 per cent in the period 1921–38 (Table 5.5). One of the reasons for this acceleration was the continued growth of the textile industry; in the period 1901–20 its growth rate was higher than the growth rate of total manufacturing, and in the period 1921–38 it was only slightly lower. A more direct and important reason for the accelerated growth of manufacturing was the growth of the heavy and chemical industries. The combined growth rate of these industries rose from 5 per cent in the period 1878–1900 to 10 per cent in the period 1901–38, and their relative contribution to total manufacturing growth increased from 13 per cent to 40–61 per cent. Heavy and chemical industries' share of total manufacturing output (at constant prices) increased from 14 per cent to 51 per cent during the period 1877–1938.

The change-over from light industries to heavy and chemical industries as the leading sector took place rapidly in Japan; before the growth of the former slowed down, the growth of the latter had already begun to accelerate. This brought about an increase in the growth rate of manufacturing. This can be contrasted with the British experience. In Great Britain during the period 1907–35 textiles, foods and tobacco's share of total manufacturing output decreased by 9 per cent (from 48 per cent to 39 per cent), and machinery, vehicles, metals and chemicals' share increased by only 4 per cent (from 36 per cent to 40 per cent).[14] In Japan there was a 22 per cent decrease (from 68 per cent to 46 per cent) in the former and a 22 per cent increase (from 21 per cent to 43 per cent) in the latter.[15] One reason for the decline in British textiles was the competition from Japanese industry which had superior technology and lower wages. Faced with such competition, Britain should have concentrated on establishing heavy and chemical industries as the leading sector. The failure to effect this change-over resulted in the slow rate of economic growth which characterizes contemporary Britain.

5.2.3   The Maturity of Manufacturing

After a sharp drop due to the Second World War, the manufacturing production index began to increase, and surpassed its highest pre-war and wartime levels in 1955. Its rate of growth in the 1950s and 1960s was unprecedentedly high (14–16 per cent) and although it fell to 5 per cent in the 1970s it was still high (3.9 per cent in 1971–87 – see

Table 5.5) compared with the developed countries of the west.

The rate of growth differed among sub-industry groups; it was only 1.1 per cent for light industries and 5.2 per cent for heavy and chemical industries during the period 1971–87 (Table 5.5). The relative contribution of heavy and chemical industries to total manufacturing growth in this period was 92 per cent, compared with only 5 per cent for light industries (Table 5.6). As a result, in the period 1955–87 light industries' share of total manufacturing output (at constant prices) decreased from 35 per cent to 14 per cent, and heavy and chemical industries' share increased from 39 per cent to 75 per cent (Table 5.7).[16]

The machinery industry was the most important of the three sub-industries (metals, machinery and chemicals) that compose the heavy and chemical industries and in the period 1971–87 this industry alone accounted for 60 per cent of the growth of total manufacturing industries.

5.3 TECHNOLOGICAL PROGRESS

5.3.1 Three Categories of Borrowed Technology

As was argued earlier (Ch. 3, Sec. 1), the growth of the pre-war Japanese economy was heavily dependent on borrowed technology. In this section we explore the concept and history of borrowed technology and identify factors responsible for the successful absorption of technology in Japan.

Akira Ono divided borrowed technology into three categories.[17] His first category is unmodified modern technology. In Figure 5.3 this is represented by the unbroken portion of the production function (F). If the wage rate in the developed countries is w_1, the capital-labour ratio represented by the point P_1 is selected, because it maximizes the rate of profit.[18] However, it is more difficult for a latecomer to substitute capital for labour and vice versa. As a result, latecomers which adopt such technology are restricted to the production function curve B_1B_1 linked at point P_1. Nevertheless this category of technology is often borrowed by latecomers, because modification of certain technology is virtually impossible. Even when modification is possible, many latecomers lack the social capability to accomplish it. Also, national pride sometimes demands the introduction of the most modern technology.

Ono's second category is modern technology introduced after capital-saving modifications. In this case the latecomer develops a portion of the production function, represented by B_2B_2 in Figure

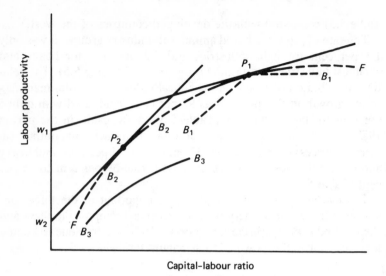

FIGURE 5.3   Types of borrowed technology

5.3, by reconstructing imported capital equipment. This is the most profitable technology for a country with a wage rate w_2. (Note that technology B_2B_2 is more profitable than technology B_1B_1 despite its lower labour productivity, because more labour with low wages can be exploited.) This technology is sometimes developed by combining elements of traditional technology inherited from pre-modern society (B_3) and modern technology borrowed from developed countries (B_1).

Ono's third category is older and less efficient technology (B_2) from the traditional sectors of the developed countries. Both the second and the third categories result in a lower level of labour productivity than the first category (B_1), but a higher level than the latecomers' traditional technology (B_3) and are most profitable to latecomers with an abundant labour force. Such technology is referred to as 'intermediate and appropriate technology'.[19]

5.3.2   Examples of Borrowed Technology

The three categories of borrowed technology can be illustrated by examples from Japanese history.[20] The first category (unmodified modern technology) was the most common in Japan. Typical examples are found in the public utilities sector. English railway technology was introduced in Meiji Japan without modification. Construction of the first railway between Shinbashi (Tōkyō) and Yokohama, begun in 1870 and completed in 1872, was directed by an English engineer, Edmund Morel. Many other foreign engineers were also employed on this project (nineteen in 1870 and sixty-two in 1871). Furthermore, almost all the equipment was imported, including locomotives made entirely in England (though some had previously been used in India). Even the sleepers and tickets were imported.

Electric generating and transmitting technology was introduced from the USA and Germany. The five power plants of the Tōkyō Electric Light Company (TELC) installed direct-current dynamos made in the USA (1887–90) and the Asakusa Thermal Generation Plant of TELC employed six German-made alternators (1895). The Ōsaka Electric Light Company (OELC) began supplying alternating-current electricity, based on technology from the USA, in 1889. The fifty-cycle alternating current which is now standard in the eastern half of Japan came from Germany. In western Japan, however, the sixty-cycle current became standard after the OELC imported alternators from the USA in 1897. The existence of two different electric generation systems in Japan caused considerable inconvenience and diseconomies during this period, and still does so today. Several attempts at standardization have been made, but in vain.

Among the manufacturing industries, there are many examples of the same type of technology introduction (borrowing). This includes the cotton industry which was the leading industry before the Second World War. Machinery imported from the UK was used in the seventeen cotton-spinning mills constructed with the guidance and assistance of the government at the beginning of the Meiji Era (including the two publicly-owned mills and ten spinning mills. Among these, ten factories were driven solely by water and one factory was driven by a combination of water and steam engines. This was because of the rarity and high price of coal at that time and because the government encouraged the use of water power. In other words, as far as the power source was concerned, the technology for the spinning factories was intermediate technology and appropriate technology.

However, the management of these factories ended in failure. Therefore, considering the result, it may be said that the technology was not 'appropriate'. It was with the establishment of Ōsaka Bōseki (Ōsaka Spinning Co.) in 1882 that modern cotton-spinning technology became established in Japan. This machinery consisted of sixteen Mules (10,500 spindles) made by Platt and Co. in England driven by steam power. As a result of this success, many cotton-spinning factories were set up in various parts of the country. These technologies were the best of their time. The fact that this introduction (borrowing of technology) was successful derives from the lessons learnt from the earlier failure and to the fact that there was a basis for accepting mass production, with the domestic market having been expanded. This means that for the introduction of the first category type of technology to be successful, it is necessary to have the correct conditions for it.

A good example of the second category is machine filature technology. Tomioka Filature (founded in 1870) was equipped with the most modern technology, which had been introduced from France (B_1). Because this capital-using technology was too expensive for small-scale Japanese plants it was not widely used. However, in 1875 the Nakayama Company in Nagano Prefecture combined this technology with traditional Japanese technology – *zakuri* (sedentary reeling) – (B_3) and created a new reeling technique (B_2). This made possible to save capital by substituting water wheels for steam engines, wood for iron in machinery and ceramics for metal in cocoon-boiling basins and steam pipes. As a result, capital costs decreased substantially: from 190 000 yen for the Tomioka Filature with 300 basins, to only 1900 yen for the Nakayama Company with 100 basins. Without this modification the rapid spread of machine filature technology and the expansion of the silk reeling industry could not have taken place.

It took sixteen years for the establishment of the cotton spinning industry from the technology introduction at the end of the Tokugawa Era (the construction of the Initial Three Spinning Mills) to the establishment of Ōsaka Spinning, but for the reeling (filature) industry, it required only five years from the establishment of Tomioka Filature to the appearance of Suwa-style reeling. This difference is related to the difference between the introduced technology B_1 and the existing technology B_3. In spinning, the difference between introduced technology and hand-spinning (or pattern-spinning, an extension of hand-spinning) was extremely large and a combination of the two was impossible. But in the case of reeling, the difference between the modern technology and sedentary reeling was not so great and it was possible to merge them. Also, the technicians and general workers of the reeling industry could easily learn to use modern technology.

The third category is illustrated by the introduction of (silk) weaving technology. Three students from Nishijin, Kyōto, brought the technology necessary to build the hand loom with batten apparatus[21] from Lyon, France, to Nishijin in 1873. They did not bring the most modern weaving technology, the power loom[22] (B_1), probably because they thought the production of the power loom was impossible given the level of engineering expertise in Japan. The batten apparatus (B_2) could be easily made by local carpenter. It was fitted to the traditional hand loom (B_3) and increased efficiency in weaving. While B_2 technology was being improved, the treadle loom was invented. Its spread eventually opened the way for the adoption of the power loom[23] (B_1).

5.3.3 Gerschenkron's Model

Gerschenkron introduced a model to explain the development of European latecomers based on his study of France, Germany and Russia.[24] The model was summarized by Henry Rosovsky as follows:[25]

1. Prior to industrialization there is a period of tension between the actual state of economic activities and the great promise inherent in development.

2. Industrialization is more promising in proportion to the backlog of technologies. The traditional view that in backward countries labour is cheap and capital is expensive is not true: an industrial work force, i.e. a stable and disciplined work force, may be extremely expensive.

3. In the face of competition from more advanced countries, backward countries adopt the most modern and most labour-saving technologies. As a result, they tend to concentrate development in a sector where technological progress has been particularly rapid. Backward countries in nineteenth-century Europe concentrated on 'newer' industries like iron and steel rather than cotton textiles which had been the foundation of England's industrialization.

4. Backward countries industrialize both through large units of production and a 'revolutionary' industrial spurt.

Here we will examine the applicability of this model to Japan and features that distinguish her history from western history.

First, Gerschenkron's hypothesis that there is a period of tension prior to industrialization is supported by the example of Japan; great political and social turmoil preceded and followed the Meiji Restoration. The military and economic threat from the advanced countries stimulated nationalism and rapid modernization. Second, the tendency of backward countries to grow rapidly by exploiting the 'backlog of technology' has already been shown to apply to Japan. Third,

Gerschenkron's hypothesis about the size of productive units (paragraph 4 above) agrees with our observation that Japan's industrialization coincided with the growth of large-scale production units. In fact Japan's industrialization was revolutionary in the sense that it was accomplished by the adoption of entirely new foreign technology.

On the remaining points, the Gerschenkron model is not applicable to Japan. First, Japan's industrialization was not founded on modern industries using the most up-to-date technology. The moving force behind Japan's economic development was the traditional textile industry, which employed labour-intensive technology. The choice of the textile industry in the early years meant that the abundant labour supply was employed. Unlike the postulation in Gerschenkron's model, Japan had an excellent work force.

Second, although what occurred in Japan agrees basically with Gerschenkron's hypothesis that industrialization implies large-scale production, the number of small-scale enterprises did continue to grow. The development of large-scale and small-scale enterprises was not mutually exclusive. The increase in income that resulted from the development of large-scale enterprises increased the demand for the traditional consumer products supplied by small-scale enterprises,[26] because the traditional Japanese consumption pattern remained unchanged during the pre-war period.

In spite of the different pattern of industrialization in Japan and western developed countries, however, the historical sequence of the introduction of technology was similar. The transition to more modern and more capital-using technology occurred at a rapid pace in Japan as the rapid increase in the capital – labour ratio in manufacturing confirms (Ch. 6, Sec. 3). Also, Japan's decision to concentrate on the textile industry and introduce capital-saving modifications to imported technology was not unique. In the USA, for example, the New England textile industry was a leading sector during the early phase of industrialization. The problem of the limited supply of coal in New England was solved by using water power rather than steam power. Moreover, as Nathan Rosenberg has pointed out, American manufacturers often made modifications when they introduced technology from England.[27]

One important point in Gerschenkron's hypothesis which Rosovsky did not mention is that the banks and the government in latecomer countries were the organizers of industrialization. The applicability of this hypothesis to Japan is discussed in Section 5.4.

5.3.4 Social Capability to Absorb Modern Technology

The availability of unexploited technology in itself does not, of course, guarantee the emergence of a modern economy. As Kuznets pointed out, it is also necessary to have the capability to absorb new technology.[28] The successful introduction of western technology in Japan can be understood only through study of this capability.

Japan's capability to absorb modern technologies resulted from a number of factors but unfortunately limited space means that we will have to confine our discussion to only two.[29] First we will discuss human resources, especially engineers. At the beginning of industrialization, Japanese industry relied heavily on the guidance of foreign engineers. These engineers were gradually replaced by Japanese engineers trained at factories and educational institutions in Japan and other countries. The most important Japanese institutions were Kōbu University (University of Engineering, established in 1877),[30] the Tōkyō Artisan School (established in 1881),[31] and several schools for the study of industry. The engineers studied foreign technical treatises and actual imported machinery, and then copied what they saw, often adding modifications. The local carpenters who produced appliances such as battens, treadle looms and machine filatures also played an important role. Without them the rapid spread of the improved hand looms and machine filatures in the Meiji Period would have been possible.

A second important factor was the research and development (R & D) which took place before the actual application of modern technology. However, only after the outbreak of the Second World War was R & D conducted on a large scale. The interruption of machinery imports and technological information from abroad during this war forced large enterprises to expand their R & D activities. The R & D of small-scale enterprises was also important; they were often members of trade associations, which had research institutions for developing technology appropriate for small-scale enterprises.

Three concluding comments are appropriate. First, Japan's 'cultural receptivity', developed through her long history of introducing culture and technology from China, facilitated the introduction of western technology.[32] Second, educational improvements meant that Japan's social capability to adopt new technology increased during industrialization. The number and quality of engineers increased as a result of the development of higher education. As a result the level of

R & D activities increased a great deal. Third, present-day developing countries can learn from Japan's experience. Those countries which have a large 'backlog' of unexploited technology must strive to increase their social capability to adopt it.

5.3.5   Technological Progress in the Post-war Period

The 'residual' of the growth rate of mining and manufacturing (λ), shown in Figure 5.4, demonstrates that technological progress was very rapid in the period from the mid-1950s until the late 1960s. This rapid technological progress resulted largely from the introduction of technology developed in western countries during and after the Second World War. The growth rate of the number of cases of introducing technology (χ) increased, reaching a peak in 1960 and then decreased. In the late 1960s λ began to decrease, largely as a result of this, probably due in turn to a decrease in the backlog of unexploited technology. There is a high correlation between λ and χ ($\bar{r} = 0.852$) for the period 1956–87.[33]

There was more R & D in the post-war than the pre-war period, but technology borrowing continued. The reason for this can be seen by noting two findings. The first is the close relation between λ and the growth rate of real R & D expenditure (y) since 1963, which implies that R & D played an important role in raising the technological level of industry. The correlation between λ and y is estimated to be 0.795 for the period 1956–87. The second important finding is the correlation between x and y, which is estimated to be 0.802 for the same period. This implies that R & D in Japan did not substitute for, but complemented borrowed technology.

These conclusions are confirmed by the data in Table 5.8 on the growth rate of labour productivity (λ), the ratio of payments for technology import to output (x), and the ratio of R & D expenditure to output (y) for manufacturing sub-industry groups in the five years 1984–8. Industries where productivity increased rapidly (such as machinery and chemicals) also tended to have a high level of both technology borrowing and R & D. Industries with a high level of technology borrowing also did extensive R & D.[34] The estimated correlations ($\bar{r}$) among the three variables are as follows: 0.638 (between λ and x), 0.763 (between λ and y) and 0.873 (between x and y).

I would like to make two comments here.

First the relation between the pattern of technological innovation in Japan and that in the rest of the world. Rapid technological

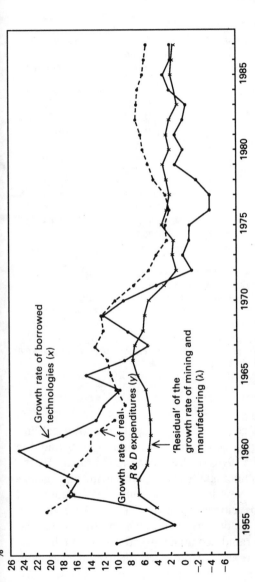

FIGURE 5.4   Growth rates of technology borrowing and real R & D expenditure, and 'residual' of the growth rate in the mining and manufacturing industries in Japan 1954–87

Notes:

x = the growth rate in the number of cases of technology import.

y = the growth rate of R & D expenditure divided by R & D deflator (1985 = 1).

λ = the growth rate of total factor productivity.

The figures are the annual growth rate based on seven-year moving averages (five-year averages for real R & D in 1955).

Sources:

The number of cases of technology import: 1950–74 – Nakamura, 1979, pp. 54–5, 1975–89 – KGY, 1991, p. 100.

Nominal R & D expenditure and its deflator: 1953–74 – Kagaku Gijutsuchō, 1979, pp. 307, 360; 1975–89 – KGY, 1991, pp. 25, 43. (Deflator for 1953–62 – Extrapolated from the R & D deflator in 1963 based on GNP deflator.)

λ: Table 5.2.

TABLE 5.8   Growth rate of labour productivity, ratio of payments for imported technology and ratio of R & D expenditure to output in the manufacturing industry in Japan 1984–8

	Growth rate of labour productivity λ	Payments for technology, ratio of imports to output x (%)	Ratio of R & D expenditure to output y (%)
Textiles	0.97	0.103	1.36
Foods and tobacco	0.97	0.120	1.70
Iron and steel	1.25	0.130	4.83
Non-ferrous metals and products	1.25	0.478	60.30
Metal products	1.07	0.055	1.63
Machinery	1.26	0.504	10.01
Chemicals	1.17	0.305	7.45
Ceramics	1.15	0.277	4.18
Miscellaneous	1.11	0.063	1.06
All manufacturing	1.17	0.307	6.27

Notes:
λ = ratio of labour productivity in 1988 to labour productivity in 1984. Labour productivity = ratio of the production index to the number of workers.
x = ratio of payments for technology import net value added to × 100.
y = ratio of R & D expenditure to net value added × 100. Averages for 1984–88.

Sources:
Production index: Same as Table 5.5.
Net Value added and the number of workers: *Kōgyō Tōkeihyō* (Census of Manufactures) (KTN, 1986, pp. 293–4; 1990, pp. 281–2).
Payments for technology (imports), and R & D expenditure: KGY, 1990, p. 67, 1991, pp. 44–5, 94–5.

introduction (borrowing) combined with rapid technological improvement in manufacturing industries up to the 1960s, and the slow-down of these after the 1970s were not confined to Japan. By the 1960s, many prominent technologies such as petrochemistry, nuclear power, pharmaceuticals, television and computer electronics had been developed in the developed countries. These were quickly spread around the world helped by favourable international relations, and they promoted rapid economic growth in many countries although there were differences in the pace of economic growth. However, there were no revolutionary technological innovations that might have influenced economic growth after the 1970s, and the economies of all countries have slowed down. It is necessary to understand that the high level of growth in Japan and its later slow-down is part of the great wave of global technological innovation.

Second is the change in technological strategy in Japan. Throughout the entire period of modern economic development, Japan has placed more emphasis on the introduction of technologies rather than on innovation. This was an appropriate strategy as long as there was a large technological gap between the developed countries and Japan. However, it has now became inappropriate since the technological gap has disappeared and, in some areas, Japan has taken the lead. Japan is expected to take over the major part of the role previously undertaken by the USA and other developed countries, by investing a greater amount of funding for the development of creative technologies. The export of technologies from Japan has been increasing tremendously. According to an estimate by the Bank of Japan (Nihon Ginkō), the ratio of the amount received for technology exports to the amount paid for technology imports was 0.007 in 1953, 0.13 in 1970 and rose to 0.38 in 1989. (According to estimates by the Management and Coordination Agency (Sōmuchō), the ratio was 1.00 in 1989.) Most recent figures are: the UK: 0.92 in 1987; the former West Germany: 0.54 in 1989; and France: 0.59 in 1989, which were comparable to that in Japan. The ratio for Japan, however, is much inferior to the one for the USA (5.26 in 1989),[35] and more determined effort for technological development is desired.

5.4 INDUSTRIAL ORGANIZATION AND INDUSTRIAL POLICIES

5.4.1 Industrial Organization in the Pre-war Period

The most conspicuous feature of the industrial organization of pre-war Japan was the *zaibatsu* (literally 'money cliques', but might better be described as 'family-controlled conglomerates').[36] Each *zaibatsu* was a group of enterprises dominated by a single family; the *zaibatsu* family controlled a holding company that dominated several principal operating companies. These companies, in turn, controlled many subsidiaries. Some *zaibatsu*, such as Mitsui, Mitsubishi and Sumitomo were active in a wide range of industries (including mining, manufacturing, commerce and banking). Yasuda was involved in banking, but not mining and manufacturing. Other *zaibatsu*, such as

Asano, Furukawa and Nakajima, specialized in only one industry (cement, non-ferrous metals and aeroplanes, respectively) and did not own banks.

Several *zaibatsu*, usually referred to as the 'old *zaibatsu*', had a long history: the Mitsui and Sumitomo *Zaibatsu* grew up from big merchant houses of the Tokugawa Era; the Mitsubishi, Yasuda, Ōkura, Asano and Furukawa *Zaibatsu* were also originally merchant families. The latter five were able to expand as a result of close co-operation with the Meiji government; they benefited particularly from the disposal of public mines and factories in the mid-1880s. All these families became *zaibatsu* during the 1910s. Nakajima, Nissan and other 'new *zaibatsu*' developed with the munitions industry in the Shōwa Period, especially during the 1930s. Cartelization occurred in various industries during the Depression that followed the First World War, with the objective of increasing profits, and was accelerated by the Important Industry Control Law in 1931. It gave the government power to encourage compulsory cartelization and increased its control over industry. Many mergers also occurred during this period. The Ōji Paper Manufacturing Company merged with the Fuji Paper Manufacturing Company and Saghalin Industries in 1933, and the public Yawata Iron Works absorbed five private companies – Kamaishi, Wanishi, Mitsubishi, Kyūshū and Fuji – and became a giant private company, called Japan Iron and Steel, in 1934. Mergers were most conspicuous in the banking industry; the number of banks decreased from 2036 in 1920 to 895 in 1930 and to 69 in 1945.[37] The banks which survived were mainly owned by the four biggest *zaibatsu*. The *zaibatsu* established control over industry through control of the banking system. In 1946 the four biggest *zaibatsu* (Mitsui, Mitsubishi, Sumitomo and Yasuda) owned about 25 per cent of total paid-in capital of incorporated enterprises; if the holdings of six small-scale *zaibatsu* (Ōkura, Asano, Nomura, Furukawa, Nakajima and Nissan) are also included the figure rises to 35 per cent.[38]

Marxists generally emphasize the harm caused by the *zaibatsu*. This view was also expressed in a report by the Zaibatsu Mission dispatched from the USA immediately after the Second World War. The leader of the Mission, Corwin Edwards, was of course not a Marxist, but an economist who sympathized with the New Deal and antitrust. The report said that

Japan's industries had been 'under the control of a few great combines . . . enjoying preferential treatment from the Japanese government' . . .

The concentration of industrial control 'promoted the continuation of a semi-feudal relationship between labor and management, held down wages, blocked the development of labor unions . . . obstructed the creation of firms by independent entrepreneurs, and hindered the rise of a middle class in Japan.' 'The low wages and concentrated profits . . . produced by such a structure have been inconsistent with the development of a domestic market . . . and in consequence, Japanese business felt the need to expand its exports. This drive for exports . . . has been an outstanding motive of Japanese imperialism . . . and aggression.'[39]

Marxists hold that the growth of the *zaibatsu* fostered militarism and finally brought about Japan's invasion of neighbouring countries. Their reasoning is as follows: The growth of the *zaibatsu* brought about a difference between the productivity and wages of large enterprises, and of agriculture and smaller enterprises, and thus unequal income distribution. As a result the domestic market did not grow, and Japan was forced to invade other countries to create new markets for her products.

We agree that the distribution of income became less equal during the period of rapid industrialization (Ch. 11, Sec. 3). However, there is no evidence to support their claim that the domestic market was small. On the contrary, our statistics show that both personal consumption and capital formation (especially the latter) increased to a significant extent and that, in general, effective demand exceeded production capacity. The latter fact is verified by the high rate of price inflation in Japan relative to other developed countries (Ch. 11, Sec. 1).

What was the relationship between the growth of *zaibatsu* and the growth of militarism? Dore, Rosovsky and Ohkawa have argued that the increasing inequality of income produced dissatisfaction among farmers and workers in small enterprises. These people, and low-ranking military officers mainly from farming backgrounds, were at odds with the *zaibatsu* and the government. The young officer rebels of the 1930s[40] were a typical result of this confrontation. The ruling class attempted to maintain national unity and divert attention from distress at home by promoting the invasion of China and thus creating an environment of international tension.[41] The attempt to expand the Japanese Empire had two other important goals. The first was to secure opportunities for emigration to relieve over-population and employment problems at home (Ch. 8, Sec. 1). The second was to secure a stable source of food, raw materials and fuels; there was a shortage of food by the 1920s and raw materials and fuels were becoming more and more in demand due to industrialization.

Few references have been made to 'positive' contributions of the *zaibatsu*. Ohkawa and Rosovsky have argued that the *zaibatsu* were efficient organizers of technological innovation:

> The *zaibatsu* were leaders in the development of technologically more sophisticated industries. They were major importers of Western technology and innovators. They provided a low-income Japan with the possibility of exploiting scale economies, and their diversification permitted what Lockwood has called 'combined investment,' i.e. the simultaneous development of complementary industries. *Zaibatsu* also economized what must have been a scarce factor, i.e. individuals capable of running modern businesses, and through the operation of their affiliated banks they were most adept at mobilizing capital resources. Given that the issue of that day, as now, was growth rather than economic democracy, there developed in Japan a certain kind of bigness that was unacceptable elsewhere but quite suitable in this setting.[42]

5.4.2   Industrial Organization in the Post-war Period

Immediately after the Second World War the occupation army – in effect, the US Army – took measures to democratize the Japanese economy.[43] In 1945 it declared its intention of dissolving the *zaibatsu*, because they were believed to have fostered militarism in the pre-war period; during the years 1946–7 eighty-three companies were identified as holding companies and twenty-one of them were dissolved because they were family companies. The *zaibatsu* leaders, including members of the founding families, were barred from business.

In 1947 two new democratization measures were taken. The main instrument of the first of these was the Anti-Monopoly Law, modelled on a US law but much more strictly applied. This law prohibited holding companies, company ownership of stocks and bonds, directors of one company holding office in another concurrently, cartelization, and so on. The Fair Trade Commission (*Kōsei Torihiki Iinkai*) was established to enforce this law. Revisions in 1949 and 1953 greatly weakened the law; company ownership of stocks and bonds, and concurrent office-holding in more than one company were now permitted. 'Anti-depression cartels' and 'rationalization cartels' were also authorized. In 1977, however, the law was again strengthened: fines were introduced for unauthorized cartels, and price rises 'in concert' had to be reported to parliament.

The main instrument of the second measure was the Law for Elimination of Excessive Concentration of Economic Power of 1947. However, although this law designated 325 companies to be partitioned into smaller units, only eighteen companies were actually affected as the Cold War made the reconstruction of the Japanese economy imperative. Japan Iron and Steel became two companies (Yawata and Fuji), and Mitsubishi Heavy Industries was broken into three companies (Eastern Japan, Central Japan and Western Japan).

Although relaxed after the occupation army's change of policy, these attempts at economic democratization brought about a drastic transformation in the industrial organization of Japan; the monopoly of the large enterprises was weakened, entry into industries became easier and competition increased. Furthermore, the purge of *zaibatsu* executives gave opportunities to young and able businessmen.[44] It is widely believed that these transformations helped make possible Japan's high rate of economic growth after the mid-1950s.[45]

Banks, however, were almost untouched by the dissolution of the *zaibatsu*. After the dissolution *zaibatsu*-affiliated enterprises became affiliated to banks. The growth of the heavy and chemical industries necessitated this because the huge amount of capital they needed could not be financed internally. Companies had no choice but to depend on loans from banks (Ch. 10, Sec. 3). Thus, six 'business groups' (*kigyō keiretsu*) appeared in the 1950s, with the Mitsubishi, Mitsui, Sumitomo, Fuji, Daiichi Kangyō and Sanwa banks at their respective centres.[46] The members of each group hold each other's stock and exchange information.

Although the formation of these business groups is sometimes referred to as the revival of the *zaibatsu*, the ties among their members are much looser.[47] First, unlike the *zaibatsu* which had a holding company, the business group does not have a central organization to control its members. Bank control of the business group is far less effective than the control *zaibatsu* exercised through holding companies. Enterprises within the group sometimes compete with each other and loans from affiliated banks are sometimes smaller than those from other banks. Second, there are many big companies which do not belong to any group. New Japan Iron and Steel (Yawata and Fuji Iron Works), Matsushita Electric, Hitachi Factory, Sony and Honda, which all grew rapidly during the period of high economic growth, are not associated with any business group.

Due to the relaxing of the Anti-Monopoly Law in 1949 and 1953 the number of cartels increased from 79 in 1954 to 1079 in 1966. Since then the number of cartels has decreased; by 1980 it had fallen to less than 500.[48] The concentration ratio declined from 1950 to the mid-1960s and increased thereafter.[49] The decline in the 1950s and early 1960s is attributable to the rapid expansion of markets which made it easier for new entrants to become established. The increase in the late 1960s and the 1970s was due to the increasing number of mergers. The most important mergers were those of Mitsubishi Heavy Industries in 1964, and Yawata and Fuji Iron Works (now New Japan Iron and Steel) in 1970.

Have these changes in industrial organization (the emergence of business groups, cartelization and mergers) reduced competition among firms? The answer appears to be in the negative; in spite of the changes the Japanese economy is still very competitive.[50] Formation of business groups has intensified competition, and cartelization has sometimes been unsuccessful. Furthermore, oligopoly resulting from mergers has not necessarily reduced competition. (For instance, the automobile industry, composed of several big companies such as Toyota and Nissan, was characterized by fierce competition, which led to the spectacular growth of this industry.) As Shinohara has emphasized, oligopolistic industrial organization is very competitive.[51] A high degree of competition has been a basic element in the rapid growth of the Japanese economy.

5.4.3   General Trading Companies and Subcontracting

Our survey of the industrialization of Japan would be incomplete without a mention of the general trading companies and the subcontracting system that characterize Japanese industry. The general trading company deals with exports and imports of various commodities. It was an important component of the *zaibatsu* in the pre-war period and remains important to business groups today. Mitsui Bussan, for example, deals with sale of the products of the Mitsui Group just as it dealt with those of the Mitsui *Zaibatsu*. With the exception of Mitsui Bussan (established in 1876), nearly all the general trading companies were formed during and immediately after the First World War (Ch. 7, Sec. 3).[52] Mitsubishi Shōji, for example, was formed in 1918. In 1947 both Mitsui Bussan and Mitsubishi Shōji were dissolved by the occupation army. Later the government attempted to strengthen the general trading companies in order to promote exports. Mitsui Bussan and Mitsubishi Shōji were revived in 1954–5 and virtually all present-day trading companies had been revived by the mid-1950s.

These companies played an important role during the rapid expansion of international trade. In 1972 51 per cent of total exports and 75 per cent of total imports were handled by the ten largest trading companies.[53] Their activities are not limited to commodity trade; they are also involved in activities such as manufacturing, transportation, construction, overseas business and the development of natural resources. General trading companies do not exist in other developed countries and have therefore attracted considerable international attention.

The well-developed subcontracting system is another important feature of Japanese industrial organization.[54] By the subcontracting system we mean the system in which large manufacturing companies (known as *oyagaisha* – literally parent companies) consign the production of certain products or parts to their subsidiaries (*kogaisha* – literally child companies). This system emerged after the First World War because small enterprises had lower wage costs than large enterprises (Ch. 9, Sec. 3). Parent companies were able to reduce production costs by indirectly making use of the cheap labour of their child companies. (This can be viewed as a labour-using – i.e. capital-saving – modification of technology by the parent companies.) During depressions parent companies decreased their orders to these subcontractors, and reduced the prices of their products. Hence, the subcontracting system also worked as a buffer for the parent companies against business fluctuations. The system developed further in the munitions industry during the Second World War, but it is only since the rapid economic expansion of the mid-1950s that it developed into its present mature state. An increase in competition among large companies forced them to improve the quality of their products, which necessitated a rise in the technological capability of the subcontractors. Parent companies began to give financial, technological, managerial and sales assistance to their child companies. Thus the present-day subcontracting system is not, like the pre-war system, characterized by exploitation of subcontractors by parent companies; it has contributed to increased efficiency in industry through vertical integration. Opinion in foreign countries about this kind of vertically aligned system is divided. One viewpoint is that this system is effective and that the system should be introduced freely. The other view attacks the system by regarding it as a symbol of the closed nature of the Japanese market. It is immediately necessary for Japan also to assess the merits and the demerits of this system.

5.4.4   The Role of the Government in Pre-war Industrialization

The government's significant role in the early Meiji Period has been described as 'policies to promote industrialization' (*Shokusan Kōgyō Seisaku*).[55] These policies can be divided into two groups. One group includes policies that made possible the structural changes necessary for subsequent capitalistic development. These included the construction of social overhead capital and the introduction of the limited company and a modern monetary system (Ch. 2, Secs 1 and 2). The second group of policies was aimed at the introduction of modern production techniques. The government operated some important businesses itself and made an effort to foster private industries by, for example, the distribution of imported machines to cotton-spinning companies and subsidies to marine transport (Ch. 2, Sec. 2). However, government-run mines and factories were business failures and, with the exception of munitions factories, were disposed of to the private sector. The costs incurred in the trial-and-error process of introducing new technology were shared by government-operated and private establishments.

The Meiji government responded very well to the 'challenge' of industrialization, which at first glance seems to support the Marxist hypothesis that the industrialization of Meiji Japan was carried out by the government; i.e. that it was characterized by 'capitalization from above'.[56] However, there are three criticisms we can make of this hypothesis.[57] First, the positive response of the private sector to government policies was an important prerequisite for successful industrialization. This response was positive because of many factors: the enthusiasm of most entrepreneurs to introduce new industries and technology, the availability of a source of savings that could finance this, the earlier development of traditional industries (agriculture and commerce), the close relationship between the government and the private sector.[58]

Second, the playing of a major role by the government during the early years of industrialization happened not only in Japan, but also in the European latecomer countries. Gerschenkron argued that banks and governments in the latecomers in the nineteenth century developed 'institutional instruments', which worked as organizers of industrialization.[59] In the eighteenth and nineteenth centuries paternalistic regimes in France, Prussia and Austria invested large sums in pilot plants.[60] A similar pattern was seen in Russia under Peter the Great (1682–1725). The similarity between the Japanese and European experiences suggests that the importance of the actions of the government to Japanese industrialization has been overrated.[61]

Third, the role of government changed fundamentally after the early Meiji Period. It is misleading to make generalizations about the government's role from this 'abnormal' period. The basic attitude of the government after this period was '*laissez-faire*'.[62] After the Meiji Period, government ownership of factories was limited primarily to the Yawata Iron Works, and this was transferred to the private sector in 1934. About the role of the government from the late Meiji Period until the Second World War Lockwood wrote:

> A study of the whole process of economic growth in modern Japan leads to the conviction that the real drive and momentum lay in large measure outside the realm of national political ambition and State activity. At most the latter only accelerated a process of industrialization which was latent in the whole conjuncture of forces at work.[63]

We are in basic agreement with this view. This does not imply, however, that the role of government can be completely ignored. The government provided the private sector with indispensable services (Ch. 10, Sec. 2). The government's activities stimulated private activities (or at least did not hinder them).

5.4.5 Post-war Industrial Policies

The government's post-war industrial policies grew out of its intervention in the private sector during the war and the period of turmoil that followed. The 1937 Material Mobilization Plan made it possible for the government to exercise significant control over the scale and structure of the economy by rationing foreign currencies to the various industries. In 1938 the National General Mobilization Law was passed, introducing conscription, fixing wages and giving directives on the production and distribution of goods. After the Second World War the extreme shortage of commodities made direct control by the government inevitable.

The so-called 'industrial policies', which are often cited as a major reason for Japan's rapid economic growth, have seldom been clearly defined. They may be said to include all measures by the government (especially – Ministry of International Trade and Industry, MITI – Tsūshō Sangyōshō) to promote the growth of industry. These include:[64]

1. Financial aid to important industries (e.g. the subsidies and low-interest loans provided through government financial institutions such as the Japan Development Bank (1951) and the Japan Export-Import Bank (1951)).

2. Protection of infant industries by imposing high duties on imports and establishing non-tariff barriers.

3. Preferential allocation of foreign currencies to important industries to make it possible for them to import goods and advanced technology (since 1949).

4. A special accelerated depreciation system for imported machinery (since 1952). This reduced the tax burden of companies and made it possible to increase investment in new plants and equipment.

5. Encouragement to adopt foreign technology. Technical cooperation with overseas companies was encouraged by the Foreign Capital Law of 1950.

6. 'Administrative guidance', which economists in other countries have recently described as being unique to Japan: This system enables the government to exercise direct influence over Japanese enterprises by giving certain information, advice and instructions to them informally rather than taking formal legal action. Administrative guidance has enabled the government to promote mergers, control production by forcing a reduction in operations and mitigate excessive competition by controlling increases in equipment. The government is able to exert pressure on private companies by virtue of its formal legal power to authorize, approve, and supervise industry

The industrial policies adopted by MITI, in the mid-1950s, were intended to make the heavy and chemical industries the leading sector in economic development.[65] The choice of these industries was inconsistent with traditional economic theory, which teaches that labour-intensive industries have an advantage over capital-intensive heavy and chemical industries in a capital-scarce and labour-abundant society. MITI rejected these theories because it believed that heavy and chemical industries would have a comparative advantage over light industries in the future, (1) because the demand for capital goods and consumer durables (both products of the heavy and chemical industries) would increase considerably because of their high income elasticity, and (2) because technical progress in heavy and chemical industries would increase the competitiveness of their exports faster than in light industries.

MITI's industrial policy changed in the early 1970s; in 1971 MITI published a report called *The Basic Direction of Trade and Industry in the 1970s* which emphasized 'knowledge-intensive industries' in the place of the heavy and chemical industries. These new industries included:

1. Research and development-intensive industries (computers, aircrafts, industrial robots, atomic power-related industries, fine chemicals, large-scale integrated circuits).
2. Industries which employ very advanced manufacturing techniques (office communication equipment, numerically counted machine tools, pollution prevention machinery).
3. Fashion industries (high-quality clothing and furniture, electronic musical instruments).
4. Knowledge industries (information management services, information supplying services, computer software, system engineering, consulting).

There were two reasons for this change of policy. First, the balance-of-payments surplus had increased significantly and since the latter half of the 1960s there had been considerable 'trade friction' with other countries. In this situation the policy of strengthening international competitiveness by increasing economies of scale had to be abandoned. Second, domestic needs such as environmental control, improvements in education and replacement of social overhead capital have increased.

In 1980 MITI published a report called *Trade and Industry Policies for the 1980s*. This report covers a far wider scope than the 1971 report. It predicted that the 1980s would be a period during which Japan developed more reliable sources of energy and became less dependent on oil. It also predicted that the 1980s would be a period of departure from an oil-oriented society and would see the development of highly sophisticated technology, using new materials and systems. It decisively played down the role of heavy and chemical industries.

Economists are divided over the issue of whether these policies have been successful or not. C. Johnson concludes the MITI's policies made important contributions to heavy and chemical industries during the period of high economic growth,[66] while Ryūtarō Komiya and Yutaka Kōsai point out that MITI's administrative guidance has sometimes been unsuccessful.[67] H. T. Patrick and H. Rosovsky said that

> Government intervention generally has tended (and intended) to ac-
> celerate trends already put in motion by private market forces. . . . Care-
> ful examination of Japan's postwar trade and industrial development in
> comparison with general world performance indicates that the Japanese
> pattern was not unique at all.[68]

It was clearly the rapid introduction of foreign technology and
capital formation, both accomplished by the private sector, the
brought about Japan's unprecedented high economic growth rate.
However, the government's industrial policies had some positive
influences: By allocating public funds to certain private industries the
government 'designated' them key (or growth) industries. This encouraged private financial institutions to extend credit to these
industries.[69] Also, there are several examples of cases in which cartels
and mergers were successfully arranged as a result of a recommenda-
tion by MITI.

SUMMARY OF THE CHAPTER

'Industry' (the *M* Sector) has grown at a very fast pace compared to
other industries and its contribution to overall economic growth has
been high; industrialization has formed the core of modern economic
growth. This statement could refer to any capitalist country, but in
Japan it was especially true. Primary industry's share of GDP fell at a
faster rate in Japan than in any other country and the share of the *M*
Sector increased especially rapidly. Its rapid growth resulted from a
high rate of technological progress and a rapid increase in demand for
its products.

In recent years (the 1970s) the service industry (*S* Sector) has had a
higher rate of growth of nominal output than other sectors. As a
result there has been an increase in the *S* Sector's share of total
output at current prices. This phenomenon, which parallels the
earlier experience of the western developed countries, may mark a
turning-point in modern economic growth.

The manufacturing industry has been crucial to industrialization.
Its development began with the development of light industries during the early phase of industrialization. The success of import substitution and export promotion in the textile industries (silk reeling,
cotton spinning and weaving) saved, and earned foreign exchange,
and thereby helped make the development of heavy and chemical

industries possible. The development of heavy and chemical industries necessitated increased imports of capital equipment, raw materials and fuels. Heavy industrialization began in the post-First World War period and gained momentum in the period immediately after the Second World War. It pushed up the growth rate of the manufacturing industry and the economy as a whole, and the upward trend in the standard of living that accompanied economic growth raised the demand for consumer durables, thus facilitating further heavy industrialization.

Technological progress accounts for much of the growth of the *M* Sector. Technological development in Japan was based on the importation and adaptation of foreign technology. Some modern technology was borrowed with little modification (e.g. railways and electricity), some was introduced after capital-saving modifications (e.g. silk-reeling) and in some cases older technology in limited use in foreign countries was imported (e.g. looms). Foreign technology was introduced relatively quickly, because of Japan's relative backwardness and her social capability to absorb it. Gerschenkron's hypothesis regarding relative backwardness and the importation of technology is supported by what happened in Japan, but his model to explain the development of western latecomer countries requires modifications if it is to be applied to Japan. Japan differed from the former in that labour was abundant and capital was scarce, so that the labour-using and capital-saving light industries developed earlier. Imported technology has also been very important to Japan's post-war technological progress. However, because of the narrowing technological gap with the west, the importance of self-developed technology is gradually increasing.

The *zaibatsu* were a very prominent feature of the pre-war Japanese economy and had a big influence on its development after the First World War. The *zaibatsu* played an important part in the importation of modern technology and thus increased the pace of industrialization. They were, however, also responsible for the increasing inequality of income distribution. After the Second World War the *zaibatsu* were dissolved by the occupation army. During the period of high economic growth six 'business groups' centred on banks came to the fore. Although these groups are sometimes referred to as revived *zaibatsu*, the level of solidarity among their members is much lower than it was in the *zaibatsu*.

The government played a major role in industrialization during the early Meiji Period, but later adopted a *laissez-faire* attitude toward the private sector. The government's intervention in the private sector in the latter half of 1930s and during the war and the tumultuous period immediately after it, prepared the way for the present 'industrial policies' of the government, especially the Ministry of International Trade and Industry (MITI). MITI promoted heavy industrialization from the mid-1950s until the beginning of the 1970s, when they transferred the emphasis to knowledge-intensive industries.

FURTHER READING

Industrialization and industrial structure:
  Nakamura, 1981, ch. 4
  Ohkawa, 1979b
  Ohkawa and Rosovsky, 1973, ch. 4.
  Shinohara, 1962, ch. 2; 1968b; 1970, chs 5, 7 and 9; 1979a; 1982, ch. 1
  Shionoya, 1968
Technological progress:
  Blumenthal, 1976
  Ishikawa, 1981, ch. 4
  Minami, 1987, ch. 15
  Ohkawa and Kohama, 1989, lecture 6
  Ozawa, 1974
  Peck and Gotō, 1981
  Peck and Tamura, 1976
  Watanabe, 1968
Industrial organization and industrial policies:
  Caves and Uekusa, 1976a; 1976b
  Hadley, 1970
  Johnson, 1982
  Komiya, 1975b
  Komiya, Okuno and Suzumura, 1988
  Shinohara, 1982, chs 2 and 3
  Ueno, 1976–7
  Yamamura, 1967

6 Capital Formation and its Sources

Economic activity has two sides – production of commodities and expenditure. In national income accounting, Gross National Product (GNP) represents the former and Gross National Expenditure (GNE) the latter. Chapters 4 and 5 analyzed production activity in agriculture and 'industry', the determinants of GNP. This and the next chapter analyze expenditure. This chapter deals with capital formation (investment).

In Section 6.1 changes in the rate of growth and composition of capital formation and the determinants of the changes are examined. In Section 6.2 we study the 'effective demand effect', the impact of the rate of investment upon the rate of economic growth. In Section 6.3 we study the 'production effect', the impact of investment on production and changes in the capital-output ratio and capital-labour ratio. Finally Section 6.4 presents an analysis of funding, the factor that makes capital formation possible. Importation of foreign capital and changes in savings are also discussed in this context.

6.1 THE SIZE, COMPOSITION AND DETERMINANTS OF CAPITAL FORMATION

6.1.1 Changes in the Amount of Capital Formation

Japan's real fixed capital formation (CF) increased very rapidly in both the pre-war and post-war periods; the annual growth rate of capital formation was 5.4 per cent for the period 1889–1938 and 9.2 per cent for the period 1955–88 (Table 6.1). (In the period 1955–70 it was 14.7 per cent, but in the period 1971–88 it decreased remarkably to 4.2 per cent.) This was much higher than the rate of economic growth (Table 3.2).

TABLE 6.1 Growth rates of the components of real GNE in Japan 1889–1988 (%)

	Personal consumption expenditure PC	Government consumption expenditure GC	Gross domestic fixed capital formation				Increase in stocks I	Exports of goods and services and factor income received from abroad E	Imports of goods and services and factor income paid abroad M
			Total CF	Private PCF	Government GCF	Non-military only GCF'			
1889–1900	2.73	4.78	4.90	2.92	11.18	9.44	–	9.16	10.02
1901–10	1.61	4.27	4.84	4.50	5.54	6.88	–	7.90	5.86
1911–20	3.55	2.86	6.68	7.33	5.91	2.73	–	8.26	5.96
1921–30	2.41	5.74	0.92	-1.34	4.84	7.80	–	6.06	6.00
1931–8	2.23	5.97	10.95	11.35	10.24	-1.23	–	8.24	4.47
Pre-war average	2.53	4.68	5.42	4.61	7.58	5.55	–	7.96	6.68
1955–60	8.02	2.85	15.96	16.82	13.97	–	14.01	11.98	14.83
1961–70	8.90	6.29	13.92	14.27	12.85	–	12.05	15.04	14.16
1971–80	4.74	4.87	3.71	3.24	4.77	–	-8.09	9.96	5.83
1981–8	3.57	2.68	4.88	6.62	0.05	–	8.73	6.75	5.36
Post-war average	6.27	4.41	9.15	9.68	7.66	–	5.69	11.05	9.76

Notes:
The figures are simple averages of the annual growth rates based on seven-year moving averages of the components of GNE (five-year averages for 1938, 1955 and 1988).
The components of GNE are at 1934–6 prices for the pre-war period and at 1985 prices for the post-war period.
Increase in stocks is included in the other items of GNE in the pre-war period; therefore it cannot be estimated separately.

Sources:
Same as Figure 3.3.

The growth rate of capital formation $G(CF)$ fluctuated a great deal in the pre-war period (Figure 6.1). These fluctuations were almost synchronous with the long swings in the rate of economic growth $G(Y)$ (Figure 3.3); the peaks and troughs of $G(CF)$ closely corresponded with those of the long swings. The $G(CF)$ peak of 1908 is, however, an exception; the increase in $G(Y)$ that resulted from the increase in $G(CF)$ was small, because real government consumption expenditure (GC) decreased remarkably. In spite of this exception there is a significant positive correlation between $G(CF)$ and $G(Y)$ (Table 6.2). A close relationship between $G(CF)$ and $G(Y)$ is also manifested in the post-war period. $G(Y)$ increased for ten years after 1956, $G(CF)$ increased very rapidly in 1956–7 and decreased thereafter. In the 1970s, however, both $G(Y)$ and $G(CF)$ decreased remarkably, suggesting that the recession was caused by a drop in investment activity.

The growth rate of real government fixed capital formation $G(GCF)$ was 7.6 per cent in the pre-war and 7.7 per cent in the post-war period, while the growth rate of real private fixed capital formation $G(PCF)$ in the two periods was 4.6 per cent and 9.7 per cent, respectively. The relatively rapid increase in $G(GCF)$ during the pre-war period stemmed from the rapid expansion of military investment; the growth rate of non-military capital formation $G(GCF')$ was 5.6 per cent, only 1 percentage point higher than $G(PCF)$. Hence, private and non-military government investment actually exhibited an almost identical rate of growth in both the pre-war and the post-war period.

When changes in $G(PCF)$, $G(GCF)$ and $G(GCF')$ are compared with those in $G(Y)$, two conclusions may be inferred. First, the pattern of changes in $G(PCF)$ was similar to that of $G(Y)$ in both periods, but $G(GCF)$ did not have any correlation with $G(Y)$ in the pre-war period and had a weaker correlation than $G(PCF)$ in the post-war period. This means that the above-mentioned correlation between $G(CF)$ and $G(Y)$ resulted from the correlation between $G(PCF)$ and $G(Y)$. The long swings were caused mainly by the fluctuations in private fixed investment.

The second conclusion relates government investment to private investment and economic growth. In the pre-war period we find a negative correlation between $G(GCF')$ and $G(PCF)$ and between $G(GCF')$ and $G(Y)$, which implies that non-military government investment tended to cancel out changes in private investment and economic growth.[1] In the post-war period there were positive

130

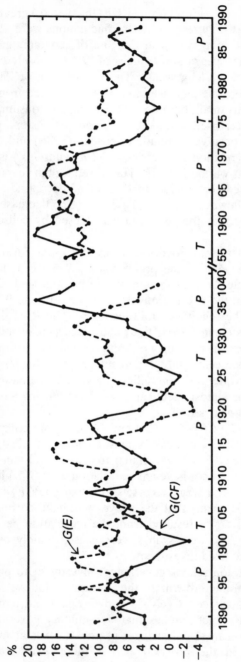

FIGURE 6.1 Growth rates of real capital formation G(CF) and real exports G(E) in Japan 1889–1988

Notes:
See Table 6.1.

Sources:
Same as Figure 3.3.

TABLE 6.2   Correlation between the growth rate of real GNE and its components in Japan 1889–1988

	Correlation between $G(Y)$ and					
	$G(PC)$	$G(GC)$	$G(CF)$	$G(PCF)$	$G(GCF)$	$G(GCF')$
1889–1938	0.463**	^{a}	0.655**	0.675**	0.192	–0.514**
1955–1988	0.979**	0.530**	0.921**	0.870**	0.905**	–

	Correlation between $G(Y)$ and		Correlation between $G(PCF)$ and		Correlation between $G(E)$ and	
	$G(E)$	$G(M)$	$G(GCF)$	$G(GCF')$	$G(CF)$	$G(D')$
1889–1938	^{a}	0.101	0.117	–0.517**	0.110	–0.464**
1955–1988	0.851**	0.884**	0.788**	–	0.689**	0.820**

Notes:
Correlation coefficients are adjusted by the degrees of freedom ($\bar{r}$).
** signifies that the correlation coefficient is statistically significant at a 1 per cent significance level.
D is domestic demand (total of PC, GC, CF, I and M).
^{a} $r^2 < 0$.

Sources:
Same as Table 6.1.

correlations between $G(GCF)$ and $G(PCF)$ and between $G(GCF)$ and $G(Y)$; government investment increased along with both private investment and economic growth. This was partly attributable to the fact that, until 1965, the issue of national bonds was prohibited and the government always strived to balance the budget. Government revenue was almost completely financed by increasing tax revenue (which increased with economic growth) and government investment, one of the components of government expenditure, had a positive correlation with economic growth because the budget was balanced (Ch. 10, Sec. 1).

6.1.2   Composition of Capital Formation

The increase in capital formation was accompanied by changes in its composition. Capital formation can be broken down into fixed capital formation (CF) and inventory investment (I). In the pre-war period it seems likely that improvements in transportation and communication caused a relative decrease in I, although reliable figures on I are not available for this period. The number of days necessary to transport commodities decreased as a result of the opening of railways (Ch. 2, Sec. 1). This certainly led to a decrease in the amount of inventory necessary. In the post-war period we do have reliable figures to show that CF increased much faster than I (Table 6.1).

Table 6.3 decomposes fixed capital formation, by sector, by industry group, and by type of capital in current prices. (The conclusions are not affected by the use of constant prices.)

1. Composition of CF by sector: In the pre-war period the proportion of PCF decreased, while that of GCF increased. The relative increase in GCF resulted from a rapid increase in military investment; the proportion of non-military investment (GCF') did not exhibit any clear trend. For the period 1955–70 the period of high economic growth, PCF's share of total capital formation increased, and in 1970–80, a period of slow growth, it decreased.

2. Composition of CF by industry group: The proportion of primary investment decreased, while that of non-primary investment increased over time. This change in investment allocation was one of the major factors responsible for industrialization.

3. Composition of CF by type of capital: In the pre-war period the share of livestock, perennial plants and residential buildings decreased. The decrease in livestock and perennial plants reflected the relative decrease in primary sector investment. The decrease in the share of residential buildings was attributable to the fact that pre-war houses were cheap to build because they used traditional materials and were constructed according to traditional patterns. Investment in producers' durable equipment and construction increased rapidly, from 53 per cent to 90 per cent of total capital formation in the period 1890–1938. These changes were the result of a relative increase in production-related social overhead capital in the non-primary sector. Thus, during the pre-war industrialization process, the composition of fixed capital changed in a manner that raised the productivity of non-primary industries and therefore the economy as a whole. This phenomenon was not unique to Japan. Kuznets showed that the proportion of inventory investment decreased while the proportion of investment in producers' equipment increased in the UK, Germany, Sweden, the USA and Canada.[2]

In the post-war period no data comparable to that for the pre-war period are available, but it is clear that the proportion of residential buildings in total investment has been increasing. Considerable numbers of residential buildings have been constructed by both the

TABLE 6.3 Composition of fixed capital formation in Japan 1890–1988 (%)

	Private v. government[a]			For industry groups[b]		For type of capital[c]			
	Private PCF	Government GCF	Non-military GCF[f]	Primary A	Non-primary M + S	Livestock & perennial plants	Producers' durable equipment	Construction	Residential buildings
1890	82.5	17.5	13.3	54.9	45.1	19.7	31.4	21.9	27.0
1900	66.8	33.2	20.2	46.5	53.5	15.4	28.6	31.0	25.0
1910	64.9	35.1	25.1	32.8	67.2	9.8	38.4	36.0	15.8
1920	68.8	31.2	20.6	20.0	80.0	5.1	46.9	35.1	12.9
1930	54.7	45.3	35.9	28.4	71.6	4.8	32.0	51.6	11.6
1938	54.0	46.0	12.3	10.1	89.9	2.8	62.1	28.3	6.8
1955	71.9	28.1	–	–	–		84.9		15.1
1960	75.4	24.6	–	–	–		85.5		14.5
1970	74.4	25.6	–	–	–		79.0		21.0
1980	69.3	30.7	–	–	–		78.4		21.6
1988	77.8	22.2	–	–	–		79.9[d]		20.1[d]

Notes:
The figures are seven-year moving averages of domestic fixed capital formation at current prices (five-year average for 1938 and 1988).

[a] Residential buildings are included
[b] Private sector. Residential buildings are excluded.
[c] Total of private and government (non-military) sectors.
[d] Three-year average.

Sources:
Pre-war period: Ohkawa and Shinohara, 1979, pp. 346–53.
Post-war period: *Ibid*, p. 363. KKKN, 1980, pp. 198–9; 1985, p. 168; 1991, pp. 250–1.

government and the private sector in response to an increase in demand stemming from rapid urbanization and an increase in the level of income.

6.1.3   Determinants of Capital Formation

Here we examine the factors responsible for private non-primary fixed capital formation (*PCF*). Government and primary investment are excluded from the analysis because of their specific characters.[3]

Expected return on capital and the level of the real capital stock (K) are two factors that influence the demand for capital. We use the real return on capital (R) and the rate of real return on capital ($r = R/K$) as indices of the expected return on capital. An increase in R or r is expected to stimulate investment activities. Previous studies of Japan have revealed that this factor has a significant effect on capital formation.[4] An increase in K decreases the necessity to expand capital equipment further. Hence, K is expected to be negatively correlated with capital formation. An empirical study of post-war Japan by Fumimasa Hamada found the expected negative correlation,[5] but a study of the same period by Tadao Uchida and Tsunehiko Watanabe revealed a positive correlation, and a study of the pre-war period by Shigeru Ishiwata showed that the sign of the coefficient on this variable depends upon the specification of the regression equation.[6]

On the supply side we analyze the effect of both nominal and real rates of interest (i and i^* respectively, where $i^* = i - G(P)$ and $G(P)$ is the rate of growth in output prices). It is expected that an increase in i or i^* will discourage capital formation. Many studies have found negative impact of i on capital formation,[7] but no attempt has been made to estimate the impact of the theoretically more appropriate variable i^*.

Estimates of the parameters of investment functions containing these variables for the pre-war and post-war periods are shown in Table 6.4. A subscript-1 attached to a variable indicates that the variable is lagged one year.

Three observations may be made here. First, the estimated parameters of r and R are very stable. This emphasizes the influence of the expected return on capital formation. Second, an increase in the rate of interest tends to decrease capital formation, and vice versa. Third, the algebraic sign of the estimated parameter on K depends on which variable is used to proxy for capital return in the pre-war

Table 6.4 Investment functions of private non-primary industries in Japan 1907–89

| | | | | Explanatory variables | | | | | |
Equation	Variable	Const.	r_{-1}	R_{-1}	i^*_{-1}	i_{-1}	K_{-1}	$\bar{R}$	d
1907–40									
(1)	PCF	−1.249 (2.40)	0.046 (2.17)	–	−0.019 (2.25)	–	0.070 (8.90)	0.854	0.46
(2)	PCF	−0.325 (2.62)	–	0.587 (4.10)	−0.011 (1.45)	–	−0.048 (1.69)	0.894	0.54
(3)	PCF	0.525 (0.50)	0.039 (1.78)	–	–	−0.183 (2.55)	0.058 (6.07)	0.860	0.41
(4)	PCF	0.562 (0.89)	–	0.557 (3.64)	–	−0.100 (1.51)	−0.048 (1.76)	0.894	0.59
1956–89									
(1)	PCF	−17 676 (4.93)	566.0 (6.20)		−182.2 (1.45)		0.142 (21.88)	0.986	0.94
(3)	PCF	−17 790 (1.63)	560.7 (4.93)			−10.752 (0.01)	0.142 (13.33)	0.985	0.69

TABLE 6.4 continued

Equation	Variable	Const.	r_{-1}	R_{-1}	i^*_{-1}	i_{-1}	K_{-1}	$\bar{R}$	d
				Explanatory variables					
(4)	PCF	12 347 (2.84)		0.412 (10.18)		−1 898 (3.81)	0.055 (10.91)	0.994	1.16

Notes:

PCF, K, r and R are at 1934–6 prices for the pre-war and at 1985 prices for the post-war period.
The units for PCF, K and R are one thousand million yen for the pre-war period, and one billion yen for the post-war period.
Units of r, i and i* are per cent.
Non-smoothed figures were used in the calculations.

Sources:

K = real capital stock (Table 5.2).
PCF = real private capital formation. The same source as that of K.
r = the real rate of profit = the nominal rate of profit deflated by the price index. Nominal rate of profit for 1907–70 – Minami and Ono, 1978a, p. 167. Nominal rate of profit for 1971–89 – calculated by multiplying the relative income share of capital by output–capital ratio.
R = rK.
i = the interest rate on loans. Pre-war – Fujino and Igarashi, 1973, pp. 470–1. Post-war – KTN, 1965, p. 173; 1979, p. 79; 1984, p. 187; 1990, p. 173.
i* = i – G(P).
P = the deflator for non-primary products (Table 11.1).

period; it is positive if we use r and negative if we use R. Therefore we cannot draw any firm conclusions about the impact of capital stock on investment. In the post-war period, however, a parameter of K is estimated as being positive in all equations, standing for the fact that an increase in capital stock has accelerated investment. This fact reflects flourishing investment activities by Japanese entrepreneurs; in the high growth period a competition in expanding production facilities, which was referred to as 'investment invites investment', and in the slow growth period necessities for rationalization of production, energy saving and anti-pollution.[8]

We can, however, state with confidence that an increase in the expected return on capital and a decrease in the rate of interest were responsible for the rapid increase in capital formation in the private non-primary industries. The increase in the expected return on capital resulted from rapid technological progress and a decline in labour's share of national income in the pre-war period (Ch. 9, Sec. 4). Historical changes in the rate of interest will be discussed in Ch. 10, Sec. 4.

6.2 THE IMPACT OF CAPITAL FORMATION ON DEMAND

6.2.1 Effective Demand Effect

Among the components of Japan's effective demand or Gross National Expenditure (GNE), personal consumption expenditure (*PC*) has always been the largest, followed by capital formation (gross domestic fixed capital formation, *CF*), exports (*E*) and government consumption expenditure (*GC*) (Table 6.5). Table 6.6 shows that, in 1988, the shares of *PC* (57 per cent), *E* (13 per cent) and *GC* (9 per cent) in GNE were much lower in Japan than the average of 103 countries (69 per cent, 28 per cent and 15 per cent respectively). On the other hand, share of *CF* + *I* (31 per cent) was much higher in Japan than in other countries. The world average is a mere 21 per cent. Thus capital formation is a more important determinant of effective demand in Japan than in other countries.

The best index of the impact of capital formation on the creation of effective demand is the relative contribution of *CF* to economic growth; i.e. the ratio of the increase in real *CF* to the increase in real GNE (Table 6.7). This ratio, 31 per cent in the pre-war period and 33

TABLE 6.5 Composition of GNE in Japan 1888–1988 (%)

	Personal consumption expenditure PC	Government consumption expenditure GC	Gross domestic fixed capital formation CF	Private only PCF	Increase in stocks I	Exports of goods and services and factor income received from abroad E	(Less) imports of goods and services and factor income paid abroad −M	Gross national expenditure GNE
1888	86.3	6.8	9.2	7.6	–	2.1	4.4	100.0
1900	85.1	8.5	11.7	7.7	–	4.4	9.7	100.0
1910	81.6	9.7	15.1	9.7	–	7.6	14.0	100.0
1920	77.7	8.6	19.3	13.1	–	11.1	16.7	100.0
1930	78.9	12.1	17.0	9.1	–	15.9	23.9	100.0
1938	63.6	13.0	26.2	14.5	–	20.1	22.9	100.0
1954	67.0	18.7	14.9	9.9	1.2	4.2	6.0	100.0
1960	65.8	13.7	22.3	15.5	1.6	5.1	8.5	100.0
1970	60.5	9.9	32.2	23.1	1.9	8.1	12.6	100.0
1980	60.9	10.0	29.3	20.1	0.5	13.3	14.0	100.0
1988	58.4	9.0	31.0	24.3	0.7	16.2	15.3	100.0

Notes:
The figures are a composition of GNE at 1934–6 prices for the pre-war period and 1985 prices for the post-war period.
The figures are seven-year moving averages of GNE (five-year averages for 1938, 1954 and 1988).

Sources:
Same as Table 6.1.

TABLE 6.6 International comparison of the composition of GDE 1988 (%)

	Personal consumption expenditure PC	Government consumption expenditure GC	Gross domestic capital formation CF + I	Exports of goods and services E	(Less) Imports of goods and services −M	Gross domestic expenditure GDE
China	56	7	38	14	15	100.0
Japan	57	9	31	13	10	100.0
Korea	51	10	30	41	32	100.0
Thailand	63	11	28	34	36	100.0
Italy	62	15	23	18	18	100.0
France	60	19	21	22	22	100.0
Former West Germany	55	19	21	33	28	100.0
UK	64	19	21	23	27	100.0
USA	67	20	15	11	13	100.0
Average of 103 countries[a]	69	15	21	28	33	100.0

Note:
[a] Including nine countries listed in this table.

Source:
WDR, 1991, pp. 194–5.

TABLE 6.7 Relative contributions to economic growth of the components of effective demand in Japan 1888–1988 (%)

	Personal consumption expenditure PC	Government consumption expenditure GC	Gross domestic fixed capital formation CF	Private only PCF	Increase in stocks I	Exports of goods and services and factor income received from abroad E	(Less) Imports of goods and services and factor income paid abroad M
1888–1900	82.7	12.6	17.9	7.8	–	10.0	23.2
1900–10	64.9	15.3	30.5	18.4	–	21.9	32.6
1910–20	69.7	6.4	27.9	20.1	–	18.3	22.3
1920–30	84.3	26.0	7.5	–6.9	–	35.3	53.1
1930–8	31.7	14.8	45.3	25.6	–	29.0	20.8
Pre-war average	57.6	14.6	30.7	16.3	–	25.0	27.9
1955–60	62.8	6.0	35.0	25.0	2.2	6.5	12.5
1960–70	57.1	7.4	38.5	28.0	2.1	10.1	15.2
1970–80	61.5	10.4	24.2	14.9	–1.9	22.2	16.4
1980–8	52.0	6.2	35.5	35.3	1.1	24.0	18.8
Post-war average	57.2	7.8	33.0	26.1	0.7	17.8	16.5

Notes:
The figures are ratios of the increases in the components of GNE to the increase in real GNE.
For further information see notes, Table 6.1.

Source:
Same as Table 6.1.

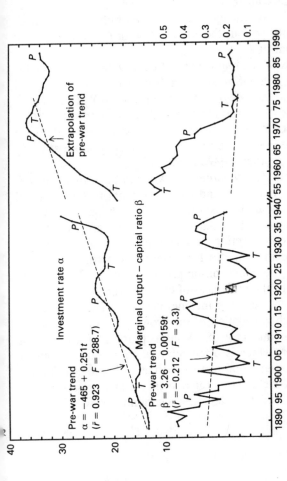

FIGURE 6.2   The investment rate (α) and the marginal output-capital ratio (β) in Japan 1889–1988

Notes:

α = gross national capital formation (CF) ÷ GNE (Y) × 100.

$\beta = G(Y) + \alpha$.

Figures for CF and Y are at 1934–6 prices for the pre-war period, and at 1985 prices for the post-war period. CF and Y are seven-year moving averages (five-year averages for 1938, 1954 and 1988).

Sources:
Same as Figure 3.3.

per cent in the post-war period, was the second highest among the components of GNE and was exceeded only by the analogous ratio for *PC*. When the post-Second World War era is divided into two periods, the contribution of *CF* was 37 per cent in the first period (1955–70) and 29 per cent in the second (1970–88), showing a decline. In contrast to this, the contribution of *E* rose from 9 per cent to 23 per cent. There was a drastic change in the source of effective demand. However, in the latter period, the contribution of *CF* still continued to be larger than that of *E*.

Still another index of the importance of *CF* to effective demand is the relatively strong correlation between the rate of growth in capital formation $G(CF)$ and the rate of economic growth $G(Y)$ (Table 6.2). In the pre-war period $G(Y)$ was more strongly correlated with $G(CF)$ than with $G(PC)$. ($G(Y)$ was not significantly correlated with $G(E)$ and $G(GC)$.) In the post-war period $G(Y)$ has been more strongly correlated with $G(CF)$ than $G(GC)$ and $G(E)$.

These indices show that economic growth has been more dependent on *PC* and *CF* than on *E* and *GC*. This confirms Ohkawa and Rosovsky's doubts about the 'export-led growth hypothesis' which asserts that exports were the 'engine' of economic growth.[9] It was domestic demand (consumption and investment), not foreign demand, that provided the impetus for economic growth. Which was more important, *PC* (personal consumption) or *CF*? Here due attention should be paid to the influences of economic growth on *PC* and *CF*. *PC* tends to increase when income increases. This may be responsible for the high correlation of the growth rate of *PC* with the overall rate of economic growth. A large portion of *CF* (capital formation), however, which is often referred to as autonomous investment, depends on external factors such as technological innovation. Thus one may conclude that the real engine of economic growth is capital formation and that Japanese economic growth has been 'investment-led'.

6.2.2   The Rate of Investment and its Significance

We have already seen that the rate of investment (the ratio of *CF* to *Y*) is larger in Japan than in other countries. Here we discuss the relationship between the rate of investment and the rate of economic growth.

The rate of economic growth $G(Y) = \Delta Y/Y$ can be rewritten as:

$$G(Y) = \frac{CF}{Y} \cdot \frac{\Delta Y}{CF}$$

Since real CF is nearly equal to the increment in real capital stock (ΔK) we have:

$$G(Y) = \frac{CF}{Y} \cdot \frac{\Delta Y}{\Delta K}$$

The first term on the right-hand side of this equation denotes the rate of investment (α) and the second the marginal output-capital ratio (β). Thus we have:

$$G(Y) = \alpha \beta$$

The variable α measures how much of present income is invested. The efficiency of investment in yielding increased production is expressed by the variable β. $G(Y)$ increases with increases in either α or β.

Figure 6.2 depicts historical changes in α and β in Japan. During the pre-war period there was a very clear upward trend in α with some fluctuation around the trend as shown by the dotted line. Peaks and troughs occurred at almost exactly the same time as peaks and troughs in the long swings (P and T in the figure). There was a great deal of fluctuation in β and these fluctuations were even more closely associated with the long swings than α. There was a slight downward trend in β, but it was not as clear as the trend in α.[10] Thus we can say that the growth in $G(Y)$ during the pre-war period was attributable to the increase in α, and the long swings were largely accounted for by the fluctuations in β. In the mid-1950s α was small, but increased from then until the 1960s, when it began to fall. This accounted for the increase in $G(Y)$ in the latter half of the 1950s and the 1960s, and the decrease in $G(Y)$ in the 1970s. As a result of the interruption of the supply of raw materials and fuels and the destruction of capital assets during the Second World War (Japan lost a quarter of her national wealth in the war) Japan's GNP fell drastically. After the war, however, the supply of raw materials and fuels increased very rapidly and total output began to grow. The capital stock recovered somewhat more slowly, however, and as a result by the mid-1950s β had grown to a very high level. This is what is usually referred to as the 'reconstruction effect' in the post-war economy. When this effect weakened, β decreased, causing a decline in $G(Y)$.

A full understanding of the impact of capital formation requires an analysis of factors that determine the marginal output-capital ratio. This ratio is influenced by a wide range of factors: the composition of investment, technological progress, industrial structure, the structure of domestic and foreign markets, the rate of capital utilization and the quantity and quality of the labour force. Also, because in the industrial structural change, β is far greater in non-primary industries than in primary ones,[11] the increase in the weighting of non-primary industries should have brought about the rise in β. However, because in reality β did not increase, this shows that there were factors that cancelled the effect of the change in composition with respect to the types of capital formation and the effect of the industrial structural change.

In order to identify the factors, Shinohara focuses on the presence of renewal investment.[12] Even if the economic growth rate is zero, investment for renewal is necessary. In this case, β is zero because it is obtained by dividing the increment of GNE, which is zero, by gross fixed capital formation, which is a plus figure. When economic growth rate rises, β increases because the proportion of renewal investment to gross investment becomes smaller. As a consequence, $G(Y)$ and β move in the same direction. This is a powerful explanation for the correlation between $G(Y)$ and β. Of course, the effect of technological progress is important, as it makes β and $G(Y)$ greater by improving the productivity of the capital.

6.2.3 International Comparison

By examining the analyses mentioned above, it becomes clear that the rapid acceleration (the accelerated increase of economic growth rate) by the end of the 1960s in Japan and its slow-down after that period were largely due to the increased investment rate and its reversal. This fact can be seen in other countries which experienced rapid acceleration.

There were rising trends of economic growth rates in Norway in the period 1880–1974, and in Italy in 1865–1974. When the $G(Y)$s for these countries are decomposed into α and β, it is seen that both α and β follow the same trend as $G(Y)$ in both countries.[13] That is, for Norway α increased from 15 per cent to 29 per cent and then decreased. The β value increased from 0.14 to 0.17 during the same period before declining. For Italy, α increased from 8 per cent to 17 per cent and then declined, and β increased from 0.08 to 0.40 before declining.

Next, it will be examined for the origin of the international difference in the $G(Y)$ value by separating $G(Y)$ into α and β for 72 countries in the world during the period 1986–90. According to Figure 6.3, it is apparent that there are correlations between $G(Y)$ and α, and between $G(Y)$ and β, and that the correlation is stronger for the former than for the latter. The difference in economic growth rate depends more strongly on the difference in marginal output–capital ratio than on investment rate. In the upper diagram Japan occupies a place below the line and in the lower diagram it occupies a place above. This is because the investment rate in Japan is relatively high when compared internationally but its marginal output–capital ratio are lower. The situations were vastly different in the 1950s and 1960s. During these periods, both α and β were large, supporting the high growth.[14] However, both α and β declined in the 1970s (the decline of the latter was especially large), bringing about a lower rate of economic growth. Moreover, it is noticed that in South Korea, Singapore and China, both α and β were large, making their growth rates high on the global scale, and that in Indonesia α was large, and in Thailand β was large, bringing about that country's relatively high growth rates.

6.3 THE IMPACT OF CAPITAL FORMATION ON PRODUCTION

6.3.1 Production Effect

Capital formation increases the capital stock which, in turn, expands production capacity. This is what we call the 'production effect of capital formation'.

The real capital stock (K) of primary industry increased at an average annual rate of 0.99 per cent during the period 1889–1938 and 7.7 per cent during the period 1956–87 (Table 4.2). The rate of growth of real GDP(Y) accounted for by the growth of capital is measured by $E_K G(K)$, where E_K is the output elasticity of capital. $E_K G(K)$ is calculated to have been 0.10 per cent and 1.7 per cent in these two periods and to have accounted for 8 per cent and 140 per cent of $G(Y)$. The relatively large contribution of $G(K)$ in the

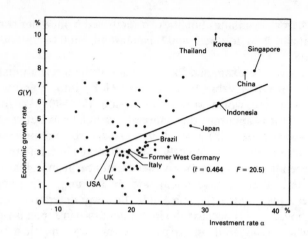

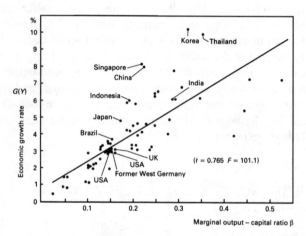

FIGURE 6.3   Relationships between the economic growth rates
$G(Y)$, and the investment rate (α), and between $G(Y)$ and the
marginal output–capital ratios (β) 1986–90

Notes:
$G(Y)$ = growth rate of real GNE.
$\propto$ = gross domestic fixed capital formation ÷ GNE × 100. $\beta = G(Y) \div \propto$.
Figures are the averages for 1986–90. Among the countries for which statistics are
available, 72 were chosen, excluding countries such as Myanmar which show unusual
growth rates due to political changes, and oil-producing countries such as Bahrain,
but including China.

Sources:
IFSY, 1991. Y of China is real GNP (ZTN, 1991, p. 31). For the $\propto$ of China, the ratio of
national income – consumption to national income is used (*Ibid.*, p. 40).

post-war period is due to the negative growth rate of the labour force $G(L)$. In the non-primary sector $G(K)$ was 5.85 per cent during the period 1908–38 and 9.3 per cent during the period 1956–87 (Table 5.2). $E_K G(K)$ is calculated to be 2.5 per cent and 2.6 per cent in these periods, accounting for 57 per cent and 33 per cent of $G(Y)$. $G(K)$'s post-war relative contribution is smaller, because $G(L)$ and the 'residual' λ (an index for the rate of technological progress) were larger in the post-war period. Thus capital accumulation, together with increases in labour force size and technological progress, have been the basic factors responsible for economic growth.

6.3.2 Capital–Output Ratio

At this point it is appropriate to analyze changes in the capital-output ratio (K/Y), the reciprocal of average capital productivity, over time. K/Y for the entire economy rose slowly from the beginning of the twentieth century until about 1930, when it began to decline (Table 6.8). For the post-war period of the 1950s and 1960s it was almost constant and it increased remarkably in the 1970s and 1980s.

Aggregate K/Y depends on the level of K/Y in each sector and their share of the economy as a whole. K/Y was higher in the primary sector (A) than in the non-primary sector ($M + S$) except during the early post-war years, because of the higher technological level in the latter. K/Y remained almost constant in the primary sector during the pre-war period, but it increased a great deal after 1960. This increase was due to the rapid mechanization of agricultural production; the stagnation of agricultural production in the 1970s further accelerated this tendency. The non-primary sector's K/Y increased slowly from the beginning of this century until about 1930 when it began to decline slowly. This decline continued in the early post-war period, but in the early 1970s it began to increase once again.

When non-primary industries are divided into M industries (mining, manufacturing, construction, transportation, communication, public utilities) and S industries (finance, commerce, service industries, etc.), it is seen that the capital–output ratio of M industries is larger than that of S industries. In 1987 these were, respectively, 2.13 and 0.95. S industries require, in comparison with M industries, less capital and they have a higher reliance on labour. Also, while the capital–output ratio of S industries is relatively stable, that of M industries varies wildly. In 1907, the capital–output ratio of M industry was 2.39 but it rose to 3.25 in 1920 and in 1938 it declined to 2.36.

TABLE 6.8   Capital–output ratio, capital–labour ratio, and labour
productivity in Japan 1907–87

	Capital–output ratio K/Y	Capital–labour ratio K/L	Labour productivity Y/L
		(Yen per worker)	
		All Industries (A + M + S)	
1907	1.71	475	278
1910	1.79	530	296
1920	1.85	829	447
1930	2.22	1 096	493
1938	1.54	1 355	683
		(000s yen per worker)	
1955	1.02	1 048	1 023
1960	0.95	1 396	1 470
1970	1.03	3 420	3 309
1980	1.47	6 945	4 740
1987	1.74	10 626	6 100

Notes:
Private sector only.
K = real gross fixed capital stock (excluding residential buildings).
Y = real GDP.
L = number of labourers.
K, Y: 1934–6 prices for the pre-war period and 1985 prices for the post-war period.

The figure are seven-year moving averages (five-year average for 1907, 1938, 1955 and 1987).

Sources:
Same as Table 4.1, Table 5.2.

After the Second World War, it declined from 1.74 in 1955 to 1.35 in 1970, but after that, it rose strongly. Its great rise from the beginning of the 1970s might be the result of desperate efforts by enterprises trying to enhance productivity against the sudden rise in prices of fuel and raw materials.

As is clear from this, the variation in the capital–output ratio of the whole economy was caused by the transformation of the non-primary industries, especially the *M* industries.

6.3.3   Capital–Output Ratio in Other Countries

With regard to the long-term trends of capital–output ratio of many countries, R. Bićanić maintains that generally the capital–output

TABLE 6.8 *cont.*

	Capital–output ratio *K/Y*	Capital–labour ratio *K/L*	Labour productivity *Y/L*
		(Yen per worker)	
Primary sector (A)			
1907	2.63	389	148
1910	2.59	409	158
1920	2.46	483	196
1930	2.70	568	210
1938	2.65	631	238
		(000s yen per worker)	
1955	1.13	519	460
1960	1.30	792	610
1970	2.49	2 848	1 142
1980	6.16	10 224	1 660
1987	8.07	16 925	2 098

Capital–output Ratio *K/Y*	Capital–labour ratio *K/L*	Labour Productivity *Y/L*
	(Yen per worker)	
Non-primary sector (M + S)		
1.23	631	515
1.39	738	531
1.67	1 284	768
2.08	1 690	813
1.85	2 041	1 104
	(000s yen per worker)	
1.00	1 442	1 444
0.89	1 711	1 918
0.93	3 553	3 815
1.27	6 527	5 133
1.54	10 006	6 494

ratio increases in the initial stages of economic development and shifts to a declining trend after that.[15]

When the estimates by R. Goldsmith and S. Kuznets for the period from the end of the nineteenth century or the beginning of the twentieth century are examined, for only three countries: Argentina, the former West Germany, and Norway, can be explained by Bićanić's hypothesis. (For the former West Germany, the variation in the capital–output ratio reached a peak in the 1920s; for Argentina in the 1910s; and for Norway at the turn of the century.) For Belgium, the USA, Australia, South Africa, Colombia, France and Canada, the capital–output ratios show declining trends from the beginning.[16]

This is probably because the rising stages of their capital–output ratios were not included in the observation period. In the initial stages of industrialization, the level of technology is low and the capital–output ratio small. But when the formation of social overhead capital such as railways, ports and harbours and communication facilities increases, the capital–output ratio rises. And then, when formation is complete and the proportion of producer's durable equipment in total capital stock increases with elevated technological standards, the capital–output ratio declines. The experience of Japan conforms well to the Bićanić hypothesis.

However, the Bićanić hypothesis does not discuss recent trends. As has been mentioned, in Japan the capital–output ratio was increasing in 1970s. A similar phenomenon can be seen for the USA. Its capital–output ratio increased from 1.1 in 1970 to 1.5 in 1981.[17] On the other hand, there are countries such as the UK for which the capital–output ratios are comparatively static. For the UK in all the years between 1977 and 1987 the ratio was 2.8.[18] It is necessary to conduct research by gathering data from more countries.

6.3.4   Capital–Labour Ratio and Labour Productivity

The capital–labour ratio (K/L) shows the extent to which the labour force is engaged in production activities using capital. If the ratio is large, then labour productivity is also large. The K/L ratio over the whole economy shows a steady upward trend throughout the period (Table 6.8). However, there are huge differences among the industries in the level of the K/L ratio and in its rate of increase. Before the Second World War, the level and the growth rate of A industries was lower than the combined $M + S$ industries, and the differences were greater. But after the war, the rise of the A industries was so prominent that in 1980 they had overcome the combined $M + S$ industries. The K/L ratio had been larger for the M industries when compared to the S industries. Moreover, the rate of increase of the K/L ratio was greater for the former than the latter both before and after the Second World War making the differences larger. In 1987, the K/L ratio of the M industries had become a little less than four times as large as that of the S industries.

I would like to add two comments on the variation of the capital–labour ratio. First is in relation to the labour market. As will be mentioned in Chapter 9, Section 2, K/L must decrease when the growth of wages is small because of over-supply of labour. Once, it was believed that this situation applied to the period before the First World War. My analysis shows that this theory is wrong. But the fact that the K/L ratio did not decrease does not imply that labour tended to be short in this period. It is possible that the K/L ratio increases in labour-surplus economies.

Second, about the relationship with labour productivity (Y/L): the ratio of K/L against K/Y. When examining K/Y throughout the period before the Second World War, the rise of the Y/L ratio was due solely to the increase in the K/L ratio. After the Second World War and until 1970, the Y/L ratio achieved a rapid increase due to the rise of the K/L ratio and the decline of the K/Y ratio. But its increase after the 1970s was due solely to the increase of the K/L ratio alone. Similar conclusions can be drawn for each category of industry. An exception is the A industries after the Second World War where, although the K/L ratio increased more quickly than in non-primary industries, its Y/L ratio remained lower than that of non-primary industries because of the tremendous increase of its K/L ratio. Because of this, the difference in productivity widened.

6.4   THE FINANCING OF INVESTMENT

6.4.1   Imports of Foreign Capital

Funds for capital formation are provided by either net imports of foreign capital or domestic savings. The ratio of net imports of foreign capital to gross domestic capital formation in the latecomer countries is shown in Table 6.9. In Japan this ratio was only slightly above zero for the period 1885–1900. During this period capital imports and exports were very limited, because the Japanese wished to deal cautiously with the western powers and because Japan was not an attractive investment prospect for the western powers.[19] If we include the reparations from the Sino-Japanese War (1894–5) in capital imports, however, we have quite a different picture; the ratio of net imports of foreign capital to gross domestic capital formation becomes 10 per cent. These reparations amounted to 360 million yen, a quarter of the national income at the time, and had the same economic significance as capital import.[20] During the first decade of the twentieth century the ratio rose to 19 per cent, the highest figure in Japanese history. Imported capital played an important role in capital formation during this period. This was because Japan succeeded in obtaining a large amount of foreign loans due to her significantly increased international status as a result of victories in the Sino- and Russo-Japanese Wars and her economic success. These funds from abroad made great contributions to the accumulation of social overhead capital, the growth of heavy industries and the strengthening of the armed forces.[21]

From the 1910s to the 1930s capital imports were cancelled out by direct investment to Japanese colonies and Japan changed from debtor to creditor. The ratio of net capital imports to gross capital formation was minus 2.3 per cent for this period as a whole. In the post-war period the ratio was also negative. Thus, the role of foreign capital in domestic capital formation was negligible for the entire period of Japanese economic development with the exception of the last two decades of the nineteenth century and the first decade of this century; capital formation in Japan was financed almost completely by domestic savings.

Most of the latecomer western countries (listed in Table 6.9) were net importers of capital. Germany, which was almost always a net exporter of capital, was an exception. Dependence on foreign capital was especially significant during the early phase of industrialization in most of these countries. In Australia and Canada, for instance, more than 30 per cent of all capital formation was financed by foreign capital. It was common for the introduction of foreign capital to stimulate industrialization among the western latecomers. However, dependence on foreign capital decreased in the course of industrialization and international capital movement slowed down substantially after the First World War.[22]

Also, many of the developing countries have been vigorously promoting the introduction of foreign capital. In particular, the role of foreign capital had been critically important for the newly-

TABLE 6.9 Ratio of net capital imports to gross capital formation in eight developed countries 1851–1989 (%)

Japan		Norway	
1885–1900	0.4 (9.9[a])	1865–74	–10.6
1901–10	19.2	1875–94	11.8
1911–20	–5.9	1895–1914	33.3
1921–30	4.2	1915–24	29.1
1931–40	–5.1	1925–34	4.2
1952–60	–0.1	1950–9	8.0
1961–70	–0.2		
1971–80	–2.3	Italy	
1981–9	–7.7		
Australia		1861–80	15.0
		1881–1900	0
1861–80	30.4	1901–10	–8.8
1881–1900	41.5	1921–30	12.2
1900/1–1919/20	12.2	1950–9	4.8
1919/20–1938/9	12.1	Germany[b]	
1950/1–1959/60	8.4		
Sweden		1851–70	–5.1
		1871–90	–11.1
1861–80	4.6	1891–1913	–4.8
1881–1900	14.3	1928	8.2
1901–20	3.8	1950–9	–13.1
1921–40	–3.8		
1941–9	0.5	Canada	
1950–9	–0.9		
		1870,1890	48.0
Denmark		1890,1900,1910	43.2
		1920,1929	21.8
1870–89	18.4	1926–30	9.3
1890–1909	17.0	1950–9	10.4
1921–30	–2.5		
1950–9	0		

Notes:
[a] Including reparations from the Sino-Japanese War.
[b] The composition of the territory which we have called Germany was, of course, different in the periods indicated.

Sources:
Net capital imports for Japan: 1885–1970 – Yamazawa and Yamamoto, 1979a, pp. 220–31. 1971–89: KKKN, 1982, pp. 264–5; 1991, p. 257.
Gross capital formation for Japan: Same as Table 6.1.
All figures for the other countries: Kuznets, 1966, pp. 236–9, table 5.3.

developed areas of NIES, Taiwan, Hong Kong, South Korea and Singapore, which achieved spectacular development after the 1970s. Foreign capital is playing an important role in the ASEAN countries of Indonesia, Malaysia, the Philippines and also Thailand, which have begun their growth since the latter half of the 1980s, following NIES. In addition to these, expectation of foreign capital has been high in China which continues to adopt a policy of opening itself to overseas countries. From the above viewpoints, there is a strong impression that the Japanese experience has been a unique one.

6.4.2   Overseas Investment

As far as dependency on foreign capital is concerned, Japan has always invested more in foreign countries than its capital imports except during the 1900s and the 1920s. The introduction of foreign capital in the 1900s was mainly to support the war effort in the Russo-Japanese War. In the 1920s, it was mainly for company and regional governmental loans. Japan's foreign investment before the Second World War was predominantly in Manchuria.

After the Second World War, during the era of high economic growth up to 1970, Japan's capital balance was only slightly in excess of exports. However, during the 1970s, Japan's overseas investment became more vigorous and in the 1980s it expanded greatly. The characteristics of this recent overseas investment will be described below.

Among these overseas investments, that is, among the outflow of long-term capital, direct investment and investment in shares are predominant. Direct investments were initially mainly towards Asian countries but later the amount towards North America (especially towards the USA) and Europe increased. In 1989 the share of direct investment in Asian regions was only 11.8 per cent but 47.5 per cent was in North America (46.5 per cent in the USA) and 19.4 per cent in Europe.[23] When examined with respect to the categories, it was mainly for light industries such as fibre products at the beginning but, reflecting the changes in industry structure of Japan, investment for manufacturing industries such as electric appliances grew gradually. As a result, electrical appliances (which are mainly manufactured in factories in Asia) are now back-imported to Japan in large quantities. It has become a common pattern that high-quality products are manufactured at factories in Japan and middle- or low-quality products are manufactured at factories overseas. Thus, a 'horizontal' division of roles is being established in Asia, with Japan acting as its core.

The most prominent direct investment is that in the automobile industry. The outflow of the automobile industry started in Asia and it is now spread over the USA and throughout the world. If we take the USA, which is the most prominent, as an example, Honda was the first to invest (production started in November 1982) and many other makers followed. Recently the phenomenon of these automobiles being back-imported to Japan has been observed. This back-importing should contribute to balancing international revenue and expenditure.

The amount of investment in shares is larger than the amount of direct investment. The major part of Japanese investment in shares is in national bonds issued by the government of the USA: this means that Japan is financing the national debt of the USA. The balance of Japanese overseas assets increased rapidly in the 1980s due to the outflow of long-term investment, and by the end of 1985 Japan has become the world's top creditor nation. On the other hand, the USA experienced a rapid increase of debt and degraded itself to a debtor nation in the same year. Japan has continued to increase overseas credits and the amount of these reached 2932 billion US dollars at the end of 1987, while the USA's debts amounted to 6637 US billion dollars.[24]

6.4.3   Savings Rates

In the next five sub-sections we will discuss savings. We begin by examining the gross and net savings rates. From Table 6.10 two conclusions may be drawn about these rates. The first is that they have shown a long-term increase. For instance, the gross rate increased from 13 per cent in the late nineteenth century to 25 per cent in 1940, and to 38 per cent in 1970. This implies that Keynes's 'absolute income hypothesis',[25] which asserts that the savings rate rises with per capita income, is consistent with the Japanese experience. During the 1970s however savings rates decreased.

Kuznets once criticized Keynes's hypothesis, asserting that the savings rate was constant in the long term in the USA.[26] This motivated further studies on the consumption function in the USA and other countries, from which it appeared that Kuznets's assertion could not be verified. Even Kuznets's own estimates of the net savings rate of some western countries since 1860 did not confirm his original claim. In Italy, Denmark, Australia, Norway and Canada the

TABLE 6.10 Savings rates and the composition of savings in Japan 1890–1987 (%)

| | Gross savings rate[a] | Net savings rate[b] | Personal savings rate[c] γ | Gross national savings | | | | |
| | | | | Net national savings | | | | |
				Households[d]	Private corporations	General government	Total	Provisions for consumption of fixed capital
1890	13.3	4.2	–	9.9		18.9	28.8	71.2
1900	13.5	5.1	4.9	32.3		2.3	34.6	65.4
1910	14.8	6.0	5.1	2.9	3.1	34.1	40.1	59.9
1920	19.0	9.6	9.0	27.9	0.2	17.9	46.0	54.0
1930	14.6	5.2	7.2	24.0	-0.5	9.7	33.2	66.8
1940	25.3	12.7	16.8[e]	116.8	20.0	-78.0	58.8	41.2
1950	22.9	17.9	–	26.2	11.3	37.4	74.9	25.1
1960	29.5	25.6	14.8	34.9	13.4	20.8	69.1	30.9
1970	37.7	27.9	17.8	32.6	15.1	16.8	64.5	35.5
1980	31.2	21.1	18.6	42.6	8.1	7.8	58.5	41.5
1987	32.7	21.8	15.0	35.4	9.8	20.2	65.4	34.6

Notes:
[a] Gross national savings ÷ GNP × 100.   [b] Net national savings ÷ NNP × 100.
[c] Personal savings ÷ personal disposable income × 100.   [e] Average for 1934–8.
[d] Private non-profit institution are included.   [e] Average for 1934–8.

All the figures are seven-year moving averages (five-year average for 1987).

Sources:
Figures for 1907, 1980 and 1987 are calculated from data in KKKN, 1982, pp. 10–11, 40–1; 1991, pp. 82–3, 94–103.
Figures for the years up to 1960 are calculated from Ohkawa et al., 1974, pp. 190–1, Ohkawa and Minami, 1975, p. 576.

net savings rate increased during this century. In the USA it decreased between the late nineteenth century and the Second World
War, but remained constant after that. In the UK it increased slightly
between the mid-nineteenth century and the First World War, but
decreased in the 1920s. Generally speaking the savings rate tended to
increase in the latecomer countries, but not in the earlier developed
countries. Therefore, the increasing savings rate in Japan was not
unique, but typical for a latecomer country.

Our second conclusion is that the savings rate is relatively high in
contemporary Japan. The gross rate was 34 per cent in 1988, higher
than the rate for other countries (Table 6.11). The average for all
thirty-five countries is 22 per cent. It should be noted that Japan's
savings rate was not high in the early years, but increased to reach its
present level.

Thus, the increase in the savings rate made possible an increase in
the rate of investment, one determinant of the rate of economic
growth. The high savings rate seen in contemporary Japan is related
to the high rate of investment, and the increase in the savings rate is
associated with trend acceleration.

6.4.4 Composition of Savings

Gross savings can be broken down into net savings and depreciation.
Net savings' share of gross savings increased from 29 per cent in the
late nineteenth century to 75 per cent in 1950, but then decreased, to
65 per cent in 1987 (Table 6.10). According to Kuznets, a relative
increase in net earnings and a relative decrease in capital depreciation
were seen in Denmark and Canada. In the UK and USA, however, a
relative decrease in net savings was seen, and Italy, Norway and
Australia did not show any clear trend.[27]

Net savings originate from households, private corporations and
the government. Net savings of households have been the most
important source of savings in Japan; in 1987, for example, they
accounted for 35 per cent of gross savings. Net savings of private
corporations are the smallest of the three components, but their
proportion of gross savings increased during the period of high
growth. The proportion of net savings supplied by the government
has fluctuated a great deal. In the other developed countries, according to Kuznets, the proportion of net savings supplied by private
corporations and the government increased, while the proportion
supplied by households decreased.[28]

TABLE 6.11 International comparison of savings rates and the composition of savings 1988 (%)

| | Gross savings rate | Net savings rate | Personal savings rate γ | Gross national savings | | | | | Provisions for consumption of fixed capital |
| | | | | Net national savings | | | | | |
				Households	Private corporations	General government	Total		
Japan	33.5	22.5	14.7	29.6	5.4	22.4	57.4		42.6
Thailand	26.6	20.2	12.9	34.0	15.7	20.2	69.9		30.1
Former West Germany	24.6	14.0	12.6	32.0	15.1	2.7	49.8		50.2
Italy	20.6	9.7	14.7	51.8	21.8	−32.1	41.5		58.5
France	20.5	9.1	7.8	24.9	13.2	0.9	39.0		61.0
The Philippines	18.0	9.4	7.7	33.7	17.8	−4.3	47.2		52.8
UK	16.9	6.0	0.4	1.4	33.1	−3.1	31.4		68.6
USA	15.2	3.4	6.6	30.7	10.4	−21.7	19.4		80.6
Average of 24 countries[a]	21.4	10.7	8.4	28.6	11.8	−2.6	37.8		62.2
Average of 35 countries[a]	21.7								

Notes:
Refer to notes of Table 6.10 for definitions.

[a] Including the eight countries listed in this table.
For some countries the figures are for 1986 or 1987.

Sources:
YNAS, 1988.

Let us compare the composition of overall savings in Japan in the most recent year (1988) where figures are available (Table 6.11). When Japan is compared with the average value of 24 countries (including itself), it has a slightly larger dependency on net savings. With regard to the details of the net savings, the proportion from corporations is small and that from various governments is large. In other countries, savings by various governments are almost always negative quantities. It can be seen from this that the financial situation of the government in Japan is relatively healthy.

6.4.5 Savings of Government and Private Corporations

Government savings expressed as a ratio of GNE, the difference between government revenue and expenditure, fluctuated a great deal in the pre-war period (Table 6.12).[29] The negative figures for the 1890s and 1900s resulted from big increases in government expenditure due to the Sino- and Russo-Japanese wars. The negative figure for the 1930s was also due to the military expansion that took place between the Manchurian Incident (1931) and the Second World War (1941). Investment exceeded savings for all periods except the 1880s and the 1910s. In the former period a tight fiscal policy was carried out by Masayoshi Matsukata (minister of finance 1881–5). In the latter period the government created savings by restraining military activity.

In the post-war period government savings increased because: (1) There was a steady increase in government revenue as a result of the high rate of economic growth. (2) Military expenditure was minimal. Government investment has also increased rapidly since the latter half of 1960s. This is because the Japanese government has emphasized capital formation more than consumption. The rapid capital formation by the government and the private sector has stimulated economic growth by creating effective demand and expanding productive capacity. The increase in government investment required increased savings. This was provided by the issuing of government bonds, which had been prohibited until 1965 (Ch. 10, Sec. 1).

In the 1970s, governmental savings decreased because of the reduction of tax revenues due to low economic growth and because of the increase in social welfare expenses. As a result, the balance between saving and investment dramatically collapsed. However, in the 1980s, the balance between saving and investment improved significantly because of the increase of tax revenue due to the economic recovery

TABLE 6.12   Ratio of government savings and investment to GNE in Japan 1886–1989

	Savings	Investment	Savings–investment
1886–90	2.7	1.6	1.1
1891–1900	–0.6	2.6	–3.2
1901–10	–0.0	3.5	–3.5
1911–20	3.9	3.4	0.5
1921–30	4.2	5.7	–1.5
1931–40	–5.4	4.1	–9.5
1951–60	6.4	7.2	–0.8
1961–70	7.3	9.0	–1.7
1971–80	3.4	6.4	–3.0
1981–9	4.5	5.3	–0.8

Sources:
Savings and investment: 1886–1970 – Ishi, 1975, p. 360, table 14.7, 1971–89 – KKKN, 1981, pp. 62–3; 1991, pp. 98–9.
GNE: 1886–1969 – Ohkawa and Shinohara, 1979, pp. 251–5; 1970–89 – KKKN, 1991, pp. 106–9.

and because of the reduction of governmental expenses following administrative rationalization.

In the corporate sector there was always more investment than saving, the ratio between the difference and the GDP being as much as 6 per cent in the 1980s (Table 6.13). The savings deficit created by the corporate sector and government was filled by family budget savings. The ratio between the savings–investment balance in the family budget to GDP amounted to a little less than 10 per cent. Family budget savings flowed into the private sector and the government (and especially towards the corporate sector) via city financial agents and post offices supporting their vigorous investment activities.

In Table 6.13, figures from the USA are shown for comparison. In the USA, although corporate savings and the corporate investments almost balanced each other (unlike Japan) the government had itself become the source of a big savings deficit through its huge budget deficit. Also the level of excess saving from the family budget was not so large as in Japan. The American savings deficit had been supplemented by the flow of funds from those excess-saving countries such as Japan and the former West Germany. In the USA, excess saving by the family budget even *decreased* between the first half and the latter half of the 1980s, and the excess of overseas savings (the net fund flow) increased by the same amount.

TABLE 6.13   Flow of funds from different sectors in Japan and the USA
1982–8 (%)

	Personal	Government	Corporate	Abroad[a]
		Japan		
1982–4	9.5	–3.1	–5.0	–1.8
1985–8	9.1	0.1	–5.8	–3.6
		USA		
1982–4	3.1	–4.5	0.0	0.7
1985–8	1.6	–4.0	–0.5	3.1

Notes:
The figures are ratios of the difference between gross savings from gross investment to
GDP. Therefore the negative figures in this Table indicate positive quantities when
seen from other countries.
[a] Net borrowing from the rest of the world.

Source:
KKKN, 1985–91.

6.4.6   Personal Savings Rate

In the following two subsections we study personal savings, a major
source of funds for capital formation. The personal savings rate (γ),
or the ratio of personal savings (PS) to personal disposable income
(PY), manifests an increasing trend (Table 6.10). (PS is the difference between PY and personal consumption, PC.) In Japan γ increased from 5 per cent in 1900 to 17 per cent in 1940 and 19 per cent
in 1980. This pattern is different from the UK, the USA or Canada,
where the rate has been almost constant from the 1920s to the
1960s.[30]

How did the rise of the γ value originate in Japan? There have been
two main explanations for this. One is Keynes's 'absolute income
hypothesis', which maintains that the ability to save increases with
improvement in the standard of living. The other is T. M. Brown *et
al.*'s 'habit-formation hypothesis', which says that because the consumption habit does not change very much, consumption will not
increase significantly when income increases. As there is a strongly
conservative element in the attitudes towards consumption among
the Japanese, it appears that Brown's hypothesis may be more
applicable.[32]

The calculated results from the consumption function (1) and the

TABLE 6.14   Personal consumption functions in Japan 1892–1989

	Equation	Variable	Constant	PY/N	$(PC/N)_{-1}$	$G(PY/N)$	$\bar{R}$	d
					Explanatory variables			
1892–1938	(1)	PC/N	4.265	0.243	0.715	–	0.993	2.08
			(1.87)	(4.58)	(11.26)			
	(2)	γ	−1.016	0.052	–	47.445	0.701	2.88
			(0.49)	(3.64)		(5.27)		
1954–89	(1)	PC/N	27.319	0.694	0.112	–	0.992	0.67
			(1.75)	(11.31)	(1.42)			

Notes:
Non-smoothed figures were used in the calculation. The unit of PC/N and PY/N is yen at 1934–6 prices for the pre-war period; 1985 prices for the post-war period.

Sources:
Same as Table 6.10.

saving function (2) are shown in Table 6.14.[33] In Equation (1), the consumption per capita (PC/N) is explained by the per capita income (PY/N) and the per capita consumption of the previous year [$(PC/N)_{-1}$]. The parameter of the variable of PY/N is larger than 0 and smaller than 1 in both before and after the Second World War. This indicates that γ rises with the increase of PY/N.[34] The parameter of the variable of [$(PC/N)_{-1}$] is positive in both periods, indicating that present consumption is influenced by that of the past. For Equation (2), the calculated results for only the period before the Second World War are shown (the result for the period after the Second World War is not shown because it is not valid statistically), where γ is explained by per capita income and per capita growth rate of income $G(PY/N)$. The same explanation applies to the parameter of the variable of PY/N, as in Equation (1). The parameter of the variable of $G(PY/N)$ is positive and it is seen that consumption does not increase as much as the increase in income because consumption follows past trends, and that, as a result, the savings rate rises when the rate of income growth rises. In conclusion, it can be said that these calculated results have proved the validity of the above two hypotheses.

A slight difference is apparent when the calculated results for the two periods are compared. In Equation (1) the parameter of (PY/N) is larger in the period after the Second World War and, in contrast to this, the parameter of (PC/N)$_{-1}$ is larger in the period before the war. The extent to which the increment of (PC/N) depends on the increment of (PY/N) and the increment of (PC/N)$_{-1}$ is shown below.

That is, the increase in consumption before the Second World War mainly due to the increase in $(PC/N)_{-1}$, and the increase in consumption after the war mainly depends on the increase in (PY/N). In other words, before the Second World War, to a large extent consumption was influenced by previous habits. After the Second World War, although the influence of past behaviour was still there, its importance had declined when compared with that before the war.

Period	$d(PY/N)$	$d(PC/N)_{-1}$
1892–1938	31.1%	68.9%
1954–1989	89.0%	11.0%

I would like to make two comments with regard to the above analyses. First, that economic growth and consumption/saving are in a mutually dependent relationship. In this Section, it has been suggested that when the economic growth rate is high, personal consumption relatively decreases and personal saving relatively increases. On the other hand, we have seen that the rise in the savings rate supports the rise in investment rate resulting in the phenomenon of acceleration of the economic growth; and that a considerable part of savings was a result of savings from family budgets, that is, personal savings. Therefore, the rise in the personal saving rate was a result of the acceleration at the same time as it was a big factor that supported acceleration.

Second, the fact that after the Second World War the saving theory did not fit well (in particular, the fact that the savings rate increased from the end of the 1960s into the first half of the 1970s, when the growth rate dramatically slowed down) indicates the necessity for considering other factors in addition to the variables that have been considered here. For the rise and fall of the rate of saving, the rise and fall of the proportion of 'bonus' income in the salary/wage income (bonus income, non-permanent income, tends largely to be saved) are considered to be a factor. And for the rise of the rate of saving in the period of low growth, the increased necessity for saving due to the rise in cost of buying residential houses should be considered as a factor. Also, for the decline of the rate of saving, the following factors can be considered: (a) ageing of the population which advanced prominently during this period (elderly people are in principle negative savers); (b) prevalence of various leisure activities because of the improvements in living standards and shorter working

hours; (c) increase in education expenses; (d) decrease in a proportion of the income of the self-employed (or the owners of small
businesses) in the overall income (the savings of self-employed
people are aimed at investment for profit, and the savings rate is
high); (e) the fact that the necessity for saving for retirement has been
decreased because of the improvement of the social security system;
and (f) the fact that consumer activity has become more vigorous
because of the development of forms of credit.[35]

6.4.7   International Comparison of the Personal Savings Rate

The rate of personal savings (γ) was 14.7 per cent in 1988, a little less
than double the average value for the 24 countries (see Table 6.11).
How can this international difference be explained? As an experi-
ment, let us focus on a variable similar to the one which was discussed
in the time-series analysis in the previous Section. These are per
capita GNP (the variable that represents personal disposable income,
and growth rate of per capita real GNP. However, there is no correlation at all between γ and these two variables. Also there can be no
meaningful correlation obtainable out of the calculation by a function
that attempts to explain γ by the two variables.[36]

In conclusion it can be said that the factors that explain the savings
rate in Japan cannot explain the international difference in savings
rates. In order to achieve an international comparison of savings
rates, research that takes the following factors in consideration is
desirable: (a) age structure of the population; (b) the proportion of
the income earned the self-employed in overall income; (c) the
proportion of the 'bonus' income in the salary/wage income; (d) ratio
between property and income; (e) cost of buying a house; (f) the
extent of social welfare systems; (g) national characteristics, and so
on.[37]

SUMMARY OF THE CHAPTER

Capital formation affects economic growth in two ways: First, it
provides funds for production equipment and hence increases the
productive capacity of the economy. We have done a brief study of
the capital-output ratio and the capital-labour ratio and found that
the former increased until 1930 and fell gradually thereafter, while

the latter showed a continuous upward trend and contributed a great deal to the rise in labour productivity.

The second way that capital formation affects economic growth is by increasing effective demand or Gross National Expenditure (GNE). About one-third of the increase in GNE was due to increases in capital formation both in the pre-war and the post-war periods. Private capital formation was substantially larger than government capital formation. From the demand side it can be said that Japanese economic growth has been led by private investment.

The investment function was estimated for the non-primary sector and investment was shown to depend heavily on returns to capital.

The rate of economic growth $G(Y)$ is the product of the rate of investment (α) and the marginal output-capital ratio (β). The upward trend in $G(Y)$ in the pre-war period is explained by the upward trend in α, while fluctuations in $G(Y)$ are explained by fluctuations in β. The upward trend in α, and hence $G(Y)$ (trend acceleration), is not unique to Japan, but can be seen in other developed countries such as Italy and Norway. This phenomenon seems to occur most often in latecomer capitalist countries.

Also, there is a correlation between $G(Y)$ and α and β for each country. That is, the international difference in the economic growth rate is the result of both the difference in the investment rate and the difference between the marginal output-capital ratio.

The analysis then shifted to the supply of investment capital. At the beginning of the twentieth century about one-fifth of investment was due to imports of foreign capital. However, dependence upon foreign capital fell sharply after that and almost all investment funds were supplied by domestic savings. The savings rate rose during both the pre-war and post-war periods and, as a result, Japan has achieved a high level of savings by international standards. The rise in savings largely reflects a rise in net savings, of which household or personal savings have been the most important. The personal savings rate (γ) has risen over the years and is today higher than any other country. The growth in γ occurred because the income level rose, and because the rise in consumption expenditure fell short of the rise in income. This may have been caused by the perseverance of traditional life-style patterns. The influence of 'habit-formation' was very strong in the pre-war period. Its influence weakened after the war, but a substantial increase in income has maintained the increase in γ. However, since the latter half of the 1970s it has been decreasing.

FURTHER READING

Capital formation:
  Emi and Ishiwata, 1979
  Fujino, 1968
  Ohkawa and Kohama, 1989, lecture 5
  Ohkawa and Rosovsky, 1973, ch. 6
  Rosovsky, 1961
  Shinohara, 1970, ch. 4
Savings:
  Blumenthal, 1970
  Komiya, 1966b
  Mizoguchi, 1970
  Odaka, 1982
  Shinohara, 1970, chs 2 and 3; 1982, ch. 10

7 Foreign Trade

Japanese industrialization has been closely linked to foreign trade. On the one hand, much of the capital equipment and almost all the raw materials and fuels which stimulated the growth of manufacturing have been imported. On the other hand, the increased competitiveness of Japanese products on the world market as a result of technological improvements in manufacturing have been important to export expansion.

In Section 7.1 changes in the quantity of trade both in absolute terms and as a share of total economic activity are analyzed, and the impact of foreign trade on economic growth and the 'export-led growth hypothesis' (i.e. the hypothesis that exports were the engine of Japanese economic growth) are discussed. Section 7.2 analyzes the relationship between foreign trade and industrialization; changes in the import and export structure are studied in relation to changes in the industrial structure. In Section 7.3 we analyze factors responsible for the growth of exports and imports.

7.1 FOREIGN TRADE AND THE NATIONAL ECONOMY

7.1.1. The Growth Rate of Foreign Trade

During the period 1889–1938 the growth rates of real exports $G(E)$ and imports $G(M)$ in Japan were 8.0 and 6.7 per cent respectively (Table 6.1). This exceeded both the economic growth rate (3.2 per cent, Table 3.2) and the growth rate of manufacturing production (5.7 per cent). During the post-war period (1956–88) $G(E)$ and $G(M)$ increased further, to 11.1 per cent and 9.8 per cent, respectively, while the economic growth rate was only 6.7 per cent and the growth rate of manufacturing production only 7.2 per cent.[1]

The increase of Japanese exports has been remarkable; Japan's

TABLE 7.1   Growth of world trade and world manufacturing 1884–1987
(%)

	Index of volume of trade	Index of manufacturing output
1884–90	3.87	3.95
1891–1900	2.51	4.17
1901–10	3.01	3.83
1911–20	0.54	–
1921–30	2.15	3.28[a]
1931–7	0.71	5.11
Pre-war average	2.11	4.06
1956–60	5.69	6.17
1961–70	8.05	6.82
1971–80	4.88	4.29
1980–7	3.97	3.07
Post-war average	6.31	5.11

Notes:
The figures are simple averages of the annual rate of growth based on seven-year moving averages (five-year averages for 1936 and 1986; three-year averages for 1937 and 1987).
[a] 1924–30.

Sources:
Index of volume of trade: To 1970 – Yamazawa and Yamamoto, 1979a, pp. 253, 255. Since 1971–YITS.
Index of manufacturing output: Pre-war – League of Nations, 1945, pp. 138–40, table V. Post-war – YIS; S.Y.

$G(E)$ has consistently exceeded the growth rate of world trade (which grew 2.1 per cent for the period 1884–1937 and 6.3 per cent for the period 1956–87, Table 7.1). As a result Japan has captured an increasing share of the world market.[2] After the opening of Japan to foreign trade in 1859, North America, Europe and east Asia were Japan's main markets. From the turn of the century until the Second World War exports to Europe and North America decreased relatively, while exports to east Asia, south-east Asia (east of Burma) and south-west Asia (west of India) increased relatively.[3] During the post-war period Japan has exported her products throughout the world.

The growth rate of world trade was 3–4 per cent between the 1880s and 1990s, while world manufacturing production grew about 4 per cent. From the 1910s, however, the growth rate of world trade declined significantly, while the growth rate of world manufacturing production increased, as a result of the rapid industrialization of newly developed countries such as Sweden, Germany and Japan. During the post-war period, however, world trade has expanded rapidly; the growth rate is more than three times that of the pre-war period. This expansion of the world market has been partially responsible for the rapid increase in Japanese exports.

7.1.2 The Relative Importance of Foreign Trade in the Japanese Economy

The ratio of foreign trade (total exports and imports) to GNE increased throughout the pre-war period. It was 18.0 per cent in the period 1885–1900, and increased to 39.1 per cent in the period 1931–40. In the post-war period, however, it was as much as 20 per cent.[4] During the post-war period, however, this ratio decreased significantly and in the 1970s it fell to the same level as at the turn of the century. According to Kuznets, the degree of dependency on foreign trade increased between the middle of the nineteenth century and the First World War among countries such as England, Italy, France, Denmark, Canada, Germany and Sweden. However he found that some new countries, such as the USA and Australia are exceptions. After that period until just before the Second World War dependency decreased among all these countries except Canada. Then after the Second World War the degree of dependency decreased greatly everywhere, without exception. Therefore it seems to correct to say that the changing pattern of dependency in Japan's foreign trade is similar to that of other developed countries.

By international standards Japan is highly independent of foreign trade. Japan's 1988 ratio of foreign trade (goods and services) to GDP was 23 per cent. This is much smaller than the average 60 per cent found in a sample of 102 countries. What accounts for differences among countries? It is presumed that the foreign trade–GDP ratio (δ) is negatively correlated with the size of GDP (Y) and population (N), but positively correlated with per capita GDP (y). Kuznets argues that the negative correlation between δ and Y or δ and N is due to the fact that large economies like the USA are virtually self-supporting, while small economies cannot grow without foreign trade.[6] The positive correlation between δ and y can be explained in two ways. First, high labour productivity may lead to increased international competitiveness and hence to a high volume of exports, which means that a high volume of raw materials and fuel must be imported. Second, high per capita income may cause demand for a wide variety of goods and thus stimulate foreign trade.[7]

The following equation is the result of an estimation of the foreign trade–GDP ratio (δ, per cent);[8]

$$ln\ \delta = 4.071 - 0.215\ ln\ N + 0.0607\ ln\ y \qquad \bar{r} = 0.583\ F = 27.03$$
$$\qquad\qquad\quad (6.91)\qquad\qquad (2.25)$$

where N is the population (1000 persons) and y is per capita GNP (dollars). The estimation was made from a sample of 102 countries in 1988. This estimation supports the hypotheses discussed above. In order to investigate factors accounting for the small value of δ in Japan we substitute the value of N and y in Japan and the world (average of 102 countries) into the estimated equation to obtain predicted values of δ (call these δ). It is 38 per cent – much larger than the actual value of δ in Japan (23 per cent). One of the major reasons for this is that Japan, located far from western developed countries, has no neighbouring countries with large production capacity and large markets. Thus Japan's small dependence on foreign trade is a result of the size of her economy and her geographical location. However, we can anticipate that Japan's dependence on foreign trade will increase because of stagnation in national industrial production the expansion of direct investment, and the development of a horizontal division of labour with the industrialization of neighbouring countries.

7.1.3　Effective Demand Effect of Exports

The expansion of exports stimulates economic growth by; (1) creating effective demand (effective demand effect), and (2) allowing an increase in imports without incurring a balance-of-payments deficit. In this subsection we discuss only the effective demand effect of exports. The best measure of the effective demand effect is the ratio of the increase in real exports (E) to the increase in real GNE (Y). This ratio was 25 per cent in the pre-war period (1888–1938), and 18 per cent in the post-war period (1955–88) (Table 6.7). It was smaller than either the ratio of the increase in personal consumption expenditure (PC) to the increase in GNE (58 per cent in the pre-war and 57 per cent in the post-war period) or the increase in fixed capital formation (CF) to the increase in GNE (31 per cent in the pre-war and 33 per cent in the post-war period). This indicates that the domestic market's contribution to effective demand has been larger than the foreign market's contribution. However, we should note that during the period after the 1970s when economic growth slowed down, the relative contribution of Japanese exports went up to 23 per cent. Nevertheless, the importance of the Japanese domestic market remained as before.

Kanamori's 'export-drive hypothesis' states that Japanese exports increased slowly when the domestic market expanded rapidly, while, during recessions, Japanese enterprises were forced to export more of their products. Although the correlations between $G(E)$ and $G(Y)$, or $G(E)$ and $G(CF)$ were not negative for either the pre-war or post-war period (Table 6.2), a more appropriate test did find a negative correlation between $G(E)$ and $G(D)$, the growth rate of total domestic demand (personal consumption, government consumption, capital formation and imports) in the pre-war period. This supports the export-drive hypothesis for that period. In the post-war period, however, a negative correlation was not found. This does not rule out the possibility that short-run 'export drives' occurred during recessions, because the growth rates $G(E)$ and $G(D)$ were calculated from smoothed series (seven-year moving averages).[9]

7.1.4 The Export-led Growth Hypothesis

At first glance the relatively rapid increase in Japanese exports appears to confirm the hypothesis, propounded by Blumenthal, Shinohara and others, that exports are the 'engine' of economic growth.[10] However, this hypothesis can be questioned on two counts;

1. Exports have a relatively limited effect on economic growth: The increase in real exports (E) accounted for a much smaller proportion of the increase in real GNE (Y) than private and government expenditure (PC and GC) and fixed capital formation (CF) during both the pre-war and post-war period (Table 6.7). Also, the correlation between $G(E)$ and $G(Y)$ was smaller than that between $G(PC)$ and $G(Y)$ or $G(CF)$ and $G(Y)$ (Table 6.2). This suggests that Japanese economic growth has relied more on the domestic market as a source of demand than the foreign market. The same conclusion was reached by Bronfenbrenner, Lockwood, Ohkawa and Rosovsky and others.[11] Lockwood argued that:

> If Japan's overseas market expanded, so too did her home market. The latter remained at all times far larger in scale. Changes in domestic tastes

and habits, and in the investment requirements of home industries, reacted upon employment and income to a much greater degree than did foreign demand for Japanese goods.[12]

2. Domestic events made export expansion possible. As we will see later, the expansion of Japanese exports resulted from the increased competitiveness of her products in the world market, which, in turn, stemmed from improvements in production equipment. During the pre-war period, for example, the Japanese cotton-spinning industry was more efficient than the UK and other countries, so that it was able to compete successfully on the world market (Ch. 5, Sec. 2). In this case, at least, export expansion was a consequence rather than a cause of industrialization.[13]

This is in sharp contrast to the experience of Canada, Australia and New Zealand in the nineteenth century. These countries exported furs, minerals, wool, wheat and other staples to developed countries. According to the 'staple theory',[14] these exports, which were the result of an increase in foreign demand, initiated economic growth in the latter half of the nineteenth century. According to this hypothesis exports really were the engine of growth in these countries. For Japan, however, although exports of primary and semi-primary products such as tea, copper, coal and raw silk in the nineteenth century played a significant role, this should not be exaggerated. The ratio of foreign trade to GNE in Japan was only 14–20 per cent, compared to 30 per cent in Canada and 40 per cent in Australia during the period 1885–1900.[15] In other words, economic growth in Japan was much less dependent on foreign trade. Furthermore, exports of raw silk, which accounted for 20–40 per cent of total commodity exports during the pre-war period, were largely the result of technological progress in Japan's silk-reeling industry (Ch. 5, Sec. 2).

The only case that definitely supports the export-led-growth hypothesis is Japan's export expansion during the First World War. Japanese exports increased because major developed countries such as the UK and Germany were not able to sustain their exports due to their participation in the war. These exports stimulated capital formation and brought forth an economic boom in Japan.

During other periods export activities were not the engine of economic growth. The engine was capital formation, which created effective demand and worked with the introduction of foreign technology to increase production efficiency and thus to stimulate exports.

7.1.5 Foreign Trade and the Balance of Payments

The second way that exports facilitate economic growth is by raising the balance-of-payments ceiling and thus allowing imports to increase. This is very important in a country like Japan, which has few natural resources and hence is dependent on the import of raw materials and fuels. Consumption goods and capital equipment have also been imported.

During the course of industrialization the volume of imports grew despite import substitution, because the demand for intermediate and finished goods increased. Imports' share of GNE increased from 4 to 24 per cent during the period 1888–1938 (Table 6.5). Exports increased at almost the same pace as imports; their share of GNE rose from 2 to 20 per cent during the same period. However, for the entire pre-war period (excluding the period 1915–19) imports exceeded exports; there was a balance-of-trade deficit (Table 7.2). This deficit was offset to some extent by unrequited transfers and capital transactions.[16]

During the post-war period both imports and exports increased

TABLE 7.2   Ratio of balance of payments to GNE in Japan 1885–1989 (%)

	Trade balance (1)	Surplus on current account (2)	Current account balance (3)	Overall balance (4)
1885–90	−0.50	−0.72	−0.60	0.00
1891–1900	−1.77	−1.88	0.48	0.17
1901–10	−1.11	−2.05	−1.73	1.34
1911–20	3.27	2.82	2.99	1.69
1921–30	−1.91	−1.60	−1.47	−0.74
1931–40	−0.70	−0.38	−0.10	−1.31
1952–60	−0.10	0.14	0.11	0.07
1961–70	0.49	0.24	0.19	0.18
1971–80	0.67	0.63	0.50	−0.25
1981–9	2.29	2.67	2.58	−0.96

Notes:
(1) = exports–imports (goods and services).
(2) = (1) + net transfers from abroad.
(3) = (2) + balance on unrequited transfers.
(4) = (3) + balance on capital transactions.

Sources:
Same as n. 4.

rapidly and imports' and exports' shares of GNE increased from 6 to 15 per cent and from 4 to 16 per cent, respectively during the period 1954–88. Until the mid-1960s the balance of trade was unfavourable. During times of prosperity the balance-of-trade situation was unfavourable due to increased imports. The government then tried to improve the balance-of-payments situation by tight fiscal and monetary policies. When a recession occurred, the government employed stimulatory policies that once again brought about increased imports. Japan did not break free from the constraints caused by balance-of-trade problems until the mid-1960s.

Thereafter, exports further expanded and in the 1970s the foreign trade/GNE ratio increased to 0.7 per cent, and in the 1980s even increased to 2.3 per cent. Japan's expansion in trade surplus has meant the spread of trade deficits in other countries. This has resulted in strong criticism by them toward Japan. These countries blamed Japan's export pressure at the expense of their local industries, so creating unemployment. However, the fact is that during this period Japan also increased overseas direct investment and security investment. As a result, the deficit in capital income expanded its range and, although the amount was trivial, the overall balance for Japan was negative. The long-term capital outflow from Japan means that it is supplementing the capital shortage in the USA and other countries.

7.1.6   The Effects of Foreign Trade

We have argued that exports expanded the market for Japanese products and that imports provided Japanese industry with raw materials and fuels not produced domestically. But foreign trade had other effects on economic growth that are not easily quantified.

Imports encouraged the introduction of modern science, technology and management.[17] The Japanese dismantled and analyzed promising products and then began domestic production of them, sometimes after making modifications (Ch. 5, Sec. 3). This 'learning from imports' can be seen as early as the Tokugawa Period (in trade with the Netherlands), but it did not become important until after the opening of the country in 1859. Although introduction of foreign products on a large scale hurt traditional industries by substituting foreign for domestic products, it motivated the establishment of new industry and created new demand.

Exports also motivated the introduction of new technology and improvements in management, stimulated capital formation, created employment opportunities and made it possible to realize economies of scale. In short, Japan's economic contacts with other countries, especially western countries, contributed more to industrialization than trade statistics suggest.

7.2 FOREIGN TRADE AND INDUSTRIALIZATION

7.2.1 Export Structure

The increase in Japanese exports was accompanied by a considerable change in their composition. In the 1870s primary products (e.g. tea, marine products, copper and coal) were the major exports, constituting 47 per cent of total commodity exports (Table 7.3). This figure declined to just 7 per cent in the 1920s and 1930s and 1 per cent in the 1970s and 1980s.

TABLE 7.3 Composition of commodity exports in Japan 1974–1990 (%)

			Manufactured products			
Period	*Primary products*	*Light industry*[a]	*Textiles only*	*Heavy and chemical*[b]	*Others*[c]	*Total*
1. 1874–80	47.1	40.7	38.6	7.6	4.6	52.9
2. 1881–90	34.1	46.4	45.0	12.0	7.5	65.9
3. 1891–1900	22.1	53.7	52.0	13.1	11.1	77.9
4. 1901–10	14.4	58.2	53.7	14.9	12.5	85.6
5. 1911–20	9.4	60.4	55.5	19.7	10.5	90.6
6. 1921–30	6.8	71.5	66.3	12.6	9.1	93.2
7. 1931–9	6.7	54.3	47.6	27.0	12.0	93.3
8. 1951–60	4.5	39.6	34.5	43.3	12.6	95.5
9. 1961–70	2.2	18.9	16.0	67.4	11.5	97.8
10. 1971–80	1.1	6.8	5.7	85.6	6.5	98.9
11. 1981–90	0.7	4.1	3.3	86.9	8.3	99.3

Notes:
[a] Foods and textiles.
[b] Metals, machinery and chemicals.
[c] Woods, ceramics and miscellaneous.
The figures are based on exports at current prices.

Sources:
Periods 1–9: Yamazawa and Yamamoto, 1979a, pp. 176–90.
Period 10: Yamazawa, 1984, pp. 240–1, appendix table 1.1.
Period 11: Preliminary estimates under some arbitrary assumptions based on KTN, 1990, pp. 241–2, 245.

Meanwhile the share of manufactured exports increased. In the Meiji and Taishō Periods manufactured exports were mainly the products of light industries, notably textiles. In the 1870s textiles' share of total exports was 39 per cent and this increased until in the 1920s it was 66 per cent. This increase in textile exports was largely the result of increased exports of fabrics. Fabrics' share of total exports rose from less than 1 per cent in the 1870s and 1880s, to more than 25 per cent in the 1920s. Textiles' share of total exports decreased during the post-war period and was only 3 per cent in the 1980s.

The heavy and chemical industries' products' share of total exports increased from 8 per cent in the 1870s to 27 per cent in the 1930s. The earliest manufactured products exported were simple ones such as matches and camphor, but the export of machinery and chemicals began after the First World War. Heavy and chemical industries' share of exports increased in the post-Second World War period – from 43 per cent in the 1950s to 87 per cent in the 1980s. These exports included ships, rolling stock, optical instruments, electrical appliances, cars and machine tools.

Thus, prior to the start of industrialization, Japan exported primary products and imported manufactured goods. Once industrialization began Japan exported primarily light industries' products, and textiles remained the major export throughout the pre-Second World War period. The heavy and chemical industries, which began to grow after the First World War, accounted for a smaller proportion of exports. This group of industries grew considerably during the post-war period and became a major source of exports. The change in the composition of exports was a result of these changes in the industrial structure.

The relationship between the structure of foreign trade and industrial structure is illustrated in Figure 7.1. Thus figure shows that the heavy and chemical industries' share of both exports and imports of manufactured goods are positively correlated with their share of output. Examining this figure more carefully we find: During periods 1–4 (1874–1910) heavy and chemical industries' share of exports and output was almost constant, and their share of imports increased rapidly. During periods 5–7 (1911–39) the rate at which their share of imports was increasing declined, but their share of output began to increase. During periods 8–11 (1951–90) their share of output increased slowly, and their share of exports increased rapidly. The expansion of the heavy and chemical industries began with imports, spread to output and then to exports.

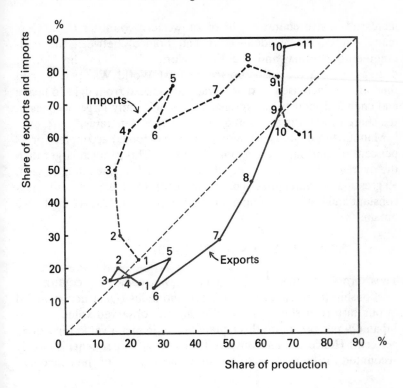

FIGURE 7.1 Relationship between Japan's heavy and chemical industries' share of foreign trade and their share of output 1874–1990

Notes:
Share of foreign trade = ratio of heavy and chemical industrys' exports (imports) to total exports (imports).
Share of output = ratio of heavy and chemical industrys' output to total manufacturing output.
The figures 1 . . . 11 stand for the same periods as in Table 7.3.

Sources:
Exports: Table 7.3.
Imports: Table 7.4.
Production: Table 5.7.

7.2.2 International Comparisons (Exports)

The pattern of changes in Japan's export structure during industrialization is similar to that of other developed countries. Manufactured goods' (excluding processed foods) share of total exports increased in five countries out of six western countries (UK, Germany, Denmark, Sweden, USA and France) between the mid-nineteenth century and the First World War.[18] In the UK, it decreased from the 1830s up to the First World War period, and thereafter it increased. Exports gradually shifted from light to heavy and chemical industries' products as the uniformly large declines in the share of exports accounted for by textiles illustrates.

Manufactured goods (excluding processed foods) accounted for 98 per cent of total Japanese exports in 1988.[19] This is much larger than the average of 81 per cent of all OECD countries (including Japan). Regressing manufactured goods' share of total exports (y) on a constant and the share of manufactures in GDP (x) for this sample, we obtain, [20]

$$y = 5.255 + 1.825x \quad \bar{r} = 0.547 \quad F = 37.73$$

Thus, cross-sectional data (of eighty-seven countries) confirm the relationship between export structure and industrial structure found in our historical statistics. Substituting the observed value of x in Japan (29 per cent) into this equation, we predict a value for y of 58 per cent. Hence, Japan's observed value of y (98 per cent) is largely accounted for by manufactured goods' large share of the economy.

7.2.3 Import Structure

Primary products' (non-processed foodstuffs, raw materials and fuels) share of commodity imports increased from only 8 per cent in the 1870s to 59 per cent in the 1930s and 61 per cent in the 1980s (Table 7.4). Today almost all imported primary products are either raw materials or fuels. The most important in the pre-Second World War period were cotton for textiles and in the post-war period mineral products (metal ores, coal and petroleum).

Manufactured goods' share of total imports fell from 92 per cent in the 1870s to less than 50 per cent in the early 1910s. Their share of total exports had reached 90 per cent by this time. Thus the focus of the economy changed from the export of primary goods and the import of finished goods, to the import of primary goods and the export of finished goods.

Next let us examine the structure of imports of manufactured goods. In the early years a large share of imports was accounted for

TABLE 7.4 Composition of commodity imports into Japan 1874–1990 (%)

Period	Primary products		Manufactured products				
	Total	Raw materials and fuels only	Light industries	Textiles only	Heavy and chemical industries	Others	Total
1. 1874–80	8.0	7.3	67.2	54.7	20.3	4.5	92.0
2. 1881–90	16.1	12.0	55.4	40.5	25.8	2.7	83.9
3. 1891–1900	35.8	25.7	30.6	18.3	31.8	1.8	64.2
4. 1901–10	45.0	32.3	19.4	9.8	34.0	1.6	55.0
5. 1911–20	52.7	40.7	10.8	3.2	35.5	1.0	47.3
6. 1921–30	55.9	37.5	14.0	5.5	27.2	2.9	44.1
7. 1931–9	59.2	41.6	9.2	2.3	30.0	1.6	40.8
8. 1951–60	80.1	62.4	2.1	0.5	16.2	1.6	19.9
9. 1961–70	70.5	57.5	3.3	1.0	23.0	3.2	29.5
10. 1971–80	74.2	59.8	4.7	3.0	16.8	4.3	25.8
11. 1981–90	60.8	47.5	4.3	4.3	24.0	10.9	39.2

Notes:
The figures are based on imports at current prices.

Sources:
Periods 1–9: Yamazawa and Yamamoto, 1979a, pp. 180–3.
Period 10: Yamazawa, 1984, pp. 242–4, appendix table 1.1.
Period 11: Preliminary estimates under some arbitrary assumption based on KTN, 1990, pp. 243–5.

by products such as textiles, that were made by light industry. The share of textile imports declined rapidly during the pre-Second World War period due to the growth of the domestic textile industry. In the post-Second World War period, however, this share increased because Japan began to import textiles from newly developed countries. The heavy and chemical industries' share of imports increased from the 1870s until the 1910s, due to an increase in the demand for capital equipment. After the 1910s their share fell steadily as a result of import substitution. (For the relationship between the growth of these industries and the change in the import structure, see Figure 7.1.)

7.2.4   International Comparisons (Imports)

Manufactured goods' share of total imports increased between the mid-nineteenth century and the First World War in the UK, Sweden and France. In Germany and the USA their share decreased until about the First World War and then increased. In Japan, however, their share has decreased, steadily, it was only 43 per cent in 1988. This is much smaller than the average of all OECD countries, at 73 per cent.[21] Japan's relatively high ratio of imports of primary products is due to: (1) her lack of natural resources, and (2) the lack of neighbouring industrialized countries with which Japan can establish a 'horizontal division of work'. However, some Asian countries commenced industrialization in the 1960s and began to export their light industries' products, and in the 1980s Japan's overseas investments increased very rapidly because of yen evaluation. Consequently, Japanese import of these products has increased significantly. In the future a horizontal division of work in which Japan exports heavy and chemical products to these countries and imports light industrial products from them and a shift of production from Japan to western countries will probably slow the decline in manufactured goods' share of Japan's imports.[22]

7.2.5   Wild Geese in Flight

Kaname Akamatsu has described Japan's historical progression from import to domestic production and to export, as a 'wild geese flying pattern'.[23] (This romantic expression calls attention to the resemblance between the pattern traced by changes in imports, production and exports and the pattern of wild geese flying in a group.) In the 1870s and 1880s imports of cotton yarn and cotton cloth increased as

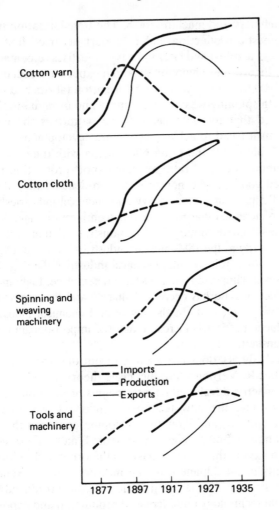

FIGURE 7.2 'Wild geese flying pattern' of economic development

Source:
Akamatsu, 1962, p. 12, figure 1.

a result of increased demand for fabrics (Figure 7.2). Soon domestic production of these products increased and began to substitute for imports, and by about 1890 domestic production exceeded imports. As production continued to increase, export of these products began, and by the first decade of the twentieth century exports exceeded imports. A similar pattern can be seen in industries such as spinning-weaving machinery and machine-tools. The transformation from imports to domestic production and to export occurred first in light industries (e.g. textiles) and later in heavy industries (e.g. machinery) as shown in Figure 7.2. The point at which exports exceeded imports was about 1900 for cotton yarn, 1905 for cotton fabrics and the early 1920s for both spinning-weaving machinery and machine-tools. Akamatsu claimed that the wild geese flying pattern is the path that latecomers must tread to achieve economic development.

Figure 7.3 illustrates the same phenomena with different data; it shows the import-demand ratio and the export-production ratio for manufactured goods. Light industries' import-demand ratio decreased throughout the pre-war period; heavy and chemical industries' import-demand ratio increased sharply in the nineteenth century and decreased sharply in the twentieth century. This demonstrates that import substitution began as early as the 1880s in light industries but did not start until the turn of century in heavy and chemical industries. During the post-war period several important changes have taken place. Light industries' export-production ratio has decreased sharply and the import-demand ratio has slowly increased. In the heavy and chemical industries the export-production ratio has increased and the import-demand ratio has remained constant.

Akamatsu's theory does not explain recent developments in light industries, but R. Vernon's 'product cycle theory' does.[24] According to Vernon, when a developed country begins production and export of a new product the new technology involved will go to other developed countries, and later to developing countries through export of technology and foreign investment. Finally, these countries will begin to export this product back to the original developer. The developments in the Japanese textile industry can be explained by this hypothesis. During the Meiji Period Japan introduced modern British textile technology and increased production and exports. Due to the relatively low-wage rate and rapid technological progress Japan's textiles gradually replaced Britain's in the world market during the pre-Second World War period. During the post-war period a considerable increase in wages made Japanese products less competitive. Many Japanese enterprises decided to invest in developing Asian countries with lower wages. Production in these countries increased rapidly and their products were exported to developed countries, including Japan. In the 1960s, Japan reverted from the production and export of textiles back to import.

The Japanese experience can thus be described by a combination of Akamatsu's and Vernon's theories.[25] These theories do not,

183

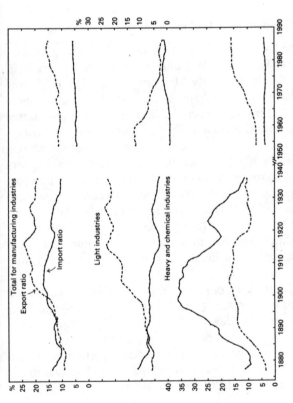

FIGURE 7.3   Import and export ratios of manufactured products 1877–1987

Notes:
Import ratio = imports ÷ (production + imports − exports) × 100.
Export ratio = (exports ÷ production) × 100.
Based on seven-year moving averages (five-year averages for 1936 and 1987) at current prices.

Sources:
See Figure 7.1.

however, explain the development of all products. Electronic calculators, electronic watches, *NC* machine tools and industrial robots were developed in Japan with no period of import or import substitution. This suggests that Japan's level of technology is now equal to other industrialized countries.

7.3   DETERMINANTS OF FOREIGN TRADE

7.3.1   The Establishment of a Trading System

Since foreign trade had been discontinued in the Tokugawa Period, its resumption necessitated the development of a system of trade in the 1870s and 1880s. In the early Meiji Period foreign trade was controlled by westerner's merchant houses which Japanese merchants were forced to use to export and import goods. In the latter half of the 1870s several Japanese trading companies, established with the government's help, began direct export-import operations (e.g. Mitsui Bussan in 1876). Direct exports' share of total exports and direct imports' share of total imports both exceeded 50 per cent by 1910. Within another ten years direct exports exceeded 80 per cent of the total, and during the 1930s direct imports reached 80 per cent of total imports.[26] These general trading companies dealt with a wide range of commodities, so that they were able to minimize risks resulting from fluctuations in demand or exchange rates, and take advantage of economies of scale.

Tōkyō Marine Insurance Company, Yokohama Specie Bank and Japan Mail Steamship Company (established in 1879, 1880 and 1885 respectively) pioneered the development of marine insurance, foreign exchange and marine transportation organizations. The latter, with assistance from the government and close relations with the trading companies grew very fast, and carried more than two-thirds of Japan's foreign trade after the First World War.[27]

7.3.2   Terms of Trade

The terms of trade – the ratio of export prices (P_E) to import prices (P_M) – increased from the 1880s until the first decade of the twentieth century and then began to fall. This trend continued, except for a few years around 1920, until the Second World War (Figure 7.4).

Shinohara and others argued that the decrease in the terms of trade was the basic factor behind the rapid increase in Japanese exports

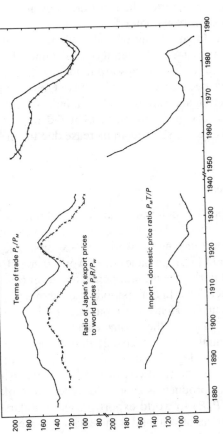

FIGURE 7.4   Terms of trade, ratios of Japan's export prices to world prices, and import prices to domestic prices 1877–1987

Notes:

P_E = commodity export prices.
P_M = commodity import prices.
P_W = commodity export prices of the world.
R = exchange rate of yen to dollars.
P = GNE deflator.
T = 1 + customs rate.

Figures for P_E/P_M, $P_E R/P_W$, and $P_M T/P$: 1934–6 = 1 for the pre-war period and 1985 = 1 for the post-war period.
The figures are seven-year moving averages (five-year averages for 1936 and 1987).

Sources:

P_E, P_M, P_W, R and T: To 1970 – Yamazawa and Yamamoto, 1979a, pp. 192–9, 252, 254–7, since 1971–YITS, 1980; p. 1220, 1988, p. 1090. ZKTG, 1980, Sep. no. 341, p. 34; 1990, Sep. no. 461, p. 53.
P: Table 11.1.

during the pre-Second World War period.[28] From the first decade of the century until the Japan's export competitiveness increased relative to the UK. As a result, Japan captured an increased share of the world export market. This pattern of expanding exports as a result of a long-term deterioration in the terms of trade is not unique to Japan. It occurred in the UK during the first eighty years of the nineteenth century and in Germany from the 1870s to the 1920s.[29] Japan's decrease in the terms of trade came later than in other developed countries because industrialization began later.[30]

After the Second World War Japan's terms of trade stabilized until around 1970. Then for the next decade and a half it declined until the first half of 1980s when it started to show an upward tendency. In the 1970s import prices increased because of the oil crises. However, mainly due to reduced production and rationalization in industry the oil crisis did not influence export prices as much as it did import prices. In the 1980s the terms of trade showed an increase due to yen evaluation.

7.3.3 Determinants of Exports

In general the volume of exports is determined by two factors; the 'income effect' and the 'price effect'. The income effect is the marginal effect of a change in world income on worldwide exports. The trade quantity index of the world (T_w), an indicator of world demand, increased at a rate of 2 per cent during the pre-war period and 6 per cent during the post-war period (Table 7.1). In both periods real exports (E) in Japan grew more rapidly than T_w. Hence the rapid increase in E in Japan cannot be accounted for solely by the income effect.

The price effect is the marginal effect of a change in the price of a country's products on its exports. Japan's share of the world market has increased due to a decline in the relative price of her products. The competitiveness of Japan's products is expressed by the ratio of her export prices in dollars ($P_E R$) to world export prices in dollars (P_w). (P_E represents export prices at yen, and R the exchange rate of yen to dollars.) In the preceding subsection we discussed the widely held belief that a deterioration in the terms of trade (P_E/P_M) brings about export expansion. Theoretically, however, it is the ratio of Japan's export prices to world export prices ($P_E R/P_w$) that decides the volume of her exports. This ratio decreased during three periods: 1901–14, 1922–37 and the post-war period excluding the 1980s. During each of these periods the price effect was significant.

$P_E R/P_w$ is P_E/P_w divided by R. P_E/P_w increased in the pre-war period, and decreased in the post-war period. *R* decreased considerably during the periods 1874–95 and 1931–3, but remained almost constant in other years. The decrease (from 1.01 dollars per yen to 0.50) between 1874 and 1895 was largely due to a decrease in the price of silver. (This effectively devalued the Japanese currency because Japan was on the silver standard. Japan went on to the gold standard in 1897.) The decrease (from 0.49 dollar per yen to 0.25) between 1931 and 1933 was caused by the abandonment of the gold standard in 1931. When the embargo on gold exports was removed at the beginning of 1930 (the 1917 parity was retained) it had caused an over-valuation of the yen, but this was adjusted by the 1931 decision. In the post-war period, *R* decreased slowly until about 1970, decreased sharply in the 1970s, and started to increase in the mid-1980s.

7.3.4 Estimation of Export Function

Here, we attempt to measure income and price effects quantitatively by estimating an export function (commodity export only),[31]

$$ln\ E = a + b\ ln\ T_w + c\ ln\ (P_E R/P_w) + u$$

where *ln* indicates natural log and *u* is an error term. Parameters *b* and *c* are the income elasticity and price elasticity of exports.

This function was estimated from data for four periods: 1885–1913, 1921–38, 1952–70 and 1971–88 (Table 7.5). The period of 1914–20 was excluded because world trade was in disarray as a result of the First World War. The post-war years (1952–88) were divided into two periods (1952–70 and 1971–88) because international circumstances were different between the former and the latter period. The signs of the parameters are as expected, and are statistically significant. The relative contributions of changes in *ln* T_w and *ln* $P_E R/P_w$ to the increase in *ln* E were calculated using these parameter estimates and are shown in the following table.

	$\Delta ln\ T_w$	$\Delta ln\ P_E R/P_w$
	%	%
1885–1913	99.1	0.9
1921–38	25.6	74.4
1952–70	78.2	21.8
1971–88	93.5	6.5

TABLE 7.5 Export and import functions 1885–1988

	Variable	Const.	$\ln T_w$	$\ln P_E R/P_w$	$\ln Y$	$\ln P_M T/P$	$\bar{R}$	d
				Explanatory variables				
				Export functions				
1885–1913	$\ln E$	0.039 (0.03)	2.327 (19.59)	−0.805 (2.54)	—	—	0.966	1.69
1921–38	$\ln E$	10.767 (6.44)	1.187 (3.39)	−1.831 (9.72)	—	—	0.920	0.89
1952–70	$\ln E$	12.262 (57.49)	1.750 (18.52)	−3.434 (6.21)	—	—	0.998	1.28
1971–88	$\ln E$	10.585 (308.00)	1.594 (10.39)	−0.352 (1.96)	—	—	0.963	0.69

189

Import functions

1885–1938	*ln M*	0.841 (0.41)	—	—	1.476 (13.40)	−1.565 (6.40)	0.973	0.61
1952–88	*ln M*	−4.547 (9.34)	—	—	1.189 (29.29)	−0.285 (3.21)	0.994	0.94

Notes:

E = commodity exports.
M = commodity imports.
Y = GNE.
T_w = world trade quantity index.
$P_E R/P_w$ = Japan–world ratio of export prices.
$P_M T/P$ = import price–domestic price ratio.
Figures for E, M and Y: Pre-war – 1934–6 prices, million yen. Post-war – 1985 prices, 1000 million yen.
Figures for T_w, $P_E R/P_w$ and $P_M T/P$: 1934–6 = 100 for the pre-war and 1985 = 100 for the post-war period.
Based on non-smoothed figures.

Sources:
E and M: to 1970 – Yamazawa and Yamamoto, 1979a, pp. 185–91. 1971–88 – Extrapolated from the 1970 figures based on the quantity index in KTN, 1990, p. 246.
T_w: Table 7.1.
$P_E R/P_w$: Figure 7.4.
Y: Figure 3.3.
$P_M T/P$: Figure 7.4.

These figures help us to understand the factors responsible for export expansion in Japan.

1885–1913: This period saw a considerable expansion in world trade; the annual compound growth rate of T_W was 3.2 per cent. Japan exported raw silk and related products that had a large income elasticity (our estimate of b was large). This meant a large income effect, which resulted in a high growth rate for E (8.3 per cent). $P_E R / P_W$ increased slightly, so that the price effect was very small.[32]

1921–38: World trade was stagnant; the growth rate of T_W decreased to 1.6 per cent from the previous period, and as a result the importance of the income effect declined. However, the competitiveness of Japanese exports increased considerably, and cotton textiles, a product which had a large price elasticity (the absolute value of c was large), became an important export. Both these factors promoted export expansion. Had raw silk and related products continued to constitute a large share of Japanese exports it is unlikely that the high growth rate observed during this period (8.5 per cent) could have been achieved.[33]

A comparison of Japan and the UK, then the world's foremost exporter, and Japan's major competitor in textiles, is enlightening. The UK's export function during the period 1920–38 was estimated to be.[34]

$$ln\ E = 6.648 + 0.228\ ln\ T_W - 0.708\ ln\ P_E/P_W\ \bar{R} = 0.675\ d = 1.12$$
$$(4.85)\quad (1.16)\qquad\qquad (3.81)$$

Estimates of parameters b and c are much smaller than in Japan. This implies that the UK's exports were relatively insensitive to increasing world demand and changes in export competitiveness. Actually the UK's export competitiveness did decline; P_E/P_W increased,[35] and brought about a slight decrease in exports.[36] The UK's export problems were the result both of the small income elasticity of the commodities she exported and a fall in the price competitiveness of her products because of slow progress in production technology.

1952–70: This period saw rapid expansion of the world market as a result of increased economic growth in many countries and factors such as the stable international political situation and the decrease in the customs duties of developed countries due to the Kennedy Round (1967–71); T_W increased at a rate of 6.9 per cent. Japan constructed and exported ships, rolling stock and other products with a high income elasticity. Japan achieved an unprecedented 15.8 per cent growth rate for E. Her export competitiveness improved slightly, but this did not have a significant impact on exports.

1971–88: The growth rate of T_w decreased to 4.6 per cent due to world-wide recessions. Japan's export competitiveness improved ($P_E R/P_W$ fell from 166 to 129, assuming 100 for 1985) as a result of improvements in production methods, in spite of unfavourable factors such as an increase in the value of the yen, and increases in wages and import prices of raw materials and fuels. However, the increased price effect was not large enough to cancel out the decrease in the income effect and the growth rate of E decreased by half from the previous period, to 7.5 per cent. It should be noted, however, that the growth rate of E was larger than the growth rate of T_w, implying that the Japanese share of the world market continued to increase.

Japanese exports will face several internal and external problems in the future. Increases in wages and import prices of raw materials and fuels will probably reduce their competitiveness, while on the external side increasing international friction over Japanese exports, and increasing pressure to import from other Asian countries with lower wages can be expected. If she is to sustain rapid export growth under these circumstances Japan will have to accept increased imports and continue to improve both technology and efficiency to maintain her export competitiveness at a high level.

7.3.5 Shinohara's Hypothesis on Exports and Economic Growth

Shinohara expressed the belief that exports played an important role in pre-war Japanese economic growth.[37] He argued that a surplus of labour during this period accelerated economic growth by reducing wage increases. This stimulated economic growth in two ways: (1) a decrease in the relative income share of labour → an increase in the savings rate → increased capital accumulation, and (2) a decrease (or a slow increase) in export prices → a deterioration in the terms of trade → increased exports. In this section we examine the latter; the economists who stress its importance refer to it as 'export-led growth'.

The importance of the decline in export prices and consequent deterioration in the terms of trade – which are crucial to the export-led growth hypothesis – has been questioned by some scholars. Kiyoshi Kojima has argued that Japanese exports expanded primarily because of an increase in foreign demand.[38] To resolve this controversy let us recall the analysis presented above: the ratio of Japan's export prices to world export prices, $P_E R/P_W$, was quite stable until the early twentieth century (it is this ratio, not the terms of trade, that influences exports directly). This suggests that increased foreign demand did play an important role in the expansion of Japanese exports. However, $P_E R/P_W$ decreased after this period, which supports Shinohara's argument.

Shinohara also emphasizes the importance of slow wage growth. Surplus labour in agriculture prevented a large increase in the wages of urban workers. Unskilled worker's wages increased very little, especially in the 1920s and early 1930s. However, the remarkable increase in Japanese labour productivity was probably a more important factor than slow wage increases in Japanese products' increased competitiveness.[39]

7.3.6 Determinants of Imports

The quantity of imports to a country is determined by the 'income effect' and 'price effect'.

The import-demand function for Japan can be written as:

$$ln\ M = a + b\ ln\ Y + c\ ln\ P_M T/P + u$$

where M, Y, P_M and P represent Japan's real commodity imports, real GNE, import prices and the GNE deflator. T is 1 + the tariff rate and $P_M T$ stands for import prices (including customs duties). The ratio $P_M T/P$ decreased during both the pre-war and post-war periods (Figure 7.4). The parameters b and c are the income elasticity (presumably positive) and price elasticity (presumably negative) of imports.

Estimates of these parameters are shown in Table 7.5. Our estimate of the parameter b was slightly lower and our estimate of the parameter c was considerably lower (in absolute value), in the post-war period. The large decrease in c is due to the fact that Japanese imports have changed from manufactured products to raw materials and fuels, which are indispensable for continued industrialization and therefore insensitive to changes in import prices. The relative contributions of an increase in $ln\ Y'$ and a decrease in $ln\ P_M T/P$ to an increase in $ln\ M$ are calculated in the following table:

	$\Delta ln\ Y$	$\Delta ln\ P_M T/P$
	%	%
1885–1938	75.4	24.6
1952–81	87.7	12.3

We find that: 1. The income effect was much larger than the price effect during both periods, because raw materials and fuels accounted for a large share of total imports. 2. The income effect increased and the price effect decreased after the Second World War. This was due to both the increase in raw materials and fuels' share of imports and the increase in the economic growth rate.

7.3.7 Foreign Trade Policies

There are a wide variety of policy instruments that can be used for export promotion.[40] Government programmes to promote export industries can be an important policy instrument. The technology imported by the Meiji government played a major role in establishing export industries. Many economists believe that post-war industrial policies were largely responsible for the increased export of heavy and chemical industries' products (Ch. 5, Sec. 4). Sometimes more direct policies to promote exports were carried out; in the 1920s and 1930s, for example, a quality control system was established for major exports such as raw silk, cotton fabrics are celluloid.

Tariffs are import policy's main tool for the protection of domestic industry. The average tariff rate increased from 1899 (they year when tariff autonomy was restored) until 1931 (Figure 7.5). (The tariff rate fell during the First World War because inflation caused a decrease in the effective *ad valorem* rates of specific duties.) After reaching a peak in 1931 the rate decreased considerably because important heavy manufactures were made exempt from tariffs and because imports from outside the trade blocs declined.

Changes in the tariff rate were accompanied by an increasing degree of differentiation among commodity groups resulting in a widening gap between the average tariff on total imports (T) and the average tariff on dutiable imports (T'). In 1899 the first tariff schedule set a rate of 0–5 per cent on raw materials, 10 per cent on semi-manufactures, 15–20 per cent on finished manufactures and more than 25 per cent on luxury goods. The schedules of 1906 and 1926 set even steeper tariff structures. The idea was to accelerate the growth of processing industries by importing raw materials at relatively low prices and limiting imports of finished goods.

Tariff protection was not limited to Japan, and there is no evidence that it was stronger in Japan than in other developed countries. Japan's tariff rate was moderate; the average rate (T) was only 24 per cent at its peak in 1931, compared to a peak of 50–60 per cent in the

194

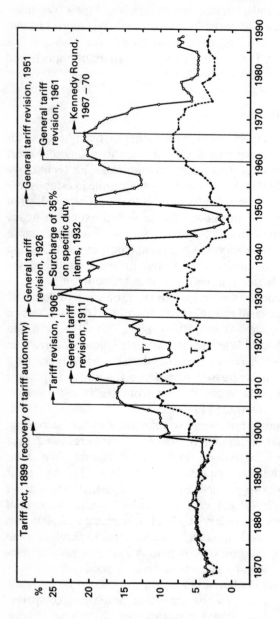

FIGURE 7.5 Customs duties in Japan 1868–1989

Note:
T = average tariff on total imports.
T' = average tariff on dutiable imports.
The figures are non-smoothed.

Sources:
See Figure 7.4.

USA.[41] Pre-war Japan is a good example of successful industrialization via the utilization of competitive pressure from imports. Furthermore, the tariff structure used in Japan (low tariffs on raw materials and higher tariffs on finished goods) was also employed in other countries.[42]

During the post-war period the average rate increased until the mid-1960s and then decreased. The increase resulted from the abolition of the tax exemption for machinery and a rise in the tariff on sugar. The later decline in tariffs was a consequence of the Kennedy Round in 1967–70 and the preferential tariff rates granted to developing countries since 1971. The average tariff rate on total imports today is only 2–3 per cent and the rate on dutiable imports about 5 per cent. These rates are similar to those of other developed countries.

Another policy instrument sometimes used to protect domestic industries is quantitative restriction on imports. It was not until 1937, however, that the Japanese government, motivated by the world-wide increase in protectionism, resorted to this policy. During the early post-war years various commodities were restricted. However, Japan became a member of GATT in 1955, and joined the world-wide free-trade movement in 1960, and the proportion of commodities whose import was not restricted increased from 41 to 93 per cent between 1960 and 1966.[43] The latter percentage is approximately the same as in other developed countries.

How far did protectionism contribute to industrial growth? The rapid industrial growth of Japan was the result of capital formation and rapid technological progress in the private sector. Protectionism facilitated (or at least did not retard) this process. Low tariffs on intermediate and capital goods encouraged manufacturing activities and tariffs on consumption goods were prohibitive. However, world history suggests that in most cases industrialization has been promoted by free trade rather than protectionism.[44]

SUMMARY OF THE CHAPTER

Japan's foreign trade grew rapidly throughout the pre-war and the post-war period. As a result, Japan's share of international markets grew steadily.

Exports contribute to economic growth by generating effective demand (external demand). In Japan such external demand was small compared to internal demand arising from consumption expenditure and fixed capital formation. The engine of Japanese economic growth was internal demand, primarily private fixed investment.

Exports also make it possible to expand import capacity. This contribution is especially important for countries that must depend upon imports for natural resources.

Industrialization changed the structure of trade. Initially Japan exported chiefly primary products and imported light manufactured goods such as textiles. During the late nineteenth and early twentieth century domestic light industries' production increased and eventually they began to export. As a result, imports of heavy and chemical industries' products increased. Since the First World War heavy and chemical industries have also engaged in import substitution and export. In the post-war period exports of heavy and chemical industries overtook those of light industries. As demand for raw materials and fuels increased, the pattern of importing them and exporting the products of heavy and chemical industries became established. Successive growth of various industries and the pattern of changes in foreign trade (from imports to import substitution and to exports) has been described as the flying-geese pattern of economic development.

During the post-war period several Asian countries where wages are low have expanded their exports of light manufactures. Developments in Japan have followed the product-cycle theory, in that she has started to import these products rather than continue producing them domestically. Since the mid-1980s Japan's overseas investment to western countries increased remarkably, and exports have been substituted gradually by Japan's production in these countries.

Between the mid-1900s and 1930s Japan's terms of trade deteriorated while the UK's terms of trade improved, as the competitive power of Japan's exports rose and England's fell. (England's ratio was crucially affected by cheap imported foodstuffs. The better terms of trade include this.) The ratio of Japanese exports to international prices fell sharply during the 1920s, 1930s and 1970s. The pre-war decrease was mainly due to the falling exchange rate. In the UK during the same period this ratio increased; while her share of world markets fell, America's, Germany's and Japan's rose rapidly. The decreased ratio in the 1970s was due to the fact that despite the world suffering an inflationary tendency caused by the oil crises Japan could keep the rise of export prices to a minimum, depending on efforts by industry to accommodate technological innovations and rationalization.

Our estimates of the export function for Japan reveal that the increase in exports prior to the First World War was primarily the result of a rise in world income. Exports increased between the wars due to their increased competitiveness, and again during the post-war period as a result of the rise in demand as rapid economic growth took place in various countries. The slow expansion of world demand during the 1970s caused many firms to raise production efficiency, and their competitiveness improved despite the rising value of the yen. In the 1980s exports are still expanding rapidly. However, expanded sale of Japanese goods in various countries has resulted in an international payments surplus in Japan and put other countries into debt. As a result, resistance to Japanese exports is steadily increasing. Japanese industry is actively urged to make foreign investment to promote local production; while industries in the USA and EC countries have intensified their tendency towards protectionist policies in trade.

Although increases in imports may be brought about by either increases in national income or a fall in the relative price of imports to domestic production, increased income has been the dominant force throughout the pre-war and the post-war period. The relative price of imported goods has fallen substantially in the post-war period and this has considerably affected the volume of imports. In the 1960s Japan liberalized commodity imports and capital inflow in face of pressure from other countries but foreign criticism has continued, the further opening of internal markets is imperative if expansion of exports is to continue. In the future Japan must increase imports of manufactured goods from the developing countries and of sophisticated industrial goods from the advanced countries.

FURTHER READING

Baba and Tatemoto, 1968
Kanamori, 1966; 1968
Krause and Sekiguchi, 1976
Lockwood, 1968, chs 6 and 7
Ohkawa and Rosovsky, 1973, ch. 7
Shinohara, 1962, ch. 3; 1982, part 2
Shionoya, 1968
Yamazawa, 1975a; 1975b
Yamazawa and Yamamoto, 1979b

Part III

Modern Economic Growth: Causes and Results

Part III

Modern Economic Growth:
Causes and Results

8 Population and Labour Supply

In Chapter 3 we said that the economic growth rate in Japan has been high (by international standards) and rising. However, if the population growth rate had been high or rising Japan might not have been able to achieve a high rate of growth of per capita gross domestic product. In Section 8.1 of this chapter changes in the population growth rate are analyzed and compared with other countries. The relationship between population growth and economic development is also discussed.

Population growth raises the productive capacity of the economy by increasing the supply of labour, labour supply, capital accumulation and technological progress together govern economic growth. Section 8.2 focuses upon the labour force, an observable proxy for labour supply. We analyze its rate of growth and discuss its determinants, particularly the labour participation rate.

8.1 POPULATION

8.1.1 The Size of the Population and the Economy

In the mid-1880s, when modern economic growth began, Japan's total population was between 37 870 000 and 39 630 000 depending on which estimate is used.[1] The total land area was 382 000 square kilometres, so that population density was 99–104 persons per square kilometre. By contrast, before the Industrial Revolution population density in Europe was only 39. In England it was 43 in 1700 and 63 in 1801.[2] Even today European countries have a population density of only 101 compared to Japan's 326 (Table 8.1).

The high population density at the starting-point of modern economic growth in Japan (it increased due to population increase thereafter[3]) had both adverse and beneficial effects on economic

TABLE 8.1 Vital statistics, population density and age composition of the population of different regions of the world 1985–90 (%)

	Vital statistics 1985–90 (%)			Population density 1989 (person/km²)	Age composition (1985) (%)			Dependent population ratio^a (1985) (%)
	Crude birth-rate	Crude death-rate	Rate of natural increase		0–14	15–64	65 or over	
World	2.7	1.0	1.7	38	34	60	6	65
Africa	4.5	1.5	3.0	21	45	52	3	93
North America	1.5	0.9	0.6	13	22	66	12	50
Latin America	2.9	0.8	1.1	21	38	58	4	73
Asia	2.8	0.9	1.9	111	35	60	5	65
East Asia	2.0	0.7	1.3	112	29	65	6	53
South Asia	3.5	1.2	2.3	173	39	57	4	77
Europe	1.3	1.1	0.2	101	21	67	13	50
Oceania	2.0	0.8	1.2	3	28	65	8	57
USSR	1.8	1.1	0.7	13	25	66	10	54
Japan	1.1	0.6	0.5	326	22	68	10	47

Note:
^a Population aged 14 years or less and 65 years or over ÷ population aged 15–64 years × 100.

Sources:
DY, 1989, pp. 117, 119.

growth. The labour–land ratio in agriculture in 1880 (the number of male workers per square kilometre of arable land) was ten times as high in Japan as in Germany and France and twenty times as high as in the UK.[4] Because of the small area of land per worker the productivity of male workers in Japan was only one-fifth of that of German and French workers and one-tenth of that of workers in the UK. As in other agricultural countries, low labour productivity in agriculture meant a low level of labour productivity in the economy as a whole. Per capita GNP in Japan was much lower than in other developed countries, even at the same stage of economic development (Ch. 2, Sec. 3).

The high labour–land ratio in agriculture meant a surplus of agricultural workers (Ch. 9, Sec. 2). However, the availability of surplus labour from the agricultural sector prevented wage increases in urban industries. Low wage rates encouraged the development of labour-intensive industries. Furthermore, low labour productivity in agriculture gave manufacturing an advantage and contributed to the development of the pattern of importing agricultural products and exporting manufacturing products.

8.1.2 The Population Growth Rate

Total population in Japan has increased at an average annual rate of about 1 per cent since the Meiji Period (Table 3.2).[5] The population growth rate increased slowly from the 1870s, reaching a peak in the latter half of the 1920s. After jumping to an abnormally high level immediately following the Second World War it decreased rapidly, and since the latter half of the 1950s it has remained at about 1 per cent. Because there has been little immigration between Japan and other countries, changes in the rate of population growth have been due almost solely to changes in birth- and death-rates. Only the 1930s and the first half of the 1940s were exceptions; during the period 1932–44 many soldiers and civilians left the country, and in 1945–6 almost $4\frac{1}{2}$ million people were repatriated.[6]

The birth-rate increased steadily, from 2.3 per cent in the early Meiji Period to a peak of 3.6 per cent in 1923, when it began to decrease. After the baby boom that followed the Second World War the birth-rate decreased sharply, to 1.8 per cent in the latter half of the 1950s. The death-rate increased slowly from the beginning of the Meiji Period until the late 1910s, when it began a long-term decline. However, the initial increase in the death-rate was smaller than the increase in the birth-rate and the latter decrease in the death-rate was smaller than the decrease in the birth-rate. Changes in the rate of population growth were mainly attributable to changes in the birth-rate.

In recent years (1985–90) the birth-rate in Japan (1.1 per cent) has been far lower than the world average of 2.7 per cent and even than that of western developed countries (Table 8.1). The developing countries of Africa, Latin America and south Asia have birth-rates as high as 3–5 per cent. Death-rates vary less than birth-rates internationally, so that there are large differences in the natural rate of population growth – it averages 1 per cent in the developed countries and 2–3 per cent in the developing countries. After the Second World War the death-rate in the developing countries was reduced by policies such as spraying DDT to control malaria. This resulted in a 'population explosion'. Many developing countries realized that the population explosion was hampering their economic development, and have encouraged birth-control. This has been successful in some countries, such as Taiwan and Singapore, but other countries still have a high birth-rate.

8.1.3 Changes in the Age Composition of the Population

As a result of changes in birth- and death-rates the age composition of the population has also changed. The proportion of the population aged 65 years or more (the elderly) was almost constant between 1865 and 1950, but has increased steadily since 1950 (Table 8.2). Much greater changes are found in the proportion of the population 0–14-year-olds (juveniles) and 15–64-year-olds (the productive age-group). The proportion of juveniles increased between 1865 and 1920, remained constant between 1920 and 1950, and decreased rapidly between 1950 and 1985. The proportion of the population in the productive age-group decreased (increased) each time the proportion of juveniles increased (decreased). These demographic changes were primarily the result of changes in the birth-rate. The increase in the birth-rate until 1920 caused a relative increase in the juvenile population and a relative decrease in the productive age-group, but a decrease in the birth-rate after 1920 terminated this trend. A further decrease in the birth-rate during the post-war period caused a relative decline in the juvenile population and a relative increase in the productive age-group and the elderly. The 'ageing' of the population today is a result of the decreasing birth-rate.

The sum of the juvenile and elderly populations is sometimes referred to as the 'dependent population', since they usually do not work and are dependent upon the productive age-group. The dependent population increased from 1865 to 1920 and decreased between 1920 and 1970. Because of the ageing of the population, however, it increased again in the 1970s and is expected to rise further in the future.

TABLE 8.2   Age composition of the population in Japan 1865–1985 (%)

	Age composition			Dependent population ratio[a]
	0–14	*15–64*	*65 or over*	
1865	31.3	63.4	5.3	57.8
1880	32.4	62.2	5.3	60.7
1900	32.9	61.7	5.3	62.0
1920	36.5	58.3	5.2	71.6
1930	36.6	58.7	4.8	70.5
1940	36.1	59.2	4.7	69.0
1950	35.4	59.6	4.9	67.7
1970	30.2	64.1	5.7	55.9
1980	24.0	68.9	7.1	45.1
1985	23.5	67.3	9.2	48.4
1985	21.5	68.2	10.3	46.6

Note:
[a] Population aged 14 years or less and 65 years or over ÷ population aged 15–64 years × 100.

Sources:
1865–1900: Yasukawa's 1972 estimates taken from Ōbuchi, 1974, p. 61, table 2.1, p. 282, table 9.1:
1920–85: *Kokusei Chōsa* (Population Census) taken from Sōmuchō, Tōkeikyoku, 1990, pp. 62–8.

Table 8.1 shows that the age composition of the populations of Japan, North America, Europe and the former USSR were similar in 1985. In the developing countries of Africa, Latin America and south Asia the proportion of juveniles was very large and the productive age-group very small. The dependent population ratio was only 50–60 per cent in the developed countries, but 80–90 per cent in the developing countries. The difference in the age composition between these two groups of countries resulted from the relatively low birth-rate in the developed countries. The high dependent population ratio, together with the high population growth rate, hampers progress in the developing countries.

8.1.4   Population Growth and the Economy

We have already pointed out that the population increased relatively slowly in Japan during modern economic growth compared to western developed countries. How did this affect economic development? Population increases tend to accelerate economic growth by increasing the supply of labour, but at the same time slow it down by increasing consumption or reducing savings and investment. It seems to us that had population increased rapidly in Japan its beneficial effects would have been small since there was already an abundant labour force, and that there would have been a large increase in the consumption of scarce capital. Therefore, the moderate population increase was probably favourable to economic development. Lockwood said:

> It is doubtful that Japan's rise as an industrial power, or her whole process of economic development, can be regarded as having been stimulated or advanced by rapid population growth in any significant fashion. Whether viewed from the standpoint of markets, of technology, or of capital accumulation, it appears to have been a decided deterrent to economic progress – certainly in per capita terms.[7]

The low rate of population growth (0.5–0.7 per cent) was a great advantage for Japan at the start of modern economic growth. Contemporary developing countries have a population growth rate of about 3 per cent.[8]

As the demand for labour increased due to economic growth, the birth-rate and the population growth rate increased. This increased the demand for food, which resulted in a food shortage and the rice riots of 1918. In the recessionary years that followed, the demand for labour decreased and disguised unemployment increased (Ch. 9, Sec. 2). In the great depression of 1930 unemployment increased considerably, and this encouraged recognition of the 'over-population problem'. For a time scholars and journalists claimed that population control was necessary, but the rate of population growth began to decline, and soon the armed forces were demanding more recruits. The government initiated a campaign encouraging people to 'have babies and increase the population', and from 1941 began giving economic benefits to large families.

The unprecedentedly large increase in population immediately after the Second World War resulted in reduced living standards and increased unemployment. In 1948 the government passed the Eugenic Protection Law legalizing abortion. The population growth rate decreased rapidly during the 1950s and the economy began to expand rapidly from the mid-1950s. Standards of living improved and unemployment declined; the population problem was resolved. However, the transformation from a labour surplus to a labour shortage around 1960 prompted some people, especially those in industry, to insist that a population increase, via a stimulation of the birth-rate and a substantial introduction of foreign workers, was necessary.

8.1.5 Age Composition and the Economy

When Japan commenced modern economic growth in the mid-1880s, she had a dependent population ratio of about 60 per cent. This is low compared to both the ratio in later years (it exceeded 70 per cent in 1920) and the figure for contemporary developing countries, which have ratios as large as 80–90 per cent.

The low dependent population ratio in Meiji Period Japan favoured economic growth for two reasons.[9] First, with a larger productive age-group, per capita GNP will be relatively large, even if GNP per labourer or GNP per productive-age person is not. Second, a low dependent ratio tends to increase savings, because the juvenile population does not save and the elderly population dissaves.

As was mentioned above, the dependent population ratio increased during the 1970s and according to some projections will increase much more. This may be detrimental to economic growth (Ch. 12, Sec. 2).

8.2 LABOUR SUPPLY

8.2.1 The Increase in the Labour Force

Japan's labour force increased at an annual compound rate of 0.52 per cent in both the period 1880–1900 and the period 1900–20,[10] and the labour supply increased from the beginning of the modern economic growth until the latter half of the 1950s (for later years see Table 8.3).[11] During the early 1970s the growth rate of labour supply fell to a low of 0.4 per cent. This fall was closely connected with the decline in the economic growth rate.

The labour participation rate (the ratio of the labour force to the population aged 15 years and over) declined between 1920 and 1975, but because the population growth rate increased until the early 1960s, the growth of the labour force accelerated. The population growth rate was 1.9–2.3 per cent in the 1950s and the first half of the 1960s, resulting in a rapid increase in the labour force. This helps to explain Japan's high economic growth rate in this period.[12] The unprecedentedly rapid population increase during the first half of the 1960s was a result of the baby boom of 1947–9. Since the early 1970s the population growth rate has been falling. Population grew only 1.1–1.3 per cent in the 1970s. This, and a decline in the labour participation rate, caused a decline in the growth rate of the labour force.

TABLE 8.3   Growth rates of population aged 15 years or over and labour force in Japan 1920–85

	Population aged 15 years or over	Labour force
1920–30	1.41	0.99
1930–40	1.34	1.35
1940–50	1.52	1.18
1950–60	1.61	1.91
1960–70	1.90	1.86
1970–80	1.19	0.71
1980–5	1.20	1.08

Notes:
Annual compound rate of growth between the two years indicated.

Sources:
Kokusei Chōsa (Population Census) taken from Sōmuchō, Tōkeikyoku, 1990, pp. 126–9.

8.2.2   The Labour Participation Rate

Table 8.4 shows that the aggregate labour participation rate in Japan decreased from 73 per cent to 64 per cent between 1920 and 1985. This decline was caused primarily by a decline in the participation rate of the 15–24 years age-group in both sexes. This was because of a rise in the numbers of children receiving higher education, as increased income allowed people to spend more on education and industrialization reduced the demand for family workers (in this case, children) in agriculture.

The labour participation rate has shown several short-term fluctuations; it declined in 1930 and 1975 due to decreasing demand for labour and rose in 1940. In 1975 the participation rate decreased significantly and noticeably slowed the increase in total labour supply. There was a rise in the female participation rate in 1940, when demand for female labourers increased as large numbers of male workers were conscripted into the armed forces. The female participation rate tends to fluctuate more because female workers enter the labour market when demand for labour increases, and return home when demand decreases. This 'fringe labour force' has 'cushioned' fluctuations in the labour market.[13]

The labour participation rate of female workers, according to Hiromi Arisawa and Iwao Ozaki (for Japan) and P. H. Douglas (for the USA), was positively correlated with their wages and negatively correlated with the wages of household heads.[14] The negative cor-

TABLE 8.4 Male and female labour participation rates in Japan 1920–85 (%)

	Male	Female	Total
1920	92.2	53.4	72.8
1930	90.5	49.1	69.8
1940	90.1	52.6	71.1
1950	83.4	48.7	65.4
1960	85.0	50.9	67.4
1970	84.3	50.9	67.1
1975	83.4	46.1	64.2
1980	82.1	46.9	64.0
1985	80.4	47.7	63.6

Sources:
Same as Table 8.3.

relation of female participation rates with wages of household heads suggests that wives and daughters are forced to work in order to compensate for a decrease in family income when men's wages fall. This relation is referred to as the 'Douglas–Arisawa law'.

According to one estimate the labour participation rate in Japan was 90.2 per cent in 1880 and 83.8 per cent in 1900,[15] it has decreased throughout this century. The labour participation rate of male workers in western countries also has declined as more children receive higher education. The labour participation rate of young females has decreased but older females' participation rates have increased in many western countries. As a result of the increased participation rates of older females in the USA the average rate for all female workers increased substantially during the post-war period.[16]

Table 8.5 compares participation rates in several countries in 1980–7. The international variation in female labour participation rates is much greater than in male labour participation rates, as a result of economic factors (e.g. income, level of industrialization) and institutional factors (e.g. religion, social practices, the social security system). The extremely high rate of labour participation among females in China (70 per cent) has come from the socialist egalitarianism since the liberation in 1949. The extremely low rate in India (30 per cent) and Pakistan (32 per cent) is due to Islamic laws regarding women's social activities. The relatively high rate of labour participation among elderly male workers in Japan (and the resulting high average participation rate; 80 per cent) partly explained by the lack of a social security system which provides an income sufficient to live on after retirement.

TABLE 8.5   International comparison of labour participation rates 1980–7
(%)

	Year	Male	Female
China	1987	84.7	69.5
USA	1987	73.9	54.2
UK	1986	71.9	48.2
Japan	1985	80.4	47.7
France	1987	65.4	45.8
Korea	1987	68.1	44.9
Former West Germany	1986	71.7	42.0
Mexico	1980	82.8	30.1
Pakistan	1981	72.4	31.8
India	1981	83.1	29.9

Note:
Labour participation rates = labour force ÷ population aged 15 years or over (16 years
or over for USA) × 100.

Sources:
YLS, 1988, pp. 27–47. For China only, Minami, 1993, table 8.4.

SUMMARY OF THE CHAPTER

The low population growth rate and the low proportion of dependent population facilitated Japan's modern economic growth. The population growth rate rose with economic growth but its rise was moderate. The exceptionally high population density Japan inherited from premodern times was a continuing problem that reduced productivity in agriculture and caused a large surplus of labour.

Despite a long-term fall in the labour participation rate the growth rate of the labour force (an indicator of labour supply) increased in the long term because of a rise in the growth rate of the productive age-group. The growth rate of the labour force was high during the 1950s and 1960s and helped sustain the high growth rate of the economy in this period. In the 1970s the growth rate of the labour force fell steeply, due to a fall in both the growth rate of the productive age-group and the labour participation rate.

FURTHER READING

Ōbuchi, 1976; 1979
Shirai and Shimada, 1979
Tachi and Okazaki, 1965
Taeuber, 1958
Umemura, 1979

9 Labour Market and Dual Structure

This chapter analyzes the changes in the labour market that have accompanied economic growth. In Section 9.1 we discuss industrialization – the rise in the importance of 'industry' in the national economy – a phenomenon that caused employment to shift from primary to non-primary industries. If the supply of labour is greater than demand the difference must become either unemployed or surplus labour. Japan absorbed a large pool of surplus labour as a result of high economic growth in the early post-war period. We analyze this process in Section 9.2. Wages and income shares are determined by demand and supply. In Section 9.3 historical changes in wages and wage differentials are discussed in relation to the dual structure theory. In Section 9.4 changes in relative income share of labour are argued.

9.1 OVERALL INDUSTRIAL STRUCTURE OF EMPLOYMENT

9.1.1 Historical Changes

The availability of jobs in a particular sector is directly related to the demand for the goods or services produced by that sector. During the period 1910–38 the annual growth rate of employment was approximately zero in the primary (A) sector and 2 per cent in the non-primary ($M + S$) sector (Table 9.1). In the period 1956–87 it was – 3 per cent and 2 per cent, respectively. The growth rate of employment in the M Sector (mining, manufacturing, construction and infrastructure industries) was much higher than in the S Sector (commerce and services) during the pre-war period, but much smaller during the post-war period.

TABLE 9.1 Growth rate of labour force, relative contribution of major industry groups to growth of labour force, and composition of labour force in Japan 1889–1987 (%)

	Primary (A)	M Sector	S Sector	Non-primary (M + S)	All industries (A + M + S)
(A) Rate of growth					
1889–1900	−0.03	–	–	1.84	0.58
1901–10	−0.33	1.55[a]	2.42[a]	1.77	0.45
1911–20	−0.56	3.38	1.33	2.24	0.64
1921–30	0.04	1.02	2.21	1.61	0.80
1931–8	−0.28	3.06	1.28	2.16	1.00
(1910–38)	−0.22	2.35	1.66	1.91	0.68
1956–60	−2.35	4.60	3.35	3.95	1.79
1961–70	−4.10	3.53	2.74	3.13	1.40
1971–80	−3.95	0.74	2.49	1.64	0.86
1981–7	−2.61	0.64	2.05	1.41	1.03
Post-war average	−3.45	2.19	2.61	2.42	1.21
(B) Relative contribution[b]					
1888–1900	−3.0	–	–	103.0	100.0
1900–10	−47.0	–	–	147.0	100.0
1910–20	−49.5	104.2	45.3	149.7	100.0
1920–30	2.3	30.7	67.0	97.7	100.0
1930–8	−13.3	80.0	33.3	113.3	100.0
(1910–38)	−17.4	69.0	48.4	117.4	100.0
1955–60	−44.8	80.6	64.2	144.8	100.0
1960–70	−69.3	94.5	74.8	169.3	100.0
1970–80	−64.3	36.0	128.3	164.3	100.0
1980–7	−24.0	25.4	98.6	124.0	100.0
Post-war average	−53.4	62.8	90.6	153.4	100.0
(C) Composition					
1888	69.9	–	–	30.1	100.0
1900	65.0	–	–	35.0	100.0
1910	60.2	18.6	21.2	39.8	100.0
1920	53.4	23.9	22.7	46.6	100.0
1930	49.5	24.4	26.1	50.5	100.0
1938	44.7	28.7	26.6	55.3	100.0
1955	37.1	29.7	33.3	62.9	100.0
1960	30.1	34.0	35.9	69.9	100.0
1970	17.2	41.8	41.0	82.8	100.0

TABLE 9.1   continued

	Primary (A)	M Sector	S Sector	Non-primary (M + S)	All industries (A + M + S)
1980	10.6	41.3	48.1	89.4	100.0
1987	8.2	40.2	51.6	91.8	100.0

Notes:
[a] 1910.
[b] Increase of sectoral employment ÷ increase in total labour force × 100.
The figures for the growth rate are simple averages of the annual growth rate.
The figures for employment are seven-year moving averages (five-year averages for 1938 and 1987).

Sources:
Pre-war period: Minami, 1973, pp. 312–13.
Post-war period: *Rōdōryoku Chōsa* (Labour Force Survey) taken from KTN, various issues. Discontinuity in this series was adjusted (see Minami, 1973, p. 91).

As a result of these differences there has been a shift in the sectoral structure of employment. The *A* Sector's share of total employment decreased from 70 per cent in 1888, to 45 per cent in 1938 and to 8 per cent in 1987. The *M* Sector's share increased from 19 per cent in 1910 to 40 per cent in 1987, while the *S* Sector's share increased from 21 per cent to 52 per cent. The increase in the *S* Sector's share during the 1970s and 1980s was particularly large (11 percentage points, from 41 per cent to 52 per cent).

There has been a decrease in the *A* Sector's share of employment and an increase in the *M* and *S* Sectors' share in all developed countries (Figure 9.1)[1] The *A* Sector's share of employment was between 50 and 70 per cent in most of these countries when modern economic growth began. (In Great Britain it was only 36 per cent in 1801[12] and 22 per cent in 1841, but it was undoubtedly much larger in earlier years.[3]) Australia is an exception: The *A* Sector's share was only 30 per cent in 1861. It increased slightly during the period 1861–81, but decreased sharply thereafter. The *A* Sector's share has declined steadily in all other developed countries. Meanwhile, both the *M* and *S* Sector's share has increased in all these countries. Since the 1920s the *S* Sector has generally increased more than the *M* Sector. In the late 1960s V. R. Fuchs argued that the USA had entered a stage of economic development where more than half of employment was not engaged in the production of commodities. He

214

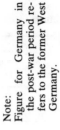

FIGURE 9.1 Major industry groups' shares of workers in employment in the developed countries 1840–1990

Note:
Figure for Germany in the post-war period refers to the former West Germany.

Sources:
Japan: Table 9.1
European countries: Mitchell, 1978, pp. 51–61.
USA: US, Department of Commerce, Bureau of the Census, 1975, p. 139.
Canada: Firestone, 1958, p. 185.
Australia: 1861–91 – Butlin, 1964, p. 194, table 40, 1901–39 – Clark, 1951, p. 428.
USA since 1970, Canada and Australia since 1950, and other countries since 1975: YLS, various issues.

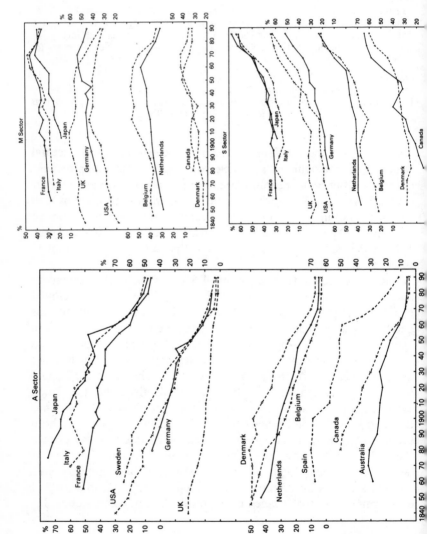

called this a 'service economy'.[4] Other developed countries such as Canada, the UK, Sweden and the Netherlands all followed the same pattern as the USA. Japan is not an exception.

That a shift in employment occurred, first, from the A to the M Sector, and later to the S Sector, was first hypothesized by W. Petty ('Petty's Law') and confirmed empirically by C. Clark.[5] This pattern is not always seen in developing countries; in many of them the A Sector's share of employment was constant for a long time and has only recently begun to decline. In developing countries the S Sector's share of employment has tended to increase much faster than the M Sector's share.[6] (This trend would be even more noticeable if farmers who are engaged in commerce on a part-time basis were included in employment for the S Sector.) However, unlike in the developed countries, this has not been the result of industrialization, but is due to the absorption of low-wage, unskilled labour by the S Sector.

Figure 9.2 depicts the relationships between sectoral shares of total employment (L_A/L, L_M/L and L_S/L) and per capita GNP in 1987 in various countries around the world, and hence the operation of Petty's Law. Initially, as per capita GNP increases L_A/L falls, while L_M/L and L_S/L rise sharply. As per capita GNP rises further, L_A/L converges to a minimum level, L_M/L begins to decrease and L_S/L continues to increase.

9.1.2 Determinants of the Industrial Structure of Employment

The ratio of employment in a particular industry (L_i) to total employment ($L = \Sigma L_i$) can be rewritten as:

$$L_i/L = (Y_i/Y) \div \left(\frac{Y_i}{L_i}\bigg/\frac{Y}{L}\right),$$

where Y_i denote GDP of industry, i. Variables without a suffix represent the total economy ($Y = \Sigma Y_i$). If we express labour productivity (Y_i/L_i and Y/L) as y_i and y we have

$$L_i/L = (Y_i/Y) \div (y_i/y)$$

The first item on the right hand side of the equation (Y_i/Y) is an index of the industrial structure of output. The second item (y_i/y) is an index of relative labour productivity. This equation shows that an

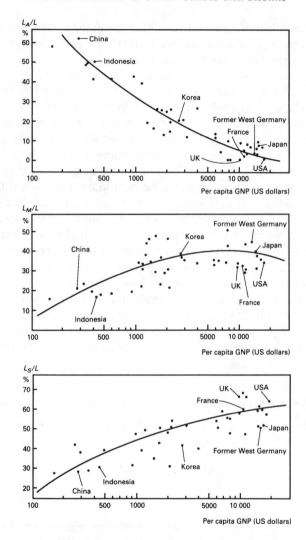

FIGURE 9.2   Relationships between major industry groups' shares of
workers in employment and per capita GNP 1987

Notes:
Where 1987 figures are not available, the figures for 1985 on 1986 are used.
For the per capita GNP the figure for 1987 is used in order to make this diagram
  comparable to Figure 5.2. The number of countries is 41.

Sources:
L: YLS, 1988. *L* for China is from Minami, 1993, table 1.2. Per capita GNP: Same as
  Fig. 5.2.

TABLE 9.2   Relative labour productivity of major industry groups in Japan
1888–1987

	Nominal			Real[a]		
	A	M	S	A	M	S
1988	0.64	–	–	0.59	–	–
1900	0.63	–	–	0.53	–	–
1910	0.61	1.72	1.51	0.52	1.38	2.02
1920	0.55	1.73	1.36	0.46	1.34	1.90
1930	0.40	1.86	1.33	0.42	1.78	1.36
1938	0.41	1.87	1.04	0.36	1.80	1.21
1955	0.45	1.53	1.13	0.45	0.99	1.62
1960	0.39	1.45	1.10	0.42	1.07	1.41
1970	0.37	1.20	1.03	0.36	1.13	1.13
1980	0.36	1.13	1.03	0.34	1.11	1.05
1987	0.33	1.14	1.00	0.33	1.14	1.00

Notes:
Refer to the text for the definition of relative labour productivity.
Labour productivity is represented by GDP per capita.
[a] At 1934–6 prices for the pre-war period, and at 1985 prices for the post-war period.
All the figures are seven-year moving averages (five-year averages for 1938, 1955 and
    1987).

Sources:
GDP: Table 5.1; Fig. 5.1.
Labour force: Table 9.1.

increase in the share of labour employed by a particular industry
can be attributed to a rise in the share of output produced by that
industry and/or a decline in the relative labour productivity of that
industry.

We have already shown that the A Sector's share of GDP (Y_A/Y)
has decreased, while the shares of the M and S Sectors $(Y_M/Y, Y_S/Y)$
have increased. These changes are major determinants of changes in
L_i/L, but Table 9.2 shows that a decline in relative labour productivity (y_i/y) in both nominal and real terms in both the A and S Sectors
has tended to raise L_i/L. This decline was brought about by limited
land area (a major factor in agricultural production), the heavy
dependence on labour in providing services, and the existence of
surplus labour in both the A and S Sectors. A rise in relative output
prices, caused by a slow increase in productivity, prevented y_i/y in
nominal term from decreasing to the same extent as y_i/y in real terms.
However, changes in relative output prices did not cancel out the

decrease in y_i/y in real terms. In the M Sector, on the other hand, y_i/y increased, both in nominal terms and in real terms, during the prewar period. However, during the post-war period, although y_i/y increased in real terms, y_i/y decreased in nominal terms due to a fall in relative output prices.

Thus we may conclude: First, the decline in the A Sector's share of employment was due solely to the decline in its share of output. The decrease in relative labour productivity was not large enough to cancel out the effect of the change in the industrial structure. Second, the rise in the M Sector's share of employment was due solely to the increase in its share of output. The increase in relative labour productivity reduced the fall in relative employment. Third, the rise in the S Sector's share of employment was the result of both an increase in relative output and a decrease in relative labour productivity.

Kuznets calculates the relative productivity of A, M and S industries from the middle of the nineteenth century up to the 1960s among six countries: Denmark, Norway, Sweden, Italy, the USA and Australia.[7] According to his calculations, the relative productivity of A and S industries decreased in the majority of these countries, both in nominal figures and in real amounts. This fact agrees with Japan's experience. Australia is the only exception here, where A industry significantly increased. In Australia, due to the development of mechanised farming for this vast land, a marked improvement was detected in its agricultural productivity.

Next, I shall analyze the differences that exist among nations in the area of their relative productivity, basing calculations on the most recent (1987) data. Table 9.3 indicates the average value of relative productivity in each group after dividing forty-one countries into six groups by their per capita GNP figures. According to Table 9.3, the relative productivity in the A industry initially decreases, because of the increase in per capita GNP, but then it goes up after reaching per capita GNP of between $2000 and $5000, the trend drawing a U-shaped curve. On the other hand, the relative productivity in the M and S industries shows their tendency to decrease relative productivity when income goes up. This tendency is more apparent in S industries than in the M industries. (In the M industry relative productivity goes up when the per capita GNP exceeds $5000–$10 000. However, the extent of this increase is much smaller when it is compared to the decrease that occurred before it reached $5000.) This analysis points up the very interesting fact that income difference

TABLE 9.3 International comparison of the relative labour productivity of major industry groups 1987

Per capita GNP (dollars)	Number of countries	A	M	S
Less than 1000	6	0.56	1.96	1.20
1000–1999	5	0.53	1.42	1.07
2000–4999	8	0.42	1.10	1.03
5000–9999	6	0.60	1.07	1.03
10 000–12 999	7	0.67	1.20	0.94
13 000 or more	9	1.19	1.12	0.97

Note:
Simple averages of the relative labour productivity (y_i/y) for all countries belonging to the respective groups.

Sources:
y_i/y is calculated by dividing Y_i/Y (Fig. 5.2) by L_i/L (Fig. 9.2).
Per capita GNP: Same as Fig. 5.2.

expands in line with economic development and this changes to a reduction when economic development reaches to a certain stage.[8]

9.1.3 Historical Changes in Primary Employment

The number of employees in primary industries decreased relatively in most of the nations. One wonders what changes can be detected in absolute numbers. The number of employees in the primary sector in Japan remained roughly constant at 15 million during the period from 1870 to the mid-1950s, then suddenly decreased (Table 9.4). An absolute decrease like this can be detected in other nations, but the time of occurrence differs from country to country. In Ireland the number had already started to decrease by 1840; also in England, the number had started to decrease by 1860. The beginning of a decrease in other countries were: 1880 in Belgium, 1900 in the USA, 1920 in France and Italy, and just after 1930 in Sweden. Most of the other developed countries started to decrease their number of employees in the primary sector just after 1940. In Japan as well as in Spain the number remained the same for a fairly long time. The rapid economic development in many nations after the Second World War made possible the decrease in the numbers in primary-sector employment, or accelerated it in these nations.

TABLE 9.4   Employment in the primary sector in the developed countries
1800–1990 (000s people)

	Japan	UK	France	Sweden	USA	Australia
1800	–	–	–	–	1 405	–
1820	–	–	–	–	2 484	–
1840	–	1 539[b]	–	–	3 594	–
1860	15 883[a]	1 982[c]	7 305[h]	664	5 911	137[c]
1880	15 918	1 694[d]	–	1 070	8 961	279[d]
1900	15 897	1 476[e]	8 245[e]	1 108	11 749	371[e]
1920	14 442	1 372[f]	9 023[f]	1 059	10 843	527[f]
1940	14 192	–	7 204[i]	733[k]	9 635	564[l]
1960	13 400	874[g]	3 907[j]	447	6 015	468[g]
1990	4 510	569	1 325	149	3 355	425

Notes:
[a] 1872; [b] 1841; [c] 1861; [d] 1881; [e] 1901; [f] 1921; [g] 1961; [h] 1856; [i] 1936; [j] 1962; [k] 1945; [l] 1939.

Sources:
Same as Fig. 9.1. The figures for Australia are unpublished estimates by Katsuo Ōtsuka.

Japan's experience, with the numbers engaged in primary industries unchanged at the beginning of its economic development, is striking. Most countries in the world experienced an increase in numbers. In particular, the tendency was significant in the USA, Australia and Finland. Although it was to a lesser extent, the same phenomenon happened in Italy, France, Sweden, Denmark, Holland and Norway. In England the figure on primary employment is available only from 1841. The number obviously increased from that year until 1851. We can imagine that this tendency to increase had already happened before 1841. In the past, there was a general recognition that the population in agricultural villages decreased dramatically because of the policy of enclosure. However, J. Chambers analysed the available data and showed that since farming in those days was labour-intensive, the agricultural revolution, which happened side by side with the Industrial Revolution, created rather than diminished a demand for agricultural labourers.[9]

The reason why Japan did not experience the phenomenon of increase in the primary employment was that Japanese villages already had a high population density at the beginning of industrialization, and therefore could not accommodate a greater labour

TABLE 9.5   Causes of changes in labour force in the primary sector in Japan 1876–1990 (000s people)

	Changes in primary labour force				Changes in non-primary labour force	
	Total increase (1)	Natural increase (2)	Net outflow (2)–(1) = (3)	Rate of net outflow (4) (%)	Total increase (5)	Dependence on primary labour force (3)/(5)=(6) (%)
1876–90	–8	72	80	0.76	109	73.4
1891–1990	9	86	77	0.51	120	64.2
1901–10	–73	68	141	0.90	180	78.3
1911–20	–73	94	167	1.10	237	70.5
1921–30	5	121	116	0.78	233	49.8
1931–40	–30	135	165	1.07	319	51.7
Pre-war average	–27	94	121	0.85	193	62.7
1951–60	–465	342	807	5.15	1 355	59.6
1961–70	–454	153	607	4.70	1 112	54.6
1971–80	–309	60	369	4.25	716	51.5
1981–90	–126	60	186	3.65	839	22.2
Post-war average	–339	154	493	4.44	1 006	49.0

Note:
All figures are annual.

Sources:
See note 10 in this chapter for details of the procedure used to estimate the natural increase and the net outflow of the primary labour force.
Employment for the two sectors is taken from Table 9.1.

force in their limited lands. This condition was completely different from that in the new countries such as the USA or Australia where the amount of cultivated land was suddenly increased by pioneering by only a small number of the population.

9.1.4   Outflow of Labour from the Primary Sector

An increase in the agricultural labour force (Table 9.5, column 1) is equal to the difference between its natural increase (new entries – retirements and deaths) (column 2) and net outflow (outflow–inflow) (column 3).[10] The table shows that during the pre-war period the size of the agricultural labour force remained almost constant, because net outflow was just large enough to compensate for the natural increase. During the post-war period the agricultural labour force decreased remarkably because net outflow accelerated.

The primogeniture system of the pre-war period meant that if the eldest son of a farmer stayed in agriculture he inherited all the land and buildings owned by his family. If he left agriculture he inherited virtually nothing.[11] As a result, eldest sons rarely left agriculture. We believe, however, that had the demand for labour in the non-primary industries increased much faster than it did, the movement of agricultural labour would have accelerated and eldest sons would have begun to leave agriculture. Our hypothesis contrasts sharply with Masayoshi Namiki's 'hypothesis of a constant agricultural labour force (or constant farm household population)'.[12] He attributes the constant agricultural population during the pre-war period solely to the primogeniture system.[13]

After the abolition of primogeniture in 1948 eldest sons began to leave agriculture and rapid economic growth from the mid-1950s increased the demand for non-agricultural labour, causing substantial migration of agricultural labourers. Also the proportion of middle- and high-school leavers who took jobs in agriculture decreased from 50 per cent in 1950, to 10 per cent in 1960 and to less than 5 per cent since 1965.[14] As a result, the average age of the agricultural population has increased.

Agriculture has supplied labour for the non-primary sector. Net outflow from the primary labour force accounted for 73 per cent of the total increase in the non-primary labour force during the period 1876–90 (Table 9.5, column 6). Migration from the primary sector accounted for 50–60 per cent of the increase in the non-primary labour force up to the 1970s, while it decreased to about 20 per cent in the 1980s.[15]

9.1.5 Changes in the Employment Structure

The number of employees (workers employed for wages and salaries) increased remarkably during the period 1920–85 (Table 9.6). The number of self-employed workers was almost constant during this period and the number of family workers (members of self-employed workers' families) increased only slightly from 1920 to 1950 and decreased thereafter. Overall, the percentage of employment accounted for by self-employed and family workers decreased, while the percentage for employees increased. This change in the employment structure has been closely related to industrialization; workers in the primary sector are almost all self-employed or family members,

TABLE 9.6   Composition of workers in employment in Japan 1920–85 (%)

	Employees	Self-employed workers	Unpaid family workers	Total[a]
1920	30.7	32.8	36.5	100.0
1930	32.4	32.7	34.9	100.0
1940[b]	41.9	26.2	31.9	100.0
1950	39.3	26.2	34.4	100.0
1960	53.9	22.1	24.0	100.0
1970	64.2	19.5	16.3	100.0
1985	75.4	15.4	9.2	100.0

Notes:
[a] Including unclassified.
[b] Civilians in Japan.

Sources:
Kokusei Chōsa (Population Census). 1920–30–Shōwa Dōjinkai, 1957, p. 40. 1940–
    Sōrifu, Tōkeikyoku, 1962, pp. 208–9. 1950–70–Sōrifu, Tōkeikyoku, 1980, p. 87.
    1985–Sōmuchō, Tōkeikyoku, 1990, p. 145.

whereas in the non-primary sector almost all are employees. Furthermore, the proportion of employees in both the *M* and *S* Sectors increased rapidly during the period 1920–85.

The argument that the modernization of the employment structure resulted from economic development could be explained by comparing it to other nations' experiences. Modern nations such as the USA or the former West Germany have quite a high ratio of employees while the ratio of the self-employed and people engaged in family businesses is high in the developing countries such as Thailand or Indonesia (Table 9.7). The proportion of employees in total employment (η) among the thirty countries where the figures can be obtained is closely correlated with per capita GNP (y).[16]

$$\eta = 42.742 + 0.00295y \qquad \bar{r} = 0.848 \; F = 71.5$$

The proportion which is calculated from the above expression ($\hat{\eta}$) is 89 per cent, exceeding the actual score (η) of 74.9 per cent. It is possible to say that the modernization of the labour market in Japan is delayed compared to the process of economic development which is measured against per capita income. When the fact is considered

TABLE 9.7 International comparison of composition of workers in employment 1984–90 (%)

		Employees	Self-employed workers	Unpaid family workers	Total[a]
USA	1989	91.0	8.1	0.3	100.0
Former West Germany	1987	88.4	8.6	3.0	100.0
UK	1987	79.3	10.3[b]	–	100.0
Japan[c]	1990	75.7	13.8	8.1	100.0
France	1987	74.7	11.3	3.3	100.0
Italy	1989	62.8	21.5	3.8	100.0
South Korea	1989	57.6	28.1	11.7	100.0
Thailand	1984	24.2	30.2	43.4	100.0
Indonesia	1988	25.7	41.9	29.6	100.0

Notes:
[a] Including unclassified employees.
[b] Including unpaid family workers.
[c] Figures from the Rōdōryoku Chōsa (Labour Force Survey).

Sources: KTY, 1991, pp. 35–41.

that only thirty years have passed since the excess number of labourers disappeared, delayed modernization might be quite an expected phenomenon in Japan.

9.2 SURPLUS LABOUR AND THE TURNING-POINT

9.2.1 The Labour Force – Supply and Demand

The post-war movements of two indicators of the excess supply of labour; the rate of unemployment (U – the ratio of the number unemployed to the total labour force) and the ratio of applications for jobs to openings (V) (Table 9.8) demonstrate that the labour surplus decreased sharply during the period 1955–65, when rapid economic growth brought about an increase in the demand for labour. The surplus increased during the 1970s and the first half of the 1980s, a period of slow economic growth, but it turned into a decrease by the late 1980s.

Table 9.8 also shows another index (U'), the ratio of the number

TABLE 9.8 Rate of unemployment and the ratio of applications for jobs to openings 1955–90 (%)

| | Unemployment rate | | Ratio of applications to openings |
	U	U'	V
1955	2.6	5.9	1.04
1960	1.6	3.2	0.60
1965	1.1	2.0	0.28
1970	1.2	1.8	0.15
1975	2.0	2.7	0.27
1980	2.0	2.9	0.51
1985	2.6	3.6	0.56
1990	2.1	2.8	0.39

Notes:
U = (number of unemployed ÷ number in labour forces) × 100.
U' = (number of unemployed ÷ number of employees) × 100.
V = junior and senior high-school leavers only.

Sources:
U and the number of employees: *Rōdōryoku Chōsa* (Labour Force Survey) from RTN, various issues.
V: *Shokugyō Antei Gyōmu Tōkei* (Report of Employment Exchange Activities) from RTN, various issues.

unemployed to 'employees'. This is a better index of surplus labour than U, because the main cause of unemployment is employees losing or leaving their jobs. U' decline more rapidly than U during the period 1955–65 and rose more slowly during the 1970s due to changes in the employment structure.[17]

The 1930 Population Census is the only data available on unemployment at the national level during the pre-war period. From this data U was calculated to be 1.07 per cent and U' 3.21 per cent in that year.[18] These figures are very low compared to those for the early post-war period. Although part of the difference between 1930 and the post-war years is due to a difference in the method of enumeration,[19] it seems reasonable to believe that the rate of unemployment was not very high during the pre-war period, especially when we remember that 1930 was a depression year. However, this does not imply that there was not an unemployment problem in pre-war Japan. Rather, surplus labour seems to have been absorbed by the low-productivity agriculture and service sectors. We believe that surplus labour disappeared some time during the high economic growth of the post-war period.

9.2.2   Concept and Theory of Surplus Labour and the Turning-point

Before a discussion of the point at which surplus labour disappeared we review W. A. Lewis's concept and theory of surplus labour in developing countries,[20] because we believe it is of great use in explaining the Japanese experience. In his model the economy is composed of two sectors: the capitalist sector (C Sector) and the subsistence sector (D Sector). The former, unlike the latter, is characterized by the modern managerial principle: profit maximization. The C Sector is composed of modern large-scale enterprises, the D Sector of agriculture and small-scale enterprises. Figure 9.3 illustrates the historical development of the D Sector. In the early phase of economic development, when the C Sector is very small, a large part of the labour force has to be absorbed by the D Sector, resulting in a low land–labour ratio. The technological level of this sector is low and capital accumulation delayed. As a result, average productivity (AP) and marginal productivity (MP) are low. If MP is lower than the subsistence level of income (SL) wages are equal to SL due to the traditional family wage-setting system. Under this system goods necessary for subsistence are provided for family workers as long as they stay in the household. If these necessities are not forthcoming, their ability to survive is threatened and they may be unable to work. Consequently, wages (implicit wages) tend to be equal to the prevailing subsistence level in the society.

If wages are equal to the subsistence level of income ($w = SL$), the C Sector can attract D Sector workers by providing wages equal to w plus some increment to cover costs for migration. In this case we say that 'unlimited supplies of labour' (USL) or 'surplus labour' exists in the D Sector. As long as surplus labour exists, C Sector wages remain at a constant level and the growth of this sector tends to accelerate. In reality, SL and therefore w has shown a tendency to increase, but the increase has not been very significant.

The difference between total labour supply and employment in the C Sector is absorbed by the D Sector. When employment in the C Sector increases, employment in the D Sector tends to decrease.

Determination of wages

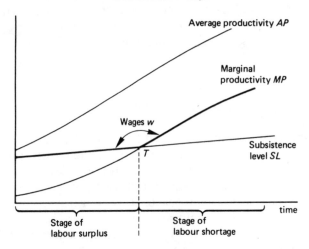

Stage of labour surplus | Stage of labour shortage

Determination of relative share of labour

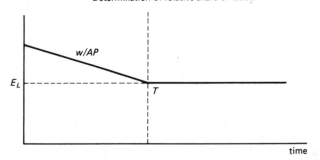

FIGURE 9.3   Model of turning-point theory

This, along with technological improvements and capital formation in the *D* Sector causes an eventual increase in the *MP* of the *D* Sector. Once *MP* exceeds *SL* (the economy passes point *T* in Figure 9.3), *w* is determined by *MP*. '*w* increases rapidly as *MP* increases and pushes up wages in the *C* Sector. As a result, the previously unlimited supplies of labour become 'limited'. The change from a labour sur-plus to a labour shortage leads to an increase in wages and it becomes more difficult to maintain a high rate of growth. The point in time at which this structural change in the labour market takes place is called the 'turning-point' (T). A substantial increase in wages and an improvement in workers' living standards can be realized only after this turning-point is passed. Hence, the turning-point is critical to a country's economic development.

9.2.3   The Turning-point in Japan

Lewisian theory is sometimes referred to as the 'classical approach' because, according to it (as in the classical theory of Malthus, Ricardo and others), wages remain at the subsistence level during the early phase of economic development. This theory has been challenged by the 'neoclassical approach' of D. W. Jorgenson, J. Williamson and others, who assert that wages and their marginal product in agriculture have been equal during all phases of economic development. Japan has been closely involved in this dispute, both sides claiming that the Japanese experience supports their theory.

Lewis suggested that Japan would reach the turning-point sometime in the 1950s as a result of the rapid decline in the crude birth-rate following the Second World War.[21] However, in spite of the decline in the birth-rate, the growth rate of the labour force was much higher in the 1950s and 1960s than in the pre-war period (Table 8.3).

J. C. H. Fei and G. Ranis concluded that the turning-point had already been reached by the end of the First World War, after finding that:[22] (1) the capital–labour ratio in non-primary industries decreased until 1916–19 and then rose, (2) real wages of industrial workers increased rapidly after 1919. However, these studies can be questioned on two counts: (1) there is no theoretical reason to believe there is a connection between the capital–labour ratio and the disappearance of surplus labour. Furthermore, using more up-to-date techniques and data we found no evidence of a decrease in the capital–labour ratio (Table 6.8). (2) Fei and Ranis's data on wages include skilled manufacturing workers. Skilled workers, presumed to have been in short supply during all periods of economic growth, are not considered in the Lewisian theory of the turning-point.

Jorgenson criticized Lewis and Fei–Ranis, asserting that there was no evidence of the existence of surplus labour even before 1917.[23] However, the evidence he gives does not in fact rule out its existence. For instance, he argued that the agricultural labour force should decrease when there is surplus labour. But theoretically the agricultural labour force can increase or decrease regardless of a labour surplus.

A comparison between wages (w) and marginal labour productivity (MP) in agriculture gives relevant data on the turning-point. As Figure 9.3 illustrates, $w = SL$ will be the prevailing relationship before the turning-point and $w = MP$ after it. MP is calculated by multiplying average labour productivity (AP) by the output elasticity of labour (E_L) in Table 9.9.[24] During the pre-war period w was much larger than MP, which implies that there was surplus labour.[25] During the post-war period w has been approximately equivalent to MP, suggesting the absence of surplus labour. However the assumption that E_L has been constant throughout the post-war period is not realistic, so that Table 9.9 alone is insufficient to locate the exact turning-point. Hence we studied the correlation between agricultural wages and average labour productivity (a proxy for MP) in different regions in Japan during the post-war period. The correlation was not positive until the late 1950s. After 1957 we find significant positive correlation indicating that wages are determined by MP.[26]

It is expected that w will not increase significantly before the turning-point, but will increase rapidly after it. Agricultural wages deflated by the consumer price index (general or rural) were almost constant until 1916. They increased rapidly during the period 1916–20, and decreased rapidly thereafter (Figure 9.4). The increase during the period 1916–20 and the decrease in later years were due to changes in the demand for labour. The supply of unskilled workers was limited during the boom years after the First World War, but unlimited during the recession that followed. As a result, real wages remained almost constant throughout the pre-war period. The annual rate of growth in real wages for the period 1896–1938 is 0.2 per cent when we use the general consumer price index and −0.3 per cent when we use the rural index. Real wages increased spectacularly during the post-war period. During the period 1954–87 wages grew at an annual rate of 4.0 per cent and 4.2 per cent, and the growth rate of wages actually accelerated in the late 1950s (Figure 9.4).

From the empirical evidence we conclude that the turning-point was around 1960.

Since the mid-1950s rapid economic growth has caused the demand for labour in the non-primary sector to increase sharply. As a result there has been an unprecedented migration from agriculture (Table 9.5). The M Sector's share of the annual increase in non-primary employment was 56 per cent and the S Sector's 44 per cent for the

TABLE 9.9   Labour productivity and wages in the primary sector in Japan 1900–87

	Output elasticity of labour E_L	Average labour productivity AP	Marginal labour productivity $MP = E_L \cdot AP$	Wages w	Wage–productivity ratio w/AP (%)
		(yen per capita)			
1900	0.170	130	22	108	83
1910	0.170	158	27	105	66
1920	0.170	196	33	122	62
1930	0.183	210	38	163	78
1938	0.294	238	70	118	50
		(000s yen per capita)			
1955	0.562	460	259	219	48
1970	0.562	1142	642	495	43
1987	0.562	2098	1179	896	43

Notes:

AP, *MP* and *w*: 1934–6 prices for the pre-war period and 1985 prices for the post-war period.

The deflator for *AP*, *MP* and *w* is represented by the agricultural price index.

The figures are seven-year moving averages (five year averages for 1938, 1955 and 1987).

Sources:

E_L and *AP*: *Table 4.1*.

w: 1897–1940–Umemura *et al.*, 1966, pp. 220–1.

1952–70–Minami, 1973, p. 298. Since 1971–Extrapolated from the 1970 figure based on the figures in NBCT, 1991, p. 219.

period 1955–60 (Table 9.1). There were 689 000 openings for middle- and high-school leavers in the *M* Sector and 349 000 in the *S* Sector for the period 1956–60.[27] Clearly the *M* Sector absorbed more surplus labour than the *S* Sector.

9.2.4   The Turning-point in Other Countries

Kindleberger's is perhaps the most impressive study of turning-points in countries other than Japan.[28] He argued that in the early half of the nineteenth century England had a high economic growth rate due to the existence of surplus labour, but that in the latter half of the century the growth rate declined as surplus labour was absorbed. In contrast, he said, in the USA there was a virtually unlimited supply of land and a limited supply of labour in the first half of the nineteenth century, while in the latter half of the century fertile land was scarce and labour unlimited. Germany, Italy, Switzerland and the Netherlands, he said, had high economic growth rates in the 1950s as a result of surplus labour, but by the early 1960s the surplus had been absorbed and their growth rates slowed down. He concluded that Lewisian theory on developing economies was more applicable to developed than developing countries.[29]

Fei and Ranis have conducted several studies on developing countries. They concluded that the turning-point was reached in 1965–6 in Taiwan and in 1966–7 in South Korea.[30]

9.2.5 Surplus Labour and Economic Growth

Shinohara has emphasized the importance of surplus labour to economic growth. He argued that there are two ways in which surplus labour accelerates economic growth.[31] The first is on the supply side. Surplus labour leads to slower wage increases, a decline in labour's share of income, and an increase in the savings rate and the rate of capital accumulation. The second is on the demand side. Slower wage increases lead to a fall in export prices and a corresponding increase in exports. Since we have already discussed the latter (Ch. 7, Sec. 3), here we will confine ourselves to the former.

If we accept the hypothesis that surplus labour causes wage (w) increases to lag behind productivity (AP) increases, it follows that this will lead to a decline in labour's share of income ($\pi = w/AP$). (Changes in labour's share of income will be studied in Section 4.)

That a decline in labour's share will lead to an increase in the savings rate and capital accumulation can be deduced from the assumption, made in the 'Cambridge School' savings function, that wages are all consumed and profits are all saved and invested, or, to put it another way, that the rate of savings from non-wage income is much higher than from wage income. To test this assumption we have estimated a savings function for the non-primary sector, including labour's share as one of the independent variables, for data on 1906–40.[32]

232

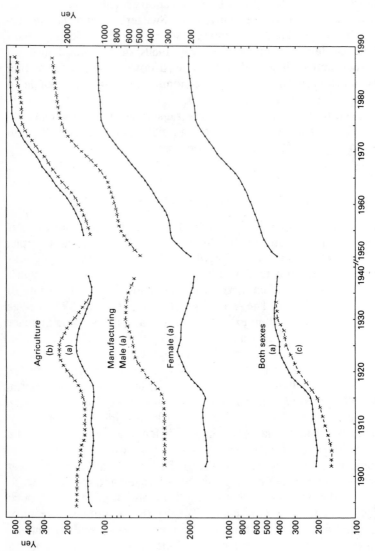

FIGURE 9.4 Real wages in agricultural and manufacturing industries in Japan 1885–1987

Notes:

Agricultural wages: Annual wages of annual contract workers in agriculture.

Manufacturing wages: Annual wage earnings of production workers in establishments with 30 or more workers.

The figures for both the pre-war and the post-war periods are at 1934–6 prices.

Deflators: (a) – The general consumer price index (P_C). (b) – the rural index (P_{CR}). (c) – the urban index (P_{CU}).

The figures used were seven-year moving averages (five-year averages in 1938 and 1987).

Sources:

Agricultural wages: Table 9.9.

Manufacturing wages: Until 1970 – Minami, 1973, pp. 306–7. Since 1971 – Estimated using same data sources and methodology as for pre-1970 period.

P_C: Nominal personal consumption expenditures ÷ real personal consumption expenditures. Real personal consumption expenditures – Fig. 3.3. Nominal personal consumption expenditure – estimated in a similar way to the real figure.

P_{CR} and P_{CU}: Until 1970 – Ono and Watanabe, 1976, p. 387. Since 1971 – Extrapolated from the 1970 figures based on the series in NBCT, 1978, p. 253; 1991, p. 219 and the series in KTN, 1979, p. 313; 1990, p. 319, respectively.

$$\frac{S}{N} = 79.931 + 0.379 \, \frac{Y}{N} - 2.816 \, \pi \quad \bar{R} = 0.915 \quad d = 0.65$$
$$(6.87) \qquad (4.60)$$

where S, Y and N stand for real private gross savings, real GDP (a proxy for personal disposable income) and population, all for the non-primary industries, π is labour's share of Y. The parameter for Y/N (the marginal propensity to save) is positive and less than unity. The negative parameter for π implies that the decline in labour's share was partly responsible for the increase in the savings rate (S/Y). Increased savings allowed an acceleration of capital formation.

There is another possibility that has not been considered by Shinohara: the decline in labour's share may have directly promoted capital formation. The rate of return on capital $(r = (1 - \pi)Y/K)$ increases when π falls, which may stimulate investment by raising the expected rate of return on capital. (The estimate of the investment function in Table 6.4 revealed a positive correlation between investment and return on capital.) Thus, the decline in labour's share may have accelerated both savings and investment and hence stimulated economic growth. If so, trend acceleration was caused partly by the existence of surplus labour.

9.2.6   Labour Shortage and Economic Growth

The change-over from a labour surplus to a shortage brought about several important changes. First, the decline in labour's share of national income came to a halt. This may well have discouraged savings and investment and helped bring about the end of trend acceleration.

Second, the increase in wages paid to unskilled workers caused a decline in the international competitiveness of Japan's labour-intensive textile industry, which had been a leading industry during the pre-war period.

Third, the increased wages paid to unskilled workers raised production costs and hence commodity prices of agricultural and small-scale enterprises, which lead to inflation. Thus, the inflation of the high-growth period could be described as an unavoidable side effect of solving Japan's chronic employment problem (this is discussed in detail in Ch. 11, Sec. 1).

9.3 WAGES, WAGE DIFFERENTIALS AND DUAL STRUCTURE

9.3.1 Changes in Real Wages Over Time

As has already been shown, real agricultural wages remained almost constant during the pre-war period as a whole, but increased during the post-war period, whereas real manufacturing wages for both sexes increased rapidly for several years after 1915. After 1922 female manufacturing wages began to decline, but male wages continued to increase slowly until the Second World War (Figure 9.4). Agricultural wages followed a similar pattern to female manufacturing wages, which implies that the latter, almost all unskilled, came from the same labour market as the former. During the post-war period all manufacturing wages increased considerably, but the growth rate of female wages was higher than that of male wages.

Next let us examine the change in real wages for the whole economy. Table 9.10 shows the weighted averages of real wages for the *A* Sector and real wages for the *M* and *S* Sectors. (These figures were worked out one the supposition of the labour income of self-employed and family workers in each Sector being equal to the wages of employees in each Sector.) That increased during the late 1910s and the 1920s, but decreased in the 1930s. The average growth rate throughout the period 1900–38 was as large as 1.4 per cent. However, we can detect rapid growth after the Second World War. In particular, including the time of high economic growth, the late 1950s and the 1960s saw a growth rate of 7–8 per cent and although the growth rate slowed down after that, even in the 1980s wage increases have kept to a rate of 2 per cent.

The growth rates of real wages (from the middle of the nineteenth century to the present) in France, Germany, Sweden, the UK and the USA are shown in Table 9.11. During the post-war years real wages grew much more rapidly in Japan than in any of these countries as a result of her higher economic growth rate. During the pre-war period also the growth rate of real Japanese wages was higher than in these countries, but only slightly; the difference in economic growth rates was minimal and there was surplus labour in Japan.

In the UK the growth rate of real wages was higher during the period 1864–89 than later years (1890–1910, 1929–35 – Table 9.11). According to Deane and Cole, however, the real wages of agricultu-

TABLE 9.10   Growth rate of real wages in all industries in Japan 1900–87
(%)

	(1)	(2)
1900–9	0.16	–0.23
1910–20	3.18	3.94
1921–30	1.72	1.43
1931–8	0.02	–0.01
(1900–38)	1.39	1.42
1956–60	7.34	7.35
1961–70	8.29	8.23
1971–80	4.67	4.63
1981–7	2.01	1.62
(1956–87)	5.64	5.52

Notes:
The rate set during 1934 and 1936 was kept both before and after the Second World
War. It is the average of real wages in the A Sector and real wages of the M and S
Sectors, the weighted average figure of the number of employees in each industry
every year. In the case of wages in the A Sector, the figures were worked out by
applying annual wages of annual contract workers in agriculture to all the labourers.
Wages in the M and S Sectors were found by dividing the total annual wages and
salaries (including labour evaluation of self-employed and family workers) of
employees by the number of workers. (1) figures were worked out by deflating the
wages of the A, M and S Sectors by P_C, the general consumer price index; and (2)
figures were found by deflating wages of the A Sector by P_{CR} (the rural consumer
price index), and deflating wages of the M and S Sectors by P_{CU} (the urban
consumer price index). The figures are simple averages of the annual growth rate
based on seven-year moving averages (five-year averages for 1908, 1938, 1955 and
1987).

Sources:
Agricultural annual contract workers' wages: Table 9.9. M and S Sectors' wages:
estimated figures, Minami and Ono 1978a, pp. 165–6. However, in 1971 and thereafter the figures were worked out by linking them with an index of the employees'
income that appeared in KKKN (various issues) divided by the number of
employees. P_C, P_{CR}, P_{CU}: Figure 9.4.

ral and construction workers in the UK were constant or declined
during the last four decades of the eighteenth century.[33] In Japan we
know that real wages did not begin to increase until the First World
War. Therefore we may conclude that real wages remained almost
constant during the early phase of industrialization in both Japan and
the UK.

TABLE 9.11   Growth rate of real wages in five western countries
1864–1988 (%)

	France	Germany	Sweden	UK	USA
1864–89	1.14	1.10	2.64	1.95	2.07
1890–1910	0.77	1.19	1.63	0.54	1.19
1929–35	2.03	0.81	1.58[a]	–1.76[a]	0.86[a]
1954–70	4.43	5.15[c]	3.68	2.73	3.00
1971–88	3.19[b]	2.37	0.39	4.30	–0.37

Notes:
The figures are for wages in the major industries (manufacturing for the USA) deflated
by the cost-of-living index.
They are simple averages of the annual growth rate based on seven-year moving
averages (five-year average for 1985 in France and 1988 for the other countries).
[a] 1925–35.
[b] 1971–85.
[c] Former West Germany.

Sources:
To 1960: Phelps Brown, 1968, appx 3.
Since 1961: Extrapolated from the 1960 figures based on the series in YLS, 1970, 1975,
1981 and 1991.

9.3.2 Wage Differentials

Our study of real wages demonstrated that their growth rate differed
from industry to industry, because, we believe, of the difference in
the rate of increase between the wages of skilled workers and those of
unskilled workers. To test this hypothesis we will use here two indices
of wage differentials.

The first is the ratio of manufacturing wages to agricultural wages.
The manufacturing industries are an index of modern industry and
employ a large number of skilled workers such as managers, technicians and office workers, while the agricultural industry is seen as a
typical traditional industry which mostly unskilled labourers. When
we compare the difference in real wages (Figure 9.4), it is obvious
that the ratio of manufacturing wages to agricultural wages increased
significantly during the pre-war period. The ratio was 0.6 at the
beginning of the 1900s, became 0.4 in about 1920 and further reduced
to 0.3 in the late 1930s. The second index we use is the ratio of wages
in large manufacturing establishments to wages in small manufacturing establishments. (Large enterprises are more dependent on skilled
workers than are small enterprises.) In 1909 and 1914 there was little
difference in the wages of large and small enterprises (Table 9.12),

TABLE 9.12   Manufacturing industry wage differentials by size of
establishment in Japan 1909–14

Size (number of production workers)	1909	1914
5–9	100	93
10–29	97	86
30–49	94	81
50–99	94	84
100–499	97	84
500–999	94	91
1 000 or more	100	100
Average	97	88

Notes:
100 represents the largest size group.
The figures are based on the daily wages of production workers.
Gas and electric utilities are included.

Sources: *Kōjō Tōkeihyō* (Census of Manufactures) from Minami, 1973, p. 172, table
8.1.

but by 1932 there was already a significant difference (Table 9.13).
This led Mataji Umemura to conclude that wages first began to differ
according to the size of enterprises during the 1920s.[34] His hypothesis
was supported by Kōnosuke Odaka's study of wages in different
occupations in northern Kyūshū.[35]

This hypothesis has received criticism on two counts. It has been
argued that the change in wage differentials during the 1920s was
merely a cyclical phenomenon. Kōji Taira argued that wage differentials increased during downswings and decreased during upswings.[36]
A second line of argument is that wage differentials already existed in
1909 and 1914. Yasuba examined the same statistics as Umemura in
more detail, and claimed that he could identify wage differentials
according to the size of the enterprise in these years.[37] Working on
the assumption that the composition of workers by sex and industry
group did not vary, he calculated that in 1909 there was a 20 percentage point difference between wages in the smallest and the largest
enterprises and that by 1914 it had increased to 30 percentage points.

In spite of these criticisms there is no doubt that the increase in the
wage differential between large and small enterprises in the 1920s was
larger than in other periods. The 1920s was a period of major qualitative change in the economy. Large-scale enterprises improved their

facilities and carried out rationalization. Unskilled workers were replaced by skilled workers; the former were discharged while the latter were granted lifetime employment and seniority wage systems were introduced.[38] As a result, skilled workers became more scarce and unskilled workers more abundant; the wage differential increased.

As we can see from Table 9.14, the wage differential increased again during the first half of the 1950s.[39] According to Akira Ono, however, this was the result of a change in the composition of labourers in different industry groups in status (production workers or non-production workers), sex and age-group. He found that the differential is constant for these years when the labour force is standardized with respect to composition.[40] The wage differential decreased during the period 1958–65. In the 1970s and 1980s it showed a slow increase, caused by a retardation of wage increases in the recessions in small and medium-sized enterprises.

The amount of the wage differential between skilled and unskilled workers depends on whether we cite different sectors (agriculture or non-agriculture) or size. However, we can generalize as follows: During the pre-war period, especially during the recession, wage differentials increased because there was a virtually unlimited supply of unskilled workers. During the post-war period wage differentials narrowed in the late 1950s and the early 1960s, when the supply of labour was limited.[41] There was only a small increase in differentials during the recession of the 1970s. This was because there was a labour shortage resulting from the long-term structural change in the labour market which began around 1960.

9.3.3 Dual Structure of the Economy

By 'dual structure' in an economy we mean the existence of two distinct sectors, one which has modern technology, a high capital–labour ratio, high labour productivity and wages, and one which has all the opposite characteristics.[42] In this subsection we discuss the dual structure of the Japanese economy.

If the ratio of labour productivity in the A or S Sector to labour productivity in the M Sector is less than unity, we say a productivity differential exists. Table 9.2 shows that the real productivity ratio decreased steadily during both the pre-war and the post-war period in both sectors.[43] The nominal productivity ratio also decreased during the pre-war period, but it was constant in the A Sector and increased in the S Sector during the post-war period. The narrowing differential in the nominal productivity ratio during the latter period was due to a large increase in product prices in the *A* and *S* Sectors relative to the *M* Sector.

The difference in productivity among industry groups has increased in Japan, because surplus labour in traditional industries has tended to hinder increases in productivity.[44] However, the difference in productivity has diminished during the post-war period. A similar pattern has been found by Kuznets and Ohkawa in other developed countries.[45]

The increased difference in productivity (Y/L) in Japan is the result of changes in the capital-labour ratio (K/L) in the different sectors. During the pre-war period K/L increased very slowly in the *A* Sector. Since K/L grew more quickly in the non-primary sector, an increase in the difference between the productivity of primary and non-primary industries resulted (Table 6.9). During the post-war period K/L has increased very rapidly in the *A* Sector, but the productivity differential has increased. The *A* Sector's K/L ratio exceeded the *S* Sector's by the mid-1960s and *M* + *S* Sector's by the mid-1970s. However, there has also been a big increase in the capital-output ratio (K/Y) in the *A* Sector and as a result the differential in Y/L between the primary and non-primary industries has not yet decreased. However, further narrowing of the differential in K/L will, however, probably bring about a narrowing of the Y/L differential in the future.

The widening wage differential during the pre-war period was associated with the widening differential in Y/L and the constant wage differential during the post-war period with a narrowing nominal productivity differential.

9.3.4 Dual Structure of Manufacturing

Table 9.13 shows the wage differential between large and small manufacturing enterprises in 1932. It also reveals that there were differentials in Y/L and K/L: the differential between the largest and smallest enterprises was 70 percentage points for w, 80 percentage points for Y/L and 90 percentage points for K/L. A similar pattern can be seen in 1957 (Table 9.15).

However, the large wage differential would have little significance were it not for the fact that small and medium-scale enterprises (1–499 persons) employed a very large portion of all workers. Their share of total employment increased during the pre-war period and it

TABLE 9.13   Manufacturing industry wage differentials, labour productivity, capital–labour ratio and relative income share of labour by size of establishment in Japan 1932

Size (amount of capital, yen	Wages w	Labour productivity Y/L	Capital– labour ratio K/L	Income share of labour (%) wL/Y
99 or less	26	12	5	90
100–499	30	20	10	63
500–999	33	23	12	62
1 000–1 999	38	26	13	64
2 000–4 999	45	31	15	62
5 000–9 999	54	41	16	57
10 000–49 999	68	54	21	53
50 000–99 999	78	60	27	55
100 000–499 999	84	70	36	51
500 000 or more	100	100	100	43
Average	65	55	39	50

Notes:
w, Y/L and K/Y: 100 represents the largest size group.
w = wages and salaries.
Y = net value added.
K = fixed capital stock.
Li = number of workers.

Sources:
Kōgyō Chōsasho (Surveys of Manufacturing) for Ōsaka Prefecture, Tōkyō City, Yokohama City, Nagoya City, Kōbe City and Ōsaka City, from Umemura, 1961, p. 209, table 30.

remained stable during the post-war period (Table 9.16). It is somewhat surprising that the capacity of these enterprises to absorb employment did not decrease during the latter period. Another significant factor is that the proportion of workers employed by small and medium-size enterprises decreased during economic upswings (1910s, 1930s and 1960s), but increased during downswings (1920s and 1970s). This suggests that they have, together with agriculture and services, served to 'cushion' fluctuations in the labour market.

What was the situation in other developed countries? Asao Mizuno found that wages and productivity varied a great deal according to the size of enterprises in Italy, France and Denmark, and concluded that differentials according to size are not unique to Japan.[46] However, differentials in wages and productivity are much smaller in the USA, the UK and the former West Germany than Japan (Table 9.17).

TABLE 9.14 Manufacturing industry wage differentials by size of establishment 1950–90

	Size (number of regular workers)		
	5–29	30–99	100–499
1950	–	67.3	83.1
1955	–	58.8	74.3
1960	46.3	58.9	70.7
1965	63.2	71.0	80.9
1970	61.8	69.6	81.4
1980	58.0	65.4	80.5
1990	55.2	60.3	77.0

Notes:
100 represents the largest size–group, with five hundred workers or more.
Figures are the total wages for regular workers.

Sources:
Rōdōshō (Ministry of Labour), *Maigetsu Kinrō Tōkei* (Monthly Labour Statistics), RTN, various issues.

Small enterprises were very important to the economies of some European countries: The proportion of workers employed by firms with 1–49 workers was 42.9 per cent in Denmark in 1958, 33.6 per cent in the former West Germany in 1956, 43.8 per cent in Italy in 1951 and 47.1 per cent in the Netherlands in 1950,[47] all of which are similar to Japan (49.4 per cent in 1960). The proportion of workers employed by small firms was negligible in the USA (17.2 per cent in 1958) and the UK (11.7 per cent in 1958), but even in these countries the figure was greater earlier in their history. In the UK, for instance, small firms employed 21.9 per cent of all workers in 1935.

To summarize, differences in wages and productivity according to the size of the firm, and dependence on small enterprises to absorb surplus labour are the international rule; the USA and the UK are exceptions to the rule.

9.3.5 Theories of Dual Structure

Two theories have been developed to explain differentials in w, K/L and Y/L. The first suggests they are related this way: differential in K/L leads to differential in Y/L, which in turn leads to differential in w; the second that they are related in the opposite way, $w \rightarrow K/L \rightarrow Y/L$.

Miyazawa and Shinohara's 'capital concentration' hypothesis forms

TABLE 9.15   Manufacturing industry wage differentials, labour productivity, capital–labour ratio, and relative income share of labour by size of establishment in Japan 1957

Size (number of workers)	Wages w	Labour productivity Y/L	Capital–labour ratio K/L	Income share of labour wL/Y (%)
1–9	35	21	11	35
10–29	41	32	12	45
30–49	44	39	14	42
50–99	48	47	18	38
100–199	53	55	25	36
200–299	57	63	32	34
300–499	62	78	47	30
500–999	70	87	63	30
1 000–1 999	79	103	91	29
2 000–4 999	91	120	106	28
5 000–9 999	87	97	86	38
10 000 or more	100	100	100	37
Averages	59	58	44	34

Notes:
w, Y/L and K/L: 100 represents the largest size-group.
Y = gross value added.
K = fixed capital stock.
L = number of employees.
w = wage earnings.

Source:
Estimates by the *Keizai Kikakuchō*, *Keiza Kenkyūjo* (Economic Planning Agency, Research Institute of Economics) from Ohkawa and Rosovsky, 1973, p. 87, table 4.8.

the basis for the first theory.[48] This hypothesis suggests that differentials in productivity and wages occur because of the differential in the rate of interest paid by large and small enterprises. Proponents of this theory claim that large enterprises can easily expand their capital by loans from banks at a low rate of interest, but small firms cannot. They claim that this resulted in a differential in K/L, which lead, in turn, to a differential in Y/L and hence w.

The second theory was put forward by Jūrō Teranishi and the author. We have worked on the assumption that large enterprises employ primarily skilled workers, small enterprises mainly unskilled workers.[49] In the 1920s the supply of unskilled workers increased, and their wages declined relative to skilled workers' wages. As a result, small firms had lower average wages than large firms (i.e. a

TABLE 9.16 A breakdown of workers in employment in manufacturing by size of establishment in Japan 1909–88(%)

	Size (number of workers)		
	1–49ᵃ	*50–499*	*500 or more*
1909	45.7	33.6	20.7
1914	40.0	34.9	25.1
1919	33.9	34.6	31.5
1930	37.0	37.4	25.6
1940	36.5	27.4	36.2
1950	48.8	26.8	24.4
1960	49.4	36.9	13.7
1970	40.5	33.5	26.0
1988	45.7	34.9	19.4

Notes:
ᵃ 5–49 persons for the pre-war period.

Sources:
Kōjō Tōkeihyō and *Kōgyō Tōkeihyō* (Census of Manufactures).
Pre-war-Tsūshō Sangyō Daijin Kanbō, Chōsa Tōkeibu, 1961, pp. 180–1. Post-war–KTH, various issues.

wage differential appeared). This, we believe, led to differentials in K/L and Y/L, because large enterprises found it profitable to employ labour-saving technology but small enterprises did not.

Proponents of the first theory have to make the assumption that large enterprises draw from a different labour market to small enterprises in order to explain persistent wage differentials. For the second theory we have to assume that unskilled labourers cannot be substituted for skilled labourers. Although there is an element of truth in both of these assumptions, both tend to over-simplify the case, particularly with regard to recent developments. The first assumption has become less tenable since the passing of the turning-point because it has meant that both large and small enterprises compete for new workers. The second assumption is no longer strictly true, because the widespread introduction of automated manufacturing systems has made it possible in many cases to replace skilled workers with unskilled workers. In spite of these changes, however, there is still a difference between the wage levels, productivity and capital-labour ratios of large and small enterprises. The greater incidence of

TABLE 9.17 A breakdown of workers in employment in manufacturing by size of establishment in four developed countries 1954–85

Scale (number of workers)	Japan (1985)		USA (1977)		UK (1954)		Previous West Germany (1977)	
	Wages	Productivity	Wages	Productivity	Wages	Productivity	Wages	Productivity
1–9	29.3	43.4			–	–	–	–
10–49	39.8	54.7	64.9	66.3	77.3	79.9	73.4	71.4
50–99	45.4	58.4			80.4	80.9	73.9	74.5
100–499	66.5	71.0	81.0	70.7	86.6	83.6	78.4	80.1
500–999	81.3	84.0			95.1	89.3	87.2	86.1
1 000 or more	100.0	100.0	100.0	100.0	100.0	100.0	100.0	100.0

Sources:
Census of manufactures of the respective countries, from KRT, 1992, p. 175, table 1.11.

lifetime employment and seniority wage systems in large-scale enter-prises may account for these differences.

9.3.6 Japanese Employment Practices

Lifetime employment and seniority wage systems apparently orig-inated in large Japanese enterprises during the 1920s. It is usually assumed, explicitly or implicitly, that these two systems are unique to Japan. Recent studies have, however, provided evidence to the contrary.[50] They show that the slope of the 'age–wage profile' (the relation between wage increases and age) for non-production workers in Japan is not significantly different from western countries, although the age-wage profile for production workers is steeper in Japan. Many of these studies have suggested that these two systems have created, during the course of industrialization, an 'internal labour market' that determines employment and wages within an enterprise independently of the 'external labour market'.

While the importance of 'Japanese employment practices' has been over-emphasized in the past, the fact that the age-wage profile in western countries and Japan is nearly the same does not mean that their employment and wage systems are alike. Japan's seniority wage system is designed to compensate for increases in living costs incurred as workers' children grow up. Wage differentials by age-group in western countries are designed to reward improvements in skill re-sulting from long service.

Japan's employment practices, whether they are unique to Japan or not, have contributed to economic growth during the post-war period by stabilizing relations between labour and management. This has often been pointed out by writers comparing labour-management relations and economic growth in western countries and Japan.

9.4   RELATIVE INCOME SHARES

9.4.1   Relative Income Shares in Non-Primary Industries

Labour's share of income in non-primary industries has been esti-mated by Ono and the present author. Labour's share is the ratio of returns on labour (W) to total income (Y), where Y is the sum of W and profit (R). W is equal to the sum of wages and salaries actually paid to employees, returns on labour of self-employed workers and returns on labour of family workers. The return on labour of self-

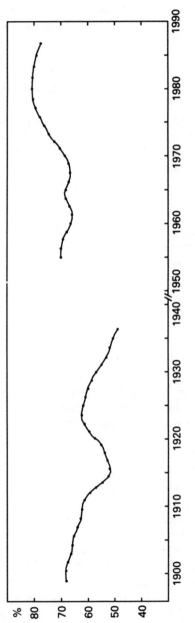

FIGURE 9.5 Income share of labour in non-primary industries in Japan 1899–1987

Notes:
Seven-year moving averages (five-year averages for 1938, 1955 and 1987).

Sources:
Prior to 1971: Minami and Ono, 1978a, p. 164.
After 1971: Extrapolated from the 1970 figure based on the index of w/y, where w and y stand for wage income and labour productivity respectively. The variable y is calculated by dividing the total factor income by the number of workers, and w is calculated by dividing the total compensations for labour by the number of employees. All figures are from KKKN, various issues.

employed workers and that of family workers were estimated under some assumptions. The estimates were carried out by industry group. Figure 9.5 shows the result for non-primary industry as a whole. Major findings are listed below:

1. The ratio of income share decreased rapidly. At the beginning of the twentieth century it even reached 70 per cent but then decreased to 48 per cent in 1938.
2. Labour's share in the post-war period has been much larger than it was during the pre-war period (65–80 per cent).
3. Labour's share in the post-war period declined initially. Then during the high economic growth period it was relatively stable before increasing again at the end of the 1960s. It declined again during the 1980s.

The trend of long term decline pointed out in (1) was due to the fact that the wage increase was smaller than the productivity increase due to the existence of surplus labour. Let us examine this point closely. In the stage where surplus labour exists, wages (w) will be equivalent to subsistence level (SL). Therefore, when the average productivity (AP) increases, the income share of labour (w/AP) will decrease (Figure 9.3).

The gap in labour share between the post-war and pre-war periods pointed out in (2) was due to the fact that non-agricultural sectors received a substantial rise in wages because of economic democratization that happened just after the Second World War: agrarian reform (this increased farmers' opportunity costs which meant the increase of values in labour supply towards non-agricultural sectors); the organization of labour unions; and the destruction of the *zaibatsu* system.

The trend of decrease in 1950s can be understood as a prolongation of the trend during the pre-war period. This is because surplus labour still existed in the 1950s. (The trend that existed during the pre-war period shifted upwards because of the various reforms in the system after the Second World War.) However, around 1960, at the turning-point, the income share stopped the trend of decline. The trend of increase since the end of the 1960s is a result of small productivity increase in an era of low economic growth.

The decline of income share during the pre-war period probably functioned in favour of capital formation and promoted economic growth, but on the other hand it also caused significant inequality in the income distribution system. The high income share of labour which occurred after the Second World War largely contributed towards a realization of an equal society.

9.4.2 Income Shares in Agriculture

Estimation of income shares in agriculture is very difficult, because most labourers are either self-employed or unpaid family workers. Hence we have to make bold assumptions in order to estimate returns on self-employed and unpaid family workers from the data available. Saburō Yamada's estimates suggest that labour's share of income was almost constant from the 1880s to the 1930s.[52] However, the ratio of agricultural wages to labour productivity (w/AP in Table 9.9), which is equal to labour's share if w is equal to average returns on labour, underwent a long-term decline from the late nineteenth century to the end of the pre-war period.[53] It followed, therefore, the same pattern as labour's share in the non-primary industries and it can also be explained by the existence of surplus labour.

9.4.3 Experience of Other Developed Countries

Labour's share of income in the economy as a whole has increased in the long term in the UK, the USA, France and Germany, but has remained constant in Canada since the mid-nineteenth century (Table 9.18).

Hence the experience of western countries is quite different from that of pre-war Japan (where labour's share declined in the long term). It seems that the key factor in explaining this difference is the existence of surplus labour in Japan. This implies that in countries (like Italy), where there was a labour surplus, labour's share of income would be expected to have behaved more or less as it did in Japan. Verification of this hypothesis must await historical studies of these countries comparable to our study of Japan.

SUMMARY OF THE CHAPTER

The distribution of workers among industries has changed a great deal during the course of modern economic growth since the mid-1880s. The share of workers in the primary sector (A) fell and the share of those in the manufacturing (M) and service (S) sectors rose.

TABLE 9.18   Income share of labour in six western countries
1853–1975(%)

UK		France	
1860–69	54	1853	56
1905–14	54	1911	64
1920–9	66	1913	67
1954–60	75	1920–9	71
1961–75[b]	82	1954–60	81
USA		**Germany**	
1899–1908	76	1895	53
1919–28	74	1913	61
1929	73	1925–9	79
1954–60	81	1954–60[a]	71
1961–75[b]	83	1967–75[ab]	83
Switzerland		**Canada**	
1924	65	1926–9	81
1954–60	74	1954–60	81

Notes:
The figures are for all industries.
[a] The former West Germany.

Sources:
Estimates by Kuznets, who assumes that returns to labour of self-employed workers
are equal to per capita income of employees. Kuznets, 1966, pp. 168–9, table 4.2.
[b] Yasuba, 1980, p. 232.

The rise in the S Sector's share during the 1970s was especially
conspicuous. Thus the labour force shifted from A to M and then to
S. This pattern, known as Petty's Law, is discernible in all developed
countries. Evidence of Petty's Law can also be observed in international cross-section analysis – as per capita income increases, the
labour force shifts from A to M to S. The distribution of the labour
force depends upon both the composition of industrial production
and relative efficiency in different industries, and the former has been
the predominant factor in Japan.

In most developed countries the size of the agricultural labour
force rose during the early phase of economic growth, but in Japan it
remained constant as a result of the high labour–land ratio; net
outflow was, in the long term, equal to the natural increase in the
labour force. The net outflow of agricultural labour was, however,
affected by changes in the demand for non-agricultural labour. The

decline of the agricultural labour force that occurred in almost every developed country was delayed in Japan, but finally began during the post-war period, when rapid economic growth brought about a large-scale outflow of agricultural labour.

Although the rate of unemployment in Japan has been low, it would be a mistake to say that unemployment has not been a serious problem. During the pre-war period and the early post-war period a large amount of surplus labour existed in low productivity sectors. As a result, the real wages of unskilled labour did not rise and a differential in the wages of skilled and unskilled labour arose. However, rapid economic growth from the mid-1950s led to a sharp rise in the demand for unskilled labour. This absorbed the surplus labour. There was now a labour shortage, as the economy passed the Lewisian turning-point around 1960. As a result, real wages of unskilled workers rose sharply and the wage differential between skilled and unskilled labour narrowed.

A dual structure – the coexistence of a sector which is technologically modern, with high productivity and wages and another which is technologically backward, with low productivity and wages – is clearly visible in the Japanese economy. Nominal and real productivity in the A and S Sectors rose only modestly compared to the M Sector and as a result the productivity differential widened. However, with the rapid increase in the product prices of the A and S Sectors during the post-war period, the nominal inter-sector productivity differential has narrowed. The inter-sector productivity differential has followed an inverse U-type path during the course of modern economic growth. A productivity differential according to size of enterprises can also be observed in the manufacturing industry and a wage differential has existed since the late 1920s. Although scholars disagree about the causal relationship between productivity and wage differentials, there is no doubt that the two are closely related. Differentials between large and small enterprises narrowed somewhat with the advent of a labour shortage, but they persist to this day.

Labour's share of total income followed similar paths in the non-agricultural and agricultural sectors. Prior to the Second World War labour's share of income underwent a long-term decline; and the existence of surplus labour meant that wage increases lagged behind productivity increases. After the passing of the turning-point the decline in labour's share ceased and it has been stable since. The developed countries of the west differ from Japan in that labour's share has been stable. It was the existence of surplus labour in Japan that brought about this difference.

FURTHER READING

Labour force:
  Cole and Tominaga, 1976
  Hatai, 1980
  Ichino, 1980
  Minami, 1973, ch. 6.
  Shirai and Shimada, 1979

Surplus labour and dual structure:
  Broadbridge, 1966
  Minami, 1973
  Miyazawa, 1964
  Ohkawa, 1972, parts 1 and 2
  Shinohara, 1968a; 1970, ch. 8

Wages and relative income shares:
  Koike, 1978
  Minami and Ono, 1979; 1981
  Ohkawa, 1968
  Ono and Watanabe, 1976
  Shimada, 1981
  Taira, 1970
  Umemura, 1980
  Yasuba, 1976

10 Public Finances and the Financial System

In this chapter we discuss government activities and finance. Section 10.1 discusses the importance of government expenditure in the economy and changes in the structure of government revenue and expenditure, and in Section 10.2 we evaluate the influence of government financial activities, particularly in connection with economic growth. In Section 10.3 we turn our attentions to changes in the financial system, the circulation of capital and overloan/overborrowing. Finally, in Section 10.4 we discuss changes in the amount and structure of the money supply, and changes in the Marshallian k, which regulates the demand for currency.

10.1 THE SIZE AND STRUCTURE OF PUBLIC FINANCES

10.1.1 Size

Comparing real government expenditure (central plus local, excluding where they overlap) with real GNE in Figure 10.1, we know that government activity has increased more rapidly than the economy as a whole. Figure 10.1 also reveals that before the Second World War there was considerable fluctuation in government expenditure, largely due to changes in military expenditure. The latter, and as a result the former, increased in steps with each successive war (Sino-Japanese, Russo-Japanese, Manchurian Incident, Pacific War). Although military expenditure decreased after each war, government expenditure did not decrease to the same extent. There was a tendency for part of the expenditure involved in the war to become a permanent feature of the government financial structure.[1] According to A. T. Peacock and J. Wiseman the same phenomenon can be seen in the UK; they have christened it 'the displacement effect of war'.[2] The result in

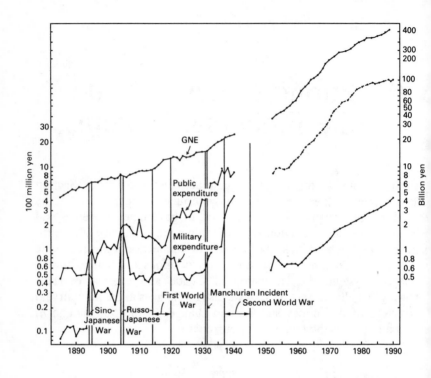

FIGURE 10.1   Real GNE and real public expenditure in
Japan 1885–1990

Notes:

All the figures are deflated by the GNE deflator (1934–6 = 1 for the pre-war period,
1985 = 1 for the post-war period).

The public financial expenditure here is the total of those from central and local
government. I have avoided overlapping them. All the figures are the fiscal year
figures (the pre-war GNE figure, however, is the calendar year figure).

The figures are non-smoothed.

Sources:

Real GNE – Estimated by the same method and from the same sources as the calendar
year statistics in Figure 3.3.

Public expenditure and military expenditure: Pre-war – Emi and Shionoya, 1966, pp.
169, 171, 186–9. Post-war – KTN, 1990, p. 215.

both countries has been an increase in the size of public finances with each war.

Since the Second World War military expenditure (defence spending) in Japan has been negligible (less than 1 per cent of GNE) and relatively constant, so that there has been little fluctuation in government expenditure.

Next let us look at changes in government expenditure as a proportion of GNE (Table 10.1). It rose from 12 to 37 per cent in the pre-war period, mainly as a result of the displacement effect, and fell to about 20 per cent after the war, when military expenditure fell. From the end of the war till 1965 budget deficits were not permitted; had they been, frequent tax reductions would have been necessary to prevent a rapid increase in revenue from taxation, and the ratio of government expenditure to GNE would have remained virtually constant. As it was, during the 1970s and 1980s the ratio rose sharply. In the former decade the private sector's share of GNE fell because of the recessions, and in the latter, government expenditure on social welfare increased.

Another indicator of government activity is the expenditure of general government (according to the concept of national accounting of the Economic Planning Agency), the sum of current purchases of goods and services (i.e. GC–government consumption), government capital formation (GCF), and transfers (T). The ratio of general government expenditure to GNE has followed a similar pattern to that of government expenditure to GNE (Table 10.1).

An absolute and relative increase in government expenditure can be seen in the history of all developed countries. In the UK the ratio $(GC + GCF)/GDP$ increased from 7.3 per cent in 1861–80 to 19.1 per cent in 1901–20, and decreased to 14.6 per cent in 1921–38. In the post-war period it was at a high level – 20 per cent or more.[3] The 'cheap government' advocated by Adam Smith was abandoned even in the UK when faith in the free market economy eroded. In the countries which developed after the UK a wide range of government activity was necessary to enable them to catch up with her. A. Wagner referred to the tendency for public finances to expand with economic development as 'Gesetz der wachsenden Staatsausgeben'.[4]

How does the position of public finances in Japan compare with other countries? The ratio of government expenditure to GNP was 16 per cent in Japan, the second lowest after former West Germany, and only half of the highest ratio of Italy (Table 10.2). The relatively small size of public finances in Japan is associated with the low rate of

TABLE 10.1 Composition of public finances in Japan 1888–1988(%)

	Public expenditure[a]	Tax burdens – national income ratio[b]	GC	GCF	GC + GCF	T[c]	GC + GCF + T	GCF	GCF
	GNE		GNE	GNE	GNE	GNE	GNE	CF	GC
1888	12.1	11.0	6.7	2.4	9.1	1.9	11.0	17.5	35.8
1900	17.2	9.7	7.3	5.3	12.6	1.6	14.2	32.9	72.6
1920	18.1	9.6	6.6	6.2	12.8	1.1	13.9	31.0	93.9
1938	36.8	10.7	11.8	13.0	24.8	1.7	26.5	45.8	110.2
1954	21.0	20.0	9.5	6.5	16.6	3.8	20.4	29.6	68.4
1970	19.5	19.0	7.9	8.9	16.8	6.4	23.2	25.6	113.2
1988	26.8	27.6	9.2	6.6	15.8	12.8	28.6	22.2	71.9

Notes:

The figures are seven-year moving averages (1938, 1954 and 1988 figures are five-year averages).

[a] Both numerators and denominators are fiscal year figures.

[b] The ratio of national government tax and the local government tax against national income. Both numerators and denominators are fiscal year figures. Only the denominator (NDP at market prices) in the pre-war period is the calendar year figure.

[c] Only the numerator is the fiscal year figure.

Sources:

Public expenditure: Table 10.1.

Tax burdens–national income ratio: In the pre-war period, this was worked out by dividing the national tax and the local tax (Nippon Ginkō Tōkeikyoku, 1966, pp. 136–7 and pp. 152–3) by NDP (Ohkawa et al., 1974, p. 202). In the post-war period, the figure is taken from KTN, 1990, p. 215.

GC, GCF, CF, GNE: These were estimated by following the method used in the estimation of real GNE in Figure 3.3 and their structural elements. Namely, the figures during the period of 1970–90 were from KKKN, 1991, pp. 106–9, and KKK, no. 88, p. 164. For the period 1952–69 the figures were worked out from the series by Ohkawa and Shinohara, 1979, p. 255, based on the figure for 1970.

T: Before 1961, the figures are from Emi and Shionoya, 1966, pp. 172–3. For the period 1962–4, the figures are from KSH, 1963, p. 144. After 1965, the figures are from KKKN, 1983, pp. 30–3 and KKKN, 1991, pp. 14–15.

TABLE 10.2   Ratio of public expenditure to GNP, and of taxation to national income in six developed countries 1989(%)

	Italy	UK	USA	France	Japan	Former West Germany
Ratio of public expenditure to GNP	33.2	26.2	22.3	21.9	16.3	12.9
Ratio of taxation[a] to national income	30.6	41.3	25.7	33.9	27.5	29.6
Ratio of taxation and non-tax burdens to national income	45.8	50.3	36.8	59.4	38.3	52.8

Notes:
Statistics for Japan and the USA are on a fiscal year basis.
[a] Central and local government taxation.

Source:
KHT, 1991, pp. 87–8, 91–2.

taxation, only about 80 per cent of the UK rate, even when charges other than actual taxation (e.g. fees for education, health insurance schemes, expressway tolls) are taken into account.

Thus, despite an expansion of government activity in recent years, it remains less important in Japan than other countries; relatively speaking government in Japan can be described as cheap.[5] It is cheap largely because the burdens of defence and social welfare are light.

10.1.2   The Composition of Government Revenue

In the pre-war period government revenue consisted mainly of income from taxation and government securities (Table 10.3). In the early part of modern economic growth taxation accounted for over 80 per cent of government revenue, but this fell steadily to just over 30 per cent in 1940. After the war revenue from government securities was minimal, and the proportion from taxation increased sharply, to over 70 per cent in the 1950s. Subsequently it fell again, to between 50 and 60 per cent in the 1970s and 1980s, as the proportion from government securities and social security payments increased. The proportion of revenue from government enterprises remained low and almost constant throughout both periods. The proportion from social security payments was extremely low before the war, but increased after it, as the social welfare system improved.

Next we will analyze central government taxes[6] (Table 10.4), and

TABLE 10.3   Composition of government revenue in Japan 1873–1986(%)

Fiscal year	Taxes	Profits from government enterprises	Others	Revenue from issue of government securities[a]	Total
	Current revenue				
1873	75.2	4.1	3.6	17.1	100.0
1900	75.8	6.2	7.1	10.9	100.0
1920	58.2	10.4	13.0	18.4	100.0
1940	33.1	5.1	6.9	54.9	100.0
1960	70.1	6.4	18.3	5.2	100.0
1986	55.7	2.6	31.1	10.6	100.0

Notes:
The figures are seven-year moving averages (five-year average for 1986) of the totals
for central and local government and government enterprises.
[a] Difference between new issues and redemptions.
Seven-year moving averages.

Sources:
Until 1970: Ohkawa and Shinohara, 1979, pp. 376–8.
Since 1971: All items other than government securities–KKKN, 1983, 1991. Government securities–KOTN, 1989, p. 4; CZY, various issues.

TABLE 10.4   Composition of tax revenue in Japan 1872–1989(%)

Fiscal year	Land tax	Income tax	Corporation tax	Business tax	Inheritance tax	Total
	Direct taxes					
1872	90.1	–	–	–	–	90.1
1900	34.6	4.3	1.2	3.9	–	44.0
1920	10.2	23.5	11.8	6.6	1.1	53.2
1940	0.9	34.0	11.7	2.6	1.6	50.8
1960	–	25.5	34.6	–	0.9	61.0
1989	–	37.7	32.1	–	3.4	73.2

Fiscal year	Liquor tax	Sugar excise	Customs duties	Gasoline excise	Commodity tax[a]	Others	Total
	Indirect taxes						
1872	1.5	–	3.3	–	–	5.1	9.9
1900	38.0	1.3	10.9	–	–	5.8	56.0

T<small>ABLE</small> 10.4   continued

	Indirect taxes						
Fiscal year	Liquor tax	Sugar excise	Customs duties	Gasoline excise	Commodity tax[a]	Others	Total
1920	22.6	6.8	11.1	–	–	6.3	46.8
1940	8.9	3.2	2.9	0.3	–	33.9	49.2
1960	15.1	–	6.7	6.8	4.9	5.5	39.0
1989	3.5	–	1.6	3.3	5.9	12.5	26.8

Notes:
The figures are seven-year moving averages (five-year average for 1989), central
   government only.
[a] Consumption tax after 1989.

Sources:
Pre-war: Nippon Ginkō, Tōkeikyoku, 1966, pp. 136–7.
Post-war: KTN, 1990, p. 219; ZKTG, 1991, p. 321.

then government securities. In the early Meiji Period land taxes were
the most important form of taxation, particularly after the reforms of
1873–81; they accounted for 90 per cent of all taxation. However,
because they were assessed against the value of the land, revenue
from them did not increase at the same rate as the increase in
agricultural output. This inelasticity relative to incomes meant that
they could not meet the increasing demands of the treasury. Indirect
taxes (e.g. on alcoholic beverages, sugar) were raised to supplement
them, but a more income-elastic tax was required – income tax. It was
introduced in 1887 and raised considerably in the 1920s and again
in 1940. The principle of making income tax the core tax was
strengthened after the Second World War by the SCAP (the occupation authorities). As a result, the percentage of income tax in the
overall tax revenue increased greatly.

However, the increase of income tax also brought problems to
light. Namely, in this tax system it was expected that the burden on
salary earners, whose income figures were easy to ascertain would
become greater and the burden on farmers and self-employed workers in commerce and industry decrease. Because of this, the action of
reducing income tax was taken for salary earners in almost every
year. However, the feelings of being under the imposed heavy taxes
among salary workers were worsened and caused their strong discon-
tent. In order to solve this problem the government introduced the

consumption tax in 1989, in which almost all consumer goods and services are taxed, as a collateral tax for the reduction of income tax.

The modernization of the tax structure has followed a similar pattern in many countries. H. Hinrichs presented a model to show how, as 'traditional societies' progress towards 'modernity', traditional direct taxes – land taxes, poll taxes – are replaced by customs duties and modern forms of direct taxation such as income tax and corporation tax.[7] This model basically fits what happened in Japan.[8]

Before the war the rate of taxation in Japan (the ratio of taxation to the national income – Table 10.1) was about 10 per cent. After the war it rose to almost 20 per cent and has since remained virtually constant as a result of deliberate government policy – annual changes in basic allowances and tax reductions. In the 1980s, however, it increased to become 28 per cent in 1988.

When current revenue does not meet expenditure the government may issue securities (national and local government bonds). In the early Meiji Period, before the introduction of modern taxation, large amounts were issued. 51.9 per cent of the cost of the Sino-Japanese War and 82.4 per cent of the cost of the Russo-Japanese War was paid for from issues of securities.[9] Revenue from this source accounted for 36.5 per cent of government revenue in 1895, and 67.8 per cent in 1905.[10] Later the government began to redeem securities and the figure fell. Since the 1920s, however, it rose sharply once more, when securities, were issued to raise capital to save enterprises from bankruptcy and ease the atmosphere of panic prevalent at that time. Especially in the 1930s even more were issued as part of Takahashi's reflationary policies, particularly in 1932, when many were bought by the Bank of Japan. Securities issued from about 1937 were once more for the purpose of military expansion. In 1940 revenue from securities accounted for 53.6 per cent of government revenue.[11] After the war revenue from this source was negligible; only the issue of local, not national, bonds was permitted until 1965. After this date the amount of government securities, and their share of government revenue, gradually increased; it reached 24.4 per cent (figure for a single year in 1980).

10.1.3   The Composition of Government Expenditure

In the pre-war period government expenditure consisted mainly of current purchases of goods and services (*GC* – see Table 10.5). When military expenditure was high its share of government expenditure

TABLE 10.5 Composition of government expenditure in Japan
1870–1987(%)

Fiscal year	Current expenditure			Capital formation	Total
	Current purchases of goods and services	Military expenditure[a] only	Transfers		
1870	53.1	26.6	29.5	17.4	100.0
1900	65.9	33.7	11.5	22.6	100.0
1920	65.4	39.2	7.7	26.9	100.0
1940	82.9	80.2	5.7	11.4	100.0
1960	41.9	5.1	20.2	37.9	100.0
1987	44.6	3.0	41.8	21.8	100.0

Notes:
The figures are seven-year moving averages (five-year average for 1870 and 1987) of
the totals for central and local government and government enterprises.
[a] National defence expenses for the post-war period.

Sources:
Military expenditure: To 1960–Emi and Shionoya, 1966, pp. 186–9. Since 1961–KSTN,
1973, KKKN, 1983, 1991.

Other statistics:
To 1970–Ohkawa and Shinohara, 1979, pp. 370–2.
Since 1971–KKKN, 1983, 1991.

rose, and vice versa. After the war current purchases' share of
government expenditure fell because of a sharp drop in military
(defence) expenditure, and it has continued to decline since, as
transfers and capital formation have increased.

Government consumption expenditure's share of GNE rose gradually in the pre-war period, from 7 per cent in 1888 to 12 per cent in
1938 (Table 10.1). Since the war it has been about 9 per cent. How
does this compare with the developed countries of the west? The first
thing that is apparent is that Japan is not the only country in which
the figure rose during the pre-war period (Table 10.6). The second is
that it has also risen in the post-war period in western developed
countries, and is now considerably higher in these countries than in
Japan. The average for 103 countries in 1988 was 15 per cent, compared with 9 per cent in Japan (Table 6.6).

GCF's share of GNE rose in the pre-war period, especially in the
1920 and 1930s (Table 10.1). This was due to increasing urbanization,
the rebuilding necessitated by the Great Kantō Earthquake (1923),

TABLE 10.6   Ratio of government current expenditure to GNP in seven western countries 1870–1989(%)

	1870	1913	1938	1950	1960	1989
France	–	–	13.0	12.9	13.3	18.3
Germany	–	–	23.1	14.4	13.6	18.7
Italy	9.7	9.8	16.3	11.1	14.5	16.8
Sweden	4.7	5.6	10.4[a]	13.9	17.7	26.2
UK	4.9	7.2	13.5	15.6	16.6	19.4
Canada	4.6	8.1	10.9	10.6	14.4	18.8
USA	3.7[b]	4.2	10.1	10.6	17.2	17.9

Notes:
[a] 1938–9.
[b] 1969–78.

Source:
Maddison, 1964, p. 103, table iv.1; 1989 – NA, 1991, p. 119.

and the increase in the number of civil engineering projects in the early Shōwa Period. (This was part of Takahashi's reflationary policies. He issued 'red-ink' bonds and distributed capital generously, in the hope of promoting economic recovery. These highly praised measures were similar to the USA's 'New Deal'; it could be said that they carried out Keynesian theory before it has been expounded.[12])

GCF's share of GNE has been much higher since the war, and is now at an internationally high level (Table 6.6). Almost the same thing can be said of the ratio of *GCF* to *CF* and that of *GCF* to *GC*.[13] Thus, the most significant aspect of government expenditure in Japan in recent years is that capital formation has been greater than current expenditure and has accounted for a greater proportion of the economy.

We can therefore say that both government activity and the overall economy have been geared to economic growth.

Transfers (*T*) accounted for a large proportion of government expenditure in the early Meiji Period (Table 10.5), because enormous sums had to be paid in compensation to ex-*samurai* families. From late Meiji until the Second World War the proportion fell,[14] except for a short period at the beginning of this century when compensation was paid to bereaved families after the Russo-Japanese War. Since the Second World War the proportion has increased rapidly as the social welfare system has improved. However the ratio of transfers to GDE is still considerably lower than in many other countries.[15]

TABLE 10.7   Subsidies to different industry groups in Japan 1880–1940(%)

Fiscal year	Primary	Con- struction	Mining and manufac- turing	Electri- city, gas and water	Trans- portation and commu- nication	Others	Total
1880	0.2	71.3	–	–	12.8	15.7	100.0
1900	4.4	4.3	–	2.0	83.0	6.3	100.0
1920	21.2	26.5	14.1	2.8	31.3	4.1	100.0
1940	52.1	3.9	25.1	3.0	5.7	10.2	100.0

Notes:
This table includes only subsidies in the general account budget.
The figures are seven-year moving averages (five-year average for 1940).

Source:
Emi and Shionoya, 1966, pp. 180–3.

Apart from the period immediately after the Second World War, subsidies, one of the components of transfers, have been negligible. In the pre-war period by far the greatest proportion of subsidies were allotted to the construction industry (Table 10.7). Many were grants from the ministry of home affairs to local government bodies for projects designed to prevent flooding or landslides; this might be described as investment in agriculture and forestry. From 1890 to about 1920 subsidies went mainly to transport and communications, the greatest single beneficiary being marine transport. From the 1920s subsidies to construction and agriculture increased, particularly for agriculture. In 1940, just before the outbreak of the Pacific War, subsidies for agriculture amounted to more than half the total. This represented an attempt by the government to relieve the increasing impoverishment of rural communities, caused by the decline in the increase in agricultural output due to importation of rice. Immediately after the Second World War the government began giving subsidies to key industries in an effort to bring about economic recovery. In 1950 subsidies accounted for 9.2 per cent of government expenditure.[16] As the economy revived the figure fell, but rose gently since the 1960s, mainly because of increased road construction.

10.2   PUBLIC FINANCES AND THE ECONOMY

10.2.1   The Role of Public Finances

Public finances affect the economy in four ways:

1. Provision of current services. The government and other public organizations provide a wide range of services necessary for the smooth-running of industrial activities and people's daily routines.

2. Creation and regulation of effective demand. Through taxation and other channels the government obtains revenue from the people, and invests it in consumption expenditure (GC) or capital formation (GCF). Increases in GC and GCF are in effect increases in effective demand. The increase in GC and GCF during the period 1888–1938 accounted for 29.0 per cent of the increase in real GNE and 14.7 per cent during the period 1955–88 (Table 6.7). How large are the effective demand effects of the government sector compared to those of private sector? The ratio of the increase in GC to the increase in PC (personal consumption expenditure) was 25.4 per cent during the period 1888–1938, and 13.6 per cent during 1955–88. The ratio of the increase in GCF to the increase in PCF (private capital formation) was 88.3 per cent and 26.4 per cent respectively. The ratio of government to private capital formation was high, particularly in the pre-war period. With the sharp fall in military expenditure after the Second World War, the private sector took the lead in capital formation as it began to expand rapidly.

Rosovsky has stressed the role of government expenditure (especially capital formation) in creating demand in Japan.[17] There is, however, a physical limit to increases in investment, and it must be remembered that government and private investment compete with each other; an increase in one may preclude an increase in the other. When government investment is directed to military objectives it is, from an economic viewpoint, a waste of scarce resources, which could be used to stimulate the economy were they used to increase private investment.[18] Hence we do not consider the government role here to have been particularly significant.

Next let us turn to regulation of effective demand. In Ch. 6, Sec. 1, we compared the growth rates of the components of effective demand and found that in the pre-war period the growth rate of non-military government capital formation (GCF') had a negative correlation with the growth rate of PCF and the economic growth rate. GCF' tended to offset cyclical fluctuations in PCF; when increases in private investment were small government investment was increased in order to maintain demand, and when people were eager to invest it was moderated.

Since the Second World War the growth rates of *GCF*, *PCF* and the economic growth rate have been positively correlated. Government investment has ceased to offset business cycles; in fact it actually served to increase their length. It was, of course, increased in times of recession and moderated when the economy 'overheated', but the main instrument for dealing with business cycles since the war has been monetary policy[19] (fiscal policy has played no more than a supporting role). This was perhaps inevitable as long as budget deficits were not permitted; there was very little room for manoeuvre. Japan's 'built-in stabilizer', although it is a somewhat different mechanism than those in other countries, has also served to offset business fluctuations. In most developed countries, when a recession occurs, increased expenditure on transfers (especially unemployment benefits) helps to prevent it from deepening. In Japan, where the level of unemployment is low, government revenue is a more important stabilizing factor. When the economy overheats, the increase in revenue from taxation is greater than the increase in GNP, so that demand in the private sector falls. The extremely progressive nature of income tax in Japan markets this mechanism very effective.[20]

The capital for government investment comes partly from taxation and partly from a system for providing treasury loans and investment known as the *zaisei tōyūshi*, which will be discussed in Section 10.3.

3. Expansion of productive capacity. Capital formation by the government increases the capital stock, and hence the productive capacity of the economy. In the prewar period government capital accounted for 30 to 40 per cent of the total capital stock, and the proportion rose gradually.[21] However the government capital stock included capital for military purposes; if we exclude this, its proportion of the total, and the rise, are both smaller.[22] The majority of non-military capital was social overhead capital, the formation of which is usually beyond the means of the private sector, so that the government's role in this sphere was vital.

Finally, government subsidies to key industries also contributed to increases in productive capacity.

4. Redistribution of income. This takes place on both the revenue and the expenditure side. The progressive nature of income tax means that the high income bracket's tax burden is greater relatively

than that of the lower income bracket's.[23] Government expenditure goes to households in the form of transfers – pensions, relief for the destitute, unemployment benefits, etc. However, as mentioned above, the ratio of expenditure on transfers to GNE is lower in Japan than western developed countries, so that redistribution of income due to government expenditure could be said to be relatively insignificant.[24]

The effect of government activity is often indirect and is a question of quality rather than quantity, so that its evaluation presents problems. However it is our opinion that (1) provision of current services and (3) expansion of productive capacity have been relatively important in Japan.

10.3   FINANCIAL ORGANIZATIONS

10.3.1   The Development of the Financial System

The Meiji government strove to introduce a modern financial system to support modern economic growth.[25] In 1872 the regulations for the establishment of 'National Banks'[26] were issued, and by 1876 four had been founded. The most important was the First National Bank established in 1873 by two financial organizations, Mitsui and Ono, with government aid; government deposits accounted for a large proportion of its capital. In 1876 the regulations were relaxed somewhat, and between 1877 and 1879 nearly 150 new National Banks were established. Various smaller financial institutions sprang up in this period, the most important of which were private banks set up by merchants and financiers; 'quasi-banking companies' (*ginkō ruiji kaisha*)[27] were smaller again. The Mitsui Bank was the first private bank, established in 1876 when the Mitsui family concern segregated its financial business from its commercial activities.

By the early 1880s the private banks' total debit balance was equal to that of the National Banks, their role was equally important and their sources of capital and lending activities were in effect the same. From the mid-1880s the demand for banking services increased as the pace of industrialization increased, and all banks began to expand rapidly. By a new set of regulations, issued in 1890, all private banks and quasi-banking companies were renamed Ordinary Banks (*futsū ginkō*), as opposed to National Banks, and most National Banks became Ordinary Banks themselves when their current licences ran out. At the same time industrialists began founding their own banks to raise capital for their companies independent of established banks. In 1895, for example, the Mitsubishi *Zaibatsu* and the Sumitomo *Zaibatsu* converted their financial departments into banks. The links between the banks and the *zaibatsu* became closer and closer, particularly in the 1920s, when small and medium-size banks were gradually taken over by the five big banks (Mitsui, Daiichi, Mitsubishi, Sumitomo, Yasuda), all of which were directly involved in *zaibatsu* activities.

Meanwhile the government founded a number of banks for specific purposes. First, and most important for economic development, was the Bank of Japan, established in 1882; it began issuing convertible notes in 1885. The Yokohama Specie Bank, established in 1880 and later given greater powers, was controlled by the government. It handled all the financial aspects of foreign trade, and gave low-interest loans to export industries. During the period 1897–1901, to provide long-term loans for agriculture, industry, electric power and transport, they founded: the Nippon Kangyō (*kangyō* means 'promotion of industry') Bank, the Hokkaidō Takushoku (*takushoku* means 'opening up new land') Bank, Nippon Kōgyō (industrial) Bank and forty-six Provincial Agricultural and Industrial Banks.

Table 10.8 illustrates how rapidly all these institutions expanded.

TABLE 10.8 Indicators of development of banks in Japan 1873–1990

	Loans	Deposits	Capital[a]
	million yen		
1873	3	3	2
1900	810	576	300
1920	9 521	8 829	1 639
1940	21 692	34 284	1 456
	000s million yen		
1960	8 183	8 872	186
1980	136 475	15 298	1 839
1990	441 169	43 624	7 681

Notes:
[a] Paid-in capital for the pre-war period.

Sources:
Pre-war: Nippon Ginkō, Tōkeikyoku, 1966, pp. 194–5.
Post-war: KTN, 1979, pp. 87–90; 1990, pp. 42–6.

R. Cameron analyzed changes in total bank assets in several developed countries and found that they had increased rapidly in Japan and Russia, but slowly in France. He suggested that this was related to the countries' respective economic growth rates, and concluded that the development of the banking system had played a decisive role in industrialization.[28] He said that, in France, government policy on currency and banking had hindered the freedom and hence the development of banks and had been partially responsible for the slow progress of industrialization there, while in Japan and Russia the banking system had not been restricted by regulations, but rather encouraged by the government, and had promoted industrialization. However, it must be remembered that in Japan and Russia the development of the banking system was the result, as well as a cause, of economic growth.

During 1946–7 SCAP, having judged that the banking system (via 'indirect financing' – described below) had been deeply involved in the invasion of Asia, took several measures to reduce its power. They freed most of the private company stock which had been held by the *zaibatsu*, limited the amount private companies could receive in loans from banks and forbade financial institutions from buying company stock/bonds, restricting the right to do this to stockbrokers. The Yokohama Specie Bank became the Bank of Tōkyō, losing most of its former powers, the Nippon Kangyō Bank and the Hokkaidō Takushoku Bank became ordinary commercial banks, and several other 'special' banks were closed down. These reforms, however, were not all carried through. The Reconversion Bank, established in 1947, lent on an increasingly large scale. Between 1949 and 1951 four of the special banks were allowed to reappear under different names (the People's Finance Corporation, the Housing Loan Corporation, the Export-Import Bank, the Japan Redevelopment Bank) and after 1951 new finance corporations were established in rapid succession. The financial system regained its former powers, and contributed to the high growth of the post-war period.

Although the financial system in Japan has developed greatly since the Second World War, as mentioned above, and has been supporting economic growth, this has only been possible under the widely-applied governmental regulations. However, with the position of Japan in the world financial market rising, the necessity of re-examining the Japanese financial system became obvious. The easing or withdrawal of governmental regulations relating to financial business and the abolition of classification (specialization or division of labour) among various financial institutions.

Revenue from national bonds, postal savings and life insurance is used for government investment, and under the *zaisei tōyūshi* plan, conceived in 1953, the government lends to the parts of the private sector that have difficulty obtaining loans: areas where long-term low-interest loans are required, areas where the risk factor is great, areas where factors such as pollution prevention are involved, small companies with a low credit rating, companies in areas where it takes considerable time to reach the profit-making stage.

The government's financial activities date back to the founding of the postal savings system in 1875. It was not, however, until after the Second World War that, with the founding of the various finance corporations and banks controlled indirectly by the government (e.g. the Export–Import Bank, the Japan Redevelopment Bank), that government financial activities expanded rapidly and exerted a significant influence on the economy. The money was used mainly for key industries and transportation and communication areas at a time of high economic growth. Since then, however, the weighting to spend these money was raised in the areas of living related; housing and environment.

10.3.2 The Circulation of Capital

What, then, has been the Japanese banking system's main contribution to the economy? Perhaps it is that it has expedited saving and investment and their smooth distribution to different sectors, enabling the effective use of the nation's capital. As we mentioned earlier (Ch. 6, Sec. 4), the surplus on personal savings (savings minus investment) flowed to companies and to the government.

When the government, or companies, require investment over and above accrued savings, it must come in the form of either direct investment by the public, or borrowings from financial institutions. The former method means issues of securities, and we refer to it as 'direct financing'; the latter we refer to as 'indirect financing'. We have already discussed how this works in the case of the government; here we will discuss company finances. First let us look at changes in the capital structure of Japanese companies (Table 10.9). The ratio of equity (bank balances, stock) to the total was 53–58 per cent in the 1920s and 1930s. This figure was halved after the war, and by the 1980s was only 24 per cent. The proportion of externally-raised capital (bonds, borrowings, notes, bills and accounts payable) has increased. Capital from company bonds, as we said, comes directly from the public, and company credit (notes, bills, accounts) is also a form of direct financing. The proportion of borrowings (indirect

TABLE 10.9   Composition of corporate capital in Japan 1928–89(%)

		Externally-raised capital					
	Equity	Sub-total	Corporate bonds	Borrow-ings	Notes, bills and accounts payable	Others	Total
1928–35	57.5	42.5	18.5	6.0	5.6	12.4	100.0
1936–43	52.7	45.3	10.2	6.5	15.9	12.7	100.0
1950–60	33.1	66.9	4.6	31.0	15.3	16.0	100.0
1961–70	22.0	78.0	5.5	34.8	21.0	16.7	100.0
1971–80	16.1	83.9	6.2	36.6	19.9	21.2	100.0
1981–89	23.6	76.4	9.6	30.9	17.8	18.1	100.0

Sources:
1928–64: Nippon Ginkō, Tōkeikyoku, 1966, pp. 336–9.
1965–89: KKB, all issues.

financing) was only 6–7 per cent in the 1920s and 1930s, but after the war it increased sharply, to 31–37 per cent. A comparison with the USA, the UK and the former West Germany in recent years (Table 10.10) reveals that the proportion of equity is much lower in Japan than in the other three, while the proportion of borrowings is much higher.

Having discussed the composition of the capital stock, let us turn our attention to its circulation, looking first at the channels through which capital is supplied to industry (Table 10.11). The proportion of internally-generated capital was greater after the war than before, and has been rising since, due to an increase in depreciation and, to a lesser extent, retained profits. The ratio of externally-raised capital was greater before the war, when more stocks and shares were issued. The proportion of borrowings rose from a mere 28 per cent before the war to almost 60 per cent during and after it. In the first half of the 1980s it was 36 per cent, which is considerably higher than in the USA, the UK, former West Germany and France (1986–9 – Table 10.12).

10.3.3   Overborrowing and Overloan

Three factors account for Japanese companies having become extremely dependent on borrowings after the war, a phenomenon which is often referred to as 'overborrowing':[29]

TABLE 10.10 Composition of corporate capital in three western countries 1956–87(%)

	Equity	Externally-raised capital					
		Sub-total	Corporate bonds	Borrowings	Notes, bills and accounts payable	Others	Total
Japan (1987)	26.2	73.8	11.2	29.6	15.4	17.6	100.0
USA (1956)	61.5	38.5	20.3	2.3	5.5	10.4	100.0
UK (1977)	44.4	55.6	a	21.2	24.5	a	100.0
Former West Germany (1984)	32.1	67.8	0.4	a	a	a	100.0

Notes:
a Unknown

Sources:
KKB, 1987, pp. 8–9.

TABLE 10.11 Supply of funds for industry in Japan 1931–85(%)

	1931–40	1941–50	1951–60	1961–70	1971–80	1981–85
Internally-generated	36.8	28.6	42.7	48.6	48.8	60.0
Retained profits	9.6	10.0	15.6	18.7	7.0	13.2
Depreciation	27.2	18.6	27.1	29.9	41.8	46.8
Externally-raised	63.2	71.4	57.3	51.4	51.2	40.0
Stocks and shares	31.1	9.8	8.1	4.8	3.2	3.1
Industrial bonds	4.3	2.7	2.5	1.8	2.1	1.4
Borrowings	27.8	58.9	46.7	44.8	45.9	35.5
Private	27.3	53.4	41.5	40.5	40.3	33.2
Government	0.5	5.5	5.2	4.3	5.6	2.3
Total	100.0	100.0	100.0	100.0	100.0	100.0

Sources:
HKT, 1957 pp. 25–6; KTN, various issues.

TABLE 10.12   Supply of funds for industry in four western countries
1986–9(%)

	USA	UK[a]	Former West Germany	France
Internally-generated	85.3	60.3	79.4	51.0
Externally-raised				
Borrowings	14.7	39.7	20.6	49.0
Securities	15.2	26.8	15.5	27.0
Others	–2.7	12.9	5.1	22.0
Total	2.2	0.0	0.0	0.0
	100.0	100.0	100.0	100.0

Notes:
[a] 1986–8.

Source:
KHT, 1991, p. 69.

1. The slow development of the stock market. The stock exchange in Japan has been extremely speculative in nature since its founding in the Meiji Period and has therefore been shunned by most savers, who have preferred time-deposit accounts at banks. For this reason the stock market's development has been considerably slower than that of the capital market.

2. Differences in the cost of raising capital. The government's low-interest-rates policy and a taxation system which allows interest payments to be set against tax has meant that the costs incurred in raising loans are low. In contrast, new issues of stock can be costly because they are issued, not at market prices, but at par value. Furthermore the tax on dividends is, like income tax, progressive. Also, the increase in the corporate income tax rate resulted in the raising of capital cost by inside finance, or the increase of capital stock.[30]

3. Availability. Rapid economic growth has meant that the increase in the demand for capital has also been rapid.

Ryūichirō Tachi and Katsunosuke Moroi analyzed pre-war and post-war company finances and came to the conclusion that the third factor was the most important;[31] overborrowing, they said, stemmed mainly from the inability to meet rapidly increasing demands for investment from internally-generated capital.

Because companies increasingly raised capital by loans from the

City Banks, the latter's loans increased at a greater rate than their deposits and their equity, so that they had to supplement the difference with loans from the Bank of Japan. This we refer to as 'overloan'.[32] During the period 1986–90 the ratio of banks' loans to their deposits was 104.5 per cent, compared with 114.5 per cent for the former West Germany, 107.8 per cent for France (1986–9), 94.9 per cent for the USA, 86.0 per cent for the UK and 38.1 per cent for Italy.[33]

It is of course impossible here to say what is normal, and whether Japan's 'indirect financing system' was in fact abnormal. What can be said with safety is that had there not been a system which could supply abundant capital to companies, economic growth would have been much slower.

Overborrowing and overloan in the postwar period made the financial system increasingly indirect, and while indirect financing was the outcome of economic growth and the increased demand for capital, at the same time it served to provide financial support for further high growth. H. Wallich and M. Wallich wrote: 'Japan's growth probably would not have been possible without the overborrowing that has been the centerpiece of enterprise finance.'[34]

10.4 MONEY – SUPPLY AND DEMAND

10.4.1 Money Supply and Financial Policy

An important function of the Bank of Japan is to maintain the money supply at an appropriate level. It can supply money in four ways:

1. Through a deficit on general government. The Bank of Japan lends to the government by buying government securities or making short-term loans. The buying of securities by the public or the ministry of finance's deposit bureau serves merely to redistribute capital in the private sector, whereas when the Bank of Japan buys them it is actually creating capital which is passed on to the private sector. This was very important in the pre-war period, especially the 1930s, when under finance minister Takahashi, substantial amounts of securities were bought by the Bank of Japan. The money supply increased rapidly, capital was in plentiful supply on the private market and interest rates fell significantly, stimulating investment activity (changes in interest rates on City Bank loans – a good indicator of overall movements in interest rates – are shown in Figure 10.2). Since

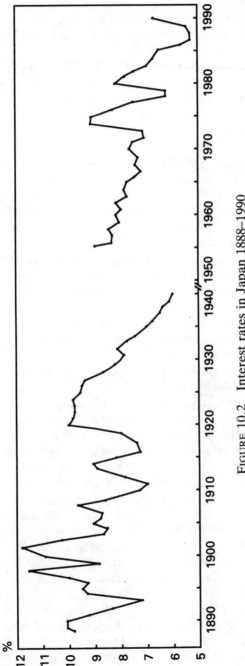

FIGURE 10.2   Interest rates in Japan 1888–1990

Notes:
The figures are interest rates on the loans of all banks. The figures are non-smoothed.

Sources:
Same as Table 6.4.

the war money has not been supplied in this way; government securities were not issued until 1965, and those issued since 1965 have not been bought by the Bank of Japan.

2. A balance-of-payments surplus. The Bank of Japan buys gold and currency from the Foreign Exchange Fund Special Account. The amount increased from the late 1960s due to a consistent balance-of-payments surplus, but it had been negligible before that (Table 10.13). This is not an area that can be regulated by the Bank of Japan.

3. Buying operations. The Bank of Japan may buy government or other securities held by financial institutions. This used to be of little importance because of the underdevelopment of the stock market, but it has gradually become more important since the introduction of the 'New Scheme for Monetary Control' in 1962, under which the Bank of Japan began actively purchasing securities.[35]

4. Lending to City Banks – discounting of bills and loans on bills. This has been the most important way of supplying money in the post-war period; a considerable proportion of cash currency has been supplied through Bank of Japan loans. Hence the Bank of Japan's lending policy has become a vital part of government financial policies. The Bank of Japan regulates the supply and demand of cash currency by adjusting its official discount rate. To supplement this traditional method of regulating credit it also carried out 'window guidance'; it guided the lending activities of the financial institutions it dealt with and thus regulated increases in loans. Window guidance was frequently used to help tighten the money supply until its abolition in 1991. From the mid-1950s to the mid-1960s adjustment of the bank rate plus window guidance was frequently used to deal with balance-of-payments deficits. When the increase in imports required by the rapidly expanding domestic economy brought about a worsening in the balance-of-payments position and a reduction in foreign currency reserves, the government raised the bank rate to curb domestic demand. When the balance-of-payments position improved it was lowered and the economy was allowed to expand.[36]

Next let us turn to movements of interest rates on loans and discounting, which of course have fluctuated with the changes in the bank rate in the post-war period (Figure 10.2). They declined from the mid-1950s until 1973, and this was one reason for the rapid increase in private equipment investment in this period. During the period 1974–5 they were high due to tight money measures (particularly the high bank rate) introduced to deal with the price inflation

TABLE 10.13 Composition of increases in the money supply in Japan 1951–90 (000s million yen)

	Treasury funds				Bank of Japan credit				
	General government fund	State bonds	Foreign exchange funds	Sub-total	Loans	Sale and purchase of securities, and bills purchased	Sub-total[a]	Reserve deposits	Total
1951–60	-31.7	–	58.7	56.5	38.6	1.9	40.5	-15.8	81.2
1961–70	228.2	-310.1	102.9	23.6	185.3	325.5	522.3	-113.7	432.2
1971–80	5569.4	-5 378.6	601.3	792.1	-2.4	907.5	1 213.6	-373.2	1 632.5
1981–90	5906.6	5 553.1	15.9	369.4	397.4	1 197.9	1 544.2	131.5	2 045.1

Notes:
All figures are per annum.
[a] Including other items.

Sources:
HKT, 1966, pp. 9–10; KTN, 1973, pp. 9–10; 1981, pp. 15–16; 1990, pp. 33–4.

which followed the 'oil shock' of 1973. Inflation was eventually brought under control, but the economy stagnated. Then the bank rate was lowered and interest rates feel sharply. The low-level of official interest rate in the second half of the 1980s caused the 'bubbling' of the economy, which was calmed down by decreases for several times in the official interest rate in 1989.

Finally we must mention the 'low-interest-rates policy'.[37] This consisted of keeping interest rates (on deposits, government and company bonds, loans, discounting) low by various legal and administrative measures. This policy resulted in private companies investing more and an increase in the demand for capital. This in turn lead to an increase in loans from City Banks (overborrowing), an increase in their borrowing from the Bank of Japan (overloan) and a further increase in the money supply. There was a chronic shortage of capital as high growth continued and the banks gave priority to large companies for loans (credit rationing),[38] helping them to expand even more. Thus the low-interest-rates policy helped maintain economic growth by bringing about an increase in investment in private companies and by influencing the distribution of capital.[39]

10.4.2   The Growth Rate of the Money Supply

A narrow definition of money (M_1) is cash currency plus deposit money (current accounts + deposits of notice + special deposits – cheques – bills). These deposits are regarded in the same light as money because they can be withdrawn at any time. M_2, a wider definition of money, includes the same items plus time deposits. Although the latter cannot be withdrawn during a fixed period of time (usually one year), loans can be made against them, so that they are regarded as quasi-money. Postal savings, which are very important in Japan, consist of both kinds of deposits.

In both the pre-war and post-war periods the annual growth rate of M_2 (9 per cent, 15 per cent) was higher than that of M_1 (7 per cent, 13 per cent) (Table 10.14).[40] The annual growth rate of M_2 in the USA during the period 1892–1938 was 5.46 per cent.[41] The growth rate of cash currency issued by the Bank of England was 0.69 per cent for the period 1847–1900 and 8.24 per cent for 1901–37.[42] It could therefore be said that the growth rate of the money supply in Japan was high in the pre-war period. In the post-war period also it has been higher than in any of the developed countries of the west; the figure for the USA was between a quarter and a third of Japan's (Table 10.15).

TABLE 10.14   The growth rate of the money supply and the Marshallian k 1878–1988 (%)

	$G(M_1)$	$G(M_2)$	$G(k_1)$	$G(k_2)$
1878–1938	6.95	9.43	–	–
1889–1938	8.47	10.15	1.32	3.00
1956–88	12.63	15.30	0.52	2.96

Notes:
$k_1 = M_1/Y$.
$k_2 = M_2/Y$.
Y = GNE at current prices. Figures for M_1 and M_2 include the government.
The figures are simple averages of the annual growth rate based on seven-year moving averages (five-year averages for 1938 and 1988).

Sources:
M: Pre-war – Unpublished estimates by Fujino and Teranishi.
Post-war – SJK, varioun issues.
Y: See Table 10.1.

TABLE 10.15   Growth rate of the money supply in the developed countries 1955–89 (%)

	M_1	M_2
Italy	14.5	15.0
France	9.9	12.8
Denmark	10.8	10.4
UK	8.7	10.7
Former West Germany	8.2	10.0
Canada	8.4	10.5
Netherlands	7.8	10.6
Sweden	6.1	10.8
Australia	7.8	10.9
USA	5.3	7.3

Notes:
The figures are simple averages of the annual growth rate.

Sources:
IFSY, 1972; 1991, pp. 90–1, 94–5.

Hence it seems fair to say that the Bank of Japan has responded positively to the people's demand for money. It has of course meant that inflation has become a permanent feature, but it has provided the financial backing necessary for private investment and economic growth.[43]

10.4.3   Demand for Money – the Marshallian k

The growth rates of M_1 and M_2 fluctuated considerably in the pre-war period, but have remained consistently high in the post-war period. How can this be explained? First we must look at changes in demand, focussing on the following relationships:

$$M_1 = k_1 Y$$
$$M_2 = k_2 Y$$

where Y represents nominal GNE (GNP) and k is the Marshallian k. If we regard these equations as pre-ante demand functions, k represents the amounts of currency necessary when Y is at a certain level. The value of k_1 increased gradually in both the pre-war and post-war periods; the value of k_2 increased rapidly (Table 10.16).

$G(M)$, the growth rate of M, is equal to the sum of $G(k)$ and $G(Y)$, the growth rates of k and Y. In both periods $G(k_1)$ was 1–2 per cent and $G(k_2)$ 3–4 per cent (Table 10.14), $G(Y)$ was 7 per cent in the pre-war period and 12 per cent in the post-war period. In other words, the increase in the money supply was caused mainly by the increase in the level of economic activity. A comparison of the fluctuations in $G(M)$, $G(k)$ and $G(Y)$ reveals that in the pre-war period the changes in $G(M)$ were caused mainly by the changes in $G(Y)$, whereas in the post-war period they were the result of changes in $G(k)$.

How are we to account for the rising trend of the Marshallian k and its cyclical fluctuations? Yoshio Suzuki put forward several factors to explain the post-war rise in the value of k_2,[44] it is our opinion that two of them also applied before the war:

1. Currency is a luxury commodity; when income levels rise, a greater proportion of income tends to be held in the form of cash balances.
2. The development of the financial market brought about increased trading in assets.

Cyclical fluctuations in k_2 are governed by changes in people's preferences. If their preference for currency becomes stronger the value of k_2 will rise, while if their preference for securities and material assets becomes stronger, it will fall. The preference for currency is governed by interest rates on deposits, the preference for securities by the yield from them and the preference for material

TABLE 10.16 The Marshallian *k* in Japan and the USA 1888–1938

	Japan[a]		USA[b]	
	k_1	k_2	k_1	k_2
1888	0.304	0.350	–	–
1890	0.282	0.332	–	0.296[c]
1900	0.306	0.389	–	0.354
1920	0.466	0.870	0.274	0.408
1938	0.510	1.306	0.367	0.533

Notes:
[a] See Note, Table 10.14.
[b] Ratios of money supply to GNP.
[c] Three-year average.
The figures are seven-year moving averages (five-year average for 1938).

Sources:
Japan: Same as Table 10.14.
USA: US, Department of Commerce, Bureau of the Census, 1975, pp. 224, 992–3.

assets by the anticipated profits when they are used. Hence the value of k_2 is determined by t (time trend), i (interest rates on deposits), r (the yield from securities) and s (anticipated profits from material assets). Suzuki excluded i from his calculations because it was virtually constant. For r he used the yield from Japan's Telegram and Telephone Companies' bonds, and for s the ratio of profits to capital for all incorporated enterprises. Using the quarterly data for the period 1960–73 he obtained the following results:

$$k_2 = 87.319 + 0.254t - 0.951r - 9.913s \quad \bar{R} = 0.962$$
$$d = 0.31$$

The fitting of the equation was good and the signs (plus/minus) of the parameters all agreed with theory.

We used the same method for the pre-war period, except that instead of t we used real GNE per capita (y) in some cases, and included i (using interest rates on postal savings). Because there are no appropriate statistics for s we excluded it (we made the assumption that the changes for s paralleled those for r). For r we used the yield on company bonds (r_1) and stocks (r_2).[45] The results of our calculations show that the signs of all the parameters are as we expected and that the parameters are statistically significant (Table

TABLE 10.17   Functions of the Marshallian k 1906–40

Equation	Variable	Const.	t	y	i	r_1	r_2	$\bar{R}$	d
				Explanatory variables					
(1)	k_2	0.288	0.004	–	0.029	–0.019	–	0.752	0.94
		(2.90)	(5.23)		(1.77)	(1.47)			
(2)	k_2	–0.757	–	6.371	0.097	–	–0.012	0.942	0.53
		(3.55)		(16.51)	(2.87)		(1.67)		

Notes:
t = time trend (1906 = 1).
y = per capita GNE (1934–6 prices, 1000 yen).
i = interest rate on postal savings (%).
r_1 = rate of return on corporate bonds (%).
r_2 = rate of return on stocks (%).

Sources:
k_2: Same as Table 10.14.
y: Same as Figure 3.3.
i, r_1 and r_2: Fujino and Akiyama, 1977, pp. 226, 383, 546.

10.17). We believe that we have shown that k rose as a result of the increase in income per capita, the rise in interest rates on deposits and the fall in profits from financial assets.

Next let us compare the trends for k with other countries, first with pre-war USA[46] (Table 10.16). Unfortunately we only have figures for k_1 in the USA for a short period, but these figures do suggest that it rose faster there than in Japan. k_2 also rose (1.8-fold) in the USA, but more slowly than in Japan (3.9-fold) during the period 1890–1938. As a result, by the end of the nineteenth century there was only a slight difference between the value of k_2 in the two countries and by 1938 it was 2.5 times greater in Japan than in the USA. In Table 10.18 Japan is compared with eleven western countries in the post-war period. From it three generalizations can be made: First, the values of k_1 and k_2 have been higher in Japan than in most of the other countries. Second, the value of k_2 has risen in all the countries between 1955 and 1988, and particularly rapidly in France.

The Bank of Japan's Economic Research Department explains these trends in the following way:[47] k_2 is the product of the extent of savings of financial assets (the ratio of the balance of financial assets to GNP) and the strength of preference for cash deposits (the ratio of M_2 to the balance of financial assets). In Japan the slow development of the market for government and company bonds has meant that there is a strong preference for cash deposits, so that the value of k_2 is high. The rapid increase in savings and investment, reflected in the

TABLE 10.18 The Marshallian k in the developed countries 1955–88

	k_1			k_2		
	1955	1970	1988	1955	1970	1988
Japan	0.276	0.371	0.325	0.616	1.063	1.590
UK	0.310	0.191	0.346	0.466	0.381	0.833
Italy	0.298	0.490	0.361	0.468	0.772	0.673
France	0.334	0.307	0.272	0.347	0.463	0.696
Former						
West Germany	0.160	0.158	0.197	0.303	0.510	0.619
USA	0.345	0.219	0.166	0.465	0.645	0.615

Notes:
$k_1 = M_1/\text{GDP}$.
$k_2 = M_2/\text{GDP}$.
The figures are five-year averages for 1955 and 1988, seven-year averages for 1970.

Source:
Japan: Same as Table 10.14.
Other countries: Same as Table 10.15.

extent of savings of financial assets, resulted in a rapid increase in the value of k_2.

SUMMARY OF THE CHAPTER

1. In the pre-war period the size of public finances fluctuated considerably (because of fluctuations in military expenditure), but since the war it has been relatively constant. Taxation accounted for the overwhelming majority of government revenue in the early Meiji Period, but from the latter part of the period the proportion of revenue from government securities rose. Since the Second World War very little revenue has come from government securities; the majority has been from taxation. Pre-war fluctuations in government expenditure were caused mainly by increases and decreases in military expenditure, which accounted for a large part of current purchases; the proportion of capital formation and that of transfers fell. After the war the proportion of current purchases fell due to a sharp reduction in military expenditure; the proportion of capital formation and transfers rose. The proportion of capital formation, and to a lesser extent transfers, have continued to increase, with rising demands for social overhead capital and improvements in social welfare.

Compared with other developed countries government finances (as a proportion of GNP) are on a small scale, and the rate of taxation is low in Japan, while capital formation accounts for a high proportion of government expenditure.

2. The rapid development of Japan's financial system has been closely tied up with economic growth, and its development has been particularly significant because a considerable proportion of industrial capital consists of loans from financial institutions ('indirect financing'). Since the war financing has become more indirect and this has lead to 'overborrowing' and 'overloan'. The rapid increase in the demand for capital could not be met by companies 'internally', and issues of stock and bonds did not increase significantly because of the slow development of the stock market. The increase in loans to companies by City Banks could not be met from their balances on deposits, and they came to rely on loans from the Bank of Japan.

The stock of money increased rapidly throughout the pre-war and post-war periods. In the former it was supplied mainly by the Bank of Japan's buying of government securities and expanding its credit; since the war the latter of these two methods has been the most important. The increase in the demand for money can be explained by the rise in the value of the Marshallian k and the rapid increase in nominal output. Because the Marshallian k's value has risen comparatively quickly it is now higher than in most other countries.

At first sight it appears that the main instrument for government regulation of effective demand in the post-war period has been monetary policy (the Bank of Japan's control over interest rates plus its 'window guidance'), and that fiscal policy (adjustment of government expenditure) has played a very minor role. However, it must be remembered that passive fiscal policy – Japan's 'special' built-in stabilizer – has also been very effective.

FURTHER READING

On public finances:
  Ackley and Ishi, 1976
  Emi, 1963
  Emi and Ishi, 1979
  Fujita, 1966; 1975–6
  Ishi, 1974

Komiya, 1966c
Patrick, 1968

On the financial system:
Fujino, 1968
Goldsmith, 1983
Nishikawa, 1974
Patrick, 1967
Suzuki, 1980
Tachi, 1966
Wallich and Wallich, 1976
Yamamura, 1972

11 Prices and Living Standards

In the first half of this chapter we discuss prices. In Japan real output has increased rapidly, but so have prices; economic growth accompanied by inflation has characterized the Japanese economy. In Section 11.1 we look first at various indicators of price changes in an attempt to discover the causes. In Section 11.2 we discuss changes in the price structure (relative prices of different sectors of the economy) and the causes, and then the significance of inflationary growth.

In the second half we analyze long-term changes in living standards. Has the welfare of the people increased during the course of modern economic growth? If it has, how does the increase in Japan compare with that in other countries? To answer these questions, first (in Section 11.3) we look at changes in incomes and consumption. Then (in Section 11.4) we discuss housing and other stock bearing on living standards, and qualitative aspects such as life-expectancy and the environment. Finally we attempt an overall evaluation of the beneficial and detrimental effects of economic development in Japan.

11.1 PRICE CHANGES AND THEIR CAUSES

11.1.1 Growth Rate of General Prices

Economic growth in Japan has been accompanied, in both the pre-war and the post-war period, by rapidly rising prices. The growth rate of the GNE (GNP) deflator, the most comprehensive indicator of prices, was 3.8 per cent during the period 1889–1938 and 5.0 per cent during 1956–88 (Table 11.1). The pre-war figure is much higher than in most other developed countries. During the period 1863–1935 the growth rate of the GNP deflator for France was 5.21 per cent, 2.11 per

TABLE 11.1 Growth rates of various price indexes in Japan 1889–1988
(%)

	1889–1938	*1956–1988[a]*
(A) *Deflators by expenditure item*		
Personal consumption expenditure (*PC*)	3.91	5.01
Government expenditure (*GC*)	3.61	7.20
Fixed capital formation (*CF*)	3.14	3.67
Exports (*E*)	1.58	1.45
Imports (*M*)	3.03	2.15
Gross national expenditure (GNE)	3.84	4.97
(B) *Deflators by industry group*		
Primary (*A*)	4.09	4.71
M Sector	2.96	3.43
Mining and manufacturing	3.01	1.98
Construction	3.49	6.71
Infrastructure	2.06	4.21
S Sector	4.03	6.12
Non-primary (*M* + *S*)	3.35	4.89

Notes:
The figures are simple averages of the annual growth rate based on seven-year moving
   averages of deflators (five-year averages for 1938).
[a] 1956–87 for Panel B.

Sources:
The deflators were calculated by dividing expenditure and output at current prices by
   expenditure and output at constant prices.
Figures for expenditure are from Figure 3.3. Figures for output are from Table 5.4.

cent for Sweden, 1.44 per cent for Germany, 0.92 per cent for the UK
and 0.34 per cent for the USA.[1] The post-war figure for Japan,
although higher than the pre-war figure, is approximately in the
middle of the table of developed countries. For the period 1955–88,
France, the UK, Italy, Denmark, Sweden and Australia show higher
growth rates (6–10 per cent) than Japan. The USA, the Netherlands
and Belgium show slightly lower growth rates (about 4 per cent) than
Japan.[2]

In the pre-war period the growth rate of Japan's GNE deflator
described a series of long swings (Figure 11.1), which coincided almost
exactly with the long swings in the economic growth rate discussed in
Chap. 3, Sec. 2. Particularly worthy of our attention is the sharp rise
in prices during the post-First World War boom, and the sharp fall in
the recession that followed. The growth rate of the price indices

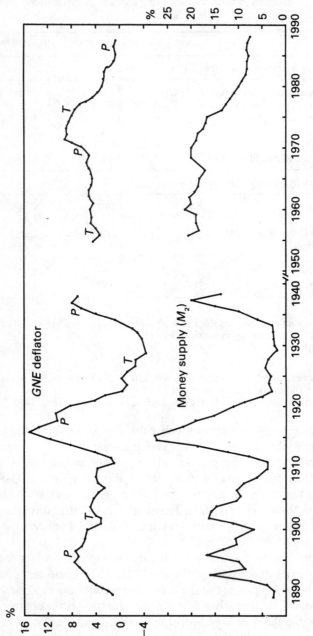

FIGURE 11.1   Growth rates of GNE deflator and money supply in Japan 1889–1988

Note, Source: See Table 11.1 and Table 10.14.

reached 15 per cent in the former (based on seven-year moving averages), the second highest figure after the hyper-inflation immediately after the Second World War,[3] while in the latter it was a minus figure. It was the first time that prices had fallen in absolute terms since Matsukata's deflationary measures of 1881–5.

We have no estimates for the Second World War and immediately after, but we do know that there was an unprecedented rise in prices. The situation improved gradually once economic recovery began to get under way and in the mid-1950s the growth rate of the GNE deflator was less than 4 per cent. It rose again in the 1960s and was very high in the early 1970s. The economic growth rate showed a rising trend from the mid-1950s to the late 1960s, when it was positively correlated with the growth rate of prices, and then began to fall. It was not correlated with the growth rate of prices in the 1970s, when we saw a new phenomenon, 'stagflation' – recession coupled with price inflation.

In 1973–4, we saw 'runaway inflation', when the government's inappropriate reaction to the rise in the value of yen brought about excess liquidity, and the 'oil shock' stimulated investment activity. A subsequent tight money policy and a decrease in import prices due to yen revaluation caused a decline in the growth rate of prices. The growth rate was only 1 per cent in the latter half of the 1980s; now Japan is one of the countries with stable prices.

11.1.2 Causes of Price Changes

To explain price inflation we test two hypotheses: cost-push and demand-pull. The cost-push hypothesis signifies that a rise in $G(l)$, the growth rate of labour costs per unit of output, brings about a rise in $G(P)$, the annual growth rate (over the previous year) of P, the GNE deflator.[4] l is the ratio of total wages paid to real output, and hence is also the ratio of w (money wages per capita) to y (real productivity).

The demand-pull hypothesis stands for that $G(P)$ is affected by the balance of supply and demand for commodities. Here we use two indicators to represent excess demand: the reciprocal of the inventory-sales ratio, φ, and $G(Y)$, the growth rate of real GNE.[5] Our use of φ is justified, because when excess demand increases the amount of unintended inventory decreases, and when excess supply increases it increases. There was also, we believe, a positive relationship between $G(O)$ and excess demand.

We have estimated price adjustment functions where $G(P)$ is explained by $G(l)$, $1/\varphi$, and $G(Y)$ (Table 11.2). The parameters for excess demand for 1903–39 and 1954–88 (with non-smoothed figures – Panels A and C), calculated from equations (2) and (3), were not statistically significant, while according to equation (1) $G(l)$ on its own accounted for most of $G(P)$. For the post-war period all parameters were estimated statistically significant in equations (2) and (3). Panels B, D and E were used to supplement A and C. In Panel B (seven-year moving averages, 1910–37) the parameter for $1/\varphi$ from equation (2) had the wrong sign, but the parameters for $G(l)$ and $G(Y)$ from equation (3) were both statistically significant. In Panel D (non-smoothed figures, 1954–70) the parameters for $G(l)$, $1/\varphi$ and $G(Y)$ were all statistically significant. Hence the effect of changes in demand was significant except during the 1970s and 1980s. This indicates that in the 1970s and 1980s the effect of low production costs was significant; Panel E (non-smoothed figures, 1971–88) demonstrates that $G(l)$ on its own accounted for $G(P)$ to a considerable extent.

Having determined that the fluctuations in $G(P)$ during the period 1910–37 (Panel B, equation (3)) can be explained by $G(l)$ and $G(Y)$, let us next ask how much these two growth rates contributed to its rise in this period. $G(Y)$'s contribution was in fact greater than $G(l)$'s ($\Delta G(Y)$ − 59.2 per cent, $\Delta G(l)$ − 40.8 per cent, calculated from Table 11.2, Panel B, equation (3)). During the period 1954–70 $G(l)$'s contribution was large 64.7 per cent; $G(Y)$'s contribution was 35.3 per cent – calculated from Panel D equation (3) of Table 11.2.

To summarize, it appears that pre-war and post-war price movements were affected similarly by fluctuations in production costs and in the supply and demand for commodities. In the 1970s and 1980s, however, the effect of the latter was negligible, the effect of the former dominant. However, caution is called for; the delineation of the period and the choice of data (especially the indicators of excess demand) could alter the results considerably.

11.1.3 Inflation and the Money Supply

Monetarists assert that the money supply is an important factor in deciding the rate of inflation. When we compare the growth rate $G(P)$ of GNE deflators and the growth rate $G(M_2)$ shown in Figure 11.1, the correlation can be detected in the pre-war period but the correlation weakens after the Second World War. This is shown

TABLE 11.2 Price adjustment functions 1903–88

| | Equa-tion | Vari-able | Const. | Explanatory variables | | | $\bar{R}$ | d |
				$G(1)$	$1/\phi$	$G(Y)$		
(A) 1907–39 (Non-smoothed figures)	(1)	$G(P)$	2.243 (2.13)	0.625 (6.92)	–	–	0.752	1.64
	(2)	$G(P)$	-1.655 (0.25)	0.605 (6.24)	3.195 (0.59)	–	0.746	1.63
	(3)	$G(P)$	2.282 (1.90)	0.616 (7.32)	–	0.008 (0.04)	0.744	1.75
(B) 1910–37 (Seven-year moving averages)	(1)	$G(P)$	1.589 (3.65)	0.706 (11.37)	–	–	0.894	0.38
	(2)	$G(P)$	6.469 (1.70)	0.750 (10.68)	-4.095 (1.29)	–	0.897	0.42
	(3)	$G(P)$	0.335 (0.43)	0.670 (11.40)	–	0.499 (2.14)	0.897	0.49
(C) 1954–88 (Non-smoothed figures)	(1)	$G(P)$	1.674 (4.11)	0.636 (11.62)	–	–	0.798	2.04
	(2)	$G(P)$	-1.582 (0.96)	0.636 (12.15)	2.980 (2.03)	–	0.903	2.21
	(3)	$G(P)$	-0.262 (0.37)	0.683 (13.45)	–	0.252 (3.15)	0.917	2.04
(D) 1954–70 (Non-smoothed figures)	(1)	$G(P)$	2.681 (2.94)	0.515 (2.80)	–	–	0.547	2.18
	(2)	$G(P)$	-29.930 (1.94)	0.738 (3.76)	25.708 (2.12)	–	0.657	2.39
	(3)	$G(P)$	-1.313 (0.74)	0.592 (3.69)	–	0.395 (2.52)	0.696	1.97
(E) 1971–88 (Non-smoothed figures)	(1)	$G(P)$	0.995 (2.46)	0.671 (14.86)	–	–	0.961	1.81

Notes:
P = GNE deflator.
l = unit labour cost = $w \div y$.
w = per capita wages for the entire economy.
y = real labour productivity = real GDP $\div$ employment.
ϕ = inventory rate = inventory $\div$ total value of shipments (pre-war) or amount of sales (post-war).
  (1934–6 = 1 for the pre-war and 1985 = 1 for the post-war period).

Sources:
P: Same as Table 11.1.
w: See Figure 9.4.
Real GDP: See Table 5.4.
Real GNE: See Figure 3.3.
Employment: See Table 9.1.
ϕ: Pre-war – Fujino and Igarashi's estimates (1973, pp. 430–1, 448–9) based on the statistics for Ōsaka City. Post-war – Since 1968: the manufacturing products inventory index by the Tsūshō-Sangyōshō (Ministry of International Trade and Industry) (KY, 1985, p. 6; 1991, p. 6). Up to 1968 ϕ is estimated based on the 1968 figure by linking the ratio of the amount of inventory to the amount of sales for the corporate enterprises of all industries (HKTNS, various issues).

TABLE 11.3   Correlation between growth rate of GNE deflator and growth
rate of money supply in Japan 1886–1888

	$G(M_1)$	$G(M_1)_{-1}$	$G(M_2)$	$G(M_2)_{-1}$
1886–1940	0.415**	0.647**	0.414**	0.622**
1955–1988	0.265	0.493**	0.283	0.547**

Notes:
The correlation coefficient is adjusted by the degree of freedom ($\bar{r}$). The growth rates
are based on non-smoothed figures.
** signify that the correlation coefficient is statistically significant at the 1 per cent
level.

Sources:
GNE deflator: Table 11.1.
M_1 and M_2: Table 10.14.

clearly by the correlation coefficients in Table 11.3.

The fact that $G(M)$ and $G(P)$ were closely correlated in the pre-war period does, however, necessarily support the monetarist view. The following interpretation is also possible: $G(P)$ was high, $G(Y)$ rose and as a result (here we assume that the value of the Marshallian k did not fall) the demand for money and therefore $G(M)$ increased. In order to avoid criticisms such as this monetarists have made calculations with a time lag between $G(P)$ and $G(M)$. Shōzaburō Fujino, for example, found from monthly data that in both the pre-war period and the post-war period until 1962 fluctuations in $G(M)$ were reflected 4–6 months later in $G(P)$.[6] The conclusion in a Bank of Japan survey, based on quarterly data, was that fluctuations in M_2 were reflected in prices 3–6 months later between 1957 and 1970, and 9–12 months later between 1970 and 1974.[7]

We have used annual data and made our own calculations, setting a time lag of one year (Table 11.3). We found that there was a significant correlation, clearer than in calculations without a time lag, both for the pre-war and the post-war periods. This result tells us that we cannot deny the point of view held by the monetarist, that the increase and decrease of money supply influences the rate of inflation to some extent.[8]

11.2   THE PRICE STRUCTURE AND INFLATIONARY GROWTH

11.2.1   Price Structure in the Demand Side

The GNE deflator is the weighted average of several expenditure deflators. Let us compare the growth rates of individual prices (Table 11.1). First, when the deflator of the fixed capital formation (*CF*) is compared with the deflator of personal consumption expenditure (*PC*), it can be detected that the growth rate of personal consumption expenditure was larger than fixed capital formation, both for the pre-war and the post-war periods. As a result, the relative rate of personal consumption expenditure against fixed capital formation was increased. This is because, based on the fact that *PC* includes the products of traditional industries such as agricultural products and foods, and *CF* includes the products of modern industries such as machinery, productivity of modern industry has suddenly increased and made the relative price of products made by the traditional industries low.

According to the research done by R. A. Gordon, the relative price of *CF* against *PC* in the USA, the UK, Canada, Sweden and Denmark was increased in the pre-war period. In the post-war period (from the 1950s until the end of the 1980s), the relative price of *CF* was increased in the seven out of a total of eleven developed countries (in addition to the above-mentioned five countries: Italy, France, Australia, Holland, Belgium and the former West Germany). Therefore Japan can be said to be one of the minority countries.

Second, when the deflators of exports (*E*) and imports (*I*) are compared, it will be found that the growth rate of exports is smaller for both the pre-war and the post-war periods. Moreover, the increase in the rate of export prices was much lower than the increase in the rate of deflators of *PC* and *CF*, and it was also lower compared to the increased rate of the mining and manufacturing industry price index. This indicates that the increase of productivity and the decrease of the relative price of export industries among manufacturing industries (textile industries in the pre-war period and machinery industries in the post-war period) were particularly significant. As a result, the terms of trade (the ratio of export prices to import prices) decreased and exports increased (Chap. 7, Sec. 3). From this, we can see that behind changes in price structure on the expenditure side, there are changes in price structure on the production side, namely the relative prices among different industries.

11.2.2   Relative Sectoral Prices

A and S Sector prices have risen relative to M Sector prices (P_A/P_M, P_S/P_M) in both the pre-war and the post-war period (Figure 11.2). Particularly remarkable has been their continuing rapid rise in the post-war period. How can these trends be accounted for?

Figure 11.2 shows the changes in relative labour costs per unit for the three sectors (l_A/l_M, l_S/l_M), which have followed a similar pattern to relative prices. There has been a strong correlation between P_A/P_M and l_A/l_M, and between P_S/P_M and l_S/l_M in both the pre-war and the post-war period (Table 11.4). A rise in the relative unit cost of labour may be caused by a rise in relative wages (w), or a relative fall in real productivity (Y). The significant (positive) correlation was not found between relative prices and relative wages (w_A/w_M, w_S/w_M), in both the pre-war and post-war periods. On the other hand, there was a significant negative correlation between relative prices and relative productivity (Y_A/Y_M, Y_S/Y_M). In other words although relative prices have increased due to the rise of relative costs in both A and S Sectors, the effects of a relative decrease in real productivity was larger than the relative increase of wages.

If we regard the A and S Sectors as the traditional sector, and the M Sector as the modern sector, we can say that productivity in the modern sector has improved rapidly due to technical progress, while the traditional sector has consistently lagged behind in this respect. In the pre-war period the difference between wages in the modern and the traditional sectors increased (the former being the higher) and this served to partially cancel out the change in relative productivity, but nevertheless the relative prices of the traditional sector rose. In the post-war period the wage differential narrowed, and the rise in the relative prices of the traditional sector was greater. The difference in the rate of productivity increases, or the rate of technical progress, has been the major factor in the relative price change.

11.2.3   Inflationary Growth

Here we discuss two aspects of price fluctuations that are closely tied up with economic growth:

1. The fact that in both the pre-war and the post-war period

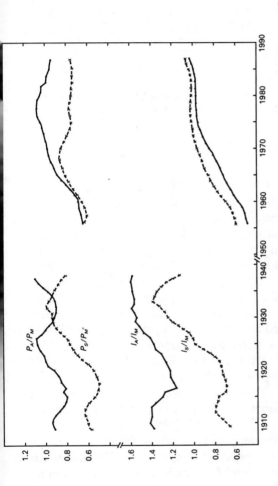

FIGURE 11.2 Relative prices and unit labour costs of major industry groups in Japan 1909–87

Notes:

P = output price index (1934–6 = 1 for the pre-war and 1985 = 1 for the post-war period).

l = unit labour cost = per capita wages ÷ (real GDP ÷ employment).

The figures are seven-year moving averages (five-year averages for 1938 and 1987).

Sources:

Same as Table 11.1.

w: Same as Figure 9.4.

Real GDP: Same as Table 5.1.

Employment: Same as Table 9.1.

TABLE 11.4   Correlation between industry groups' relative prices and their determinants 1906–89

	l_A/l_M	y_A/y_M	w_A/w_M
P_A/P_M			
1906–40	0.404**	−0.427**	0.235
1953–89	0.541**	−0.899**	−0.587

	l_S/l_M	y_S/y_M	w_S/w_M
P_S/P_M			
1906–40	0.899**	−0.860**	0.573**
1953–89	0.981**	−0.843**	0.175

Notes:
Refer to notes, Table 11.3.

Sources: Same as Figure 11.2.

economic growth has been accompanied by inflation. Except for two periods, 1881–5 and the 1920s, prices have risen continuously; Japan provides a typical example of 'inflationary growth'. This indicates that demand has consistently exceeded supply, or that investment has consistently exceeded savings. This has occurred because it has become easier to pass on increased production costs into higher prices and also because prices, and therefore profits, have increased faster than production costs. Increased profits have in turn lead to further increases in savings and investment. (This process has contributed to economic growth and trend acceleration.) However, inflation in Japan has been comparatively mild, and confidence in the yen has been maintained except during the period immediately after the Second World War.[11] This contrasts with the Soviet Union in the 1930s where rapid economic growth took place, but was accompanied by runaway inflation.

2. The changes in the relative price of agricultural and industrial products. In the pre-war period it remained fairly constant. Rapid agricultural growth until about 1910 enabled self-sufficiency in foodstuffs, and from then until the Second World War the rise in agricultural prices was contained by the importation of cheap agricultural products from the colonies. This not only kept the relative price stable, it also contributed to limiting the rise in general prices. This again contrasts with the Soviet Union of the 1930s; agricultural output there could not keep pace with industrialization and excess

demand caused agricultural prices to rise sharply.[12]

In the post-war period agricultural prices in Japan rose considerably, pushing up prices in general and consumer prices in particular. This was the result of increased production costs in agriculture, and government subsidies that allowed these costs to be passed on into prices. The post-war rise in agricultural prices has certainly increased the cost of living but at the same time it has served to raise agricultural wages, and reduce the difference between them and wages in the non-agricultural sector.

11.3 LIVING STANDARDS

11.3.1 Increases in Incomes and Consumption

The welfare of the people of a country depends on both quantitative and qualitative factors. First let us consider the former. The growth rate of real GNE (GNP) per capita in Japan was 2.1 per cent during the period 1889–1938, and 5.7 per cent in the period 1955–88 (Table 3.2). During her modern economic growth era Japan has had the second highest rate of growth after Sweden (Table 3.1). GNP, however, includes such items as depreciation, taxation and corporate reserves, which do not constitute income for households. A more apposite indicator of living standards is personal disposable income, which excludes these items, but includes transfers of income. The growth rate of personal disposable income per capita (PY/N) differed little from the growth rate of GNE. It was 2.3 per cent during the period 1895–1936 and 4.1 per cent during the period 1956–87.[13]

Another indicator of living standards is personal consumption expenditure per capita (PC/N). This grew at 1.5 per cent during the period 1889–1938,[14] a lower figure than the growth rate of GNE per capita. Consumption expenditure's share of GNE fell during this period. How does this growth rate compare with other developed countries? PC/N in the USA (2.1 per cent 1889–1948) and Sweden (2.3 per cent 1882–1948) was considerably higher than in Japan. In Germany (1.4 per cent 1851–1913) and Canada (1.3 per cent 1870–1930) it was similar to Japan, and in the UK (0.8 per cent 1880–1939), Italy (0.5 per cent 1861–1940) and Norway (0.9 per cent 1865–1930) it was considerably lower, so that the figure for Japan was approximately equal to the average of the western developed countries.[15] During the period 1956–87, however, PC/N in Japan was 3.8 per cent,

TABLE 11.5   Living standards in seven developed countries 1988–9

	Per capita personal disposable income (1988)	Per capita consumption expenditure (1988)	Manufacturing wage rate (1989) (dollar/hour)
	(000s dollars)		
Japan	15.5	13.3	10.7
USA	14.9	13.9	11.5
Former West Germany	11.8	10.4	10.2
France	11.6	10.2	6.8
Italy	10.8	9.3	6.9
UK	9.7	9.4	8.1

Sources:
Personal disposable income, personal consumption expenditure, YNAS, 1980.
Wage rate: KHT, 1991, pp. 3–4, 43–6, 110–2, 168.
Figures for income, consumption and wage rate, are represented by the currencies of
   respective countries converted to dollars according to the exchange rates.

compared to the UK (2.2 per cent), Canada (2.4 per cent), and the USA (2.1 per cent).[16]

The standard of living in Japan has improved in both the pre-war and the post-war period, but before the war surplus labour kept the rate of wage increases below the economic growth rate and traditional consumption patterns remained dominant, so that improvement was not rapid. Since the war, however, due to rapid economic growth, the transition to a labour shortage and the adoption of western consumption patterns, living standards have risen more rapidly here than in any other country in the world. How does the standard of living in Japan today compare with other countries? According to three indicators (personal disposable income per capita, personal consumption expenditure per capita, the manufacturing wage rate – Table 11.5), in 1988–9 it was much higher than in the UK, and comparable to previous West Germany or the USA. Nevertheless, as price levels in Japan are relatively high when compared to other countries, the GNP per capita measured by average purchasing power prices and wage levels for actual labour hours remain 75 per cent (1989) and 57.1 per cent (1987) respectively of those of the USA.[17] But when we recall that in 1870 Japan's GNP per capita was

TABLE 11.6   Composition of consumption expenditure in Japan 1880–1987
(%)

	Food	Clothing	Housing	Lighting and fuel	Others
1880	65.9	7.9	6.7	5.3	14.2
1900	64.0	7.9	7.8	2.9	17.4
1920	59.3	13.8	7.4	4.1	15.4
1938	49.0	13.7	11.9	4.3	21.1
1950	56.4	12.3	4.6	4.9	21.8
1970	33.8	9.7	4.9	4.4	47.2
1987	26.1	7.2	4.8	5.9	56.0

Notes:
The figures are based on seven-year moving averages (five-year average for 1938 and 1987).

Sources:
To 1972: Ohkawa and Shinohara, 1979, pp. 338–45. Since 1973: the *Kakei Chōsa* (Family Income and Expenditure Survey) by the Sōmuchō, Tōkeikyoku (Management and Coordination Agency, Statistics Bureau) (KTN, 1955, pp. 295–6; 1972, p. 279; 1973, p. 281; 1991, pp. 323–4).

only 36 per cent of the USA's and 25 per cent of the UK's[18] it brings home to us how much the times have changed.

11.3.2   Changing Consumption Patterns

Table 11.6 shows the changes in consumption that have taken place in the past one hundred years.[19] Let us look first at Engel's coefficient, the proportion of consumption expenditure going on foodstuffs. It has declined, slowly during the pre-war period, rapidly during the post-war period. This has, of course, been the case in all developed countries. In Germany it fell from 45.7 per cent in 1851–60 to 38.4 per cent in 1911–13, in Sweden from 37.7 per cent in 1864 to 32.1 per cent in 1938, and in the USA from 35.8 per cent in 1869 to 24.9 per cent in 1924–33.[20] Its fall in Japan in both the pre-war and the post-war period, however, has been steeper than in these countries, and Engel's coefficient is now at a similar level in Japan as in other developed countries.[21]

The proportion spent on housing has increased, because urbanization has raised the relative price of rents. The proportion spent on other items – leisure, education, commuting, health and hygiene – has increased, particularly since the war.

TABLE 11.7   Gini coefficient for Japan 1923–86

	Yamaguchi Prefecture			
	Three cities and towns	*Five villages*	*Japan*	
1923	0.536	0.523	1963	0.361
1930	0.525	0.477	1968	0.354
1937	0.563	0.476	1973	0.350
			1979	0.336
			1986	0.356

Sources:
Pre-war: Estimates based on the local tax data by Minami and Ono (1987, p. 337, table 2).
Post-war: Estimates by Terasaki (1990, p. 27) based on the *Kokumin Seikatsu Kisochōsa* (Basic Survey of National Life) by the Kōseishō (Ministry of Welfare).

11.3.3   Income Distribution

We feel that a discussion of income distribution is necessary here, because the same national income distributed more equally means increased welfare. Unfortunately we do not have reliable data for the whole country on the household income of all income groups in the pre-war period. There are data on Class 3 national income tax, but this only concerns the higher income brackets. It is possible to make fairly accurate estimates from the records of a local government household tax[22] levied by most cities, towns and villages, but few of these document have been studied. Akira Ono and the author have recently been accumulating data from cities, towns and villages all over the country, which we hope will give us a better idea of pre-war trends.

Here, as one example, I will introduce the estimated results gained in Yamaguchi Prefecture (Table 11.7). First, it can be noted that the Gini coefficients of the three cities and towns are much higher than those of the five villages. There is no doubt that income distribution in cities was far less equal compared to that in agricultural villages. Second, when the changes that happened in the Gini coefficients of the three cities and towns are focused on, we can understand that income distribution in the 1920s was more equal, but then became unequal in the 1930s. In the 1930s industrialization progressed rapidly, one of the negative consequences being unequality. In contrast, income distribution was equalized in rural areas. Third, we see that the estimated Gini coefficient produced by pooling the samples of three cities and towns and five villages was 0.532 in 1930.[23] (The reason for this figure being slightly higher than the Gini coefficient for three cities and towns, or the Gini coefficient for five villages, is that there is a big gap between the income per household in urban areas and in rural areas. In the same year the income per household in the three cities and towns was 1.55 times higher than the income per household in the five villages.) These Gini coefficients were significantly higher than the ones in the post-war Japan or the ones in the developing countries today. Although I have not finished measuring the income distribution of Japan as a whole, even once it was completed I would think that the above-mentioned result would not be very influenced by it. This is because each of the following facts, which can be found in the national labour market, supports my reasoning that income distribution in the pre-war period was very unequal and this unequality was intensified by industrialization.[24]

1. The productivity differential and the wage differential between agricultural and non-agricultural sectors were larger compared to the ones in the post-war period. These differentials were expanded in the pre-war period.
2. The relative labour share of income in the non-agricultural sector was extremely low compared to the post-war period. This ratio was decreased in the pre-war period.
3. Each wage differential in the urban industries (for instance, the wage differential depending on the scale of each enterprise) was large compared to the one in post-war period. This was expanded in the pre-war period.
4. The cityward drifting of population continued.

When we come to the post-war period a considerable amount of data is available, and much research has been done on it.[25] According to Yasuhiko Terasaki's calculations the Gini coefficient for Japan in 1963 was 0.36, much lower than our estimates for Yamaguchi Prefecture in the pre-war period (Table 11.7). While it is not suggested that Yamaguchi Prefecture is representative of the whole country, there seems to be little doubt that income distribution has become much more equal since the war, initially because of SCAP's democratization measures and the fall in the value of the wealthy's financial assets in the severe inflation immediately after the war.[26] In the 1960s the Gini coefficient fell again, probably due to the reduced wage differentials as the labour surplus became a shortage, and the end of the downward trend in labour's share of income in the non-agricultural sector. The Gini coefficient showed no definite trend since the 1970s.

To summarize, income distribution became more unequal in the pre-war period, but has taken two great strides towards equality since the war, the first immediately after it, the second during the 1960s[27] (after regressing during the 1950s[28]). Kuznets argues that during the long process of modern economic growth income distribution at first becomes more unequal, but later the trend is towards greater equality.[29] By examining the Japanese experience in comparison with this hypothesis, which is referred to as the reversed U-shaped hypothesis, we can the following comments. The increasing trend in inequality during early industrialization was clearly seen in Japan, but the decreasing trend in later years was not so obvious. A substantial decrease in inequality was noticed immediately after the Second World War through structural changes such as the resolution of *zaibatsu* and spread of trade unions, and not as a consequence of economic development. (The decrease in inequality after the 1960s was due to the transition of the economy from having a labour surplus to a labour shortage, but this decrease was quite small compared with the drop from the pre-war to the post-war period.)

F. Paukert estimated the Gini coefficients of various countries in the world in or near to 1965, and after cross-sectional analysis identified Kuznets curves.[30] According to his study, when GDP per capita reaches 200–300 dollars the rise in the Gini coefficient changes to a decline, and the critical point is at 0.5. However, Japan's figure of 0.36 (1963) is much lower than one would expect with this figure for GDP per capita (500–1000 dollars). The Gini coefficient of the three countries with the highest GDP per capita (Denmark, Sweden and the USA – over 2000 dollars) was higher, 0.37. Differences in statistical sources and methods make international comparison of Gini coefficients a hazardous exercise, but we can say that without doubt the degree of equality in income distribution in Japan in 1963 (and probably in recent years) was not inferior to the developed countries of the west.[31]

Table 11.8   Residential capital stock per capita in Japan 1885–1989

	Gross capital stock (1934–6 prices, yen)	Net capital stock
1885	196	–
1900	243	–
1920	233	–
1940	226	–
	(1965 prices, 000s yen)	(1985 prices, 000s yen)
1955	196	–
1969	291	427
1989	–	1 499

Sources:
Gross capital stock: Ohkawa and Shinohara, 1979, pp. 366–9.
Net capital stock: KKKN, 1982, pp. 750–1; 1985, p. 368; 1991, p. 410. Population: See Figure 3.3.

11.4   LIVING STANDARDS: CHANGES IN STOCK, QUALITATIVE MEASUREMENT

11.4.1   Increases in Stock

Progress in the area of housing in Japan has been much slower than with the other two basic necessities, food and clothing. Housing stock's share of gross capital stock fell from 51 per cent in 1885 to 22 per cent in 1940,[32] whereas in the USA it remained virtually unchanged between 1900 (42 per cent) and 1945 (41 per cent).[33] Capital formation in Japan was concentrated on productive areas, at the expense of non-productive ones. This helped maintain a high rate of growth, but it did nothing to improve the housing situation; real housing stock per capita showed no distinct trend during the pre-war period (Table 11.8).

Since the war some improvement has been seen. Housing capital's share of total capital has fallen during the period of high growth rate (36 per cent in 1955 and 22 per cent in 1969), but thereafter it was almost stable (22 per cent in 1988). Housing capital per capita increased during the period 1955–89, especially since the 1970s. The size of units of accommodation also increased. The number of *tatami* mats[34] per household rose from 3.50 in 1948 to 9.55 in 1988.[35] The quality of housing has also improved steadily. However, housing in Japan remains inferior to housing in the west. In 1988 there was little difference in the number of people per room (0.7 in Japan, 0.6–0.9 in western developed countries).[36] But there was a big difference in quality.

One of the main reasons for the slow progress in housing has been the shortage of available land, while urbanization and a rise in the number of mortgages increased the demand for land and raised its price sharply in urban areas.[37] The cost of construction has also risen significantly. After the Second World War, there were three different periods of time when Japan experienced jumps in land value: in the middle of the 1960s (around the time of the Tōkyō Olympics); at the beginning of the 1970s (the time of the 'reconstruction of Japanese islands' boom); and in the second half of the 1980s (the time of the Bubble Economy). For the first two periods the increase in land values was spread over the whole country, but in the second half of the 1980s the increase mainly happened in the large cities. Towards the end of the 1980s, property prices in the large cities has risen to such an extent that it was impossible for the average worker to buy a house. Inequality in land property values between urban and rural areas was caused by a regional imbalance of increases in land values. This is in surprising contrast to the fact that there had not been many changes in income on financial assets between urban and rural areas since the middle of the 1970s.[38]

The increased purchase of consumer durables, particularly electrical products and cars, has been remarkable in the post-war period, as their prices have fallen and incomes have risen. Vacuum cleaners and washing-machines have reduced the burden of housework and allowed housewives to join the labour force or increase their leisure time. Television, record players and cars have been a source of considerable pleasure to the people. On the detrimental side the increased number of cars has also served to exacerbate environmental pollution.

11.4.2 Living Standards: a Qualitative Picture

There has been a beneficial and a detrimental side to modern economic growth. Progress in medicine and hygiene and improved living standards have increased life-expectancy. According to the first 'life table', for 1891–98, it was 43 for males and 44 for females.[39] By 1988 it was 76 and 82 respectively, the highest figures in the world. The quality of life has also been enhanced by the rapid development of transport and the media and the increase in leisure time and activities.

TABLE 11.9 Ratio of real GNE to land area and of energy consumption to land area and to real GNE in Japan 1955–88

	Real GNE	Energy consumption	Energy consumption
	Land area (million yen/km²)	Land area (tons/km²)	Real GNE (tons/million yen)
1955	116		
1960	172	292	1.69
1970	460	893	1.94
1980	716	1 168	1.63
1988	983	1 289	1.31

Notes:
Real GNE: At 1985 prices.
Energy consumption: In coal equivalent.

Sources:
Real GNE: Figure 3.3.
Land area and energy consumption: KHT, 1983, pp. 5–6, 167; 1991, p. 173.

On the minus side we can cite the damage to the natural environment. As we said in Ch. 8, Sec. 1, urbanization, combined with population density, adversely affected the urban environment, and industry and automobiles have polluted the air and the water. The figures in Tables 11.9 and 11.10 underline the causes. Real GNE per acre of land has increased rapidly and is presently the highest figure in the world, with the former West Germany. Consumption of fuels, particularly oil, has increased rapidly; the consumption of energy per acre of land is higher in Japan than most of the other developed countries. As a result, the amount of sulphur dioxide discharged into the air, and the concentration of organic matter in rivers increased apace until the latter half of the 1960s,[40] when regulations were introduced to combat pollution, and companies began investing much money in pollution prevention. There has been a considerable decrease in the amount of sulphur dioxide discharged since 1967, and in the concentration of organic matter in rivers since 1970. Meanwhile much effort has been put into energy conservation since the 'oil shock' of 1973. The amount of energy consumed per acre of land has declined, and energy consumption as a ratio of GNE is now the lowest among the developed countries.

The extent of social security is another important factor in determining the welfare of the people. Real expenditure on social security, and its share of national income, has increased in both the pre-war

TABLE 11.10   Ratio of GNE to land area and of energy consumption to land area and to GNE in seven developed countries 1988

	GNE Land area (000s/dollars/km²)	Energy consumption Land area (tons/km²)	Energy consumption GNE (tons/million dollars)
Japan	7 833	1 289	165
Former West Germany	4 829	1 366	282
UK	3 433	1 152	336
Italy	2 766	639	249
France	1 743	374	215
USA	521	263	504
Canada	48	28	580

Note:
Energy consumption: In coal equivalent.

Sources:
KHT, 1991, pp. 3–4, 31, 173.

and the post-war period (Table 11.11), and the increase was especially rapid in the 1960s and 1970s when the people demanded improvements. How does Japan compare with other developed countries in this respect?[41]

Figure 11.3 indicates that the ratio of the social welfare level in each country against GDP increases markedly when the GNP per capita increases. The figure at this point for Japan is well below the line and indicates that the Japanese social welfare system is lagging significantly behind her achievements in economic growth.

Since the Second World War, Japan's total annual working hours have steadily decreased, from 2432 hours in 1960 to 2043 hours in 1975, but have remained around 2100–2200 hours since then. This is 200 hours longer than those of the USA and the UK, and 400 hours longer than those of Germany and France.[42] In addition, commuting hours for Japanese workers are much longer than the hours their US or European conterparts spend travelling,[43] while their time for leisure is shorter than the time spent in America or Europe. The reduction in labour hours is an area for improvement in the Japanese economy; an area of top priority in order to restore the success as an economic power to her people as well as in areas such as land and property prices, and the imbalance in prices between Japan and the rest of the world.[44]

TABLE 11.11 Real social security expenses per capita and the ratio of social security expenses to national income in Japan 1890–1987

Fiscal year	Real social security expenses per capita (yen)	Social security expenses-national income ratio[a] (%)
1890	0.2	0.2
1900	0.4	0.3
1920	1.0	0.5
1938	3.7	1.2
1955	14.4	5.7
1970	60.0	6.3
1987	209.6	14.3

Notes:
Social security expenses are deflated by the consumer price index (1934–6 = 1).
The figures are seven-year moving averages (five-year average for 1938; three-year average for 1987).
[a] National income for the pre-war period is for calendar years.

Sources:
Social security expenses: Pre-war period – Emi and Shionoya, 1966, pp. 203–5. Post-war period – Shakaihoshō Kenkyūjo, 1973, p. 6; KTY*, 1990, p. 285.
National income: Pre-war period – Ohkawa and Shinohara, 1979, pp. 273–5. Post-war period – KY, 1980, p. 41; 1991, p. 41.
Consumer price index: Figure 9.4.

11.4.3 Fruits of Modern Economic Growth

Is it possible to evaluate the overall effect of modern economic growth, in a way that takes into account both beneficial and detrimental aspects? NNW (net national welfare) is an attempt to do this quantitatively. It consists of personal consumption expenditure (minus expenditure that is not really personal, e.g. commuting expenses) plus an imputed wage for leisure and housework, and the value of services stemming from ownership of consumer durables, minus expenditure on pollution control. In 1970 NNW was 426 000 yen per capita, 92 per cent of NDP (Net Domestic Product).[45] It was lower than NDP because of the detrimental effect of environmental pollution. The growth rate of NNW per capita was 4.5 per cent during 1955–60, 6.6 per cent during 1960–5, and 7.5 per cent during 1965–70. Thus, although lower than the growth rate of real GNE per capita (due to environment pollution), the growth rate of NNW per capita was accelerating. The growth rate of NNW per capita during 1970–5 was 7.8 per cent,[46] still accelerating and higher than the growth rate

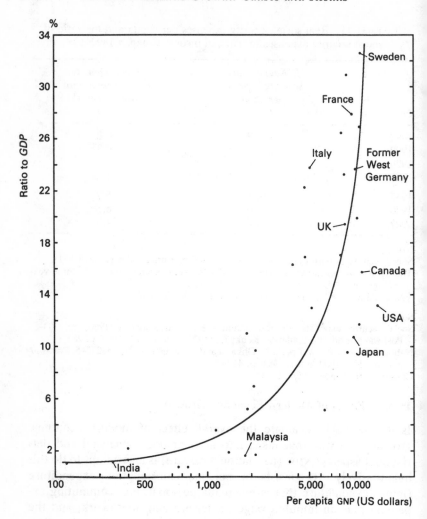

FIGURE 11.3 Relationship between ratio of social security expenses to GDP and per capita GNP 1983

Notes:
For some countries where the 1983 figure is not available, the 1982 figure was used.

Sources:
Ratio of social security expenses to GDP: KTY, 1990, pp. 208–9.
Per capita GNP: WDR, 1985, pp. 174–5.

of GNE per capita, which was by then decelerating. The detrimental effect of pollution and the number of road deaths had been reduced, and leisure time had increased.

Here we wish to emphasize two points:

1. The welfare of the people of Japan increased steadily as a result of modern economic growth. The improvement in living standards brought about by economic growth has been much greater than the harm it has caused. This indicates that the proponents of zero growth are mistaken.

2. In the 1970s, when the economic growth rate fell, the increase in the welfare of the people continued to accelerate, due to efforts to reduce factors detrimental to that welfare. These efforts were the result of the realization that rapid economic growth, such as that of the 1960s, did not necessarily lead to the greatest possible increase in the welfare of the people.

Here then we have two lines of guidance for the future direction of the Japanese economy:

1. The effective exploitation of growth potential is a precondition for increasing the welfare of the people.

2. The rate of growth of that welfare can be increased even when the economic growth rate is falling, by reducing the harm caused by economic growth.

To guarantee the greatest possible increase in welfare, economic expansion, not zero growth, must be the ultimate objective of economic policy.

SUMMARY OF THE CHAPTER

Japan provides an excellent example of inflationary growth; economic growth here has always been accompanied by rising prices. Since the war the growth rate of general prices has been about average for the developed countries, but during the pre-war period it was easily the highest.

Inflation facilitates increases in profits and stimulates savings and investment. In Japan it has occurred because of excess demand on the commodity market and the rise in production costs per unit. The latter rise took place because money wages increased more rapidly than real productivity (this was particularly noticeable in the ten years from the late 1960s).

The price of agricultural products relative to industrial ones has risen rapidly since the war. Increases in productivity have been much greater in industry, while wages have increased much faster in the agricultural sector. In other words, the widening of the productivity differential between the traditional and the modern sector has led to a relative increase in the prices of the former. These changes in the price structure have been more conspicuous since the war, but the same trend can be seen in the pre-war period.

The basic determinants of the welfare of the people are income and consumption. Both real income per capita and real consumption per capita have increased steadily during the period of economic growth, and particularly since the war. Their growth rates since the war have been the highest in the world. However, in both the pre-war and the post-war period the increase in consumption per capita has been smaller than the increase in income per capita. In the pre-war period this was largely because consumption patterns remained relatively unchanged. As consumption expenditure has increased its structure has changed considerably. Engel's coefficient has fallen and the proportion spent on clothing, housing, education, leisure and other items has increased. These trends have also been particularly noticeable since the war.

We believe that the distribution of income became more unequal in the pre-war period. It became more equal immediately after the war with democratization, and again during the 1960s when the labour surplus changes to a shortage, wage differentials narrowed, and labour's share of GNP ceased to decline.

The welfare of the people depends not only on income flow, but also on capital stock, and the most important item of stock in this context is housing. The accumulation of housing stock has been slower than that of capital for productive purposes, but since the war housing stock per capita has increased steadily, and the housing situation is improving. However it is also the case that the increase in land values in large cities has become a serious social problem. The quality of life is also an important determinant of welfare. It has improved in some respects (e.g. life-expectancy), but has deteriorated in others (e.g. the environment), largely due to urbanization.

A century or so of economic growth has raised incomes, but it has impaired the environment. It is of great importance that we evaluate the beneficial and detrimental aspects of economic growth unemotionally, before we begin to plot the future course of the economy.

FURTHER READING

On prices:
  Minami and Ono, 1975
  Noda, 1979
  Watanabe, 1977

On consumption and income distribution:
  Mizoguchi, 1970
  Mizoguchi and Takayama, 1984
  Odaka, 1982
  Ono and Watanabe, 1976

On welfare and social securities:
  Jinushi, 1975–6
  Maruo, 1972

On urban and environmental problems:
  Mills and Ōta, 1976
  Shōji and Miyamoto, 1977

Part IV

Summary and Conclusions

12 Modern Economic Growth: Retrospect and Prospect

In the introductory chapters (Chs 1–3) we discussed the initial conditions for modern economic growth and the growth process. Then, in more specific terms (Chs 4–11), we elucidated various aspects of the mechanism of economic growth. In Section 12.1 of the present chapter we summarize the conclusions derived from the preceding analyses and, by comparing Japanese experience with the experience of the developed countries of the west and the developing countries, we discuss the distinctive features of Japanese economic development. In Section 12.2 we discuss the future prospects of the Japanese economy.

12.1 A RETROSPECTIVE VIEW OF MODERN ECONOMIC GROWTH

12.1.1 Pre-war Economic Growth

At the starting-point of modern economic growth in the mid-1880s a huge gap existed between the Western Powers and Japan. However, agricultural technology had made great strides during the Tokugawa Period (1603–1867) and a considerable amount of commercial capital had been accumulated in the cities. Furthermore, progress had been made in the formation of social overhead capital (e.g. the transportation network and irrigation facilities). The *terakoya* education system also had been diffused far and wide. In the Meiji Period (1868–1912) a powerful central government carried out a series of modernization measures: the abolition of the system of social ranking, the liberalization of domestic and foreign travel, the introduction of compulsory education, the formation of more social overhead capital (e.g. railways and communications), the establishment of government factories and the protective nurturing of some private firms. Development in the traditional sectors continued, along with the introduction of modern industries and technology. The heritage from the Tokugawa Period, together with the foundations for economic growth developed during the early Meiji Period, enabled Japan to propel the economy on the road to modern economic growth over a period of about twenty years starting from the mid-1880s.

Nevertheless, the growth process from this period until the Second World War was by no means a smooth one. Economic growth rates showed 'long swings' of about twenty years' duration. These swings demonstrated a rising trend, a phenomenon referred to as 'trend acceleration' of economic growth. As a result, Japan's growth rates exceeded the world average.

If we divide the sources of demand into domestic and foreign, the former are seen to be more important. Although Japan's export growth rate exceeded the growth rate of world trade and provided a large market for domestic industry, the growth rate of domestic demand – that is, personal consumption expenditure, government expenditure and capital formation – exceeded that of exports. Particularly remarkable was the expansion of domestic capital formation. The proportion of domestic capital formation to gross national expenditure (GNE) – that is, the investment rate – grew steadily, reaching high levels at the end of the pre-war period. This was one of the factors that caused trend acceleration.

The investment activity was due primarily to expectations of high returns to capital. The expected high returns were a result of buoyant demand which often exceeded supply (thus breeding inflationary growth), the relative ease with which technology could be introduced from the developed countries and the tendency of wages to lag behind productivity increases due to the pressure of agricultural 'surplus labour'. The sharp decline of interest rates in the 1930s was combined with great savings, thus stimulating investment still further without leading to severe inflation. The ratio of gross savings to gross national product (GNP) increased, and personal savings, the most important component of net savings, grew more rapidly than personal disposable income. The growth in consumption expenditure lagged behind the rise in personal disposable income, mainly because consumption patterns in areas such as food and housing changed very little.

Next, we shall consider supply. Dividing the economic growth rate into the growth rates of population and of per capita production, we observe rising trends for both. The rise in the population growth rate was caused by an increase in birth-rates until the 1920s, and a decline in death-rates thereafter. The rise in the growth rate of per capita production was a result of the modernization of the industrial structure and productivity increases in industry.

The modernization of the industrial structure is evident from the decline in the proportion of agriculture in the gross domestic product (GDP) and the corresponding increase in the proportion of GDP accounted for by the M Sector (mining, manufacturing, construction, transport, communications and public utilities) and the S Sector (commerce, services, etc.). The growth of the M Sector – that is, industrialization – appears particularly important; indeed it constitutes the core of modern economic growth. The growth of the manufacturing sector was immense and provided commodities to meet the increase in domestic demand that resulted from population growth and the rise in per capita incomes, and also provided exports for overseas markets. Although the importance of agriculture declined steadily, its contribution to the initial growth of the economy was considerable. Above all, agriculture provided sufficient supplies of foodstuffs to prevent agricultural prices rising relative to those of industrial goods. Since industrial wages were kept low by the existence of surplus labour, increased profits ensued.

Increases in productivity took place in every industry, but the most remarkable were in manufacturing, due principally to rapid capital formation and technological innovation – which are, of course, intimately related. Capital formation has been discussed above. Rapid technological progress stemmed mainly from 'borrowed technology' from the US, the UK, Germany, etc. At the start of modern economic growth, there was an immense technological gap between Japan and the western developed countries. Taking advantage of this technological backlog Japan borrowed the technology necessary for growth and appropriate from the point of view of factor endowment. Japan's technological borrowing can thus be considered a classic example of the benefits, of 'relative backwardness'. Japan's successful introduction of technology was facilitated by the availability of entrepreneurs and technicians who took a positive interest in the adoption of modern industry, science and technology, workers who quickly became familiar with modern equipment, and the existence of appropriate financial and distributional mechanisms. Rapid technological progress in manufacturing raised labour productivity and lowered export costs relative to world levels, so that exports expanded rapidly.

The above description may give the impression that Japan had few problems in her modernization process, but this was not so: (1) Political leadership was neither unified nor stable; friction between the military and non-military elements within the government was frequent. Nor was economic policy always consistent; the suddenness of the transition from the Ōkuma fiscal policy to the Matsukata fiscal policy in the Meiji Period, and from the Inoue fiscal policy to the Takahashi fiscal policy in the Taishō and Shōwa Periods have become legendary. (2) Successful introduction of modern technology came only after the accumulation of experience marked by numerous failures. Technology borrowing did not always take place systematically, and the long-term national economic interest was not always considered. For example, the introduction of modern agricultural and spinning technology from western countries in the early days of the Meiji Period failed, and borrowing from two sources, the USA and Germany, resulted in the existence of different frequencies in the electric power network, and caused considerable inconvenience. (3) There was also strong opposition to the introduction of compulsory education and it took some time before it was accepted. Even the construction of railways and communications systems aroused opposition, and did not proceed smoothly initially. (4) Rapid industrialization may have been responsible for making the distribution of income less equal and increasing dissatisfaction among the people, with helped put Japan on the path to war and destruction.

To summarize, the relatively high economic growth and trend acceleration that characterized the pre-war period were due primarily to buoyant investment activity and the rapid introduction of new technology. Gross capital formation is a component of effective demand and net capital formation augments capital stock and raises productive capacity. Technological innovation shifts the production function upward, thus raising productive capacity; it also raised the level of expected returns to capital thus stimulating further investment. As a result of population increases the labour force grew. Surplus labour available in agriculture prevented a rise in wages and assured the maintenance of high returns to capital, facilitating increased investment and bringing about an acceleration of economic growth. Moreover, the constant pressure of demand became a strong stimulus for the expansion of production equipment.

It has been shown that the effect of exports on the growth of demand was less important than the effect of capital formation and consumption expenditure. However, exports also contributed by allowing growth to continue without being checked by balance-of-payment constraints. Exports also enabled the introduction of new technologies and the import of raw materials, which are very important to Japan.

12.1.2 Post-war Economic Growth

Although completely impoverished as a result of the Second World War the Japanese economy recovered, partly as a result of the demand for military supplies for the Korean War during the first half of the 1950s. From the second half of that decade until the end of the 1960s high growth took place. However, the growth rate began to show a declining trend in the 1970s.

The increase in the growth rate until the late 1960s was partly an extension of the trend acceleration in the pre-war period. The investment rate was a carry-over from the increasing trend in the pre-war period, as was the growth in productivity. This cannot fully account for the extremely high economic growth rate of the post-war period, however. In the post-war period the investment rate and the productivity growth rate rose much faster than in the pre-war period. It seems that much of the high economic growth rate of the post-war period must have been due to factors peculiar to this period. Growth was caused by both domestic and foreign factors. On the domestic side one can cite high returns to capital, high savings rates, rapid increases in private investment made possible by the government's low-interest-rate policy; modernization of equipment, remarkable increases in productivity as a result of rapid capital formation; rapid expansion in exports due to the decline in export prices relative to those of other countries (which, in turn, resulted from productivity increases); and a larger portion of government expenditure that could be directed to the expansion of industrial productive capacity as a result of the sharp decline in military expenditure. On the foreign side one can point to the effect on Japan of the fast pace of technological innovation in the developed countries, and to Japan's export market expansion, which was caused partly by the relatively liberal world trade (compared to pre-war) and the full-employment policies introduced by developed countries to raise their economic growth rate.

Rapid economic growth swelled the demand for unskilled labour in Japan so that, by the 1960s, the labour surplus had become a shortage. This was one of the important by-products of modern economic growth. As a result, the wages of unskilled labour, found mostly in agriculture and in small and medium-sized firms, increased rapidly. Capital formation tended to occur primarily in large firms; small and medium-sized firms were slow to introduce modern equipment. This created a big productivity differential between large and small firms. Increases in wages raised production costs in agriculture and the small and medium sized firms, and caused a corresponding increase in their product prices. As a result, consumer prices rose quickly, while wholesale prices remained stable. Thus it can be said that the inflation in this period was one of the consequences of high growth. Another consequence was environmental pollution. Although pollution had also been observed in the pre-war period, its widespread occurrence became a considerable social problem in the 1960s.

At the beginning of the 1970s the Japanese economy experienced a transition and a sharply declining trend was observed in economic growth rates. Although it recovered slightly in the middle of the 1980s the economic growth rate did not subsequently reach even half of that of its period of high economic growth.

There were several factors to account for this low economic growth rate: the world-wide stagnation of technological innovation; the decreased opportunity to introduce new technology because of the disappearance of the difference in technical knowledge between Japan and other developed countries; changes in economic policy by developed countries to aid their own economic growth; changes in the heavy chemical industry due to the rapid increase in oil prices; and the critical shortage of labour.

12.1.3 The Consequences of Economic Growth

As a result of a century of economic growth Japan's GNP has increased remarkably, and is now second only to the USA. Per capita GNP also increased rapidly, and by the middle of the 1970s exceeded that of the UK, and even that of the USA by the end of the 1980s. When one remembers that Japan's per capita income in the 1870s was only a quarter of that of the UK and a third of that of the USA one realizes just how fast her growth has been. Per capita consumption and real wages also increased, though at a slower pace, leading to improved living standards. Food intake has improved both in quality and quantity, and expenditure on consumer durables, education, leisure and services have risen. Moreover, income distribution has become more equal. These changes are the benefits of modern economic growth and industrialization, though it should be remembered that improvements in living standards have been primarily a post-war phenomenon. There are costs, of course, notably environmental pollution in the big cities; but there can be little dispute that for Japan the net benefits of industrialization are positive.

12.1.4 A Comparison with Other Developed Countries

Here we discuss the distinctive characteristics of Japanese modern economic growth by comparing it with the historical experiences of the other developed countries and with the post-war experience of the developing countries. From preceding chapters the reader will have noticed that the emphasis has been on the similarity rather than the uniqueness of the Japanese experience. This is because the uniqueness of Japan has often been exaggerated. To illustrate this we will compare Japan with the UK, the first successful case of industrialization:

1. Japan's economic growth rate, from the start of modern economic growth up to the 1960s, showed a rising trend. During this period, the UK's economic growth rate did not show any clear trend, but trend acceleration is evident during the latter half of the eighteenth century and the nineteenth century.

2. Ohkawa's hypothesis to explain the successful start of modern economic growth in Japan asserted the 'concurrent growth' of agriculture and non-agriculture. But, as we saw earlier, recent research suggests that in both Japan and the UK agricultural and industrial growth began before and continued into the initial period of modern economic growth. In this respect there is no fundamental difference between the two countries' historical experience.

Thus, we wish to stress two points: First, many widely held views of Japan and other developed countries have not been subjected to rigorous quantitative tests. When subjected to such tests these views often require modification or complete rejection. Second, we believe it is not appropriate to compare different countries at an identical time in history. It is more useful to compare them at a similar stage of economic development. Thus, trend acceleration did not occur during the same period in the UK as it did in Japan, but at a similar stage of industrial development. We have shown in this book that Japan's industrial growth rate, far from declining during the inter-war years, increased, because of the smooth transition from light to heavy industries. It has been pointed out that this contrasts with British industry, which stagnated when it failed to make the transition. However, this does not imply that the British economy lacked the ability to transform during other periods. In the latter half of the eighteenth century and the nineteenth century the UK was able to modify her economy and trend acceleration took place.

What then are the distinctive characteristics of Japan's economic history? The most important is the exceedingly high level of population density in the initial period of modern economic growth. This meant that agricultural productivity was lower than that of developed countries at a similar stage of development, resulting in lower per capita GNP. Furthermore these initial conditions would later determine Japan's pattern of economic growth:

1. Due to the high labour–land ratio agriculture could not absorb more labour. This contrasts sharply with the experience of some western countries. The agricultural labour force continued increasing until 1850 in the UK and until 1900 in the USA.

2. Due to the high labour–land ratio agriculture was at a disadvantage relative to industry, so the course taken to achieve economic growth concentrated on industrialization. Because of the lack of raw materials industrialization meant importing them and exporting manufactured articles.

3. Productivity in agriculture was lower than in industry and many members of the agricultural labour force were employed only because of family loyalties; there was in fact a surplus. Because of this surplus the rise in industrial wages was lower than that of productivity, so the relative income share of labour declined. This raised returns to capital, which in turn stimulated investment. It also raised the capacity to save, the ultimate source of investment. Thus it can be considered to be one of the factors which caused trend acceleration.

However, it cannot be claimed that these phenomena are peculiar to Japan.

1. The agricultural labour force did not increase during modern economic growth in some countries; it was constant after 1845 in Belgium and decreased in Ireland after 1840.

2. Modern economic growth was caused by industrialization in all

advanced countries. The UK was a typical case; it began importing raw materials and exporting manufactured articles very early.

3. Surplus labour probably existed in Italy and other parts of Western Europe. Estimates of income distribution in other countries have not yet shown the long-term decline in labour's share observed in Japan, but when research progresses in countries where surplus labour existed it will probably be demonstrated that it was not peculiar to Japan.

Clearly, a comparison of Japanese economic history with that of other developed countries is no easy task. However, in order to bring to light the distinctive characteristics of Japan, or any other country's economic history, it must be attempted. This book is no more than a first step in that direction. In the future there will probably be a great deal more research into comparative economic history.[1]

12.1.5 A Comparison with Developing Countries

Japan grew rapidly by taking advantage of the technological backlog of the developed countries. There is a huge technological gap between present-day developing countries and developed countries, so that it ought to be possible for the former to take advantage of their relative backwardness. However, if we compare them with Japan when it first decided to modernize, Japan is seen to have been several stages ahead, economically and culturally.[2] Agricultural technology was fairly advanced and was able to meet the increased demand for food created by industrialization. Furthermore the growth of the agricultural sector meant the accumulation of capital that would later finance the industrialization process. Rural industries had also progressed and provided a basis for the transplanting of modern industries. With the development of industry the domestic market grew and was able to finance large-scale production in factories. Education had been widely diffused, the level of literacy was high and an efficient political system had been established. In other words, the difference in 'social capability' to absorb technology explains the great difference in the economic performance of Meiji Japan and present-day developing countries.[3]

Also, a word about the extent of the *disadvantages* arising from relative backwardness is necessary when comparing Japan with the developing countries. In the latter the death-rate has declined due to the introduction of medical technology from the developed countries and this has increased pressures from over-population. Moreover, as new products from developed countries poured into developing countries' markets, the level of consumption increased and the capacity to save declined. This was not the case with pre-war Japan. The death-rate declined, not sharply, but slowly, as a result of an improvement in living standards, and the demonstration effect was not strong. Therefore population growth was not rapid and did not prevent increases in saving.

Many other factors advantageous to Meiji Japan come to mind: the small land area, the homogeneity of the people and the language, all of which facilitated unification and the interchange of information, the moderate climate, abundant rainfall, the people's patience, industriousness and avidity for research, the absence of a rigid class system and the absence of a religion that restrained economic activity. The fact that Japan, unlike many other Asian countries (e.g. India, Indonesia, the Philippines), has never been colonized is also significant. When these things are taken into consideration it appears quite natural that Japan was the first Asian country to achieve modern economic growth.

What lessons, then, can developing countries learn from the Japanese experience? This question is difficult to answer, because the international environment in the Meiji Period was so different from today, and there are immense differences between the developed and the developing countries in terms of climate, culture, race and religion. However, the following points may provide some guidance:

1. Before the promotion of industrialization, or rather along with it, agriculture and commerce, social overhead capital and education must be developed to a sufficient level to enable the absorption of modern technology.

2. The choice of industries emphasized in an industrialization strategy must be appropriate. Densely populated, low-wage, capital-scarce Japan chose the labour-intensive textile industry and succeeded. Had Japan chosen capital-intensive industries right from the beginning, industrialization might have encountered serious problems.

3. It is important for developing countries to choose and develop appropriate technology for themselves. Japan developed capital-saving technology by combining borrowed and indigenous technology. From the foreign technology available she chose to borrow only that which was most capital-saving.

12.2 FUTURE PROSPECTS OF ECONOMIC GROWTH

Forecasting the future of economic growth is a task beset with difficulties, and it is not the objective of this book. However, we may conclude by considering a few of the more fundamental factors which might influence the pattern of change in the years to come.

12.2.1 Natural Resources and Technological Innovation

Natural resources, including land, are fundamental in classical economic theory. However, in neoclassical theory, technological progress and capital formation play the key role, and natural resources have come to be considered merely supplementary. From the end of the 1960s, however, the problem of natural resources once more began to attract attention, and it again became a popular subject of research for economists. The trend reached its peak with the publication of *Limits to Growth* (1972) by the Club of Rome,[4] which warned that, because exploitable natural resources are limited, mankind is heading towards destruction within a century due to food scarcity, the exhaustion of natural resources and the pollution of the environment. The 'oil crisis' of 1973 increased pessimism.

In Japan, where the raw materials for industry are almost all imported, the problem is especially acute.[5] Oil is the principal energy source, and a large supply of it, at stable prices, was crucial to the rapid heavy industrialization of the post-war period. The oil crisis caused considerable disruption and a substantial fall in oil prices in the near future is unlikely. This has necessitated counter-measures such as the development of energy-conserving technology and energy substitutes, and the nurturing of low-energy-consumption industries.

Japan is a small country; it is the most densely populated country in the world, with the highest GNP per square metre of land. Therefore, the pollution spawned by industrialization and urbanization has become a bigger problem than in any other country. Experience has demonstrated that to a certain degree pollution can be controlled, but it will become increasingly necessary to control strictly the emission of noxious substances from factories and cars, use different energy sources and encourage industry to take pollution control measures. For this reason, a rise in production costs and a decline in the rate of economic growth would appear to be inevitable.

The important point that technological innovation made a decisive contribution to modern Japanese economic growth will continue to be recognized. However, the possibility of the introduction of technology from overseas which has in the past supported Japan's technological innovation, will not be as great in the future, since the gap between the other developed countries and Japan (where technical knowledge is concerned) has now disappeared. Japan's future technological innovation will depend on her own technological development. In order to speed up this development there will be an urgent requirement not only to allocate large sums for R & D, but also to reorganize the R & D system, and to train technicians and researchers who have flair and originality to undertake new research projects. But producing excellent technicians and researchers with these qualities will not be possible without radical reforms in the Japanese school university system and its educational content.

12.2.2 Population and Labour Supply

One can speak with more certainty about the future of population growth in Japan. Growth will slow down sharply and, while it will not reach zero, it will be close to it by the year 2015. The growth rate of the over-65 population will, however, increase, and the proportion of those over 65 in the total population is expected to rise from 11.6 per cent in 1989 (Table 8.2) to 16.3 per cent in the year 2000 and to an all-time high of 24 per cent between the years 2020 and 2050.[6]

How will this affect the economy?[7]

1. The decline in the population growth rate and the ageing of the population will cause a slowdown in the increase in labour supply. This will intensify the labour scarcity problem, and hinder economic growth, as increased wages cause returns to capital to decline and private investment to fall.

2. The ageing of population will diminish increases in labour productivity. The productivity of the economy as a whole depends on labour mobility between industries (assuming there are differences in productivity) and the level of productivity in each industry. In Japan the lifetime employment system means that inter-industry labour movements occur mainly as a result of the choice of industry of school-leavers and graduates. Therefore, the decline in the numbers of school-leavers and graduates will greatly reduce the mobility of the labour force as a whole. Some fear that, with the ageing of the labour force, efficiency will suffer, but the effect here will vary from industry to industry. For example, in the service industries, where experience

is required, the ageing of the labour force will not necessarily lower efficiency. But in industries such as construction, where physical strength is a basic requirement, the scarcity of young labour will surely create problems.

3. The ageing of the population will also adversely affect savings. In childhood we are pure consumers, but, once we leave school and begin working, the situation changes. As our salaries increase we save more. When we retire, however, our earnings cease and we have to live on savings and pensions. This constitutes a burden on saving. Because of this 'savings life-cycle' the ageing of the population will almost certainly lower the savings rate. This will in turn reduce capital formation.

4. The ageing of the population will swell society's expenditure on pensions and welfare. Government expenditure on industry-related fields will decline.

Thus, demographic factors will probably reduce economic growth rates by preventing increases in labour supply and labour productivity.

Another important factor is the potential labour force for industry existing in the agricultural sector. In the past a very large proportion of the non-primary sector demand for labour has been supplied by young people deserting agriculture, and, as a result, primary industry's proportion of the total labour force had declined to 6.7 per cent in 1992.[8] Furthermore, the agricultural labour force is ageing, and in the 1970s the nominal productivity of the agricultural sector rapidly increased relative to other industries. All this suggests that the agricultural labour force exodus must be nearing its limit,[9] and this is another factor that will hinder economic growth.

12.2.3   International Economic Environment

During Japan's post-war period of rapid economic growth the international environment was exceptionally favourable. There was a high degree of free trade, stable prices and a plentiful supply of raw materials. However, fundamental changes have taken place in recent years and they may affect Japan's economic development. The raw-material problem was discussed above. Automobile exports have shown how a sudden surge in exports can trigger off an international reaction, and lead to trade protectionism. This is a serious problem not only for Japan, but for the world as a whole. Thus it is important that Japan practise self-restraint with exports and increase industrial imports. Japan must acknowledge the extent of her inflence on the world and the role she plays in world development.

12.2.4   Tasks for the Modern Japanese Economy

The two key phrases, 'a welfare economy' and 'an economy open towards the outside' could be used to express the Japanese economy for the future.

'A welfare economy' refers to an economy which makes improvements in people's welfare its first priority; an economy which takes a serious view of consumers' needs. The idea of making economic growth the first priority is now outdated. The idea has been abandoned as a result of a serious problem of labour shortage; the rise of raw fuel prices; increased public demand for environmental preservation, anti-pollution policies and the provision of social capital for the improvement of living standards; increased government expenditure on welfare because of the ageing of the population; and serious economic conflicts in the international arena. However, even when quantitative growth slows down, it is possible to improve public welfare standards by narrowing wage differentials and increasing division of labour to deal with the labour shortage; decreasing work hours; decreasing productivity differentials among industries by extending microelectronics technology to service industries, where technological progress was lagging; accumulating social capital for environmental preservation, anti-pollution policies, and the improvement of living standards; and enriching the social welfare system.

With the shift from a growth-oriented to a welfare-oriented economy it will become possible, for the first time, to enjoy the fruits of economic growth. From this point a hundred years of modern economic growth begins to take on meaning.

The shift to 'an economy open towards the outside' was inevitable, because of the shift from being 'a small country' to being 'a large country'. Now Japan produces 10 per cent of the world GNP and is 'a great country' in terms of the world's largest foreign net assets influencing world economic trends by her economic operations. Until now Japan has always acted passively (conservatively), depending on the movement of other countries (in particular the trends of the developed countries) not only in economic affairs but also in political and cultural fields. However, this type of attitude is not appropriate for 'a large country'. Japan now should behave positively, based on

her own independent ideas. As a guideline for Japan's future behaviour, I would like to propose four major areas for consideration.

First, Japan should understand the economic difficulties faced by
other countries and consider aid for them. It will be necessary to offer
financial aid and technological co-operation to some countries such as
the former Communist countries where the introduction of the prin-
ciples of competition is not smooth; developing countries struggling
to make the first steps in development; and the countries with annual-
ly worsening accumulating debts.

Second, Japan should actively co-operate in the maintenance of a
free trading system. The USA, which led the system until the 1970s,
can no longer play this role because of an increased deficit in her
current account balance, and protectionism beginning to take hold.
Japan, as an economic power, should have the responsibility of
making great efforts to maintain a free trading system by looking
again at the conditions for exporting; preventing the increase of
protectionism in the world; and further opening the market for
agricultural products.

Third, Japan should co-operate in the maintenance of the international monetary system. The former Communist countries and the
developing countries where large amounts of investment are needed
for economic reform, countries with accumulating debts such as
Latin-American countries, and the USA, which has a huge deficit of
savings, are the countries hoping for a share of surplus Japanese
funds. If this does not happen, the operation of the world economy
may suffer negative consequences. For instance, if the funds for
Central and South American countries are stopped, banks in the
USA who funded them will become bankrupt and there is a strong
possibility of causing a world financial panic.

Fourth, Japan should internationalize and modernize its national
economic system. Although the policy of protecting the agricultural
industry is adopted by many governments, the preservation of a low
productivity sector is a waste of natural resources from the public
economy point of view, and Japan's protection of its agricultural
industry should be decreased as much as possible. Japan's pre-
modern distribution system should be reformed so that the principle
of competition operates. The 1991 amendment (of the 'Large-Scale
Retail Shops Law',[10] which was intended to restrict the expansion of
large-scale shops such as department stores and supermarkets in
order to protect the large number of small shops) should be looked
upon as a good try by the Japanese government at this type of reform.

Also the manner of allocating contracts in the construction industry must be mentioned;[11] in Japan the allocations are not made on an open bidding system but determined by private consultation; the subcontractors typically take turns in receiving contracts. Even though some merit can be seen in this system, if the system is difficult for most of the world to understand, then it should be regarded as intolerable internationally. Furthermore, radical reforms should be necessary to clarify the cloudy rules in the securities and financial business and the tightly-knit structure of industry and government. It is hoped that Japan will carry out these tasks of her own accord, and not just because of pressure from other countries (especially from the USA). Some tasks may cause pain to the economic system, but Japan should accept this as a necessary part of the duties of a 'large country'.

Appendices

APPENDIX A: CHRONOLOGY OF JAPANESE HISTORY

Tokugawa Period 1603–1867

1603	Tokugawa feudal regime begins
1616–41	The introduction of measures which 'closed the doors' to foreign countries
1853	The visit of American Commodore M. C. Perry to Uraga, Kanagawa Prefecture
1854	The US-Japan Peace Treaty (Kanagawa Treaty)
1858	The Commercial Treaties (Ansei Treaties) concluded with five western countries
1859	Foreign trade begins, with the reopening of three ports to foreign countries

Meiji Period 1868–1912

1868	The Meiji Restoration
1869	Abolition of the social ranking system
	Restrictions on domestic travel abolished
	The *daimyō* (feudal lords) surrender their lands to the emperor
1870	Japan's first telegraphic communication service (Tōkyō-Yokohama)
1871	Japan's first postal service (Tōkyō-Ōsaka)
	Farmers permitted to grow the crops of their choice
1872	The ban on the sale of farmland lifted
	The introduction of compulsory education
	Japan's first railway opened by JNR (Shinbashi-Yokohama)
	The introduction of conscription
1873	The Land Tax Revision Law
1876	Commutation of the pensions of the *samurai* class
1877	Reduction of the land tax rate
	The Satsuma Rebellion
1880–84	Public factories sold to the private sector
1881–85	Matsukata Minister of Finance
1882	Bank of Japan established
1885	Bank of Japan begins issuing convertible banknotes

331

1889	The Constitution promulgated
1890	The first general election
1894–95	The Sino-Japanese War
1894–99	Westerners' extra-territorial privileges abolished
1896	The Navigation Law and the Construction-Bounty Law
1897	Gold standard adopted; silver standard abandoned
1899	Partial restoration of tariff autonomy
1904–05	The Russo-Japanese War
1906	Major local railways nationalized
1910	Korea annexed by Japan
1911	Tariff autonomy fully restored
	The Factory Law (executed in 1916)

Taishō Period 1912–26

1917	Embargo on gold exports
1918	Rice riots
1923	The Great Kantō Earthquake
1925	The Universal Suffrage Law

Shōwa Period 1926–

1928	The Law for Maintenance of the Public Peace
1929–30	Inoue Minister of Finance
1930	Embargo on gold exports lifted
1931	The Important Industry Control Law
	The Manchurian Incident
1931–36	Takahashi Minister of Finance
1931	Embargo on gold exports reintroduced (end of the gold standard and beginning of the managed currency system)
1932	Manchuria (Manchukuo) founded
	The 5.15 Incident
1936	The 2.26 Incident
1937	The Sino-Japanese War begins
1938	The National General Mobilization Law
1938–50	Electric power industry controlled by the government
1941–45	The Pacific War
1945–52	Occupation by Allied Powers
1945	Decision to dissolve the *zaibatsu* (carried out in 1946–7)
	The Trade Union Law
1946	Emergency Financial Measures
	The Labour Relations Adjustment Law
	The New Constitution promulgated
	The Differential Production Scheme introduced
1946–47	Agricultural land reforms
1947	The Labour Standards Law
	The Anti-Monopoly Law
	The Law for Elimination of Excessive Concentration of Economic Power

1949	The Dodge plan
	Yen-dollar exchange rate fixed at $1 = ¥360
1950–53	The Korean War
1951	The Peace Treaty with the Allied Powers
	The US–Japan Security Treaty
1952	Japan becomes a member of IMF
1955	Japan becomes a member of GATT
1956	Japan becomes a member of UN
1960	Double the National Income Plan introduced
1962	Liberalization of foreign trade and exchange begins
1964	Japan becomes a member of OECD
1965	The first post-war national bond issue
1967	Liberalization of capital movements begins
1970	Land area for rice cultivation reduced
1971	Free-floating yen–dollar exchange rates
1972	Okinawa returned to Japan

APPENDIX B: MAP OF JAPAN

Prefectures and cities which are referred to
in the text:

1 Aomori
2 Akita
3 Yamagata
4 Fukushima
5 Gunma
6 Saitama
7 Tōkyō
8 Kanagawa
9 Fukui
10 Nagano
11 Aichi
12 Kyōto
13 Ōsaka
14 Hyōgo
15 Hiroshima
16 Nagasaki
17 Kagoshima

Notes and References

1 INTRODUCTION

1. The arguments depend largely on Encyclopaedia Britannica 1974, pp. 34–57.
2. The distinguishing feature of Japanese rooms is the *tatami* (straw) mat floor. See note 34, ch. 11.
3. Stringed instruments.
4. From 1641 the only Europeans allowed to live in Japan were a small group of Dutch at Dejima in Nagasaki. A few Japanese intellectuals continued their studies of the west through contacts with these people.
5. The long and disastrous war with China which began from an incident in 1937.
6. For the concept of modern economic growth, see Kuznets, 1966, ch. 1; 1973, pp. 247–51. 'Modern economic growth' is one factor in 'modernization', together with political modernization (democratization), social modernization (realization of freedom and equality) and cultural modernization (realization of rationalism) (Tominaga, 1990, p. 49). See the above volume for details of modernization discussions.
7. For the concept of industrialization, see Landes, 1969, ch. 1.
8. The concept of the beginnings of modern economic growth brings to mind W. W. Rostow's concept of an 'economic take-off'. He believed that all advanced nations went through a period of about twenty years when the investment ratio increased sharply, and he referred to this as 'the take-off' (1960, ch. 1; 1978, part 5). In actual fact, however, the investment ratio of these countries (including Japan) rose gradually over a long period (Kuznets, 1963; Ohkawa, 1969, part 4, ch. 1).
9. Ohkawa and Rosovsky, 1965, p. 53.
10. Minami, 1987, p. 74, table 4.6.
11. Changes in the total horsepower capacity by engine-type were discussed in detail in Minami, 1987, pp. 115–24.
12. Ohkawa and Rosovsky, 1965, p. 52.
13. Minami, 1987, p. 111, figure 6.1.
14. Shinohara, 1972, p. 145.
15. Teranishi, 1982, pp. 219–20; Ueno and Teranishi, 1975, pp. 372–3.

2 READINESS FOR MODERN ECONOMIC GROWTH

1. The feudalism in western (that is, European) countries and Japan had a common characteristic of a hereditary system of feudal lands. This had been a continuous element in forming a basis for economic growth (Rosenberg and Bindzell, 1986, pp. 60–1).
2. Emi, 1963, p. 113.
3. Nippon Ginkō, Tōkeikyoku, 1966, p. 130.
4. The credit for the victory over inflation is generally attributed to Matsu-kata, but the major part of his financial policies were in fact a con-tinuance of Ōkuma's revised policies (Teranishi, 1982, p. 127).
5. The Japanese abacus is a complicated affair and requires considerable training, but a skilled operator can make difficult calculations on it rapidly. Even today it is preferred to an electronic calculator by many.
6. Rosovsky, 1966, p. 106.
7. Dore, 1965, p. 321.
8. Ibid., p. 291.
9. Ibid., p. 292.
10. Crawcour, 1965, pp. 35–6.
11. Monbushō, 1963, p. 180.
12. Landes, 1969, p. 342.
13. Monbushō, 1963, pp. 192–3.
14. Dore, 1965, p. 296.
15. Tsuchiya, 1954. Ranis (1955) also argues along these lines. For an outline of their respective views, see Yamamura, 1974, pp. 137–43.
16. Hirschmeier, 1964, ch. 5; Yamamura, 1974, ch. 7.
17. Ishikawa, 1974, p. 107.
18. Yamamura, 1974, pp. 143–59.
19. Horie, 1965, p. 196. The comparative roles of Confucianism in Japan and Protestantism in Europe in the fostering of the entrepreneurial spirit is a very interesting area of study. In a recent publication Michio Morishima has emphasized the significance of Confucian ethics in Japan's economic success (1982).
20. Ishikawa, 1967, p. 99.
21. Minami, 1973, p. 312.
22. Crawcour, 1965, p. 41.
23. Ibid., p. 36.
24. Landes, 1965, p. 115.
25. Smith, 1959, ch. 7.
26. Umemura *et al.*, 1966, p. 226.
27. The evaluation of the extent of the progress of 'manufacture' in Japan is a controversial area. See Shōda, 1971, pp. 16–17.
28. Minami, 1987, pp. 45–7.
29. The frame for throstle spinning had revolving tubes made of tin plate, one inch in diameter and five to seven inches long. Raw cotton was stuffed into these tubes, and the thread was made by pulling it through them and winding it over the bobbins.
30. Shinohara, 1972, pp. 141, 188. Tōyōkeizai Shinpōsha, 1935, pp. 2, 55.
31. There are several interpretations of the sale of government enterprises

(Smith, 1955, pp. 87–8). Smith's own view is that the government's financial position was the deciding factor (1955, p. 100). Some economists also see the occasion of the sale of these factories as the start of the growth of the *zaibatsu*. This will be discussed in Ch. 5, Sec. 5.

32. Shinohara, 1972, pp. 144–5.
33. The growth of industry in agricultural areas – 'proto-industrialization' or 'rural-centred pre-modern growth' was stressed by Smith, 1973, pp. 157–8, and Saitō, 1985.
34. Horie, 1965, pp. 201–2.
35. For a summary of this view and its main proponents, see Hanley and Yamamura, 1977, ch. 1.
36. Ibid., p. 9.
37. Shinbo, 1978.
38. Umemura, 1981, pp. 29–30.
39. Crawcour, 1965, pp. 28, 44.
40. Hayami, 1975, p. 49.
41. Umemura, 1981, pp. 11–13.
42. Ibid., pp. 25–7.
43. Kuznets, 1958, pp. 140–1.
44. Rosovsky said: 'She [Japan] was not so far along economically as the early industrializers of Western and Central Europe or the U.S.A. in their pre-industrial phases.' (1966, p. 110).
45. For the concept of relative backwardness, see Gerschenkron, 1962, p. 8.
46. Maddison, 1969, p. xvi, table 1. Agriculture's share of the total labour force in Japan is calculated from Minami, 1973, p. 312.
47. Ohkawa suggests that the difference in GNP per capita between Japan and other countries would be smaller if it could be estimated from the point of view of purchasing power; i.e. if differences in price levels could be taken into consideration (1979a, p. 7).
48. Deane and Cole, 1962, p. 142, table 30.
49. Minami, 1973, p. 312. The proportion employed in agriculture only was 69 per cent.

3 AN ANALYSIS OF THE GROWTH RATE DURING MODERN ECONOMIC GROWTH

1. The period examined is only up to the mid-1960s but this will be sufficient for the analysis of the 'catch-up' process of Japan in relation to more advanced countries.
2. Gershenkron, 1962, pp. 6–8.
3. Kuznets, 1958, p. 145.
4. We will not take up the question of long swings in other countries here, but much research has been done; e.g. Kuznets, 1971, pp. 43–50.
5. The '*P*' and '*T*' of the long swings in Figure 3.3 were decided upon after comparing both the smoothed and non-smoothed GNE growth rates, so they are not always exactly at the highest or lowest point of the upswing or downswing.

6. The first research on this subject was in Ohkawa and Rosovsky, 1962.
7. Shinohara, 1962, pp. 85–6; 1979, p. 113.
8. Fujino, 1965, part 5; 1966, pp. 67–77; 1968, pp. 60–8.
9. Ohkawa and Rosovsky, 1973, p. 204.
10. Minami, 1965, p. 204.
11. See Ch. 4, note 8.
12. KKKN, 1980, p. 78.
13. This is the reason for setting 1987 as the last year (P) of the rising phase. However, this period setting is only a tentative one and it will require many years to definitely determine it.
14. Ohkawa and Rosovsky, 1973, p. 40.
15. Factors 1 and 2 were pointed out by Shinohara (1970, pp. 8–11). See Ch. 6, Sec. 2 for a discussion of the 'reconstruction effect' – how the recovery from low levels of production affected the post-war economy.
16. Hirschmeier and Yui, 1975, p. 294.
17. Maddison, 1984, pp. 69–70.
18. Maddison, 1989, pp. 87–8.
19. For the period before 1970, see Mitchell, 1978, pp. 407–22, and for the period after that year, see YNAS.
20. Ohkawa has acknowledged that this phenomenon is not unique to Japan (1978, p. 8).

4   AGRICULTURE DURING INDUSTRIALIZATION

1. For a historical discussion of agricultural growth, see ibid. part 1; Hayami and Ruttan, 1971, pp. 153–64; Ogura, 1967.
2. Hayami, 1975, p. 125, fig. 5.3.
3. Hayami, 1975, p. 128.
4. NTN, first issue, pp. 630, 632.
5. Ohkawa and Rosovsky, 1973, p. 103.
6. Hayami and Ruttan, 1971, pp. 218–28.
7. See note 4 above.
8. All the land belonging to absentee landlords and all except 1 *chō* (almost 1 hectare) of resident landlords' land was forcibly purchased by the government and sold very cheaply to farmers. As a result the proportion of tenant farmers fell from 27 to 28 per cent for 1910–47 to 5 per cent in 1950 (Kayō, 1958, pp. 94, 139). For further discussion of these reforms and their effect, see Dore, 1959; Kawano, 1969.
9. The cultivated land utilization rate declined from 133.9 per cent to 102.8 per cent between 1960 and 1989, and the total planting area declined, from 8 130 000 to 5 430 000 hectares (Nōrin Tōkeikyōkai, 1991, p. 64).
10. Some species of rice can be ruined by excessive application of fertilizers.
11. For the effect of technological progress in the fertilizer industry on agricultural production, see Hayami, 1973, pp. 102–15. The relationship between the development of electric power industry, chemical industry, and agriculture is discussed by Fujino (1965, ch. 21).
12. On BC technology and M technology, see Ohkawa, 1972, pp. 130–4; Ohkawa and Rosovsky, 1973, pp. 99–100; Yamada and Ruttan, 1980, pp. 511–13.

13. According to Ohkawa's production function calculations for rice and *mugi* (wheat and barley), the sum of the labour, capital and land coefficients was 0.979 for 1937–9, and 1.023 for 1940–1, suggesting that returns to scale were constant. See Minami, 1981a, p. 360, table 3.

14. For the relation between the development of machinery industries and mechanization in agriculture, see Hayami, 1973, pp. 115–27.

15. According to Yoshimi Kuroda and Taiji Yoshida's calculations of macro-production functions, returns to scale were constant during 1954–6, but during 1965–7 increasing returns to scale prevailed. See Minami, 1981a, p. 361, table 6.

16. This point is stressed by Shigeru Ishikawa (1967, ch. 2, sec. 2).

17. Ohkawa, 1972, pp. 166–7, 170; Ohkawa and Rosovsky, 1964, p. 68.

18. Ohkawa, 1972, p. 268.

19. Hayami, 1975, pp. 210–12.

20. Smith, 1959.

21. Nakamura, 1966, ch. 4. Here the Hitotsubashi Series means the estimates in Ohkawa *et al.*, 1957.

22. Umemura *et al.*, 1966.

23. Nakamura, 1966, ch. 5.

24. Hayami and Yamada, 1969, p. 110, table 2.

25. Nakamura, 1966, ch. 7.

26. Smith, 1959, chs 7 and 13.

27. Umemura *et al.*, 1966, pp. 226–7.

28. Hayami and Yamada, 1969, pp. 112–25. Also see Rosovsky, 1968.

29. Nakamura's estimates for the rice yield (and hence production) in 1920 are based on government statistics, and are therefore the same as *LTES*.

30. See note 27 above.

31. E.g. Chambers and Mingay, 1966; Deane, 1965, ch. 3; Mingay, 1963.

32. The figure for 1885 is from the source for Table 5.4. The figure for 1880 was obtained by a simple extrapolation of the trend for 1885–1900.

33. The source is the same as Figure 5.1.

34. Agriculture's relative contribution can be expressed as follows: (A = real GDP of agriculture, Y = total GDP)

$$\frac{\Delta A}{\Delta Y} = \left(\frac{\Delta A}{A_0} \middle/ \frac{\Delta Y}{Y_0} \right) \cdot \frac{A_0}{Y_0}$$

Here $\Delta A = A - A_0$ and $\Delta Y = Y - Y_0$. (The zero indicates the starting-point of the modern period.) Thus the part in parentheses represents agriculture's relative rate of growth and A_0/Y_0 represents agriculture's share of GDP at the starting-point.

35. This is calculated using the equation in note 34. The figure for the relative rate of growth (1805–35) and agricultural production's share in 1801 are taken from Deane and Cole, 1962, pp. 166, 170.

36. It is accepted that industrial wages may have been higher than agricultural wages because of the physical and social costs of movement to the towns and differences in the cost of living between rural areas and towns. This does not, however, affect the discussion below.

37. The direct concern of industrial managers was, of course, w/P_M, not w/P_A.

38. Lewis, 1958a, pp. 432–5; Fei and Ranis, 1964, pp. 155–9. This is also discussed in Maynard, 1962, chs 2 and 3; Minami, 1973, pp. 53–4.
39. The relative price between agriculture and the manufacturing industries was stable at 0.81–0.86 between 1880 and 1920 (the ratio of the price of agricultural products to the price of industrial products – 1934–36 = 1, the seven-year moving index (Ohkawa *et al.*, 1967, pp. 16–17 and pp. 192–3).
40. The relative price between agriculture and the manufacturing industries (see note 39 above) was 0.89 in 1930 and 1.02 in 1937.
41. Shinohara, 1961, pp. 313–14.
42. Minami and Ono, 1978b, pp. 28–9.
43. Nōrin Tōkeikyōkai, 1991, p. 28.
44. The relative price between agriculture and the manufacturing industries was 2.4 in 1970 and 2.8 in 1986 (see note 39 above).
45. Yamazawa and Yamamoto, 1979a, pp. 117, 119.
46. Fujino, Fujino and Ono, 1979, pp. 160–5.
47. Strictly speaking T_f is the difference between agricultural taxes and subsidies.
48. Mundle and Ohkawa, 1979; Ohkawa *et al.*, 1978; Ohkawa and Rosovsky, 1964; Ranis, 1969; Fujino, 1965, ch. 19; Teranishi, 1982, ch. 4.
49. Teranishi, 1982, pp. 293–4.
50. These problems are acknowledged by Teranishi (1982, p. 256).
51. A *tanomoshikō* is a group of people who agree to each put a certain amount of money into a pool, and then draw lots to decide which member of the group will borrow the total sum. This process is repeated by the group at regular intervals.
52. Deane, 1965, p. 49.
53. There are research findings on a relative comparison among Asian countries including Japan (Ishikawa, 1990, ch. 5).
54. The figures below are from Teranishi, 1982, p. 260, table 4.6.
55. Later, subsidies to agriculture increased. In 1940 they accounted for 52 per cent of total subsidies (Table 10.7). These increases were measures to deal with the problem of the impoverishment of agricultural communities and to prevent food shortages.
56. Deane, 1965, p. 51.

5 INDUSTRIALIZATION

1. Strictly speaking, the rapid growth of the economy was due both to the rising industrial growth rate and the increasing share of industry in the total economy.
2. US Department of Commerce, Bureau of the Census, 1975, p. 667 (Mitchell, 1978, pp. 179–82).
3. Shinohara, 1962, pp. 7–14.
4. Ohkawa and Rosovsky's study of non-primary industries revealed no significant changes in labour quality in either the pre-war or the post-war period. The effect of the change in capital quality was found to be very small in the pre-war period, but more significant in the post-war period

(1973, pp. 51–8). Tsunehiko Watanabe has concluded that the contribution of improved labour quality to economic growth was very small in the post-war period (1970, p. 174).

5. Kendrick, 1961, pp. 136, 152.
6. International comparisons of the 'residual' of overall economic growth have been made by Denison (1967), Denison and Chung (1976) and others.
7. Kaneda, 1969, pp. 404–5; Mizoguchi, 1970, pp. 265–88.
8. Assuming that consumption expenditures O_A, O_M and O_S have a constant relation to value added of industries A, M and S ($\bar{O}_A$, $\bar{O}_M$ and $\bar{O}_S$), changes in O_A/O and O_M/O and O_S/O explain the changes in $\bar{O}_A/O$, $\bar{O}_M/O$ and $\bar{O}_S/O$ ($\bar{O}_A + \bar{O}_M + \bar{O}_S = \bar{O}$).
9. Tōyōkeizai Shinpōsha, 1935, pp. 2, 55.
10. Value of production: Shinohara, 1972, pp. 141–3, 188–9, 194–5. Value of exports: Tōyōkeizai Shinpōsha, 1935, pp. 2, 50, 72.
11. E.g. Norman, 1940, pp. 125–6.
12. Shionoya, 1968, pp. 77–8.
13. Landes, 1965, p. 171; 1969, p. 174.
14. Deane and Cole, 1962, p. 175, table 40; p. 178, table 41.
15. Based on non-smoothed figures calculated from the statistics in Table 5.17.
16. The rate of accommodating heavy and chemical industries in Japan was among the highest in the world, comparable rates being found for the former West Germany, Sweden and Singapore. See Minami, 1993, fig. 5.2.
17. Fujino, Fujino and Ono, 1979, pp. 178–82.
18. Necessary conditions in order to maximize the rate of profit ($r = (Y - wL)/K$) (Y = output, L = labour force, K = capital stock, w = wage rate) are $r = Y/K$ and $w = Y/L$. This implies that, in the state of equilibrium, r is equal to the slope of a line tangent to the curve F and w is equal to the point at which that line intercepts the vertical axis.
19. For this concept, see Ishikawa, 1981, pp. 349–54.
20. For details, see Minami, 1987, ch. 15.
21. A batten is a flying shuttle – a piece of apparatus used to supply the woof quickly. It was invented in England in 1733.
22. The power loom (i.e. a loom operated by mechanical power) was invented in England in 1785. It was widely used in France in the early 1870s.
23. The treadle and power looms are similar pieces of machinery, the main difference between them being the way mechanical power is applied. Although the treadle loom was used in Europe before the power loom, there is no evidence of it being imported to Japan. It seems likely that it was 'invented' in Japan by someone who had studied the imported power loom's mechanism.
24. Gerschenkron, 1962, pp. 5–30.
25. Rosovsky, 1961, pp. 91–104.
26. This relationship was emphasized by Nakamura, 1966.
27. Rosenberg, 1972, p. 61.

28. Kuznets, 1968, pp. 391–2.
29. For details, see Minami, 1987, ch. 15.
30. This became the Department of Engineering of the University of Tōkyō in 1886.
31. This became the Tōkyō University of Engineering in 1929.
32. Bronfenbrenner, 1961, p. 13.
33. This conclusion remains the same if we use λ' in place of λ.
34. The same conclusion has been reached by Blumenthal (1976, p. 252) and Peck and Gotō (1981, p. 231).
35. KGY, 1991, pp. 162–3. Because the trade in technology is affected by past transactions such as payment for patents, it is questionable to use it at the present time as an index for the influence (that is, the participation power/ability) of technology.
36. For the *zaibatsu* and their dissolution, see Hadley, 1970.
37. Nippon Ginkō, Tōkeikyoku, 1966, pp. 194–5.
38. Hadley, 1970, p. 45.
39. Nakamura, 1971, p. 24.
40. The officers who organized the attempted coups (known as the 5.15 Incident (1932) and the 2.26 Incident (1936)) because they were dissatisfied with party politics and *zaibatsu* leadership in the economy and politics. They sympathized with right-wing political factions and poor farmers. It was these incidents that helped open the way for political control by military forces and Fascist sympathizers.
41. Dore, 1959, ch. 5; Rosovsky, 1972, pp. 249–53; Ohkawa and Rosovsky, 1973, pp. 230–1.
42. Ohkawa and Rosovsky, 1973, pp. 219–20.
43. Hadley, 1970; Nakamura, 1981, pp. 23–6.
44. Hirschmeier and Yui, 1975, pp. 245–8; Ohkawa and Rosovsky, 1973, pp. 227–8.
45. E.g. Hadley, 1970, p. 442; Nakamura, 1981, p. 25.
46. The post-war business group has been described as 'one set-ism' because it includes almost all major industries, grouped round a bank (Hadley, 1970, p. 269). On business groups, see also Gotō, 1982.
47. Hadley, 1970, ch. 11; Shinohara, 1982, pp. 41–2.
48. Kōsei Torihiki Iinkai, 1981, pp. 330–1.
49. Caves and Uekusa, 1976b, p. 473.
50. The concentration ratio of Japanese manufacturing is equal to or smaller than that of the USA (Uekusa, 1982, p. 22).
51. Shinohara, 1982, ch. 3.
52. For general trading companies, see Hirschmeier and Yui, 1975, pp. 181–3; Yamamura, 1976.
53. Yamamura, 1976, p. 161.
54. For the subcontracting system, see Caves and Uekusa, 1976a, pp. 101–15; Hirschmeier and Yui, 1975, pp. 235–6.
55. For the role of government in this period, see Bronfenbrenner, 1961; Rosovsky, 1966, 1972; Smith, 1955.
56. E.g. Norman, 1940.
57. These criticisms were first made by Nakayama, 1960, pp. 2–6.
58. Rosovsky, 1972, p. 249. According to Landes the hostility between state

officials and private entrepreneurs that afflicted the economies of continental Europe was absent in Japan (1965, p. 113).

59. Gerschenkron, 1962, pp. 16–21.
60. Landes, 1965, pp. 103–5.
61. Landes, 1965, p. 105.
62. Johnson, 1982, p. 88.
63. Lockwood, 1968, p. 574.
64. Johnson, 1982, chs 6 and 7; Ueno, 1976–7.
65. Our discussion of the history of industrial policies owes a great deal to Shinohara, 1982, pp. 31–4.
66. Johnson, 1982, especially ch. 6, Shinohara (1982, chs 2 and 3) and Ueno (1976–7) also evaluate the effects of industrial policies.
67. Komiya, 1975b, pp. 218–19; Kōsai, 1981, pp. 227–8.
68. Patrick and Rosovsky, 1976b, pp. 47–8.
69. Johnson, 1982, pp. 210–11; Ueno, 1976–7, p. 29.

6 CAPITAL FORMATION AND ITS SOURCES

1. Ohkawa *et al.*, 1974, p. 33.
2. Kuznets, 1966, pp. 252–6, table 5.6.
3. Government investment, especially military investment, is subject to large fluctuations due to non-economic factors. Also because in farming households, business and household investments are combined, the theory of investment, which is used to explore investment behaviour in the capitalistic management system, does not seem applicable to primary industry. Furthermore obtaining an estimate of the rate of return on capital, one of the major factors determining investment, is extremely difficult in this industry.
4. Ishiwata, 1975, p. 28, table 1.5; Tatemoto *et al.*, 1977, p. 427.
5. Hamada, 1971, pp. 117–19.
6. Uchida and Watanabe, 1959, pp. 23–4; Ishiwata, 1975, pp. 28–9.
7. Ishiwata, 1975, p. 28; Satō, 1977, pp. 89–92; Tatemoto *et al.*, 1977, p. 427.
8. The fact that the parameter for capital stock becomes positive during a period of high growth was similarly ascertained by the calculations of Nakamura. A similar explanation was given to the one in this book (Nakamura, 1980, pp. 191–2). For investment behaviour after the First Oil Crisis, see Moriguchi, 1988, pp. 131–4, and Takenaka, 1984, pp. 24–6.
9. Ohkawa and Rosovsky, 1973, pp. 143–5. We will refer to the export-led growth hypothesis again in Ch. 7, Sec. 1.
10. If we exclude military investment, the slopes of the trends in $G(Y)$, α and β decrease:

$$G(Y) = -39.2 + 0.022t \quad \bar{r} = 0.238 \ F = 4.0$$
$$\alpha = -349 + 0.190t \quad \bar{r} = 0.918 \ F = 270.0$$
$$\beta = 4.00 - 0.002t \quad \bar{r} = -0.283 \ F = 5.4.$$

11. Ohkawa *et al.*, 1974, p. 40, table 2.7.

12. Shinohara, 1962, p. 129; 1964, pp. 159–61.
13. Mitchell, 1978, pp. 781–2. For historical changes in α and β in western countries, see Kuznets, 1966, ch. 5.
14. Kuznets's findings on the high rate of economic growth in Japan support the analysis based on Figure 6.3 (1968, pp. 410–12).
15. Bićanić, 1962, pp. 18–21.
16. Goldsmith and Saunders, 1959, pp. 30–1; Kuznets, 1971, p. 74, table 9; Feinstein, 1972, table 20.
17. The ratio of gross capital stock excluding houses (*Survey of Current Business*, vol. 65, no. 7, July 1985, PR 52–3) to GNP (Ibid., vol. 66, no. 4, April 1986, p. 25) in terms of the 1972 price.
18. The ratio of gross capital stock excluding houses to GDP at 1985 prices. Both from Central Statistical Office, 1989, pp. 243, 250.
19. Lockwood, 1968, p. 253.
20. Although reparations are included in unrequited transfers in the national economic accounts, they have the same impact on the national economy as the introduction of foreign capital. Refer to Yamazawa and Yamamoto, 1979a, p. 50.
21. The significance of capital imports in Japan has been emphasized by Yamazawa and Yamamoto (1979a, pp. 49–58; 1979b, pp. 144–5).
22. Kuznets, 1966, pp. 330–1.
23. KY, 1991, pp. 194–5. For a detailed study of the overseas investments of Japan, see Kojima, 1985.
24. KHT, 1991, p. 163.
25. A consumption function *à la* Keynes is

$$C = a + bY \quad (a > 0 \; 1 > b > 0)$$

where C and Y denote consumption and income. From this we obtain a saving function

$$S = (1 - b)Y - a$$

Therefore

$$S/Y = (1 - b) - a/Y$$

where S is savings $(Y - C)$. This shows that the savings rate S/Y increases as a result of an increase in Y.
26. Kuznets, 1937.
27. Kuznets, 1966, p. 247.
28. Ibid.
29. For a study of government savings, see Ishi, 1974.
30. Ohkawa and Minami, 1975, p. 577, appx, table 5.
31. For more on this hypothesis, see Odaka, 1982, pp. 339–40.
32. This was emphasized by Ohkawa (1974, pp. 166, 169–70).
33. For the examples of estimating consumption and saving functions by the other authors, Blumenthal, 1970, 1972a, part 1; Komiya, 1966b; Mizoguchi, 1970, part 2; Odaka, 1982; Ohkawa, 1974, ch. 7; Shinohara, 1970, chs 2 and 3; 1982, ch. 10; Tsujimura, 1968.
34. See n. 25.
35. Studies of these factors are surveyed by Mizoguchi (1988).

36. The correlation coefficient (r) between γ (average for 1986–8) and the per capita GNP (1987) was 0.239. The correlation coefficient between γ and the growth rate of per capital real GNP (average for 1986–8) was 0.147. Twenty-four countries were taken as the samples. Data for γ is from YNAS, 1988; the per capita GNP from WDR, 1989, pp. 164–5; and the population and real GNP from IFSY, 1990. Similar conclusions can be found in Blumenthal, 1972a, pp. 38–40, and in Emi and Mizoguchi, 1968, pp. 13–16. The multiple correlation coefficient (R) of the function that explains γ with two variables was 0.345.

37. Evaluations of these factors have been attempted by Emi and Mizoguchi (1968), Komiya (1966b) and Mizoguchi (1970, part 1). For the other studies, see a survey by Mizoguchi, 1988, pp. 270–2.

7 FOREIGN TRADE

1. For the statistics of manufacturing production, see Table 5.5.
2. Japan's share of the world exports of manufactures increased steadily, from 0.5 per cent in 1891–5 to 1.3 per cent in 1911–13 to 7.0 per cent in 1936–8, and to 13.9 per cent in 1988. Pre-war figures are from League of Nations, 1945, p. 157, table VII, p. 159 table IX. Post-war figures (for market economies only) are from YITS, 1981, pp. 536, 1224, 1988, p. 1080.
3. Yamazawa and Yamamoto, 1979a, pp. 9–10. Japan's trade with China, Manchuria and the Japanese colonies (Korea and Taiwan) was important. These countries formed part of the 'yen bloc', where the Japanese traded on privileged terms. In the 1930s imports from these countries accounted for 36 per cent of total imports, exports to these countries for 37 per cent of total exports (ibid. p. 9, table 1.6; p. 10, table 1.7). Japan imported rice and sugar, and exported textiles and heavy industries' products. The pattern was similar to that of European countries' trading activities with their colonies.
4. Exports and imports (goods and services): Yamazawa and Yamamoto, 1979a, pp. 214–7; KKKN, 1991, pp. 106–9. GNE: same as Table 6.12.
5. Kuznets, 1966, pp. 310–21.
6. Ibid. p. 302.
7. Blumenthal, 1972a, p. 158.
8. WDR, 1991, pp. 178–9, 194–5.
9. Hisao Kanamori posits the existence of export drive in the troughs of business cycles (1966, p. 88). This view has been criticized by Blumenthal (1972b, p. 629).
10. Blumenthal, 1972a, pp. 155–6; Shinohara, 1962, p. 74; 1979a, p. 114.
11. Bronfenbrenner, 1961, p. 22; Lockwood, 1968, pp. 369, 576; Ohkawa and Rosovsky, 1973, p. 174. Kanamori (1968, p. 325), Krause and Sekiguchi (1976, pp. 398–402) and others have denied the existence of export-led growth during the post-war period.
12. Lockwood, 1968, p. 309.
13. This was asserted by Shionoya and Yamazawa (1973, pp. 334–5).
14. The original theory was developed by D. C. North (1955) and others.

15. Kuznets, 1966, pp. 312–4, table 6.4.
16. The introduction of foreign capital was discussed in detail in Ch. 6, Sec. 4.
17. Lockwood, 1968, pp. 320–46, 572. Kuznets's argument that the beginning of foreign trade accelerated economic growth is consistent with the discussion here (1968, pp. 407–9).
18. Kuznets, 1967, pp. 46–8.
19. WDR, 1991, pp. 208–9.
20. Ibid., pp. 182–3.
21. WDR, 1991, pp. 206–7. This figure depends on the statistics excluding processed foods. The ratio becomes 60 per cent in Japan and 83 per cent in OECD countries, if processed foods are included.
22. However, the important point is that the fact that Japan imports relatively little finished industrial products is considered to be due to the closed nature of the Japanese market to overseas industries. According to E. J. Lincoln, when the ratio of imports of finished industrial products against GNP and the trade index within the industry (trading of manufactured goods in both exporting and importing within the same category of industry) are considered as the two measuring factors, trading in Japan is far less open to overseas industries even when compared to Korea and India, let alone Europe and the USA. Lincoln states that the excuses such as lack of raw materials, relatively better quality of products, and Japan being geographically isolated, (excuses that Japan uses for its small share of imports of manufactured goods) are not relevant, since the same situation also exists in Korea. See Lincoln, 1990.
23. Akamatsu, 1962.
24. Vernon, 1966.
25. Yamazawa, 1975b.
26. Yamazawa and Kohama, 1978, p. 179, fig. 1.
27. Lockwood, 1968, p. 348.
28. Shinohara, 1961, part 3; 1962, ch. 3.
29. Imlah, 1950, pp. 177–80; Kindleberger, 1956, pp. 12–13; Lipsey 1963, pp. 442–3.
30. Kojima, 1958, p. 103.
31. Export and import functions have been estimated by many authors: e.g. Baba and Tatemoto, 1968; Shinohara, 1961, ch. 13; Shionoya and Yamazawa, 1973, pp. 339–40; Yamazawa and Yamamoto, 1979a, p. 89.
32. If the period 1885–1913 is divided into two sub-periods; 1885–1900 and 1901–13, the relative contributions of the two factors discussed in the next can be calculated:

	$\Delta ln\, T_W$	$\Delta ln\, P_E R / P_W$
	%	%
1885–1900	110.2	−10.2
1901–13	88.7	11.3

The income effect was significant in both sub-periods.

33. If the parameters b and c had remained unchanged from the previous period (1885–1913), the growth rate of E for the period 1921–38 would have been 6.1 per cent rather than the actual rate of 8.5 per cent.

34. E (at 1913 prices): value of exports (Mitchell, 1978, p. 307) $\div$ P_E (Kindleberger, 1956, pp. 22–3). T_W See Table 7.1. P_W See Figure 7.4. Figures for E, T_W and P_E/P_W are indices with 100 for 1913. Non-smoothed data are used.

35. P_E/P_W (1913 = 100) decreased from 120 to 109 between 1920 and 1932, but increased thereafter and reached 151 in 1938.

36. Exports of the US and German manufacturing industries expanded very rapidly before industrialization began in Japan; they were comparable to those of the UK's industries at the beginning of the twentieth century. The UK's share of total exports of manufactures in the world decreased from 37.7 per cent in the period 1876–80, to 27.5 per cent in 1911–13, to 18.6 per cent in 1936–8, and to 3.9 per cent in 1980. Data source is the same as in note 2.

37. Shinohara, 1961, part 3; 1962, ch. 3.

38. Kojima, 1958, chs 3 and 4.

39. Lockwood, 1968, p. 149; Ohkawa and Rosovsky, 1973, pp. 178–82.

40. Our argument in this subsection is drawn from Yamazawa, 1975a; Yamazawa and Yamamoto, 1979a, pp. 77–85.

41. US, Department of Commerce, Bureau of the Census, 1975, p. 888.

42. For instance it was seen in Prussia (Crouzet, 1972, p. 123).

43. BN, 1970, p. 108. On 1 April 1990, there were 18 items listed as non-liberalized trading products, including beef and oranges. There are 53 items, such as rice, that GATT treats as being exempted from liberalization (ZKTG, August 1990, no. 460, p. 83).

44. Yasuba, 1980, pp. 200–1.

8 POPULATION AND LABOUR SUPPLY

1. Ōbuchi, 1974, p. 61, table 2.1.

2. Usher, 1918, pp. 89–90.

3. Population density reached 326 in 1989 (Table 8.1).

4. Yamada and Ruttan, 1980, table 10, A.1–10, A.6.

5. The demographers used to maintain that the registration of births and deaths were not accurate in the early days, and that the official data underestimated the birth-rate and the death-rate. Some estimates have been carried out using demographic methods. However, it is difficult to tell which, the official figures or the demographic estimates, is correct. See Ōbuchi (1974) pp. 61–7 and pp. 74–85 for the details.

6. Nippon Ginkō, Tōkeikyoku, 1966, p. 13.

7. Lockwood, 1968, p. 167. Also see pp. 160 and 162.

8. Kelley and Williamson (1974, pp. 132–7) and Minami and Ono (1978b, pp. 26–8) demonstrate the disadvantage of rapid population increase using a simulation of the pre-war period.

In the western developed countries also the population growth rate before modern economic growth was lower than in present-day developing countries (Kuznets, 1958, p. 149).

9. The same view is seen in Ōbuchi, 1974, p. 282.
10. Minami, 1973, pp. 312–13.
11. The pre-war Population Census refers to the 'usual status' of labourers, while the post-war census to the 'actual status'.
12. This parallels C. P. Kindleberger's suggestion that differences in the rate of economic growth among European countries in the 1950s and the early 1960s are accounted for by differences in the growth rate of labour supply (1967, p. 3). However it is misleading to over-emphasize the effect of labour supply; it seems to us that the growth rate of labour productivity is of greater significance in explaining the overall economic growth rate.
13. Umemura, 1971, ch. 1.
14. These studies are discussed in Obi, 1980, pp. 44–52.
15. Minami, 1973, p. 239, table 13.2, p. 312.
16. Yasuba, 1980, pp. 65–8.

9 LABOUR MARKET AND DUAL STRUCTURE

1. Kuznets has studied long-term changes in the industrial composition of employment in various countries (1966, ch. 3; 1971, ch. 6).
2. Deane and Cole, 1962, p. 142, table 30.
3. Gregory King estimated that the *A* Sector's share may have been as high as 60 per cent in England and Wales in 1688 (Rosovsky, 1966, p. 111).
4. Fuchs, 1968, p. 1.
5. Clark, 1951, p. 396.
6. Kuznets, 1971, p. 256.
7. Kuznets, 1971, pp. 289–302.
8. Kuznets, 1971, p. 211.
9. Chambers, 1953.
10. Net outflow (3) is the difference between the natural increase (2) and actual increase in agricultural labour (1). The rate of natural increase in agricultural labour was assumed to be equal to the rate of natural increase in the economy as a whole. For details, see Minami, 1973, pp. 105–7. Recently, Fumino Makino estimated the natural increase in agricultural labour without the assumption that the rate of natural increase was equal in different industries (1980, p. 364, table 1). His results were very similar to ours. We estimate that the average annual net outflow was 281 000 during the period 1929–38. Makino estimated the average to be 282 000 during the same period.
11. Yukio Masui (1969) found that the price at which members of the agricultural population were willing to supply labour to the non-agricultural sector varied according to sex and to whether it was the eldest son or not.
12. Namiki, 1959.
13. We can detect a change in the outflow of the agricultural labour force

commensurate with economic changes. This means that an outflow from the agricultural labour force is taking place to adjust the imbalance of the labour supply in non-agricultural areas. See Minami, 1973, ch. 6 on this point.

14. Minami, 1973, p. 111, fig. 6.6.
15. Much of the primary labour force has migrated to urban areas. The proportion of the total population that lived in urban areas increased from 18.0 per cent in 1920 to 37.7 per cent in 1940 (Sōrifu, Tōkeikyoku, 1982, p. 23). During the post-war period the urban population increased even more rapidly; the proportion reached 72.1 per cent in 1970 and 76.2 per cent in 1980. During the 1970s the trend towards urbanization slowed because (1) demand for labour in the urban industries decreased due to recessions, (2) there was an increase in factory construction in rural areas in order to make use of the relatively abundant land and cheap labour available there, and (3) many young workers returned to the rural areas in which they were born.

    For an analysis of historical urbanization trends, see Okazaki, 1977, ch. 4; Taeuber, 1958, part 4.
16. The numbers η and y are calculated for 1987. In some countries η was worked out from calculations for 1984–6. The source for these is in Table 9.7; WDR, 1989, pp. 164–5.
17. The Japanese rate of unemployment is low by international standards; in 1990 it was 2.1 per cent compared with 5.5 per cent in the USA, 5.8 per cent in the UK, 7.2 per cent in West Germany, 8.9 per cent in France and 11.0 per cent in Italy (KHT, 1991, pp. 109, 111).
18. The figure for U is from Minami and Odaka, 1972, p. 166, table B-2. U' was calculated by dividing U by the ratio of employees (Table 9.6) to total labour force (Table 8.3).
19. See note 11, Ch. 8.
20. Lewis, 1958a; 1958b. For more elaborate versions of this model, see Fei and Ranis, 1964 and Minami, 1973, chs 1–5.
21. Lewis, 1958b, p. 29.
22. Fei and Ranis, 1964, pp. 129, 263–4.
23. Jorgenson, 1966, p. 60.
24. Our estimates indicate that E_L increased steadily during the pre-war period and was at a high, but stable, level during the post-war period. This makes sense since the post-war level of E_L is related to pre-war growth. For more details, see Minami, 1981a.
25. On the basis of cross-sectional estimates of production functions in agriculture, Masakatsu Akino and Hayami claimed that the output elasticity of labour was equal to labour's relative share of income or $w = MP$ (1974, p. 469).
26. Minami, 1973, pp. 213–15.
27. Minami, 1973, p. 252, fig. 13.2.
28. Kindleberger, 1967, chs 1 and 2.
29. Ibid. p. 3.
30. Fei and Ranis, 1975, p. 49. Recent studies demarcate the Korean turning point much later than Fei and Ranis, say the early 1980s. For example, Choo, 1991, p. 13 and Oshima, 1991, p. 126.

31. Shinohara, 1961, part 3; 1962, ch. 3. Lewis stated that surplus labour causes a decline in labour's share of income which then raises the rate of economic growth (1958a, pp. 416–20, 448).
32. Minami and Ono, 1981, p. 323.
33. Deane and Cole, 1962, p. 21.
34. Umemura, 1961, p. 210.
35. Odaka, 1968, pp. 86–7, fig. 4.
36. Taira, 1970, part 1.
37. Yasuba, 1976, pp. 256–7.
38. Hyōdō, 1971, pp. 453–65.
39. There are many studies of the wage differential between large and small enterprises during the post-war period; e.g. Mizuno, 1973, chs. 3 and 4; Ono, 1973, part 2.
40. Ono, 1973, p. 175, fig. 8.4.
41. The view that the wage differential narrowed during the post-war period as a consequence of the change from a labour surplus to a labour shortage is widely accepted; e.g. Blumenthal, 1977, p. 167: Ono, 1973, p. 197.
42. Ohkawa has proposed that the expression 'differential structure' be used rather than 'dual structure'. The Japanese economic structure, he argues, is made up of many layers, not merely the two extremes of large and small (1972, p. 61).
43. The higher labour productivity in the S Sector in earlier years was due to pre-modern profits. These profits decreased as the distribution process was modernized and, as a result, productivity increased more slowly than in other countries (Ohkawa, 1975, p. 184).
44. Ohkawa, 1975, p. 195.
45. Kuznets, 1971, p. 294; Ohkawa, 1975, pp. 186–90.
46. Mizuno, 1973, pp. 115–17.
47. Katō, 1967, pp. 56–9, 63.
48. Miyazawa, 1964; Shinohara, 1970, ch. 8.
49. Teranishi, 1972–3, pp. 85–6; Minami, 1973, pp. 78–81.
50. Koike, 1978; Shimada, 1981; Umemura, 1980.
51. In the ratio of labour's share, changes coinciding with the long swings and trade cycles are noticeable. For details see Minami and Ono, 1981.
52. Yamada's estimates are cited in Hayami, 1975, p. 36, table 2.11.
53. Minami and Ono, 1981, p. 319, fig. 4.

10 PUBLIC FINANCES AND THE FINANCIAL SYSTEM

1. Emi, 1963, p. 44.
2. Peacock and Wiseman, 1960, pp. 24–30.
3. Pre-war period: Feinstein, 1972, T4–9, T85–87. Post-war period: YNAS.
4. For a discussion of Wagner's Law, see Musgrave, 1969, ch. 4.
5. Komiya, 1975a, pp. 107–22.
6. In the pre-war period, because most local government taxes were an extension of central government taxes, their structure was similar.
7. Hinrichs, 1966.

8. For details, see Ishi, 1979, pp. 238–47.
9. Suzuki, 1962, p. 86, table 13.
10. These figures are based on non-smoothed averages. The source is the same as for Table 10.3.
11. See the previous note.
12. Emi, 1963, p. 13.
13. The figures for *GCF/CF* in Japan, the USA, the UK, the former West Germany, and France in 1988 (1987 in the case of the UK) are, respectively, 16.9, 9, 4, 11.8 and 15.6 per cent. Also for these countries the figures of *GCF/GC* are 55.1, 8.8, 8.1, 12.1 and 16.9 per cent respectively. YNAS, 1988.
14. The decline in the proportion of transfers was linked to the rise in the proportions of current purchases and capital formation. In the UK transfers rose considerably in the late 1910s, while the proportions of current goods and services and capital goods and services declined (Peacock and Wiseman, 1960, p. 75, fig. 13).
15. The figures for *T/GDE* in Japan, the USA, the UK, the former West Germany, and France in 1988 (1987 in the UK) are 13.2, 11.5, 16.1, 20.8 and 25.6 per cent respectively. YNAS, 1988.
16. Based on non-smoothed averages. The source is the same as for Table 10.5.
17. Rosovsky, 1961, ch. 2.
18. It must also be remembered, however, that the military took the lead in technological innovation in some industries, thus helping to promote economic growth in the private sector. Yamamura (1977) asserts that the Meiji government's policy of strengthening the armed forces greatly enhanced technical progress in Japan.
19. While it is generally agreed that monetary policy was the main focus in dealing with business cycles, opinions are divided over the issue of whether the government's economic stabilization policies were effective. Ackley and Ishi assert that they were (1976, pp. 218–25).
20. See Ishi, 1976; Watanabe, 1970, ch. 8.
21. Ohkawa, *et al.*, 1966, p. 262.
22. This was because military investment increased more rapidly than non-military investment (see Table 6.1).
23. However it is probable that in the pre-war period taxation did not bring about a redistribution of income. Income tax was still negligible, and the proportion of indirect taxes, which have the opposite effect, was high. For a discussion of taxation and redistribution of income in Japan, see Ishi, 1979, ch. 2.
24. Komiya, 1975a, pp. 112–13.
25. On the pre-war financial system see Nippon Ginkō, Chōsakyoku, 1976; Patrick, 1967. On the post-war system see Nippon Ginkō, Chōsakyoku, 1976; Suzuki, 1980.
26. Japan's National Banks were modelled on the American system, after the merits of this and European banking systems had been investigated.
27. On the origins and activities of quasi-banking companies, see Patrick, 1967, pp. 246–9.
28. Cameron, 1967b, pp. 298–304.

29. On overborrowing see Suzuki, 1980, pp. 13–14; Wallich and Wallich, 1976, pp. 267–8.
30. Komiya and Iwata, 1973, p. 155.
31. Tachi and Moroi, 1965, pp. 93, 103. Shigeru Tamura, from his analysis of post-war electrical companies, concluded that the second factor was also important (1971, pp. 273, 295). Ryūtaro Komiya and Kikuo Iwata criticized Tachi and Moroi's analysis (1973, p. 317).
32. On overloan, see Suzuki, 1980, pp. 3–13; Wallich and Wallich, 1976, pp. 284–90.
33. KHT, 1991, p. 79.
34. Wallich and Wallich, 1976, p. 275; Komiya expresses the same opinion (1975a, pp. 191–2).
35. On the 'New Scheme for Monetary Control' see Suzuki, 1980, pp. 32–3.
36. This corresponded to the UK's 'Stop–Go' policy, except that in the UK the expansion phase was shorter and the economic growth rate lower.
37. On the low-interest-rates policy and the interest system, see Suzuki, 1980, pp. 37–61.
38. Banks were supposed to be able to choose to whom and what amount they wished to lend because of the excess demand for capital. This exercise of discretionary powers is known as 'credit rationing'.
39. Ackley and Ishi, 1976, p. 166; Kawaguchi, 1970, p. 405.
40. Although the calculated figures of M_1 and M_2 which are normally used do not include the government's financial activities, considering the importance of the postal savings system in Japan, the figures in this table were estimated by including the government's financial activities.
41. The growth rate of M_2 for the USA is based on seven-year moving averages. US, Department of Commerce, Bureau of the Census, 1975, pp. 992–3.
42. Based on seven-year moving averages. Mitchell, 1962, pp. 444–6.
43. Patrick, 1967, p. 274.
44. Suzuki, 1980, pp. 144–5.
45. We also did calculations where k_2 was determined by t, i and r_2, and by y, i, and r_2, and where i was represented by interest on time deposits. The results were basically the same.
46. See M. Friedman and A. J. Schwartz's (1963) well-known research on long-term fluctuations in the money supply and the Marshallian k in the USA.
47. Nippon Ginkō, Chōsakyoku, 1977, pp. 5–6.

11   PRICES AND LIVING STANDARDS

1. These are the compound growth rates for 1863 (the average of 1860–6) to 1935 (the average of 1932–8). The source is Phelps Brown, 1968, appx 3, pp. 432–52. Prices rose in France during the 1920s due to a fall in the value of the franc.
2. IFSY, 1984, pp. 124–5; 1991, pp. 164–5.
3. According to non-smoothed figures the growth rate of the GNE deflator during the period 1917–19 was 24–28 per cent. In 1974 it was 20 per cent.

4. P = prices, Y = real GNP, $\bar{Y}$ = nominal GNP, w = wages per capita, L = labour force. We get the following definitional equation:

$$P = \frac{\bar{Y}}{Y} = \frac{\bar{Y} - wL}{Y} + \frac{wL}{Y}$$

With ε as the ratio of income other than wages $(\bar{Y} - wL)$ to income from wages (wL) we get:

$$P = (1 + \varepsilon)\frac{wL}{Y}$$

$$\therefore P = (1 + \varepsilon) w/y = (l + \varepsilon)l$$

Here y is real productivity (Y/L), l is labour costs per unit (w/y).

   If we assume that the mark-up rate $(1 + \varepsilon)$ is constant, $G(P) = G(l)$ (the mark-up rate may fluctuate in the long term, but we have assumed it is constant here for the sake of simplicity). Equation (1) in Table 11.2 expresses this in general terms.

5. Both these indicators have merits and demerits: φ is a direct indicator, but for the pre-war period the only source is Ōsaka City, and for the post-war period incorporated enterprises. $G(Y)$ covers the whole of the economy, but is an indirect indicator.

6. Fujino, 1965, p. 492.

7. Nippon Ginkō, Chōsakyoku, 1975, p. 5.

8. One Japanese monetarist, Seiji Shinbo (1980) presented an econometric model of the 1970s, and discussed the effect of the money supply using simulation analysis.

9. Gordon, 1961, p. 938, table 1; p. 940, table 2; p. 941, table 3.

10. YNAS, various issues.

11. Maynard, 1962, p. 238.

12. Ibid. p. 226.

13. Sources are the same as Table 6.14. Seven-year moving averages (five-year average for 1988).

14. This was calculated from the population growth rate in Table 3.2 and the growth rate of PC in Table 6.1.

15. Ohkawa *et al.*, 1974, pp. 22–3. Gleason (1965) emphasized the importance of the increase in consumption per capita in the pre-war period.

16. Ohkawa and Minami, 1975, p. 577. The figures for post-war Japan were combined with the calculated figures from YNAS, 1988.

17. NA, 1991, p. 145; Ministry of Labour, 1988, p. 335.

18. See note 46 in Chapter 2.

19. For a detailed discussion of long-term changes in the composition of consumption expenditure, see Shinohara, 1967, ch. 1; 1970, ch. 6. Shinohara's estimated expenditure elasticities for the period 1874–1940 were 0.71 for food, 2.77 for clothing, 1.00 for housing and 0.87–1.04 for lighting and heating (1970, p. 245, table 7). Mizoguchi estimated pre-war and post-war elasticities, using time-series data and cross-sectional data (1970, part 2).

20. These figures are based on real amounts (Ohkawa, 1973, p. 244).

21. For an international comparison of Engel's coefficient in the post-war

period see Mizoguchi, 1970, pp. 255–65.

22. This tax, known as *kosūwari*, was levied on all householders and people with independent livelihoods. It was abolished in 1940.

23. Same as Table 11.7.

24. Ono and Watanabe, using similar sources and methods as the author, came to the same conclusion (1976, p. 372).

25. E.g. Mizoguchi *et al.*, 1978; Mizoguchi and Takayama, 1984; Takayama, 1980.

26. Ono and Watanabe, 1976, p. 380; Patrick and Rosovsky, 1976b, pp. 35–40.

27. The sources used for this estimate of income distribution do not include capital gains. With the rapid post-war rise in land prices the effect of capital gains on income distribution must have been considerable.

28. Takayama, 1980, p. 24, table 1.1.

29. Kuznets, 1955.

30. Paukert, 1973, pp. 174–5.

31. At the beginning of the 1980s the Gini coefficient in Japan was lower than in the UK, the former West Germany and the *USA* (Keizai Kikakuchō, 1990b, p. 271, table 3.1.8.

32. Ohkawa and Shinohara, 1979, pp. 366–8.

33. Ohkawa *et al.*, 1966, p. 27.

34. The floor of a traditional Japanese room is made up of regular rectangular blocks of rush matting called *tatami*, each 1 m 80 cm by 90 cm. The customary way of stating the area of a room in Japan is by the number of these *tatami* mats, even in a western-style room.

35. Mills and Ōta, 1976, table 10.9; KY, 1983, p. 289.

36. KY, 1991, p. 210.

37. On the question of land prices, see Komiya, 1975a, ch. 8.

38. Keizai Kikakuchō, 1990a, p. 28, fig. 1.2.4.

39. KY, 1991, p. 29.

40. Yasuba, 1980, p. 224, table 7.4.

41. For an international comparison of social security see, for example, Shinohara, 1964, part 2, appx 3.

42. KRT, 1991, p. 184.

43. The percentages of workers who spend over 60 minutes commuting to their work places are Japan 14 per cent; USA 6 per cent; the former West Germany 3 per cent; and Belgium 2 per cent (Rōdōshō, 1988, p. 348).

44. For an international comparison of levels of welfare (quantitative) see, for example, Maruo, 1972; Patrick and Rosovsky, 1976b, pp. 28–35. According to these two studies Japan was superior in terms of life-expectancy, readership of newspapers and the incidence of murder, but inferior in terms of housing and environmental pollution.

45. Economic Council of Japan, 1974, p. 16.

46. Kanamori and Takase, 1977, p. 126, table 13.

12 MODERN ECONOMIC GROWTH: RETROSPECT AND PROSPECT

1. Among comparative economic history studies centred on Japan two pieces of work (Landes, 1965, Maddison, 1969; Saitō, 1985, and Yasuba, 1980) are particularly important.
2. For a comparison of the Japanese historical experiences with present developing countries, see Minami, 1993; Ohkawa, 1976; Ohkawa and Kohama, 1989; and Ohkawa and Ranis, 1985. A study by Reynolds (1983) on the history of the third-world economies is also relevant.
3. It should also be remembered that technology introduced to Meiji Japan was much simpler than contemporary technology.
4. Meadows *et al.*, 1972.
5. For a discussion of the natural resources problem in Japan, see Itagaki, 1970.
6. Minami and Ueda, 1979, p. 7, table 3.
7. For details see Minami, 1980, and Ōbuchi, 1979.
8. RTY, 1992, p. 31.
9. It is estimated by Ohkawa and Rosovsky that the agricultural labour force ceases to move to non-agriculture when its share of the total labour force becomes slightly less than 10 per cent (1973, p. 248).
10. This law was strongly criticized by the US government as a non-tariff barrier, because restrictions on large-scale retail shops were considered to be partly responsible for the small increase in imports of foreign goods. (They presumed that imports were almost always sold in large rather than small shops.) See Itō, 1992, pp. 394–7 for details of the law. Due to the amendment in 1991, establishment and expansion of large-scale retail shops has become less restrictive.
11. This manner of allocation of contracts in the Japanese construction industry is referred to as *dangō*. This too has been taken by the US government as a non-tariff barrier, because with this system, they believe, it is almost impossible for foreign companies to take part in the allocation of contracts.

Bibliography

A PERIODICAL VOLUMES OF STATISTICS (abbreviations used in the text preceded the full reference).

BN — Nippon Kanzei Kyōkai (Japan Tariff Association), *Bōeki Nenkan* (*International Trade Annual*).

BSN — Nippon Ginkō, Chōsa Tōkeikyoku (Bank of Japan, Research and Statistics Department), *Bukka Shisū Nenpō* (*Price Indexes Annual*).

CZY — Jijishō Zaiseika (Ministry of Home Affairs, Local Finance Division) (ed.), *Chihō Zaisei Yōran* (*Manual of Local Government Finance*).

DY — United Nations, Department of International Economic and Social Affairs, Statistical Office, *Demographic Yearbook*.

GKTN — Nippon Ginkō, Chōsa Tōkeikyoku (Bank of Japan, Research and Statistics Department), *Gaikoku Keizai Tōkei Nenpō* (*Annual Report of Foreign Economic Statistics*).

GWI — United Nations, Department of Economic and Social Affairs, Statistical Office, *The Growth of World Industry, National Tables*.

HKT — Nippon Ginkō, Chōsa Tōkeikyoku (Bank of Japan, Research and Statistics Department), *Honpō Keizai Tōkei* (*Economic Statistics of Japan*).

HKTNS — Ōkurashō, Shōkenkyoku, Shihon Shijōka (Ministry of Finance, Securities Bureau, Capital Market Division) (ed.), *Hōjin Kigyō Tōkei Nenpō Shūran* (*Statistics of Incorporated Enterprises, Annual Report*).

IFSY — International Monetary Fund, Bureau of Statistics, *International Financial Statistics Yearbook*.

JDTG — Kōseishō, Daijin Kanbō, Tōkei Jōhōbu (Ministry of Health and Welfare, Minister's Secretariat, Statistics and Information Department), *Jinkō Dōtai Tōkei Geppō (Monthly Report of Vital Statistics*).

KGKCH — Sōrifu, Tōkeikyoku (Prime Minister's Office, Statistics Bureau), *Kagaku Gijutsu Kenkyū Chōsa Hōkoku* (*Report on the Survey of Research and Development*).

KGY — Kagaku Gijutsuchō, Kagaku Gijutsu Seisakukyoku (Science and Technology Agency, Science and Technology Policy

Bureau) (ed.), *Kagaku Gijutsu Yōran* (*Science and Technology Manual*).

KHT   Nippon Ginkō, Chōsa Tōkeikyoku (Bank of Japan, Research and Statistics Department), *Nippon Keizai o chūshin to suru Kokusai Hikaku Tōkei* (*Statistics for International Comparison Centred on Japan*).

KKB   Mitsubishi Sōgō Kenkyūjo (Mitsubishi Research Institute Inc.) (ed.), *Kigyō Keiei no Bunseki* (*Business Management Studies*).

KKK   Kezai Kikakuchō (Economic Planning Agency) (ed.), *Kokumin Keizai Keisan* (*National Economic Accounts Quarterly*).

KKKK   Keizai Kikakuchō, Keizai Kenkyūjo, Kokumin Shotokubu (Economic Planning Agency, Research Institute of Economics, National Income Division) (ed.), *Kikan Kokumin Keizai Keisan* (*National Economic Accounts Quarterly*).

KKKN   ——— (ed.), *Kokumin Keizai Keisan Nenpō* (*Annual Report of National Accounts*).

KOTN   Ōkurashō, Rizaikyoku (Ministry of Finance, Financial Bureau) (ed.), *Kokusai Tōkei Nenpō* (*Government Bonds Statistics Manual*).

KRT   Nippon Seisansei Honbu (Japan Productivity Centre), *Katsuyō Rōdō Tōkei* (*Labour Statistics Manual*).

KSH   Keizai Kikakuchō (Economic Planning Agency) (ed.), *Kokumin Shotoku Hakusho* (*White Papers of National Income*).

KSTN   Keizai Kikakuchō (Economic Planning Agency) (ed.), *Kokumin Shotoku Tōkei Nenpō* (*Annual Report on National Income Statistics*).

KTG   Nippon Ginkō, Chōsa Tōkeikyoku (Bank of Japan, Research and Statistics Department), *Keizai Tōkei Geppō* (*Economic Statistics Monthly*).

KTH   Tsūshō Sangyōshō, Daijin Kanbō, Chōsa Tōkeibu (Ministry of International Trade and Industry, Minister's Secretariat, Research and Statistics Department), *Kōgyō Tōkeihyō, Sangyō Hen* (*Census of Manufactures, Report by Industries*).

KTN   Nippon Ginkō, Chōsa Tōkeikyoku (Bank of Japan, Research and Statistics Department), *Keizai Tōkei Nenpō* (*Economic Statistics Annual*).

KTY   Sōrifu, Tōkeikyoku (Prime Minister's Office, Statistics Bureau) (ed.), *Kokusai Tōkei Yōran* (International Statistics Manual).

KTY*   Kōseishō, Daijin Kanbō, Tōkei Jōhōbu (Ministry of Health and Welfare, Minister's Secretariat, Statistics and Information Department), *Kōsei Tōkei Yōran* (*Welfare Statistics Manual*).

KY   Keizai Kikakuchō (Economic Planning Agency) (ed.), *Keizai Yōran* ((*Economic Statistics Manual*).

NA   Organization for Economic Cooperation and Development, *National Accounts. Main Aggregates*, vol. 1.

NBCT   Nōrin Suisanshō, Tōkei Jōhōbu (Ministry of Agriculture,

	Forestry, and Fisheries, Statistics and Information Department), *Nōson Bukka Chingin Tōkei* (*Statistics for Prices and Wages in Villages*).

NST ——, *Nōrin Suisan Tōkei* (*Statistics of Agriculture, Forestry and Fishery*).

NTN Sōrifu, Tōkeikyoku (Prime Minister's Office, Statistics Bureau), *Nippon Tōkei Nenkan* (Japan Statistical Yearbook).

RTN Rōdōshō, Daijin Kanbō, Tōkei Jōhōbu (Ministry of Labour, Minister's Secretariat, Statistics and Information Department), *Rōdō Tōkei Nenpō* (*Yearbook of Labour Statistics*).

RTY Rōdōshō, Daijin Kanbō, Seisaku Chōsabu (Ministry of Labour, Minister's Secretariat, Policy Planning and Research Department) (ed.), *Rōdōtōkei Yōran* (*Labour Statistics Manual*).

SJK Nippon Ginkō, Chōsa Tōkeikyoku (Bank of Japan, Research and Statistics Department), *Shikin Junkan Kanjō* (*Flow of Funds Accounts in Japan*).

SY United Nations, Department of International Economic and Social Affairs, Statistical Office, *Statistical Yearbook*.

WDR World Bank, *World Development Report*.

YIS United Nations, Department of International Economic and Social Affairs, Statistical Office, *Yearbook of Industrial Statistics*, vol.1, *General Industrial Statistics*.

YITS ——, *Yearbook of International Trade Statistics*, vol. 1, *Trade by Country*.

YLS International Labour Office, *Yearbook of Labour Statistics*.

YNAS United Nations, Department of International Economic and Social Affairs, Statistical Office, *Yearbook of National Accounts Statistics*, vol. 1, *Individual Country Data*.

ZKTG Ōkurashō (Ministry of Finance), *Zaisei Kinyū Tōkei Geppō* (*Monthly Report of Financial Statistics*).

ZT Ōkurashō, Shukeikyoku, Chōsaka (Ministry of Finance, Budget Bureau, Research Division) (ed.), *Zaisei Tōkei* (*Financial Statistics*).

ZTN Zhongguo, Guojia Tongji Ju (China, Statistical Bureau of the State), *Zhongguo Tongji Nianjian* (*Statistical Yearbook of China*).

B BOOKS AND ARTICLES (The asterisks denote particularly important sources which are referenced at the end of the appropriate chapters. *LTES* denotes *Chōki Keizai Tōkei: Suikei to Bunseki* (*Estimates of Long-term Economic Statistics of Japan since 1868*), 14 vols, ed. Kazushi Ohkawa, Miyohei Shinohara and Mataji Umemura.

*Ackley, Gardner and Hiromitsu Ishi 1976. 'Fiscal, Monetary, and Related Policies,' in Patrick and Rosovsky 1976a, pp. 153–247.

Agarwala, Amar Narain and Sampat Pal Singh (eds) 1958. *The Economics of Underdevelopment*, London: Oxford University Press.

Akamatsu, Kaname 1962. 'Historical Pattern of Economic Growth in Developing Countries.' *Developing Economies*, Preliminary Issue, no. 1, March–August, pp. 3–25.

Akino, Masakatsu and Yūjirō Hayami 1974. 'Sources of Agricultural Growth in Japan, 1880–1965', *Quarterly Journal of Economics*, vol. 88, no. 3, August, pp. 454–79.

*Allen, G. C. 1965. *Japan's Economic Expansion*, London, New York and Toronto: Oxford University Press.

*—— 1972 (rev. edn). *A Short Economic History of Modern Japan 1867–1937 with a Supplementary Chapter on Economic Recovery and Expansion 1945–1970*, London: George Allen & Unwin.

*Baba, Masao and Masahiro Tatemoto 1968. 'Foreign Trade and Economic Growth in Japan: 1858–1937', in Klein and Ohkawa 1968, pp. 162–96.

Bank of Japan, Economic Research Department 1973. *Money and Banking in Japan*, (translated by S. Nishimura and edited by L. S. Pressnell), New York: St Martin's Press.

Bićanić, Rudolf 1962. 'The Threshold of Economic Growth', *Kyklos*, vol. 15, fasc. 1, pp. 7–28.

*Blumenthal, Tuvia 1970. *Saving in Postwar Japan*, Cambridge, Massachusetts: Harvard University Press.

—— 1972a. *Nippon Keizai no Seichō Yōin*, Tōkyō: Nippon Keizai Shinbunsha.

—— 1972b. 'Exports and Economic Growth: The Case of Postwar Japan,' *Quarterly Journal of Economics*, vol. 86, no. 4, November, pp. 617–31.

*—— 1976. 'Japan's Technological Strategy', *Journal of Development Economics*, vol. 3, no. 3, September, pp. 245–55.

—— 1977. 'Scarcity of Labor and Wage Differentials in the Japanese Economy, 1958–64', in Kosobud and Minami 1977, pp. 153–77.

*Broadbridge, Seymour 1966. *Industrial Dualism in Japan: A Problem of Economic Growth and Structural Change*, London: Frank Cass & Co.

Bronfenbrenner, M. 1961. 'Some Lessons of Japan's Economic Development, 1853–1938', *Pacific Affairs*, vol. 34, no. 1, Spring, pp. 7–27.

Butlin, N. G. 1962. *Australian Domestic Product, Investment and Foreign Borrowing 1861–1938/39*, London: Cambridge University Press.

—— 1964. *Investment in Australian Economic Development 1861–1900*, London: Cambridge University Press.

Cameron, Rondo (ed.) 1967a. *Banking in the Early Stages of Industrialization: A Study in Comparative Economic History*, London, New York and Toronto: Oxford University Press.

—— 1967b. 'Conclusion', in Cameron 1967a, pp. 290–321.

*Caves, Richard E. and Masu Uekusa 1976a. *Industrial Organization in Japan*, Washington, D.C.: Brookings Institution.

*—— 1976b. 'Industrial Organization', in Patrick and Rosovsky 1976a, pp. 459–523.

Central Statistical Office 1989. *Annual Abstract of Statistics*, London: Her Majesty's Stationery Office.

Chambers, J. D. 1953. 'Enclosure and Labour Supply in the Industrial Revolution', *Economic History Review*, vol. 5, no. 3, April, pp. 319–43.

—— and G. E. Mingay 1966. *The Agricultural Revolution 1750–1880*, London: B. T. Batsford.

Chenery, Hollis B. 1963. 'The Use of Interindustry Analysis in Development Programming', in T. Barna (ed.), *Structural Interdependence and Economic Development*, London: Macmillan, pp. 11–27.

Choo, Hakchung 1991. 'A Comparison of Income Distribution in Japan, Korea and Taiwan', in Mizoguchi *et al.* pp. 3–25.

Clark, Colin 1951 (2nd edn). *The Conditions of Economic Progress*, London: Macmillan Press.

*Cohen, J. B. 1949. *Japan's Economy: War and Reconstruction*, Minneapolis and London: University of Minnesota Press and Oxford University Press.

*Cole, Robert E. and Ken-ichi Tominaga 1976. 'Japan's Changing Occupational Structure and Its Significance', in Patrick 1976, pp. 53–95.

Crouzet, F. 1972. 'Western Europe and Great Britain: "Catching Up" in the First Half of the Nineteenth Century', in Youngson 1972, pp. 98–125.

*Crawcour, E. Sydney 1965. 'The Tokugawa Heritage', in Lockwood 1965, pp. 17–44.

Deane, Phyllis 1965. *The First Industrial Revolution*, London: Cambridge University Press.

—— and W. A. Cole 1962. *British Economic Growth 1688–1959: Trends and Structure*, London: Cambridge University Press.

Denison, Edward F. 1967. *Why Growth Rates Differ: Postwar Experience in Nine Western Countries*, Washington, D.C.: The Brookings Institution.

—— and William K. Chung 1976. 'Economic Growth and Its Sources', in Patrick and Rosovsky 1976a pp. 63–151.

Dore, R. P. 1959. *Land Reform in Japan*, London, New York and Toronto: Oxford University Press.

—— 1965. *Education in Tokugawa Japan*, London: Routledge & Kegan Paul.

Economic Council of Japan, NNW Measurement Committee 1974. *Measuring Net National Welfare of Japan*, Tōkyō: Ministry of Finance, Printing Bureau.

*Emi, Kōichi 1963. *Government Fiscal Activity and Economic Growth in Japan 1868–1960*, Tōkyō: Kinokuniya.

—— 1971. *Shihon Keisei, LTES*, vol. 4.

*—— and Hiromitsu Ishi 1979. 'Government Accounts: Expenditure and Revenue', in Ohkawa and Shinohara 1979, pp. 195–202.

*—— and Shigeru Ishiwata 1979. 'Capital Formation and Capital Stock', in Ohkawa and Shinohara 1979, pp. 177–94.

—— and Toshiyuki Mizoguchi 1968. *Kojin Chochiku Kōdō no Kokusai Hikaku*, Tōkyō: Iwanami Shoten.

—— and Yūichi Shionoya 1966. *Zaisei Shishitsu, LTES*, vol. 7.

*Encyclopaedia Britannica, Inc. 1974 (15th edn). *The New Encyclopaedia Britannica, Macropaedia*, vol. 10, Chicago, London and other cities, pp. 34–57.

Falkus, M. E. 1977 (rep.). *The Industrialization of Russia, 1700–1914*, London and Basingstoke: Macmillan Press.

Fei, John C. H. and Gustav Ranis 1964. *Development of the Labor Surplus Economy: Theory and Policy*, Homewood, Illinois: Richard D. Irwin.

—— 1975. 'A Model of Growth and Employment in the Open Dualistic Economy: The Case of Korea and Taiwan', *Journal of Development Studies*, vol. 11, no. 2, January, pp. 32–63.

Feinstein, C. H. 1972. *National Income, Expenditure and Output of the United Kingdom 1855–1965*, London: Cambridge University Press.

Firestone, O. J. 1958. *Canada's Economic Development 1867–1953: with Special Reference to Changes in the Country's National Product and National Wealth*, London: Bowes & Bowes.

Friedman, Milton 1977. 'Nobel Lecture: Inflation and Unemployment', *Journal of Political Economy*, vol. 85, no. 3, June, pp. 451–72.

—— and Anna Jacobson Schwartz 1963. *A Monetary History of the United States 1867–1960*, Princeton, New Jersey: Princeton University Press.

Fuchs, Victor R. 1968. *The Service Economy*, New York: National Bureau of Economic Research.

Fujino, Shōzaburō 1965. *Nippon no Keiki Junkan: Junkanteki Hattenkatei no Rironteki, Tōkeiteki, Rekishiteki Bunseki*, Tōkyō: Keisōshobō.

*—— 1966. 'Business Cycles in Japan, 1868–1962', *Hitotsubashi Journal of Economics*, vol. 7, no. 1, June, pp. 56–79.

*—— 1968. 'Construction Cycles and Their Monetary-Financial Characteristics', in Klein and Ohkawa 1968, pp. 35–68.

—— 1977. 'Inflation to Shitsugyō', in Ōkita and Uchida 1977, pp. 17–48.

—— 1990. *Kokusai Tsūkataisei no Dōtai to Nippon Keizai*, Tōkyō: Keisōshobō.

——, Shirō Fujino and Akira Ono 1979. *Sen-i Kōgyō, LTES*, vol. 11.

—— and Ryōko Akiyama 1977. *Shōken Kakaku to Rishiritsu 1874–1975*, vol. 2, Tōkyō: Institute of Economic Research, Hitotsubashi University.

—— and Fukuo Igarashi 1973. *Keiki Shisū 1880–1940*, Tōkyō: Institute of Economic Research, Hitotsubashi University.

—— and Jūrō Teranishi 1975. "Shikin Junkan no Chōki Dōtai: Yobiteki Bunseki', *Keizai Kenkyū*, vol. 26, no. 4, October, pp. 334–58.

*Fujita, Sei 1966. 'Tax Policy', in Komiya 1966a, pp. 32–59.

—— 1975–6. 'Fiscal Policy in Postwar Japan', *Japanese Economic Studies*, vol. 4, no. 2, Winter, pp. 27–58.

Gerschenkron, Alexander 1962. *Economic Backwardness in Historical Perspective: A Book of Essays*, Cambridge, Massachusetts: Harvard University Press, Belknap Press.

*Gleason, Alan H. 1965. 'Economic Growth and Consumption in Japan', in Lockwood 1965, pp. 391–444.

*Goldsmith, Raymond W. 1983. *The Financial Development of Japan, 1868–1977*, New Haven, Connecticut: Yale University Press.

—— and Christopher Saunders (eds) 1959. *The Measurement of National Wealth*, London: Bowes & Bowes.

Gordon, R. A. 1961. 'Differential Changes in the Prices of Consumers' and Capital Goods', *American Economic Review*, vol. 51, no. 5, December, pp. 937–57.

Gotō, Akira 1982. 'Business Groups in a Market Economy', *European Economic Review*, vol. 19, no. 1, September, pp. 53–70.

*Hadley, Eleanor M. 1970. *Antitrust in Japan*, Princeton, New Jersey: Princeton University Press.

Hamada, Fumimasa 1971. *Setsubi Tōshikōdō no Keiryō Bunseki: Shihon Stock no Seichō to Tōshikōdō*, Tōkyō: Tōyōkeizai Shinpōsha.

Hanley, Susan B. and Kōzō Yamamura 1977. *Economic and Demographic*

Change in Preindustrial Japan 1600–1868, Princeton, New Jersey: Princeton University Press.

*Hatai, Yoshitaka 1980. 'Business Cycles and the Outflow of Labor from the Agricultural Sector: Some Comments on Namiki's Debate with Minami and Ono', in Nishikawa 1980, pp. 5–18.

Hayami, Akira 1975. 'Jinkō to Keizai', in Hiroshi Shinbo, Akira Hayami and Shunsaku Nishikawa, *Sūryō Keizaishi Nyūmon: Nippon no Zenkōgyōka Shakai*, Tōkyō: Nippon Hyōronsha, pp. 21–118.

—— and Matarō Miyamoto (eds) 1988. *Keizai Shakai no Seiritsu, 17–18 Seiki* (*Nippon Keizaishi* vol. 1), Tōkyō: Iwanami Shoten.

Hayami, Yūjirō 1973. *Nippon Nōgyō no Seichō Katei*, Tōkyō: Sōbunsha.

*—— 1975. *A Century of Agricultural Growth in Japan: Its Relevance to Asian Development*, Tōkyō: University of Tōkyō Press.

*—— and Vernon W. Ruttan 1971. *Agricultural Development: An International Perspective*, Baltimore: Johns Hopkins Press.

—— and Saburō Yamada 1969. 'Agricultural Productivity at the Beginning of Industrialization', in Ohkawa, Johnston and Kaneda 1969, pp. 105–35.

*—— 1991. *The Agricultural Development of Japan: A Century's Perspective*, Tōkyō: University of Tōkyō Press.

Henmi, Kenzō 1969. 'Primary Product Exports and Economic Development: The Case of Silk', in Ohkawa, Johnston and Kaneda 1969, pp. 303–23.

Hinrichs, Harley H. 1966. *A General Theory of Tax Structure Change during Economic Development*, Cambridge, Massachusetts: Harvard Law School.

Hirschman, Albert O. 1958. *The Strategy of Economic Development*, New Haven, Connecticut: Yale University Press.

Hirschmeier, Johannes 1964. *The Origins of Entrepreneurship in Meiji Japan*, Cambridge, Massachusetts: Harvard University Press.

—— and Tsunehiko Yui 1975. *The Development of Japanese Business 1600–1973*, London: George Allen & Unwin.

Horie, Yasuzō 1965. 'Modern Entrepreneurship in Meiji Japan', in Lockwood 1965, pp. 183–208.

Hyōdō, Tsutomu 1971. *Nippon ni okeru Rōshikankei no Tenkai*, Tōkyō: University of Tōkyō Press.

*Ichino, Shōzā 1980. 'The Structure of the Labor Force and Patterns of Mobility: 1950–1965', in Nishikawa 1980, pp. 41–66.

Imlah, Albert H. 1950. 'The Terms of Trade of the United Kingdom, 1798–1913', *Journal of Economic History*, vol. 10, no. 2, November, pp. 170–94.

*Ishi, Hiromitsu 1974. 'Long-Term Changes of the Government Saving Rate in Japan', *Economic Development and Cultural Change*, vol. 22, no. 4, July, pp. 615–33.

—— 1975. 'Seifu no Chochiku to Tōshi', in Ohkawa and Minami 1975, pp. 342–66.

—— 1976. *Zaisei Kōzō no Anteikōka: Builtin Stabilizer no Bunseki*, Tōkyō: Tōyōkeizai Shinpōsha.

—— 1979. *Sozei Seisaku no Kōka: Sūryōteki Sekkin*, Tōkyō: Tōyōkeizai Shinpōsha.

Ishikawa, Kenjirō 1974. 'Meijiki ni okeru Kigyōsha Katsudō no Tōkeiteki Kansatsu', *Ōsaka Daigaku Keizaigaku*, vol. 23, no. 4, March, pp. 85–118.

Ishikawa, Shigeru 1967. *Economic Development in Asian Perspective*, Tōkyō: Kinokuniya.

*———— 1981. *Essays on Technology, Employment and Institutions in Economic Development: Comparative Asian Experience*, Tōkyō: Kinokuniya.

———— 1990. *Kaihatsu Keizaigaku no Kihon Mondai*, Tōkyō: Iwanami Shoten.

Ishiwata, Shigeru 1975. 'Minkan Kotei Shihon Tōshi', in Ohkawa and Minami 1975, pp. 15–33.

Itagaki, Yoichi (ed.) 1970. *Nippon no Shigen Mondai*, Tōkyō: Nippon Keizai Shinbunsha.

*Ito, Takatoshi 1992. *The Japanese Economy*, Cambridge, Massachusetts and London: MIT Press.

*Jinushi, Shigemi 1975–76. 'Welfare: Social Security, Social Overhead Capital, and Pollution', *Japanese Economic Studies*, vol. 4, no. 2, Winter, pp. 59–82.

*Johnson, Chalmers 1982. *MITI and the Japanese Miracle: The Growth of Industrial Policy, 1925–1975*, Stanford, California: Stanford University Press.

*Johnston, Bruce F. 1962. 'Agricultural Development and Economic Transformation: A Comparative Study of the Japanese Experience', *Food Research Institute Studies*, vol. 3, no. 3, November, pp. 223–76.

*———— 1966. 'Agriculture and Economic Development: The Relevance of the Japanese Experience', *Food Research Institute Studies*, vol. 6, no. 3, pp. 251–312.

*———— 1969. 'The Japanese Model of Agricultural Development: Its Relevance to Developing Nations', in Ohkawa, Johnston and Kaneda 1969, pp. 58–102.

Jorgenson, Dale W. 1966. 'Testing Alternative Theories of the Development of a Dual Economy', in Irma Adelman and Erik Thorbecke (eds), *The Theory and Design of Economic Development*, Baltimore: Johns Hopkins Press, pp. 45–60.

Kagaku Gijutsuchō (Science and Technology Agency) 1979. *Kagaku Gijutsu Hakusho: Shōwa 54–Nen*, Tōkyō: Ōkurashō, Insatsukyoku.

*Kanamori, Hisao 1966. 'Economic Growth and the Balance of Payments', in Komiya 1966a, pp. 79–94.

*———— 1968. 'Economic Growth and Exports', in Klein and Ohkawa 1968, pp. 303–25.

———— and Yuriko Takase 1977. 'Keizai Seichō to Fukushi: GNP to NNW', in Ōkita and Uchida 1977, pp. 115–31.

Kaneda, Hiromitsu 1969. 'Long-Term Changes in Food Consumption Patterns in Japan', in Ohkawa, Johnston and Kaneda 1969, pp. 398–431.

Katō, Seiichi 1967. *Chūshō Kigyō no Kokusai Hikaku*, Tōkyō: Tōyōkeizai Shinpōsha.

Kawaguchi, Hiroshi 1970. 'Over-Loan and the Investment Behavior of Firms', *Developing Economies*, vol. 8, no. 4, December, pp. 386–406.

Kawano, Shigeto 1969. 'Effects of the Land Reform on Consumption and Investment of Farmers', in Ohkawa, Johnston and Kaneda 1969, pp. 374–97.

Kayō, Nobufumi (ed.) 1958. *Nippon Nōgyō Kiso Tōkei*, Tōkyō: Nōrin Suisangyō Seisansei Kōjō Kaigi.

Keizai Kikakuchō (Economic Planning Agency) 1969. *Kaitei Kokumin*

Shotoku Tōkei: Shōwa 26-Nendo–Shōwa 42-Nendo, Tōkyō: Ōkurashō, Insatsukyoku.

—— (ed.) 1990a. *Kokumin Seikatsu Hakusho, Heisei 2-Nenban*, Tōkyō: Ōkurashō, Insatsukyoku.

—— 1990b. *Keizai Hakusho: Heisei 2-Nenban*, Tōkyō: Ōkurashō, Insatsukyoku.

Keizai Kikakuchō, Keizai Kenkyūjo (Economic Planning Agency, Research Institute of Economics) 1968. *Chōki Keizai Tōkei no Seibi Kaizen ni Kansuru Kenkyū II: Fukakachi, Sanshutsu Deflator, Shūgyōshasū oyobi Shihon Stock*, Tōkyō: Ōkurashō, Insatsukyoku.

Keizai Kikakuchō, Keizai Kenkyūjo, Kokumin Shotokubu (Economic Planning Agency, Research Institute of Economics, National Income Division) 1972. *Minkan Kigyō Soshihon Stock no Suikei: Nenji Keiretsu, Shōwa 28-Nen–Shōwa 45-Nen*, Tōkyō.

—— 1977. *Minkan Kigyō Soshihon Stock: Shōwa 30–50-Nendo*, Tōkyō.

—— 1991. *Minkan Kigyō Soshihon Stock: Shōwa 40-Heisei 1-Nendo*, Tōkyō.

Kelley, Allen C. and Jeffrey G. Williamson 1974. *Lessons from Japanese Development: An Analytical Economic History*, Chicago and London: University of Chicago Press.

Kendrick, John W. 1961. *Productivity Trends in the United States*, Princeton, New Jersey: Princeton University Press.

Kindleberger, Charles P. 1956. *The Terms of Trade: A European Case Study*, Massachusetts and New York: Technology Press of Massachusetts Institute of Technology and John Wiley & Sons.

—— 1967. *Europe's Postwar Growth: The Role of Labour Supply*, Cambridge, Massachusetts: Harvard University Press.

Klein, Lawrence and Kazushi Ohkawa (eds) 1968. *Economic Growth: The Japanese Experience since the Meiji Era*, Homewood, Illinois and Nobleton, Ontario: Richard D. Irwin and Irwin-Dorsey.

*Koike, Kazuo 1978. 'Japan's Industrial Relations: Characteristics and Problems', *Japanese Economic Studies*, vol. 7, no. 1, Fall, pp. 42–90.

Kojima, Kiyoshi 1958. *Nippon Bōeki to Keizai Hatten*, Tōkyō: Kunimotoshobō.

—— 1985. *Nippon no Kaigai Chokusetsu Tōsi*, Tōkyō: Bunshindō.

Komiya, Ryūtarō (ed.) 1966a. *Postwar Economic Growth in Japan*, (translated by Robert S. Ozaki), Berkeley and Los Angeles, California: University of California Press.

*—— 1966b. 'The Supply of Personal Savings', in Komiya 1966a, pp. 157–81.

*—— 1966c. 'Japan', in National Bureau of Economic Research, *Foreign Tax Policies and Economic Growth*, New York and London: Columbia University Press, pp. 39–90.

—— 1975a. *Gendai Nippon Keizai Kenkyū*, Tōkyō: University of Tōkyō Press.

*—— 1975b. 'Planning in Japan', in Morris Bornstein (ed.), *Economic Planning, East and West*, Cambridge, Massachusetts: Ballinger Publishing Co., pp. 189–227.

—— and Kikuo Iwata 1973. *Kigyō Kinkyū no Riron: Shihon Cost to Zaimu Seisaku*, Tōkyō: Nippon Keizai Shinbunsha.

*————, Masahiro Okuno and Kōtarō Suzumura (eds) 1988. *Industrial Policy in Japan* (translated under the supervision of Kazuo Satō). Tōkyō, San Diego and California: Academic Press.

Kōsai, Yutaka 1981. *Kodo Seichō no Jidai*, Tōkyō: Nippon Hyōronsha.

*———— and Yoshitarō Ogino 1984. *The Contemporary Japanese Economy*, London: Macmillan Press.

Kōsei Torihiki Iinkai (Fair Trade Commission) 1981. *Shōwa 55-Nendo Nenji Hōkoku*, Tōkyō.

Kosobud, Richard and Ryōshin Minami (eds) 1977. *Econometric Studies of Japan*, Urbana, Chicago and London: University of Illinois Press.

*Krause, Lawrence B. and Sueo Sekiguchi 1976. 'Japan and the World Economy', in Patrick and Rosovsky 1976a, pp. 383–458.

Kuznets, Simon 1937. *National Income and Capital Formation*, New York; National Bureau of Economic Research.

———— 1955. 'Economic Growth and Income Inequality', *American Economic Review*, vol. 45, no. 1, March, pp. 1–28.

———— 1958. 'Underdeveloped Countries and the Pre-Industrial Phase in the Advanced Countries: An Attempt at Comparison', in Agarwala and Singh 1958, pp. 135–53.

———— 1963. 'Notes on the Take-off', in Rostow 1963, pp. 22–43.

———— 1966. *Modern Economic Growth: Rate, Structure, and Spread*, New Haven, Connecticut and London: Yale University Press.

———— 1967. 'Quantitative Aspects of the Economic Growth of Nations: x, Level and Structure of Foreign Trade: Long-Term Trends', *Economic Development and Cultural Change*, vol. 15, no. 2, January, pp. 1–140.

———— 1968. 'Notes on Japan's Economic Growth', in Klein and Ohkawa 1968, pp. 385–422.

———— 1971. *Economic Growth of Nations: Total Output and Production Structure*, Cambridge, Massachusetts: Harvard University Press.

———— 1973. 'Modern Economic Growth: Findings and Reflections', *American Economic Review*, vol. 63, no. 3, June, pp. 247–58.

*Landes, David S. 1965. 'Japan and Europe: Contrasts in Industrialization', in Lockwood 1965, pp. 93–182.

———— 1969. *The Unbound Prometheus: Technological Change and Industrial Development in Western Europe from 1750 to the Present*, London: Cambridge University Press.

League of Nations, Economic, Financial and Transit Department 1945. *Industrialization and Foreign Trade*.

Lewis, W. Arthur 1958a. 'Economic Development with Unlimited Supplies of Labour', in Agarwala and Singh 1958, pp. 400–49.

———— 1958b. 'Unlimited Labour: Further Notes', *Manchester School of Economic and Social Studies*, vol. 26, no. 1, January, pp. 1–32.

Lincoln, Edward J. 1990. *Japan's Unequal Trade*, Washington, DC: Brookings Institution.

Lipsey, Robert E. 1963. *Price and Quantity Trends in the Foreign Trade of the United States*, Princeton, New Jersey: Princeton University Press.

Lockwood, William W. (ed.) 1965. *The State and Economic Enterprise in Japan: Essays in the Political Economy of Growth*, Princeton: Princeton University Press.

*———— 1968 (expanded edn). *The Economic Development of Japan: Growth*

and Structural Change, Princeton, New Jersey: Princeton University Press.
LTES 1965–. Ohkawa, Kazushi, Miyohei Shinohara and Mataji Umemura (eds), *Chōki Keizai Tōkei: Suikei to Bunseki (Estimates of Long-Term Economic Statistics of Japan since 1868)*, vols 1–14, Tōkyō: Tōyōkeizai Shinpōsha.

Maddison, Angus 1964. *Economic Growth in the West: Comparative Experience in Europe and North America*, New York and London: Twentieth Century Fund and George Allen & Unwin.

—— 1969. *Economic Growth in Japan and the USSR*, London: George Allen & Unwin.

—— 1984. 'Comparative Analysis of the Productivity Situation in the Advanced Capitalist Countries', in J. W. Kendrick (ed.), *International Comparisons of Productivity and Causes of the Slowdown*, Cambridge, Massachusetts: Ballinger Publishing Co.

—— 1989. *The World Economy in the 20th Century*, Paris: Development Centre, OECD.

Makino, Fumio 1980. '1930-Nendai no Rōdōryoku Idō', *Keizai Kenkyū*, vol. 31, no. 4, October, pp. 362–7.

Marczewski, J. 1963. 'The Take-off Hypothesis and French Experience', in Rostow 1963, pp. 119–38.

*Maruo, Naomi 1972. 'A Measure of Welfare Standards of the Japanese People', *Annual of the Institute of Economic Research*, vol. 3, pp. 101–34.

Masamura, Kimihiro 1978. *Nippon Keizairon,ʿ*: Tōyōkeizai Shinpōsha.

Masui, Yukio 1969. 'The Supply Price of Labor: Farm Family Workers', in Ohkawa, Johnston and Kaneda 1969, pp. 222–49.

Maynard, Geoffrey 1962. *Economic Development and the Price Level*, London: Macmillan Press.

Meadows, Donella H. *et al.* 1972. *The Limits to Growth: A Report for the Club of Rome's Project on the Predicament of Mankind*, New York: Universe Books.

*Mills, Edwin S. and Katsutoshi Ōta 1976. 'Urbanization and Urban Problems', in Patrick and Rosovsky 1976a, pp. 673–751.

Minami, Ryōshin 1965. *Tetsudō to Denryoku*, *LTES*, vol. 12.

*—— 1973. *The Turning Point in Economic Development: Japan's Experience*, Tōkyō: Kinokuniya.

—— 1980. 'Kōreika Shakai no Mondaigun', *Keizai Seminar*, no. 301, February, pp. 70–6.

—— 1981. 'Nōgyōrōdō no Seisan Danryokusei no Chōkihenka: Suikei to Bunseki', *Keizai Kenkyū*, vol. 32, no. 4, October, pp. 358–66.

*—— 1987. *Power Revolution in the Industrialization of Japan: 1885–1940*, Tōkyō and London: Kinokuniya and Oxford University Press.

—— 1993. *The Economic Development of China: Comparison with Japanese Experience* (translated by Wenran Jiang and Tanya Jiang with assistance from David Merriman) London: Macmillan Press.

—— and Yukihiko Kiyokawa (eds) 1987. *Nippon no Kōgyōka to Gijutsu Hatten*, Tōkyō: Tōyōkeizai Shinpōsha.

—— and Fumio Makino 1983. 'Conditions for Technological Diffusion: Case of Power Looms', *Hitotsubashi Journal of Economics*, vol. 23, no. 2, February, pp. 1–20.

—— and Kōnosuke Odaka 1972. *Chingin Hendō: Sūryōteki Sekkin*, Tōkyō: Iwanami Shoten.

*—— and Akira Ono 1975. 'Price Changes in a Dual Economy', *Japanese Economic Studies*, vol. 3, no. 3, Spring, pp. 32–58.

—— 1978a. 'Yōsoshotoku to Bunpairitsu no Suikei: Minkan Hiichiji Sangyō', *Keizai Kenkyū*, vol. 29, no. 2, April, pp. 143–69.

—— 1978b. 'Modeling Dualistic Development in Japan', *Hitotsubashi Journal of Economics*, vol. 18, no. 2, February, pp. 18–32.

*—— 1979. 'Factor Incomes and Shares', and 'Wages', in Ohkawa and Shinohara 1979, pp. 205–18, 229–40.

*—— 1981. 'Behavior of Income Shares in a Labor Surplus Economy: Japan's Experience', *Economic Development and Cultural Change*, vol. 29, no. 2, January, pp. 309–24.

—— 1987. 'Senzen Nippon no Shotoku Bunpu: Kosūwari Shiryō ni yoru Yamaguchiken no Bunseki', *Keizai Kenkyū*, vol. 38, no. 4, October, pp. 333–52.

Minami, Ryōzaburō and Masao Ueda (eds) 1979. *Nippon no Jinkō Kōreika*, Tōkyō: Chikurashobō.

Mingay, G. E. 1963. 'The "Agricultural Revolution" in English History: A Reconsideration', *Agricultural History*, vol. 37, no. 3, July, pp. 123–33.

*Ministry of Foreign Affairs 1980. *The Japan of Today*, Tōkyō: International Society for Educational Information.

Mitchell, B. R. 1962. *Abstract of British Historical Statistics*, London: Cambridge University Press.

—— 1978. *European Historical Statistics 1750–1970*, London and Basingstoke: Macmillan Press.

*Miyazawa, Ken-ichi 1964. 'The Dual Structure of the Japanese Economy and Its Growth Pattern', *Developing Economies*, vol. 2, no. 2, June, pp. 147–70.

*Mizoguchi, Toshiyuki 1970. *Personal Savings and Consumption in Postwar Japan*, Tōkyō: Kinokuniya.

—— 1988. 'Nippon no Shōhikansū Bunseki no Tenbō', *Keizai Kenkyū*, vol. 39, no. 3, July, pp. 253–76.

—— *et al.* 1978. 'Sengo Nippon no Shotoku Bunpu II', *Keizai Kenkyū*, vol. 29, no. 1, January, pp. 44–60.

—— *et al.* (eds) 1991. *Making Economies More Efficient and More Equitable: Factors Determining Income Distribution*, Tōkyō: Kinokuniya.

*—— and Noriyuki Takayama 1984. *Equity and Poverty under the Rapid Economic Growth: Japanese Experience*, Tōkyō: Kinokuniya.

Mizuno, Asao 1973. *Chingin Kōzō Hendōron*, Tōkyō: Shinhyōron.

Monbushō, Chōsakyoku (Ministry of Education, Research Bureau) 1963. *Nippon no Seichō to Kyōiku: Kyōiku no Tenkai to Keizai no Hattatsu*, Tōkyō: Teikoku Chihō Gyōsei Gakkai.

Moriguchi, Chikashi 1988. *Nippon Keizairon*, Tōkyō: Sōbunsha.

Morishima, Michio 1982. *Why Has Japan 'Succeeded'?* Cambridge, London, New York. New Rochelle, Melbourne and Sydney: Cambridge University Press.

Mundle, Sudipto and Kazushi Ohkawa 1979. 'Agricultural Surplus Flow in Japan, 1888–1937', *Developing Economies*, vol. 17, no. 3, September, pp. 247–65.

Musgrave, Richard Abel 1969. *Fiscal Systems*, New Haven, Connecticut: Yale University Press.

Nakamura, James I. 1966. *Agricultural Production and the Economic Development of Japan 1873–1922*, Princeton, New Jersey: Princeton University Press.

Nakamura, Seiji 1979. *Sengo Nippon no Gijutsu Kakushin*, Tōkyō: Ōtsuki Shobō.

Nakamura, Takafusa 1966. 'The Modern Industries and the Traditional Industries – at the Early Stage of the Japanese Economy', *Developing Economies*, vol. 4, no. 4, December, pp. 567–93.

—— 1971. *Senzenki Nippon Keizai no Seichō no Bunseki*, Tōkyō: Iwanami Shoten.

—— 1980 (2nd edn). *Nippon Keizai: Sono Seichō to Kōzō*, Tōkyō: University of Tōkyō Press.

*—— 1981. *The Postwar Japanese Economy: Its Development and Structure*, Tōkyō: University of Tōkyō Press.

*—— 1983. *Economic Growth in Prewar Japan*, (translated by Robert A. Feldman), New Haven, Connecticut: Yale University Press.

—— and Kōnosuke Odaka (eds) 1989. *Nijūkōzō* (*Nippon Keizaishi*, vol. 6), Tōkyō: Iwanami Shoten.

Nakayama, Ichirō 1960. 'The Japanese Economy and the Role of the Government', *Hitotsubashi Journal of Economics*, vol. 1, no. 1, October, pp. 1–12.

—— and Miyohei Shinohara (eds) 1969. *Nippon no Keizai Hatten: Kōgyōka to Mirai*, Tōkyō: Ushio Shuppansha.

Namiki, Masayoshi 1959. 'Nōka Jinkō no Idō', in Shigeo Nojiri (ed.), *Nōson no Jinkō: Atarashii Kadai to sono Taisaku*, Tōkyō: Chūō Keizaisha, pp. 53–90.

Nippon Gakushiin (Japan Academy) (ed.) 1964. *Meijizen Nippon Nōgyō Gijutsushi*, Tōkyō: Nippon Gakujutsu Shinkōkai.

Nippon Ginkō, Chōsakyoku (Bank of Japan, Economic Research Department) 1975. 'Nippon ni okeru Money Supply no Jūyōsei ni tsuite', *Chōsa Geppō*, July, pp. 1–19.

—— 1976. *Wagakuni no Kinyūseido*, Tōkyō.

—— 1977. 'Marshall no *k* no Sūseiteki Jōshō ni tsuite', *Chōsa Geppō*, November, pp. 1–25.

Nippon Ginkō, Tōkeikyoku (Bank of Japan, Statistics Department) 1966. *Meijikō Honpō Shuyō Keizai Tōkei*.

*Nishikawa, Shunsaku 1974. 'The Banking System: Competition and Control', *Japanese Economic Studies*, vol. 2, no. 3, Spring, pp. 3–52.

—— (ed.) 1980. *The Labor Market in Japan: Selected Readings*, (translated by Ross Mouer), Tōkyō: Japan Foundation.

—— 1985. *Nippon Keizai no Seichōshi*, Tōkyō: Tōyōkeizai Shinpōsha.

—— and Takeshi Abe (eds) 1990. *Sangyōka no Jidai, Jō* (*Nippon Keizaishi*, vol. 4), Tōkyō: Iwanami Shoten.

—— and Yūzō Yamamoto (eds) 1990. *Sangyōka no Jidai, Ge* (*Nippon Keizaishi* vol. 5), Tōkyō: Iwanami Shoten.

*Noda, Tsutomu 1979. 'Prices', in Ohkawa and Shinohara 1979, pp. 219–28.

Nōrin Tōkeikyōkai (ed.) 1991. *Nōgyō Hakusho, Heisei 2-Nendoban*, Tōkyō: Nōrin Tōkeikyōkai.

Norman, E. Herbert 1940. *Japan's Emergence as a Modern State: Political and Economic Problems of the Meiji Period*, New York: Institute of Pacific Relations.

North, Douglas C. 1955. 'Location Theory and Regional Economic Growth', *Journal of Political Economy*, vol. 63, February–December, pp. 243–58.

Nurkse, Ragnar 1953. *Problems of Capital Formation in Underdeveloped Countries*, Oxford: Basil Blackwell.

Obi, Keiichirō 1980. 'The Theory of Labor Supply: Some New Perspectives and Some Implications', in Nishikawa 1980, pp. 41–66.

Ōbuchi, Hiroshi 1974. *Jinkōkatei no Keizai Bunseki: Jinkō Keizaigaku no Ichikenkyū*, Tōkyō: Shinhyōron.

*—— 1976. 'Demographic Transition in the Process of Japanese Industrialization', in Patrick 1976, pp. 329–61.

*—— 1979. 'The Aging of Population and Economic Growth in Japan', *Japanese Economic Studies*, vol. 7, no. 3, Spring, pp. 3–29.

Odaka, Kōnosuke 1968. 'A History of Money Wages in the Northern Kyūshū Industrial Area, 1898–1939', *Hitotsubashi Journal of Economics*, vol. 8, no. 2, February, pp. 71–100.

*—— 1982. 'An Analysis of the Personal Consumption Expenditures in Japan, 1892–1967', in *Essays in Development Economics in Honor of Harry T. Oshima*, Metro Manila: Philippine Institute for Development Studies, pp. 335–56.

—— 1984. *Rōdōshijō Bunseki*, Tōkyō: Iwanami Shoten.

*Ogura, Takekazu (ed.) 1967. *Agricultural Development in Modern Japan*, Tōkyō: Fuji Publishing Co.

*Ohkawa, Kazushi 1968. 'Changes in National Income Distribution by Factor Share in Japan', in Jean Marchal and Bernard Ducros (eds), *The Distribution of National Income*, London, Melbourne and Toronto: Macmillan Press, pp. 177–88.

—— 1969. *Nippon Keizai Bunseki: Seichō to Kōzō, Zōhoban*, Tōkyō: Shunjūsha.

*—— 1972. *Differential Structure and Agriculture: Essays on Dualistic Growth*, Tōkyō: Kinokuniya.

—— 1973. *'Nijūteki Seichō ni okeru Kojinshōhi'*, in Ohkawa and Hayami, pp. 227–49.

—— 1974. *Nippon Keizai no Kōzō: Rekishiteki Shiten kara*, Tōkyō: Keisōshobō.

—— 1975. 'Keizai no Hatten Kōzō: Nippon no Keiken no Kokusaiteki Igi', in Ohkawa and Minami 1975, pp. 178–209.

—— 1976. *Keizai Hatten to Nippon no Keiken*, Tōkyō: Taimeidō.

—— 1978. 'Past Economic Growth of Japan in Comparison with the Western Case: Trend Acceleration and Differential Structure', in Shigeto Tsuru (ed.), *Growth and Resources Problems Related to Japan*, Tōkyō: Asahi Evening News, pp. 3–15.

—— 1979a. 'Aggregate Growth and Product Allocation', in Ohkawa and Shinohara 1979, pp. 3–33.

*———— 1979b. 'Production Structure', in Ohkawa and Shinohara 1979, pp. 34–58.

*————, Bruce F. Johnston and Hiromitsu Kaneda (eds) 1969. *Agriculture and Economic Growth: Japan's Experience*, Tōkyō: University of Tōkyō Press.

———— and Yūjirō Hayami (eds) 1973. *Nippon Keizai no Chōki Bunseki; Seichō, Kōzō, Hadō*, Tōkyō: Nippon Keizai Shinbunsha.

*———— and Hirohisa Kohama 1989. *Lectures on Developing Economies: Japan's Experience and Its Relevance*, Tōkyō: University of Tōkyō Press.

———— and Ryōshin Minami (eds) 1975. *Kindai Nippon no Keizai Hatten: Chōki Keizai Tōkei ni yoru Bunseki*, Tōkyō: Tōyōkeizai Shinpōsha.

———— and Gustav Ranis (eds) 1985. *Japan and the Developing Countries: A Comparative Analysis*, Oxford and New York: Basil Blackwell.

———— *et al.* 1957. *The Growth Rate of the Japanese Economy since 1878*, Tōkyō: Kinokuniya.

———— *et al.* 1966. *Shihon Stock, LTES*, vol. 3.

———— *et al.* 1967. *Bukka, LTES*, vol. 8.

———— *et al.* 1974. *Kokumin Shotoku, LTES*, vol. 1.

———— *et al.* 1978. 'Agricultural Surplus in an Overall Performance of Savings-Investment', in K. Ohkawa and Y. Hayami (eds), *Papers and Proceedings of the Conference on Japan's Development Experience and the Contemporary Developing Countries: Issues for Comparative Analysis*, Tōkyō: International Development Center of Japan.

*———— and Henry Rosovsky 1962. 'Economic Fluctuations in Prewar Japan: A Preliminary Analysis of Cycles and Long Swings', *Hitotsubashi Journal of Economics*, vol. 3, no. 1, October, pp. 1–33.

*———— 1964. 'The Role of Agriculture in Modern Japanese Economic Development', in Carl Eicher and Lawrence Witt (eds), *Agriculture in Economic Development*, New York, Toronto, San Francisco and London: McGraw-Hill, pp. 45–69.

*———— 1965. 'A Century of Japanese Economic Growth', in Lockwood 1965, pp. 47–92.

*———— 1973. *Japanese Economic Growth: Trend Acceleration in the Twentieth Century*, Stanford: Stanford University Press.

———— and Miyohei Shinohara (eds) 1979. *Patterns of Japanese Economic Development: A Quantitative Appraisal*, New Haven, Connecticut and London: Yale University Press.

Okazaki, Yōichi 1966. *Nippon no Rōdōryoku Mondai*, Tōkyō: Kōbunsha.

———— 1977. *Kōreika Shakai eno Tenkan*, Tōkyō: Kōbunsha.

Ōkita, Saburō and Tadao Uchida (eds) 1977. *Kokusai Keizai Symposium: Atarashii Han-ei o Motomete*, Tōkyō: Nippon Keizai Shinbunsha.

Ono, Akira 1973. *Sengo Nippon no Chingin Kettei: Rōdōshijō no Kōzō Henka to Sono Eikyō*, Tōkyō: Tōyōkeizai Shinpōsha.

———— 1980. 'Comparative Perspectives on Labor's Share', in Nishikawa 1980, pp. 255–72.

———— 1989. *Nipponteki Koyōkankō to Rōdōshijō*, Tōkyō: Tōyōkeizai Shinpōsha.

*———— and Tsunehiko Watanabe 1976. 'Changes in Income Inequality in the Japanese Economy', in Patrick 1976, pp. 363–89.

Oshima, Harry T. 1991. 'Kuznets' Curve and Asian Income distribution', in Mizoguchi *et al.*, pp. 117–34.

*Ozawa, Terutomo 1974. *Japan's Technological Challenge to the West, 1950–1974: Motivation and Accomplishment*, Cambridge, Massachusetts and London: Massachusetts Institute of Technology Press.

*Patrick, Hugh T. 1967. 'Japan 1868–1914', in Cameron 1967a, pp. 239–89.

*—— 1968. 'The Financing of the Public Sector in Postwar Japan', in Klein and Ohkawa 1968, pp. 326–55.

—— (ed.) 1976. *Japanese Industrialization and Its Consequences*, Berkeley, Los Angeles and London: University of California Press.

—— and Henry Rosovsky (eds) 1976a. *Asia's New Giant: How the Japanese Economy Works*, Washington, D.C.: Brookings Institution.

*—— 1976b. 'Japan's Economic Performance: An Overview', in Patrick and Rosovsky 1976a, pp. 1–61.

Paukert, Felix 1973. 'Income Distribution at Different Levels of Development: A Survey of Evidence', *International Labour Review*, vol. 108, nos 2–3, August–September, pp. 97–117.

Peacock, Alan T. and Jack Wiseman 1960. *The Growth of Public Expenditure in the United Kingdom*, Princeton, New Jersey: Princeton University Press.

*Peck, Merton and Akira Gotō 1981. 'Technology and Economic Growth: the Case of Japan', *Research Policy*, vol. 10, no. 3, July, pp. 222–4.

*—— and Shūji Tamura 1976. 'Technology,' in Patrick and Rosovsky 1976a, pp. 525–85.

Phelps Brown, E. H. 1968. *A Century of Pay*, London, Melbourne, Toronto, and New York: Macmillan and St. Martin's Press.

Ranis, Gustav 1955. 'The Community-Centered Entrepreneur in Japanese Development', *Explorations in Entrepreneurial History*, vol. 8, no. 2, December, pp. 80–98.

—— 1969. 'The Financing of Japanese Economic Development', in Ohkawa, Johnston and Kaneda 1969, pp. 37–57.

Reynolds, Lloyd G. 1983. 'The Spread of Economic Growth to the Third World: 1850–1980', *Journal of Economic Literature*, vol. 21, no. 3, September, pp. 941–80.

Rōdōshō (Ministry of Labour) (eds) 1988. *Rōdōhakusho, Shōwa 63-Nenban*, Tōkyō: Nippon Rōdō Kenkyūkikō (Japan Institute of Labour).

Rosenberg, Nathan 1972. *Technology and American Economic Growth*, New York: Harper & Row.

*Rosovsky, Henry 1961. *Capital Formation in Japan: 1868–1940*, New York: Free Press of Glencoe.

*—— 1966. 'Japan's Transition to Modern Economic Growth, 1868–1885', in Rosovsky (ed.), *Industrialization in Two Systems: Essays in Honor of Alexander Gerschenkron*, New York, London and Sydney: John Wiley & Sons, pp. 91–139.

—— 1968. 'Rumbles in Rice-Fields: Professor Nakamura vs the Official Statistics', *Journal of Asian Studies*, vol. 27, no. 2, February, pp. 347–60.

*—— 1972. 'What are the "Lessons" of Japanese Economic History?' Youngson, 1972, pp. 229–53.

Rostow, W. W. 1960. *The Stages of Economic Growth: A Non-Communist*

Manifesto, London: Cambridge University Press.
—— (ed.) 1963. *The Economics of Take-Off into Sustained Growth*, London: Macmillan Press.
—— 1978. *The World Economy: History & Prospect*, London: Macmillan Press.
Saitō, Osamu 1985. *Proto-Kōgyōka no Jidai: Seiō to Nippon no Hikakushi*, Tōkyō: Nippon Hyōronsha.
Satō, Kazuo 1977. 'A Model of Investment Behaviour: Fixed Investment and Capacity in Japanese Manufacturing, 1952–1963', in Kosobud and Minami 1977, pp. 75–113.
Sekiyama, Naotarō 1942. *Nippon Jinkōshi*, Tōkyō: Shikai Shobō.
Shakaihoshō Kenkyūjo (Social Development Research Institute) (ed.) 1973. *Shakaihoshō Suijun Kiso Tōkei*, Tōkyō: Tōyōkeizai Shinpōsha.
*Shimada, Haruo 1981. *Earnings Structure and Human Investment: A Comparison between the United States and Japan*, Tōkyō: Kōgakusha.
Shinbo, Hiroshi 1978. *Kinsei no Bukka to Keizai Hatten: Zenkōgyōka e no Sūryōteki Sekkin*, Tōkyō: Tōyōkeizai Shinpōsha.
—— and Osamu Saitō (eds) 1989. *Kindaiseichō no Shidō (Nippon Keizaishi*, vol. 2), Tōkyō: Iwanami Shoten.
Shinbo, Seiji 1980. *Gendai Nippon Keizai no Kaimei: Stagflation*, Tōkyō: Tōyōkeizai Shinpōsha.
Shinohara, Miyohe 1961. *Nippon Keizai no Seichōto Junkan*, Tōkyō: Sōbunsha.
*—— 1962. *Growth and Cycles in the Japanese Economy*, Tōkyō: Kinokuniya.
—— 1964. *Keizai Seichō no Kōzō: Tenki Keizai no Bunseki*, Tōkyō: Kunimoto Shobō.
—— 1967. *Kojin Shōhi Shishitsu, LTES*, vol. 6.
*—— 1968a. 'A Survey of the Japanese Literature on Small Industry', in Bert F. Hoselitz (ed.), *The Role of Small Industry in the Process of Economic Growth*, Mouton and Paris: The Hague, pp. 1–113.
*—— 1968b. 'Patterns and Some Structural Changes in Japan's Postwar Industrial Growth', in Klein and Ohkawa 1968, pp. 278–302.
—— 1969. 'Nippon no Kōgyōka: Tōtatsuten to Shotokuchō', in Nakayama and Shinohara 1969, pp. 21–62.
*—— 1970. *Structural Changes in Japan's Economic Development*, Tōkyō: Kinokuniya.
—— 1972. *Kōkōgyō, LTES*, vol. 10.
*—— 1979a. 'Manufacturing', in Ohkawa and Shinohara 1979, pp. 104–21.
—— 1979b. 'Consumption', in Ohkawa and Shinohara 1979, pp. 159–76.
*—— 1982. *Industrial Growth, Trade, and Dynamic Patterns in the Japanese Economy*, Tōkyō: University of Tōkyō Press.
Shionoya, Yūichi 1964. 'Patterns of Industrial Growth in the United States and Sweden: A Critique of Hoffmann's Hypothesis', *Hitotsubashi Journal of Economics*, vol. 5, no. 1, June, pp. 52–89.
—— 1967. 'Kōgyō Hatten no Keitai', in Miyohei Shinohara and Shōzaburō Fujino (eds), *Nippon no Keizai Seichō*, Tōkyō: Nippon Keizai Shinbunsha, pp. 139–78.

*———— 1968. 'Patterns of Industrial Development', in Klein and Ohkawa 1968, pp. 69–109.

———— and Ippei Yamazawa 1973. 'Kōgyō Seichō to Gaikoku Bōeki', in Kazushi Ohkawa and Yūjirō Hayami (eds), *Nippon Keizai no Chōki Bunseki: Seichō, Kōzō, Hadō*, Tōkyō: Nippon Keizai Shinbunsha, pp. 331–63.

Shintani, Masahiko 1983. *Nippon Nōgyō no Seisankansū Bunseki*, Tōkyō: Taimeidō.

*Shirai, Taishirō and Haruo Shimada 1979. 'Japan', in John T. Dunlop and Walter Galenson (eds), *Labor in the Twentieth Century*, New York, San Francisco and London: Academic Press.

Shōda, Ken-ichirō 1971. *Nippon Shihonshugi to Kindaika*, Tōkyō: Nippon Hyōronsha.

*Shōji, Hikaru and Ken-ichi Miyamoto 1977. 'Environmental Pollution in Japan', *Japanese Economic Studies*, vol. 5, no. 4, Summer, pp. 3–40.

Shōwa Dōjinkai (Shōwa Study Group) 1957. *Wagakuni Kanzenkoyō no Igi to Taisaku, Dai 4-Bu, Tōkei: Tōkei kara Mita Koyō to Shitsugyō*, Tōkyō.

*Smith, Thomas C. 1955. *Political Change and Industrial Development in Japan: Government Enterprise, 1868–1880*, Stanford, California: Stanford University Press.

*———— 1959. *The Agrarian Origins of Modern Japan*, Stanford, California: Stanford University Press.

*———— 1973. 'Pre-Modern Economic Growth: Japan and the West', *Past and Present*, no. 60, August, pp. 127–60.

Sōmuchō, Tōkeikyoku (Management and Coordination Agency, Statistics Bureau) 1990. *Nippon no Jinkō: Shōwa 60-Nen Kokusei Chōsa Saishū Kekka Hōkokusho, Shiryōhen*, Tōkyō: Sōmuchō, Tōkeikyoku.

Sōrifu, Tōkeikyoku (Prime Minister's Office, Statistical Bureau) 1962. *Shōwa 15-Nen Kokusei Chōsa Hōkoku, Dai 2-Kan, Sangyō Jūgyōjō no Chii*, Tōkyō: Sōrifu, Tōkeikyoku.

———— 1980. *Nippon no Jinkō: Shōwa 50-Nen Kokusei Chōsa no Kaisetsu*, Tōkyō: Sōrifu, Tōkeikyoku.

———— 1982. *Wagakuni no Jinkō: Shōwa 55-Nen Kokusei Chōsa Kaisetsu Series No. 1*, Tōkyō: Sōrifu, Tōkeikyoku.

Suzuki, Takeo (ed.) 1962. *Zaiseishi*, Tōkyō: Tōyōkeizai Shinpōsha.

*Suzuki, Yoshio 1980. *Money and Banking in Contemporary Japan: The Theoretical Setting and Its Application*, (translated by John G. Greenwood), New Haven, Connecticut and London: Yale University Press.

*Tachi, Minoru and Yōichi Okazaki 1965. 'Economic Development and Population Growth: With Special Reference to Southeast Asia', *Developing Economies*, vol. 3, no. 4, December, pp. 497–515.

*Tachi, Ryūichirō 1966. 'Fiscal and Monetary Policy', in Komiya 1966a, pp. 11–31.

———— and Katsunosuke Moroi 1965. 'Senzen Sengo no Kigyō Kinyū', in Tachi and Tsunehiko Watanabe (eds), *Keizai Seichō to Zaisei Kinyū*, Tōkyō: Iwanami Shoten, pp. 83–105.

*Taeuber, Irene B. 1958. *The Population of Japan*, Princeton, New Jersey: Princeton University Press.

*Taira, Kōji 1970. *Economic Development and the Labor Market in Japan*, New York and London: Columbia University Press.

Takayama, Noriyuki 1980. *Fubyōdō no Keizaigaku*, Tōkyō: Tōyōkeizai Shinpōsha.

Takenaka, Hēzo 1984. *Kenkyū Kaihaitsu Tōshi to Setsubi Tōs no Keizaigaku: Keizai Katsuryoku o Sasaeru Mekanizumu*, Tōkyō: Tōyō Keizai Shinpōsha.

Tamura, Shigeru 1971. 'Wagakuni Kigyō no Shihon Kōsei', in Takuya Shimano and Kōichi Hamada (eds), *Nippon no Kinyū*, Tōkyō: Iwanami Shoten, pp. 273–96.

Tatemoto, Masahiro *et al.* 1977. 'Stabilization Model for the Postwar Japanese Economy, 1954–1962', in Kosobud and Minami 1977, pp. 414–54.

Teranishi, Jūrō 1972–3. 'A Survey of Economic Studies on Prewar Japan', *Japanese Economic Studies*, vol. 1, no. 2, Winter, pp. 47–98.

――― 1982. *Nippon no Keizai Hatten to Kinyū*, Tōkyō: Iwanami Shoten.

Terasaki, Yasuhiro 1990. 'Sekai no Shotoku Kakusa', *Nippon Keizai Kenkyū*, vol. 20, May, pp. 22–31.

Tominaga, Ken-ichi 1990. *Nippon no Kindaika to Shakai Hendō*, Tōkyō: Kōdansha.

Tōyōkeizai Shinpōsha (ed.) 1935. *Nippon Bōeki Seiran*, Tōkyō.

Tsuchiya, Takao 1954. *Nippon Shihonshugi no Keieishi-teki Kenkyū*, Tōkyō: Misuzushobō.

Tsujimura, Kōtarō 1966. 'The Employment Structure and Labor Shares', in Komiya 1966a, pp. 107–30.

――― 1968. *Shōhi Kōzō to Bukka*, Tōkyō: Keisōshobō.

――― 1974. 'Stagflation no Kaimei', in Yōichi Shinkai and Hiroshi Niida (eds), *Inflation: Readings Nippon Keizairon*, Tōkyō: Nippon Keizai Shinbunsha, pp. 98–111.

Tsūshō Sangyō Daijin Kanbō, Chōsa Tōkeibu (Ministry of International Trade and Industry, Minister's Secretariat, Research and Statistics Division) 1961. *Kōgyō Tōkei 50-Nen Shi: Shiryōhen*, Tōkyō.

Uchida, Tadao and Tsunehiko Watanabe 1959. 'Nippon Keizai no Hendō 1951–1956', vol. 9, nos 3–4, June, pp. 20–9.

Uekusa, Masu 1982. *Sangyō Soshikiron*, Tōkyō: Tsukumashobō.

*Ueno, Hiroya 1976–7. 'Conception and Evaluation of Japanese Industrial Policy', *Japanese Economic Studies*, vol. 5, no. 2, Winter, pp. 3–63.

――― and Jūrō Teranishi 1975. 'Chōki Model no Kiso to Kaidai: 2-Bumon Model no Rironteki Framework', in Ohkawa and Minami 1975, pp. 369–98.

Umemura, Mataji 1961. *Chingin, Kōyō, Nōgyō*, Tōkyō: Taimeidō.

――― 1971. *Rōdōryoku no Kōzō to Koyō Mondai*, Tōkyō: Iwanami Shoten.

*――― 1979. 'Population and Labor Force', in Ohkawa and Shinohara 1979, pp. 241–9.

*――― 1980. 'The Seniority-Wage System in Japan', in Nishikawa 1980, pp. 177–87.

――― 1981. 'Bakumatsu no Keizai Hatten', in Kindai Nippon Kenkyūkai (Study Group on Modern Japan) (ed.), *Bakumatsu Ishin no Nippon*, Tōkyō: Yamakawa Shuppansha, pp. 3–30.

———— and Yūzō Yamamoto (eds), *Kaikō to Ishin* (*Nippon Keizaishi*, vol. 3), Tōkyō: Iwanami Shoten.

———— *et al.* 1966. *Nōringyō, LTES*, vol. 9.

———— *et al.* 1988. 'Rōdōryoku', *LTES*, vol. 2.

United States, Department of Commerce, Bureau of the Census 1975. *Historical Statistics of the United States: Colonial Times to 1970*, parts 1 and 2, Washington, D.C.

Usher, Abbott Payson 1918. *An Introduction to the Industrial History of England*, London: Harrap.

*Van der Meer, Cornelis L. J. and Saburō Yamada 1990. *Japanese Agriculture: A Comparative Economic Analysis*, London and New York: Routledge & Kegan Paul.

Vernon, Raymond 1966. 'International Investment and International Trade in the Product Cycle', *Quarterly Journal of Economics*, vol. 80, no. 1, February, pp. 190–207.

*Wallich, Henry C. and Mable I. Wallich 1976. 'Banking and Finance', in Patrick and Rosovsky 1976a, pp. 249–315.

*Watanabe, Tsunehiko 1968. 'Industrialization, Technological Progress, and Dual Structure', in Klein and Ohkawa 1968, pp. 110–34.

———— 1970. *Sūryō Keizai Bunseki: Seichō o Meguru Shomondai*, Tōkyō: Sōbunsha.

*———— 1977. 'Price Changes and the Rate of Change of Money Wage Earnings in Japan, 1955–1962', in Kosobud and Minami 1977, pp. 178–97.

*Yamada, Saburō 1967. 'Changes in Output and in Conventional and Nonconventional Inputs in Japanese Agriculture Since 1880', *Food Research Institute Studies*, vol. 7, no. 3, pp. 371–413.

———— 1973. 'Nōgyō', in Emi and Shionoya 1973, pp. 107–28.

*———— and Vernon W. Ruttan 1980. 'International Comparison of Productivity in Agriculture', in John W. Kendrick and Beatrice N. Vaccara (eds), *New Developments in Productivity Measurement and Analysis*, Chicago: University of Chicago Press, pp. 509–94.

Yamamoto, Hirofumi 1972. *Ishinki no Kaidō to Yusō*, Tōkyō: Hōsei Daigaku Shuppankyoku.

*Yamamura, Kōzō 1967. *Economic Policy in Postwar Japan: Growth Versus Economic Democracy*, Berkeley and Los Angeles, California: University of California Press.

*———— 1972. 'Japan, 1868–1930: A Revised View', in Rondo Cameron (ed.), *Banking and Economic Development: Some Lessons of History*, London, New York and Toronto: Oxford University Press.

———— 1974. *A Study of Samurai Income and Entrepreneurship: Quantitative Analyses of Economic and Social Aspects of the Samurai in Tokugawa and Meiji Japan*, Cambridge, Massachusetts: Harvard University Press.

———— 1976. 'General Trading Companies in Japan: Their Origins and Growth', in Patrick 1976, pp. 161–99.

———— 1977. 'Success Illgotten? The Role of Meiji Militarism in Japan's Technological Progress', *Journal of Economic History*, vol. 37, no. 1, March, pp. 113–35.

*Yamazawa, Ippei 1975a. 'Industrial Growth and Trade Policy in Prewar Japan', *Developing Economies*, vol. 8, no. 1, March, pp. 38–65.

*———— 1975b. 'Strategy of Industrial Development: Japanese Experience', in Nagatoshi Suzuki (ed.), *Asian Industrial Development*, Tōkyō: Institute of Developing Economies, pp. 314–48.

———— 1984. *Nippon no Keizai Hatten to Kokusai Bungyō*, Tōkyō: Tōyōkeizai Shinpōsha.

———— and Hirohisa Kohama 1978. 'Shōsha Katsudō to Bōeki Kakudai', *Kikan Gendai Keizai*, vol. 33, December, pp. 176–91.

———— and Yūzō Yamamoto 1979a. *Bōeki to Kokusai Shūshi, LTES*, vol. 14.

*———— 1979b. 'Trade and Balance Payments', in Ohkawa and Shinohara 1979, pp. 134–56.

*Yasuba, Yasukichi 1976. 'The Evolution of Dualistic Wage Structure', in Patrick 1976, pp. 249–98.

———— 1980. *Keizai Seichōron*, Tōkyō: Tsukumashobō.

Youngson, A. J. (ed.) 1972. *Economic Development in the Long Run*, London: George Allen & Unwin.

Index of Personal Names

Index of Subjects